Constructing a Language

Constructing

a Language

A Usage-Based Theory
of Language Acquisition

MICHAEL TOMASELLO

HARVARD UNIVERSITY PRESS
Cambridge, Massachusetts, and London, England

Library of Congress Cataloging-in-Publication Data

Tomasello, Michael.
Constructing a language : a usage-based theory of
language acquisition / Michael Tomasello.
p. cm.
Includes bibliographical references and index.
ISBN 0-674-01030-2 (cloth)
ISBN 0-674-01764-1 (pbk.)
1. Language acquisition.   2. Cognition in children   I. Title.

P118 .T558 2003
4019.93—dc21   2002038840

Designed by Gwen Nefsky Frankfeldt

For Liz Bates

Contents

Constructing a Language

Usage-Based Linguistics

> The confusions which occupy us arise when language
> is like an engine idling, not when it is doing its work.
>
> —LUDWIG WITTGENSTEIN

NOTHING could seem less remarkable than a one-year-old child requesting "More juice" or commenting "Doggie gone." But the remarkable fact is that even these baby utterances differ from the communicative activities of other animal species in a number of fundamental ways. For example, other animals do not refer one another's attention to outside entities such as juice, they do not make disinterested comments to one another about missing doggies or the like, and they do not combine communicatively significant elements to create new meanings. But from an ethological perspective, perhaps the most astounding fact is that something on the order of 80 percent of all *Homo sapiens* cannot understand these simple utterances at all. That is, whereas the individuals of all nonhuman species can communicate effectively with all of their conspecifics, human beings can communicate effectively only with other persons who have grown up in their same linguistic community—typically, in the same geographical region.

Whatever may be the evolutionary reasons for this unique, indeed bizarre, situation, one immediate outcome is that, unlike most other animal species, human beings cannot be born with any specific set of communicative behaviors. Young children must learn during their individual ontogenies the set of linguistic conventions used by those around them, which for any given language consists of tens of thousands, or perhaps even hundreds of thousands, of individual words, expressions, and constructions. The human species is biologically prepared for this prodigious task in ways that individuals of other species are not, of course, but this preparation cannot be too specific, as human children must be flexible enough to learn not only all of the different words and conventional expressions of any language but also all of the different types of abstract constructional patterns that these languages have grammaticized historically. It thus takes many years of daily interaction with mature language users for children to attain adult-like skills, which is a longer period of learning with more things to be learned—by many orders of magnitude—than is required of any other species on the planet.

The first proposal in the modern context was that young children learn their "verbal behavior" using the same garden-variety learning mechanisms they use to learn other behaviors—which, by the way, are the same learning mechanisms used by rats and pigeons. Thus, Skinner (1957) proposed that young children learn pieces of language by means of instrumental conditioning (based on principles of association) and that they generalize to new instances by means of stimulus generalization (based on principles of induction). But in his withering review of Skinner's book, Chomsky (1959) argued that there are some principles of grammar that are so abstract and, in a sense, arbitrary that children could not possibly learn them by means of simple association and induction. Indeed, Chomsky (1968, 1980a, 1986) later argued that there are some abstract principles of grammar for which children have no reliable and unambiguous evidence at all—given that the language they experience consists of nothing more than a series of individual utterances. This is the so-called argument from the poverty of the stimulus, and Chomsky's well-known solution was to hypothesize that human beings are born with an innate universal grammar containing a number of abstract principles that guide the acquisition process.

This argument had a profound effect on researchers studying children's language in the 1960s and 1970s. The prevailing opinion at the time was that baby utterances such as "More juice" and "Doggie gone" were just that, baby utterances that rested on very concrete and seemingly non-adult-like linguistic representations such as *More X* and *X gone* (e.g., Braine, 1963, 1976). But people impressed with the argument from the poverty of the stimulus looked at these baby representations and at the formal descriptions of adult language being proposed by Chomsky and others and said, in effect: "You can't get there from here" (e.g., Gleitman and Wanner, 1982). The majority opinion in the field thus changed rather quickly to the view that children's early language was somehow undergirded by some kind of linguistic abstractions—perhaps even the same ones that underlie mature adult language. This is the so-called *continuity assumption:* that basic linguistic representations are the same throughout all stages of child language development—since they come ultimately from a single universal grammar (Pinker, 1984).

But much has happened in the last two decades in developmental psychology, linguistics, and cognitive science which suggests a re-evaluation of the situation, that is, which suggests that children *can* get from here to there, and that they can do it without the aid of any hypothesized universal grammar. There are two fundamental points: (1) children have at their disposal much more powerful learning mechanisms than simple association and blind induction; and (2) there exist plausible and rigorous theories of language that characterize adult linguistic competence in much more child-friendly terms than does generative grammar—which makes the endpoint of language acquisition seem much closer.

The first point is that modern developmental psychologists and cognitive scientists no longer think of children's learning as isolated association-making and induction, but rather they think of it as integrated with other cognitive and social-cognitive skills—in ways that Skinner and the Behaviorists (and Chomsky in his critiques) could never have envisaged. Two sets of such skills are of particular importance for language acquisition. The first set comprises various skills of *intention-reading* (theory of mind, broadly conceived). These skills first emerge in human ontogeny at around 9–12 months of age (Tomasello, 1995a) and include such things as:

- the ability to share attention with other persons to objects and events of mutual interest (Bakeman and Adamson, 1984);
- the ability to follow the attention and gesturing of other persons to distal objects and events outside the immediate interaction (Corkum and Moore, 1995);
- the ability to actively direct the attention of others to distal objects by pointing, showing, and using of other nonlinguistic gestures (Bates, 1979);
- the ability to culturally (imitatively) learn the intentional actions of others, including their communicative acts underlain by communicative intentions (Tomasello, Kruger, and Ratner, 1993; Tomasello, 1998b).

These skills are necessary for children to acquire the appropriate use of any and all linguistic symbols, including complex linguistic expressions and constructions. Indeed, they basically define the symbolic or functional dimension of linguistic communication—which involves in all cases the attempt of one person to manipulate the intentional or mental states of other persons.* Importantly in the current context, this functional dimen-

---

* The notions of communicative intention and function are correlative. Someone uses a piece of language with a certain communicative intention, and so we may say that that piece of language has a certain function.

sion enables certain kinds of abstraction processes, such as analogy, that can only be effected when the elements to be compared play similar functional (communicative) roles in larger linguistic expressions and/or constructions. Intention-reading skills are very likely unique to human beings, and they probably emerged relatively recently in human evolution (Tomasello, 1999). They are domain-general in the sense that they do not just enable linguistic communication, but also enable a variety of other cultural skills and practices that children routinely acquire (such as tool use, pretend play, rituals).

The other main set of skills is those involved in various kinds of *pattern-finding*—categorization, broadly defined. These skills also begin to emerge early in human development (some prelinguistically) and include such things as:

- the ability to form perceptual and conceptual categories of "similar" objects and events (e.g., Rakison and Oakes, in press);
- the ability to form sensory-motor schemas from recurrent patterns of perception and action (e.g., Piaget, 1952; Schneider, 1999; Conway and Christiansen, 2001);
- the ability to perform statistically based distributional analyses on various kinds of perceptual and behavioral sequences (e.g., Saffran, Aslin, and Newport, 1996; Marcus et al., 1999; Gomez and Gerken, 1999; Ramus et al., 2000);
- the ability to create analogies (structure mappings) across two or more complex wholes, based on the similar functional roles of some elements in these different wholes (Gentner and Markman, 1997).

These skills are necessary for children to find patterns in the way adults use linguistic symbols across different utterances, and so to construct the grammatical (abstract) dimensions of human linguistic competence. They are skills that are evolutionarily fairly old, probably possessed in some form by all primates at the very least (Tomasello and Call, 1997; Hauser, Weiss, and Marcus, in press). They are also domain-general, in the sense that they allow organisms to categorize many different aspects of their worlds into a manageable number of kinds of things and events (although it seems very likely that when these skills are applied to linguistic symbols—as they are in humans but not in other primate species—some novel characteristics emerge). A particularly exciting development along these lines is the creation of connectionist and other kinds of computer programs that are able to find many patterns in linguistic stimuli with only a few uncomplicated pattern-finding algorithms (Elman, 1990, 1993). This of course suggests that young children should be able to do the same thing with similar skills—or even more with more skills.

The second modern development that undermines the You Can't Get

There From Here argument is new ways of looking at the nature of language itself. Chomskian generative grammar is a "formal" theory, meaning that it is based on the supposition that natural languages are like formal languages. Natural languages are thus characterized in terms of (1) a unified set of abstract algebraic rules that are both meaningless themselves and insensitive to the meanings of the elements they algorithmically combine, and (2) a lexicon containing meaningful linguistic elements that serve as variables in the rules. Principles governing the way the underlying algebra works constitute a universal grammar, the "core" of linguistic competence. The linguistic "periphery" involves such things as the lexicon, the conceptual system, irregular constructions and idioms, and pragmatics. This dichotomy between core and periphery leads to the so-called dual process approach to language acquisition (also called the words and rules approach by Pinker, 1999), namely, that whereas children acquire elements of the linguistic periphery using "normal" learning processes, the linguistic core, universal grammar, cannot be so learned; it is an innate property of the human mind.

But in recent years a new view of language and human linguistic competence has begun to emerge. This view is represented by a group of theories most often called *cognitive-functional linguistics* but sometimes also called *usage-based linguistics* to emphasize their central processing tenet that language structure emerges from language use (e.g., Langacker, 1987a, 1991, 2000; Croft, 1991, 2001; Goldberg, 1995; Givón, 1995; Bybee, 1985, 1995, 2002; see Tomasello, 1998a, in press, and Barlow and Kemmer, 2000, for similar approaches). Usage-based theories hold that the essence of language is its symbolic dimension, with grammar being derivative. The ability to communicate with conspecifics symbolically (conventionally, intersubjectively) is a species-specific biological adaptation. But, in contrast to generative grammar and other formal approaches, in usage-based approaches the grammatical dimension of language is a product of a set of historical and ontogenetic processes referred to collectively as *grammaticalization*. When human beings use symbols to communicate with one another, stringing them together into sequences, patterns of use emerge and become consolidated into grammatical constructions—for example, the English passive construction, noun phrase construction, or -*ed* past tense construction. As opposed to conceiving linguistic rules as algebraic procedures for combining words and morphemes that do not themselves contribute to meaning, this approach conceives linguistic constructions as themselves meaningful linguistic symbols—since they are nothing other than the patterns in which meaningful linguistic symbols are used in communication (for example, the passive construction is used to communicate about an entity to which something happens).

In the usage-based approach, competence with a natural language consists of the mastery of all its items and structures, and these constitute a much more complex and diverse set of linguistic representations than the "core grammar" of formal approaches. They include the highly canonical (core), the highly idiosyncratic (periphery), and many things in between. Thus, fluent speakers of English control not only highly abstract syntactic constructions (past-tense -ed, the passive construction), but also concrete expressions based on individual words or phrases, such as ritualized greetings, idioms, metaphors, and noncanonical phrasal collocations (*I wouldn't put it past him; He's getting to me these days; Hang in there; That won't go down well with the boss; She put me up to it;* see Pawley and Syder, 1983; Jackendoff, 1996). In addition, and importantly, they also control many so-called mixed constructions that fall somewhere in between these in having both concrete and abstract elements (such as the -er construction, as in *The bigger they are, the nicer they are,* which has many unique properties along with some more regular ones). A plausible way to think of mature linguistic competence, then, is as a structured inventory of constructions, some of which are similar to many others and so reside in a more core-like center, and others of which connect to very few other constructions (and in different ways) and so reside more toward the periphery.

The implications of this new view of language for theories of language acquisition are truly revolutionary. If there is no clean break between the more rule-based and the more idiosyncratic items and structures of a language, then all constructions may be acquired with the same basic set of acquisitional processes—namely, those falling under the general headings of intention-reading and pattern-finding. If adult linguistic competence is based, to a much larger degree than previously supposed, on concrete pieces of language and straightforward generalizations across them—with many constructions remaining idiosyncratic and item-based into adulthood—then it is possible that children's early language is largely item-based and yet they can still construct an adult-like set of grammatical constructions originating with these baby constructions (given several years in which they hear several million adult utterances). If linguistic constructions are meaningful linguistic symbols in their own right, then children can use function or meaning to assist in their acquisition, just as they do in their acquisition of smaller linguistic constructions such as individual words.

In this book I proceed from the assumption that children can get from here to there, from item-based baby constructions to abstract constructions, and that they can do this with one set of acquisition processes. The assumption is justified by the fact that the cognitive and social learning skills that children bring to the acquisition process are much more powerful than previously believed, and by the fact that the adult endpoint of language acquisition comprises nothing other than a structured inventory of linguistic constructions, a much closer and more child-friendly target than previously believed. These two new advances in developmental psychology and usage-based linguistics thus encourage us to pursue the possibility that we might be able to describe and explain child language acquisition without recourse to any hypothesized universal grammar.

It should also be emphasized at the outset that, in the current view, the principles and structures whose existence it is difficult to explain without universal grammar (such Chomskian things as the subjacency constraint, the empty category principle, and the binding principles) are theory-internal affairs and simply do not exist in usage-based theories of language—full stop. There is no poverty of the stimulus when a structured inventory of constructions is the adult endpoint. Moreover, hypothesizing the existence of an innate universal grammar brings with it two major acquisition problems that are currently unresolved—and that do not exist on a usage-based view. First is the problem of cross-linguistic diversity: How can the child link her abstract universal grammar to the particularities of the particular language she is learning (the linking problem)? Second is the problem of developmental change: How can we understand the changing nature of children's language across development if universal grammar is always the same (the problem of continuity)? For these reasons as well, then, it seems worthwhile to attempt to describe and explain child language acquisition without adding the extra acquisitional problems created by an hypothesized universal grammar.

Origins of Language

The common behavior of mankind is the system of reference by means of which we interpret an unknown language.

—LUDWIG WITTGENSTEIN

HUMAN linguistic communication differs from the communication of other animal species in two main ways. First, and most importantly, human linguistic communication is symbolic. Linguistic symbols are social conventions by means of which one individual attempts to share attention with another individual by directing the other's attentional or mental state to something in the outside world. Other animal species do not communicate with one another using linguistic symbols, most likely because they do not understand that conspecifics have attentional or mental states that they could attempt to direct or share (Tomasello, 1998b). To oversimplify, animal signals are aimed at the behavior and motivational states of others, whereas human symbols are aimed at the attentional and mental states of others. It is this mental dimension that gives linguistic symbols their unparalleled communicative power, enabling them to be used to refer to and to predicate all kinds of diverse perspectives on objects, events, and situations in the world.

The second main difference is that human linguistic communication is grammatical. Human beings use their linguistic symbols together in patterned ways, and these patterns, known as linguistic constructions, take on meanings of their own—deriving partly from the meanings of the individual symbols but, over time, at least partly from the pattern itself. The process by which this occurs over historical time is called *grammaticalization* (or syntacticization), and grammatical constructions of course add still another dimension of communicative power to human languages. The process of grammaticalization depends crucially on a variety of domain-general cognitive and social-cognitive processes that operate as people communicate with and learn from one another. It is also a species-unique process—because if other animals do not use symbols, the question of grammar is moot.

Human skills of linguistic communication are also unique in the way they are acquired during ontogeny. The main point is that, unlike other animal species, the human species does not have a single system of communication. Different groups of human beings have conventionalized different systems of communication (there are more than 6,000 of them), and children typically acquire only the system(s) of their natal group(s). Children take several years to acquire the many tens of thousands of linguistic conventions used by those around them, whereas most other animal species do not learn any of their species-typical communicative signals at all.

2.1. Phylogenetic Origins

As adumbrated in Chapter 1, the Generative Grammar hypothesis focuses only on grammar and claims that the human species has evolved during its phylogeny a genetically based universal grammar. The theory is unconcerned with the symbolic dimensions of human linguistic communication. The usage-based view—or at least the version of it espoused here—is precisely the opposite. In this view, the human use of symbols is primary, with the most likely evolutionary scenario being that the human species evolved skills enabling the use of linguistic symbols phylogenetically. But the emergence of grammar is a cultural-historical affair—probably originating quite recently in human evolution—involving no additional genetic events concerning language per se (except possibly some vocal-auditory information-processing skills that contribute indirectly to grammaticalization processes).

This is not to imply that we know how language originated in human evolution, because we do not. But if we focus on linguistic symbols as primary, we may obtain some hints by looking at the communication of our nearest primate relatives—who communicate not with symbols but with vocal and gestural signals. At the very least, this comparison will help us to identify the unique features of human symbolic communication. For hints about the emergence of grammar in human evolution we need to examine various processes of grammaticalization and syntacticization as they may be inferred from historical examinations of written language and from comparative examinations within language families.

2.1.1. Primate Communication

Discerning the unique features of human symbolic/linguistic communication is sometimes made more difficult by anthropocentric accounts of nonhuman primate communication. The most important instance of this is the well-known case of the alarm calls of vervet monkeys. The basic facts are these (see Cheney and Seyfarth, 1990, for more details). In their natural habitats in east Africa vervet monkeys use three different types of alarm calls to indicate the presence of three different types of predator: leopards, eagles, and snakes. A loud, barking call is given to leopards and other cat species, a short cough-like call is given to two species of eagle, and a "chutter" call is given to a variety of dangerous snake species. Each call elicits a different escape response on the part of vervets who hear the call: to a leopard alarm they run for the trees; to an eagle alarm they look up in the air and sometimes run into the bushes; and to a snake alarm they look down at the ground, sometimes from a bipedal stance. These responses are just as distinct and frequent when researchers play back previously recorded alarm calls over a loudspeaker, indicating that the responses of the vervets are not dependent on seeing the predator but rather on information contained in the call itself.

On the surface, these alarm calls would seem to be very similar to human language. It seems as if the caller is directing the attention of others to something they do not perceive or something they do not know is present; that is, the calls would seem to be symbolic (referential). But several additional facts argue against this interpretation. First, there is basically no sign that vervet monkeys attempt to manipulate the attentional or mental states of conspecifics in any other domain of their lives. Thus, vervets also have different "grunts" that they use in various social situations, but these show no signs of being symbolic or referential in the sense of being intended to direct the attention of others to outside entities; they mainly serve to regulate dyadic social interactions not involving outside entities, such as grooming, playing, fighting, sex, and travel. Second, predator-specific alarm calls turn out to be fairly widespread in the animal kingdom. They are used by a number of species—from ground squirrels to domestic chickens—that must deal with multiple predators requiring different types of escape responses (Owings and Morton, 1998), but no one considers them to be symbolic or referential in a human-like way. An extremely important evolutionary fact in all of this is that no species of ape has such specific alarm calls or any other vocalizations that appear to be referential (Cheney and Wrangham, 1987). Since human beings are most closely related to the great apes, this means that it is not possible that vervet monkey alarm calls could be the direct precursor of human language unless at some point apes used them also—and there is no evidence of this.

Similarly and importantly, the visual-gestural communication of nonhuman primates shows no signs of referentiality or symbolicity either. Most strikingly, nonhuman primates do not point or gesture to outside objects or events for others, they do not hold up objects to show them to others, and they do not even hold out objects to offer them to others (Tomasello and Call, 1997). Once again, primate gestures are used almost exclusively to regulate dyadic social interactions such as grooming, play, fighting, sex, and travel, not triadically to direct the attention of others to outside entities or events. Relatedly, nonhuman primates use their species-typical vocalizations and gestures almost exclusively for imperative motives, to request a behavior of others, not to share attention or information with others in a disinterested manner (Tomasello, 1998b).

Finally, nonhuman primate vocalizations and gestures are not socially learned in the sense of being copied from others. Primate vocalizations are almost certainly not learned at all, as monkeys and apes raised outside their normal social environments vocalize in much the same way as those who grow up in normal social environments (although some aspects of call comprehension and use may be learned). Many nonhuman primate gestures are also not learned, but some are. However, these are not learned by imitation—by observing others using a gesture and then adopting it oneself—but rather by a process of ritualization in which individuals mutually shape one another's behavior over repeated social interactions (Tomasello and Zuberbühler, 2002). Overall, because they are not used referentially, not used simply to share attention with others, and not learned from others via imitation, the communicative signals of nonhuman primates do not seem to be socially shared (or socially constituted) in the same way as human linguistic symbols.

As a result of facts such as these, a number of primatologists and behavioral ecologists have cautioned against using human language as an interpretive framework for nonhuman primate communication (Owings and Morton, 1998; Owren and Rendell, 2001). They concur with the current analysis that nonhuman primates do not use communicative signals to convey meaning or to convey information or to refer to things or to direct the attention of others, but rather use them to affect the behavior or motivational states of others directly. If this interpretation is correct, then the deep evolutionary roots of human language lie in the attempts of primate individuals to influence the behavior, not the mental states, of conspecifics. To find the most direct precursors of human linguistic symbols as tools for directing attention, therefore, we can only look at the history of the human species since it began its own unique evolutionary trajectory.

2.1.2. Symbols and Grammaticalization

Although no one knows for certain, it is very likely that human symbolic skills arose as a more or less direct result of a biological adaptation—most likely occurring very recently with the emergence of modern humans some

200,000 years ago. According to Deacon (1998), this adaptation concerned symbolic skills directly, whereas according to Tomasello (1999) it concerned a new kind of social cognition more generally, in which human beings understood one another for the first time as intentional and mental agents—which then led them to attempt to manipulate one another's intentional and mental states for various cooperative and competitive purposes.

In any case, whenever and however they arose, human linguistic symbols are most clearly distinguished from the communicative signals of other primate species by the ways they are learned and used:

- Human linguistic symbols are *socially learned,* mainly by cultural (imitative) learning in which the learner acquires not just the conventional form of the symbol but also its conventional use in acts of communication (Tomasello, Kruger, and Ratner, 1993).
- Because they are learned imitatively from others, linguistic symbols are understood by their users *intersubjectively* in the sense that users know their interlocutors share the convention (that is, everyone is potentially both a producer and a comprehender and they all know this; see Saussure, 1916, on "bi-directionality of the sign").
- Linguistic symbols are not used dyadically to regulate social interactions directly, but rather they are used in utterances *referentially* (triadically) to direct the attentional and mental states of others to outside entities (see Grice, 1975, on the non-natural meaning of linguistic symbols).
- Linguistic symbols are sometimes used *declaratively,* simply to inform other persons of something, with no expectation of an overt behavioral response (see Dunbar, 1996, on the origins of language for purposes of gossip).
- Linguistic symbols are fundamentally *perspectival* in the sense that a person may refer to one and the same entity as *dog, animal, pet,* or *pest,* or to the same event as *running, fleeing, moving,* or *surviving—* depending on her communicative goal with respect to the listener's attentional states (Langacker, 1987a).

All these features are in contrast to the unlearned, or at least not imitatively learned, dyadic and imperative communicative signals of nonhuman primates that do not involve mental perspectives at all. In at least one reasonable hypothesis, these uniquely human features all derive—along with a host of other cultural skills involving, for example, teaching and collaborative interactions—from a single social-cognitive adaptation enabling the understanding of the psychological states of others more generally (theory of mind, broadly defined; Tomasello, 1999).

Tomasello (1999) also argued that linguistic symbols provide human beings with a species-unique format for cognitive representation. That is, when a child learns the conventional use of linguistic symbols, what she is learning are the ways her forebears in the culture found it useful to share and manipulate the attention of others in the past. And because the people of a culture, as they move through historical time, evolve many and varied purposes for manipulating one another's attention (and because they need to do this in many different types of discourse situations), today's child is faced with a whole panoply of linguistic symbols and constructions that embody many different attentional construals of any given situation. As just a sampling, languages embody attentional construals based on such things as:

- Granularity-specificity *(thing, furniture, chair, desk chair).*
- Perspective *(chase-flee, buy-sell, come-go, borrow-lend).*
- Function *(father, lawyer, man, American; coast, shore, beach).*

Consequently, as the young child internalizes a linguistic symbol—as she learns the human perspective embodied in that symbol—she cognitively represents, not just the perceptual or motoric aspects of a situation, but also one way, among other ways of which she is also aware, that the current situation may be attentionally construed by "us," the users of the symbol. The way that human beings use linguistic symbols thus creates a clear break with straightforward perceptual or sensory-motor cognitive representations—even those connected with events displaced in space and/ or time—and enables human beings to view the world in whatever way is convenient for the communicative purpose at hand.

The evolution of grammar raises a more controversial set of theoretical issues, leading to some very different hypothesized evolutionary scenarios. Generative grammarians believe that the human species evolved a genetically based universal grammar common to all peoples and that the variability in modern languages is basically on the surface only. There are a number of accounts from this perspective, ranging from Chomsky's (1986) single-mutation account to Bickerton's (1984) two-stage account to Pinker and Bloom's (1992) gradualist account. But in all these variants the basic idea is the same: that the fundamental grammatical categories and relations underlying all of the world's languages come from a biological adaptation (or set of adaptations) in the form of a universal grammar.

The alternative is the usage-based view, in which there is no need to posit a specific genetic adaptation for grammar because processes of grammaticalization and syntacticization can actually create grammatical structures out of concrete utterances—and grammaticalization and syntacticization are cultural-historical processes, not biological ones. Thus, it is a historical fact that the specific items and constructions of a given language are not invented all at once, but rather they emerge, evolve, and accumulate modifications over historical time as human beings use them with one another and adapt them to changing communicative circumstances (Croft, 2000). Most importantly, through various discourse processes (involving various kinds of pragmatic inferencing, analogy making, and so on) loose and redundantly organized discourse structures congeal into more tightly and less redundantly organized constructions (see Traugott and Heine, 1991; Hopper and Traugott, 1993). This happens both on the level of words and on the level of more complex constructions.

On the level of words, simple examples are English phrases such as *on the top of* and *in the side of* evolving into *on top of* and *inside of* and eventually into *atop* and *inside*. Often, however, this congealing process results in some structural changes as the communicative functions of some elements are reanalyzed in the context of specific constructions. Thus, case markers and agreement markers most often originate in free-standing words such as spatial prepositions, pronouns, or even nouns and verbs. A simple English example concerns the future marker *gonna*, a fusion of *going* and *to*. The original use of *going* was as a verb for movement, often in combination with the preposition *to* to indicate the destination *(I'm going to the store)*, but sometimes also to indicate an intended action that the *going to* enabled *(Why are you going to London? I'm going to see my bride)*. This later became *I'm gonna VERB*, with *gonna* indicating not just the intention to do something in the future, but futurity only (with no movement or intention necessary; on this change see Bybee, 2002). Givón's (1979) well-known characterization of this process is: today's morphology is yesterday's syntax.

On the level of constructions, instead of sequences of words becoming one word, whole phrases take on a new kind of organization; that is, loose discourse sequences become more tightly organized syntactic constructions. Again Givón's characterization is apt: today's syntax is yesterday's discourse. Some hypothetical examples based on Givón (although in many cases the historical record is not sufficiently detailed for confidence in the specifics):

- Loose discourse sequences such as *He pulled the door and it opened* may become syntacticized into *He pulled the door open* (a resultative construction).
- Loose discourse sequences such as *My boyfriend . . . He plays piano . . . He plays in a band* may become *My boyfriend plays piano in a band*. Or, similarly, *My boyfriend . . . He rides horses . . . He bets on*

them may become *My boyfriend, who rides horses, bets on them* (a relative clause construction).

- If someone expresses the belief that Mary will wed John, another person may respond with an assent, *I believe that,* followed by a repetition of the expressed belief, *Mary will wed John*—which become syntacticized into the single statement *I believe that Mary will wed John* (a sentential complement construction).

- Complex constructions may also derive from discourse sequences of initially separate utterances, as in *I want it . . . I buy it* evolving into *I want to buy it* (an infinitival complement construction).

The historical processes of grammaticalization and syntacticization derive from a number of psychological and social-communicative processes that have been well studied, most importantly automatization, functional reanalysis, and analogy. Thus, when a person says *going* and *to* together enough (and consistently for the same single function), she ends up saying *gonna* by processes of automaticity very similar to those which occur in a variety of sensory-motor skills (Schneider, 1999). The constraint on such streamlining is of course that the behavior cannot be so streamlined that it no longer serves its communicative function effectively. In situations of high predictability the reduction of phonetic content may be relatively great; in less predictable situations less reduction is possible without serious consequences for communication.

Frequency plays a large role in this process as well, as only relatively frequently used expressions will become highly predictable—which accounts for the well-known principle that the more frequently a word is used in a language the shorter it tends to be (Zipf's Law). Frequency is also crucial because, as is well known, constructions that occur frequently are often irregular. This irregularity can be maintained because items and constructions that are highly frequent can be learned and used on their own, as constructional islands, whereas items and constructions that are less frequent tend to get regularized by pattern-seeking children (or, in the limiting case, they drop out of use as children do not get enough exposures to learn them). An interesting example is the subjunctive in Canadian French, which has dropped out of active use for virtually all low-frequency verbs but has stayed in use for a small number of high-frequency verbs (Poplack, 2001; also note an even narrower pattern in English in which the subjunctive survives for most speakers only in some fixed expressions such as *If I were you . . .*).

Grammaticalization also quite often involves processes of functional reanalysis and analogy. An example from English illustrates (adapted from

Trask, 1996). Old English had a verb *lician* that meant something like "be pleasing to." Like similar verbs in many languages (such as the German *gefallen*, the Spanish *gustar*), this verb had as its subject the thing that pleased, with the person who was pleased with that item appearing in the dative case *(X is pleasing to Fred)*. The normal word order for utterances with this verb consisted of the person being pleased said before the verb (in dative case) and the thing doing the pleasing said after the verb (as subject, agreeing in number with the verb); this is presumably because in English nominals indicating people most often come before verbs (for pragmatic reasons of topicality) and nominals for inanimate objects most often come after verbs. We thus get:

Pam kynge licoden peran.
To the king-[dative] were-pleasing pears. (pears = plural subject)

During the Middle English period, however, English lost much of its case-marking morphology, and so this same utterance was normally expressed:

The king licenden peares.
The king were-pleasing pears. (no dative marking)

It is clear that *pears* is still the subject at this point since the verb agrees with it in number, and not with the singular *king* (the *-en* ending on the verb indicates plurality, as in modern-day German). Finally, the plural marking on the verb was lost too, and we were left with the modern-day:

The king liked pears.

The dative *king* has now been reanalyzed as the subject, and the former subject *pears* as a direct object. Presumably, a driving force in this particular historical development was the fact that this construction had an atypical configuration of case-marking and word order (and perhaps it became less frequent as well, creating pressure for regularization), and so the reanalysis was in some sense aided by a kind of analogy to other Subject-Verb-Object (SVO) constructions.

All of this is not perfectly understood at this point, but for the process of grammaticalization to result in complex and abstract syntactic constructions the organisms involved must be equipped with some fairly complex cognitive and social-cognitive skills, including the ability to form complex schemas and to categorize these and their internal constituents into abstract categories, as well as the abilities to make sophisticated pragmatic inferences, functional reanalyses, and analogies. It may also be that humans' relatively recent specialized speech adaptations enabled the emergence of fully linguistic communication, if for no other reason than that they enabled the very rapid production of sequences of linguistic symbols so that grammaticalization could take place (Lieberman, 1985). In any case, grammaticalization theory is able, at least in principle, to account both for the similarities among the world's languages—based on species-wide skills of cognition, vocal-auditory information processing, and pragmatic inferencing, along with commonalities among peoples in social and communicative goals—and for fundamental differences in these languages, as different speech communities use and grammaticalize different discourse sequences.*

2.1.3. Language Universals

Of crucial importance to the question of whether human grammatical competence is best explained by an innate universal grammar or by processes of grammaticalization is the question of language universals. The basic facts are these. Leaving aside for the moment nouns and verbs—which may or may not be universal in all the world's languages—virtually all linguists who are involved in the detailed analysis of individual languages cross-linguistically (known as linguistic typologists) now agree that there are very few if any specific grammatical categories and constructions that are present in all languages. Many languages simply do not have one or more of what are conventionally called relative clauses, auxiliary verbs, passive constructions, grammatical markers for tense, grammatical markers of evidentiality, prepositions, topic markers, subject markers, a copula *(to be)*, case marking of grammatical roles, subjunctive mood, definite and indefinite articles, incorporated nouns, plural markers, conjunctions, adverbs, complementizers, and on and on. The fact is that many languages (or language families) have grammatical categories and constructions that seem to be unique to them, that is, that do not correspond to any of the European categories and constructions as these have been defined over the centuries, beginning with Greek and Roman sources—who, by the way, created these grammatical entities not with the goal of psychological real-

---

* Some people may doubt that cultural-historical processes can create abstract structures such as those embodied in the grammatical constructions of modern-day languages. But, although the analogy is clearly not perfect, there are many highly abstract structures in modern mathematics that could only have been created by cultural-historical processes since they are not universal among cultures (for example, those of algebra and calculus). Again, there are many disanalogies between language and mathematics (which is more closely related, both logically and historically, to written language). The only point is that abstract symbolic systems can be created by groups of human beings working together over historical time in the domain of mathematics, and so perhaps they can also be created in similar yet different ways in the domain of language.

ity in mind, but rather as resources for the analysis of written texts and the teaching of Latin grammar.

For sure, we can force all languages into one abstract mold, which mostly means forcing the grammatical entities of non-European languages into European categories. Just as there was a time when Europeans viewed all languages through the Procrustean lens of Latin grammar, we may now view the native languages of Southeast Asia, the Americas, and Australia through the Procrustean lens of Standard Average European grammar. But why? On one reasonable view, this is just Eurocentrism, plain and simple, and it is not very good science. Foley and van Valin (1984) speculate about what our linguistic categories and theories would look like if we had begun by analyzing the languages of Southeast Asia and the Pacific Ocean and then attempted to assimilate European languages to them. The conclusion is that they would look very different. Croft (2002) also points out the "methodological opportunism" routinely employed by many linguists looking for language universals. In effect, they focus on a subset of the features that characterize, for instance, English subjects, and claim that any category in any language characterized by this subset is a subject—basically ignoring the features that don't match. From a very practical perspective, Dryer (1997) points out that when different investigators, whatever their theoretical persuasions, look long enough and in enough detail at a given language, they mostly come to agreement about the basic grammatical categories and how they work. The problems arise when they then try to decide if any of these categories correspond to such things as "subject," "preposition," and "auxiliary verb," as these have been defined for European languages. We can fight about it, but is it really a useful fight? The fact that our Greco-Roman pigeonholes do not accommodate many non-European languages in a particularly graceful way should not be surprising, since these pigeonholes were not created with those languages in mind.

Of course there are language universals. It is just that they are not universals of form—that is, not particular kinds of linguistic symbols or grammatical categories or syntactic constructions—but rather they are universals of communication and cognition and human physiology. Because all languages are used by human beings with similar social lives, all peoples have the need to solve in their languages certain kinds of communicative tasks, such as referring to specific entities or predicating things about those entities. All human beings also have the same basic tools for accomplishing those tasks—linguistic symbols, markers on those symbols, ordering of symbols, and prosodic patterns (Bates and MacWhinney, 1982)—and certain grammaticalization pathways seem to recur quite often in the service of those tasks. This leads to some language universals, for example, something like nouns and verbs as expressions of reference and predication using linguistic symbols of certain kinds. Such universals are therefore emergent phenomena, based ultimately on universals of human cognition, human communicative needs, and human vocal-auditory processing. But there is very little evidence in the typological literature for the existence of contentful language universals of the type one would normally associate with an innate universal grammar.

2.2. Ontogenetic Origins

The human adaptation for symbolic communication emerges in human ontogeny quite predictably across cultures at around 1 year of age (Tomasello, 1995a, 1999). It emerges in the context of a whole suite of new social-cognitive skills, the most important for language acquisition being the establishment of joint attentional frames, the understanding communicative intentions, and a particular type of cultural learning known as role reversal imitation. Together this new suite of skills may be referred to as skills of intention-reading, indicating the most fundamental social-cognitive ability underlying them all.

As for grammar, recent findings have demonstrated that prelinguistic infants have some astounding skills of pattern-finding when exposed to various kinds of auditory sequences, which obviously prepare them for acquiring grammatical constructions. But these skills cannot go to work in earnest until children are able to acquire some linguistic symbols in the first place, again depending on key social-cognitive developments at around 1 year of age.

2.2.1. Prelinguistic Infants

When people speak in a language that is totally unfamiliar to us, we have no way of understanding what they are trying to say. Prelinguistic infants are in an even worse situation. Not only do they not know what adults are trying to say, they do not even know *that* adults are trying to say something. They do not even know what "saying something" is. Without an understanding of linguistic symbols and how they work, it is all just noise.

Perhaps surprisingly, there are very few concrete proposals for why children start comprehending and producing language when they do, soon after their first birthdays. In a recent account of early word learning, it is claimed that "in the end, nobody knows why word learning starts at about 12 months and not at six months or three years" (Bloom, 2000: 45). The puzzle is that infants seemingly have conceptualized things they can talk about from at least 4 or 5 months of age, by which time they have, by all accounts, formed concepts of simple objects and events (see, e.g., the research reviewed by Spelke et al., 1994; Baillargeon, 1995). Infants of about this same age have also demonstrated that they can recognize word-like sound patterns when these recur in their experience in association with distinct objects (Jusczyk, 1997). And, of course, one of the best-established findings in infancy research is that even neonates are able to associate two aspects of their experience with one another, including auditory and visual experiences (see Haith and Benson, 1997, for a review). But, since 5-month-olds do not comprehend or produce language, it would seem that concepts, speech units, and associations are not enough.

It is possible that further developments in infants' ability to conceptualize the world emerge at around the first birthday, and so account for the emergence of language. But this is unlikely. The only serious candidate in this regard is infants' emerging ability to deal with so-called sortal categories like "dog" and "duck" (e.g., Xu, Carey, and Welch, 1999). But such categories are not necessary for them to learn, for example, the proper names of those around them. It is also possible that further developments in infants' ability to segment speech are involved in the initial emergence of language. But, again, this is unlikely. Although infants are indeed acquiring new speech-perception skills at around their first birthdays, these would not be necessary for them to learn single words said to them in isolation, which occur with some frequency in at least some infants' daily lives well before language begins. And there exist no serious proposals that infants' skills of association learning undergo any kind of qualitative shift at 1 year of age that would provide some new boost to their ability to acquire language.

An alternative explanation involves infants' social and communicative skills. In this case something important does indeed seem to happen at the appropriate developmental period, and it does so in a way that is correlated with the emergence of language. Thus, although human infants are social creatures from very early in development—they look selectively at schematic drawings of human faces over other perceptual patterns (Fantz, 1963); they recognize other persons as animate beings that are different from physical objects (Legerstee, 1991); they engage in "protoconversations" with adults (Trevarthen, 1979); and they mimic some body movements (Meltzoff and Moore 1977, 1989, 1994)—they are probably not so different from other primate species socially. But near the end of the first year of life something new happens in the way human infants relate to other persons, and, in the current account, this explains why the acquisition of language begins when it does.

In the current account, children begin to acquire language when they do because the learning process depends crucially on the more fundamental skills of joint attention, intention-reading, and cultural learning—which emerge near the end of the first year of life. And importantly, a number of studies have found that children's earliest skills of joint attentional engagement with their mothers correlate highly with their earliest skills of language comprehension and production (see Carpenter, Nagell, and Tomasello, 1998, for a review; and see Chapter 3 for studies of joint attention and word learning). This correlation derives from the simple fact that language is nothing more than another type—albeit a very special type—of joint attentional skill; people use language to influence and manipulate one another's attention.

2.2.2. Early Skills of Intention-Reading

At around 9–12 months of age human infants begin to engage in a host of new behaviors that would seem to indicate something of a revolution in the way they understand their social worlds. Prototypically, it is at this age that infants begin to flexibly and reliably look where adults are looking (gaze following), to use adults as social reference points (social referencing), and to act on objects in the way adults are acting on them (imitative learning). These behaviors are not dyadic—between child and adult (or child and object)—but rather they are triadic in the sense that they involve infants coordinating their interactions with both objects and people, resulting in a referential triangle of child, adult, and the object or event to which they share attention. These behaviors would seem to indicate an emerging understanding of other persons as intentional agents like the self whose psychological relations to outside entities may be followed into, directed, and shared (Tomasello, 1995a). Intentional agents are animate beings who have goals and who make active choices among behavioral means for attaining those goals, including active choices about what to pay attention to in pursuit of them.

Three manifestations of this new level of social understanding are especially important for language acquisition: (1) the joint attentional frame, (2) understanding communicative intentions, and (3) cultural learning in the form of role reversal imitation.

THE JOINT ATTENTIONAL FRAME

First, 1-year-olds' newfound ability to interact triadically with other persons enables them to participate in relatively extended bouts of social interaction mediated by an object in which both participants constantly monitor each other's attention both to the object and to themselves. These periods of joint engagement establish the common ground—what we may call the joint attentional frame*—within which adult-child communication may take place. For example, suppose a child is on the floor playing with a toy, but also is perceiving many other things in the room. An adult enters the room and joins the child in playing with the toy. The joint attentional frame is those objects and activities that the child and the adult know are part of the attentional focus of both of them. In this case, such things as the rug and the sofa and the child's diaper will not be a part of the joint attentional frame, even though the child may be perceiving them basically continuously, because they are not part of "what we are doing." In contrast, if the adult enters the room with a new diaper and readies the child for a diaper change on the rug, then the joint attentional frame may include the diapers and perhaps the rug—but not the toys because "we" have no goals with respect to the toys.

The basic point is that joint attentional frames are defined intentionally, that is, they gain their identity and coherence from the child's and the adult's understandings of "what we are doing" in terms of the goal-directed activities in which we are engaged. In one case we are playing with a toy, which means that certain objects and activities are part of what we are doing, and in another case we are changing a diaper, which brings into existence, from the point of view of our joint attention, a whole different set of objects and activities. This enables the child, as we shall see shortly, to create the common ground within which she may understand the adult's communicative intentions when the adult uses a novel piece of language—at least partly by creating a domain of "current relevance." Another crucial feature of joint attentional frames is that the child understands both the adult's and her own roles in the interaction from the same "outside" perspective—so that they are all in a common representational format (Bruner, 1983; Tomasello, 1999).

UNDERSTANDING COMMUNICATIVE INTENTIONS

Second, 1-year-olds' newfound ability to understand others' communicative intentions enables them to understand communicative intentions inside these joint attentional frames. Human infants very likely begin to understand the intentional actions of others in the last few months of their first year of life, before language begins (Gergely et al., 1995). But commu-

---

* Other terms that have been used are "joint attentional formats" (Bruner, 1981) and "joint attentional scenes" (Tomasello, 1999).

nicative intentions are a special type of intention in which an individual intends something not just toward an inert object but toward the intention states of someone else. Consequently, when an adult addresses an utterance to an infant too young to comprehend intentions, from the infant's point of view the adult is just making noise (for whatever reason). Infants this young may on occasion learn to associate one of these noises with a perceptual event in much the same way a household pet may understand that the sound *dinner* heralds the arrival of food. But this is not language. Sounds become language for young children when and only when they understand that the adult is making that sound with the intention that they attend to something. This requires an understanding of other persons as intentional agents who intend things toward one's own intentional states.

To illustrate, Tomasello, Call, and Gluckman (1997) attempted to communicate with apes and human 2-year-olds by using communicative signs that were totally novel for the subjects. In two of their experimental conditions they indicated for subjects which of three distinct containers contained a reward by (a) placing a small wooden marker on top of the correct container, or (b) holding up an exact replica of the correct container. Before this experiment, children did not know about using markers and replicas as communicative signs, but they nevertheless used these novel signs very effectively to find the reward. In contrast, no ape was able to do this for either of the novel communicative signs. One explanation of these results is that the apes were not able to understand that the human being had intentions toward their attentional states. The apes therefore treated the communicative attempts of the human as discriminative cues on a par with all other types of discriminative cues that have to be laboriously learned over repeated experiences. The children, meanwhile, treated each communicative attempt as an expression of the adult's intention to direct their attention in ways relevant to their current situation.

Said another way, the children understood something of the experimenter's communicative intentions. In one reasonable analysis, to understand your communicative intention I must understand:

You intend for [me to share attention to [X]]

Two aspects of this formulation are especially important. First, according to all analysts from Grice (1975) forward, the understanding of a communicative intention must have this embedded structure. Thus, if you physically push me down into a chair I will recognize your intention that I sit down. But if you tell me "Sit down" I will recognize your intention that I attend to your proposal that I sit down—and if I do sit down it will not be due to physical force but rather because I have changed my intentional states to comply with your proposal. The understanding of a communicative intention is therefore a special case of the understanding of an intention; it is the understanding of another person's intention toward my intentional states. Understanding this is clearly more complex than understanding another person's intention *simpliciter.*

The other important aspect of this analysis is that it readily accommodates different kinds of speech act goals on the part of the speaker and their recognition by the listener. This is accomplished by simply substituting different things for the X in the formula. Thus, in the case of an imperative such as *Sit down,* I understand that you intend for me to attend to your proposal that I sit down. In the case of an indicative, referential utterance such as *A birdie!* I understand that you intend for me to share attention with you to the bird (to attend to your already established attention to the bird). Importantly, in the case of so-called performatives or expressives such as *Hi* or *Thank you,* I understand that you intend for me to attend to your expression of happiness at seeing me or your expression of gratitude at receiving this gift. The reason performatives are important in the current context is that most theories of language acquisition basically ignore them. But they are frequently used communicative symbols, and they have a very similar intentional structure to expressions with a more clearly referential component. If performatives were nothing more than spontaneous and unreflective expressions of emotion (with referential expressions involving some extra cognitive work), there would be no reason children could not begin using them at a much younger age than referential words—but they do not.

Children understand adult communicative intentions, including those expressed in linguistic utterances, most readily inside the common ground established by joint attentional frames. Using adults to highlight the general principles involved, suppose that an American is in a train station in Hungary when a native speaker approaches and starts talking to her in Hungarian. It is very unlikely that in this situation the American visitor will understand the communicative intentions expressed in any Hungarian word or phrase; there is no common ground or joint attentional frame. But suppose now that the American goes to the ticket window, manned by another Hungarian speaker, and tries to buy a ticket. In this situation it is possible that the visitor may come to comprehend the communicative intentions expressed in some Hungarian words and phrases because the two interactants share an understanding of each other's interactive goals in terms of gaining information about train schedules, obtaining a ticket, exchanging money, and so forth—goals expressed directly through the execution of meaningful and already understood actions such as the actual exchanging of ticket and money.

The key for language understanding in such a situation would be for the native speaker to use some novel word or phrase in a context that suggested his reason for making that utterance at that time—for example, while reaching for the bills in the visitor's hand or while offering her the ticket or some change. In such cases the learner makes an inference of the type: If the speaker is using that unknown expression with communicative intention X, then it is relevant to his goal in the current joint attentional frame as I already know it (Sperber and Wilson, 1986; Nelson, 1996). Note that the establishment of a joint attentional frame between child and adult requires the child to read the adult's simple intentions in the general situation (and the adult the child's), whereas identifying the referential event symbolized in an utterance or some part of an utterance requires the child to read adult communicative intentions within that frame. The relationship between the joint attentional frame and the referential event (as one aspect of communicative intentions)—as well as the overall perceptual scene the child is experiencing—is depicted in Figure 2.1.

The general picture is thus that at around 9–12 months of age human infants begin to understand others as intentional agents like the self, which enables them to understand adult intentions on specific occasions in two especially important ways. First, infants begin to monitor the intentional states of other persons toward outside objects and so to engage with them in all kinds of joint attentional activities, including relatively extended periods of joint engagement—joint attentional frames—which serve to "scaffold" children's attention and learning. These joint attentional frames create a common intersubjective ground within which children and adults may understand one another's communicative attempts and their current relevance. Second, infants begin to monitor the intentional states of adults toward themselves and their own intentional/attentional states and so to understand the unique structure of communicative intentions. Understanding communicative intentions seems to happen most readily for young children within the confines of joint attentional frames. This dual-level structure—the establishment of joint attentional frames and the expression of communicative intentions within them—is crucial not only to basic symbol learning, but also to children's pragmatic skills in using language appropriately in different communicative contexts; for example, in children's pragmatic grounding of their own utterances in the current speech situation as defined by the listener's current knowledge and attention, as will be documented below and in Chapter 6.

ROLE REVERSAL IMITATION

Third and finally, understanding others as intentional agents enables some new and species-unique forms of social learning known as cultural learn-

(a) Perceptual situation

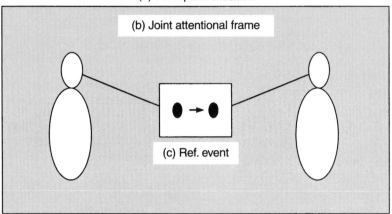

Figure 2.1. The basic adult-child communicative situation: (a) the perceptual situation (not relevant to utterance); (b) the joint attentional frame (immediate relevance); and (c) the event being referred to linguistically.

ing, which underlie children's ability to become producers of language on their own (Tomasello, Kruger, and Ratner, 1993). Children who understand that other persons have intentional relations to the world, similar to their own, may attend especially carefully to the behavioral means that these persons have devised for meeting their goals, and so may imitate their intentional actions. That is, whereas in early infancy there is some face-to-face dyadic mimicking of behaviors (Meltzoff and Moore, 1977), at 9 months of age infants begin to reproduce triadically adults' novel intentional actions on outside objects. This of course opens up the possibility of acquiring the conventional use of tools and other artifacts that presuppose or "point" to outside entities, including symbolic artifacts such as linguistic symbols.

Two recent studies have tested directly what infants understand about others' intentional actions in the context of imitative learning. In the first, Meltzoff (1995) presented 18-month-olds with two types of demonstration. Infants in one group saw the adult perform actions on objects. Infants in the other group saw the adult try but fail to achieve the end result of some target action; for example, the adult tried to pull two parts of an object apart but never succeeded in separating them. Infants in this second group thus never saw the target actions actually performed. Meltzoff found that infants in both groups reproduced the target actions equally well, that is, they appeared to understand what the adult intended to do and performed that action instead of just mimicking the adult's actual behavior. In the second study, Carpenter, Akhtar, and Tomasello (1998a) investigated infants' imitation of accidental versus intentional actions. They had 16-month-olds watch an adult perform some two-action sequences on objects that made interesting results occur. One action of the modeled sequences was marked vocally as intentional ("There!"), and one action was marked vocally as accidental ("Woops!"). Infants were then given a chance to make the result occur themselves, and what they mainly did was to reproduce the adult's intentional actions but not the accidental ones. From soon after their first birthdays, then, infants cannot help perceiving Daddy as "trying to clean the table" or "trying to open the drawer"—not simply as making specific bodily motions or producing salient changes of state in the environment—and these intentional actions are what they attempt to reproduce.

Importantly, in learning to produce an act of symbolic communication, the process of imitative learning is similar to, but somewhat different from, the imitative learning of these straightforward intentional actions. For example, if the child sees an adult operate a novel toy in a particular way and then imitatively learns to do the same thing, there is a parallel in the way the adult and child treat the toy—the child just substitutes herself for the adult. However, when an adult addresses the child with a novel communicative symbol intending to refer her attention to that toy, and the child wants to imitatively learn this communicative behavior, the situation changes. The reason is that in expressing communicative intentions in a linguistic symbol, the adult expresses her intentions toward the child's attentional state. Consequently, if the child simply substitutes herself for the adult she will end up directing the symbol to herself—which is not what is needed. To learn to use a communicative symbol in a conventionally appropriate manner, the child must engage in role reversal imitation: she must learn to use a symbol toward the adult in the same way the adult used it toward her. This is clearly a process of imitative learning in which the child aligns herself with the adult in terms of both the goal and the means for attaining that goal; it is just that in this case the child must not only substitute herself for the adult as actor (which occurs in all types of cultural learning) but also substitute the adult for herself as the target of the intentional act (that is, she must substitute the adult's attentional state as goal for her own attentional state as goal).

The result of this process of role reversal imitation is a linguistic symbol: a communicative device understood intersubjectively from both sides of the interaction. That is to say, this learning process ensures that the child understands that she has acquired a symbol that is socially "shared" in the sense that she can assume in most circumstances that the listener both comprehends and can produce that same symbol—and the listener also knows that they can both comprehend and produce the symbol (see Figure 2.2). This contrasts with the process of understanding communicative signals—for example, by nonhuman primates and presymbolic human infants—in which each participant understands its own role as sender or receiver only, from its own inside perspective. It is interesting to note that the intersubjectivity inherent in socially shared symbols, but not in one-way signals, sets up all kinds of pragmatic "implicatures" of the type investigated by Grice (1975) concerning expectations that other persons will use the conventional means of expression—that we both know they know—and not others that are more cumbersome or indirect.

The main thing to note in Figure 2.2 is the contrast between an associationistic account in which sounds are connected to objects (or concepts) in a direct, dyadic way and a social-pragmatic account in which the relationship is triadic and therefore not one of association but of intentionality (signifier-signified). Using linguistic symbols in utterances is a social act, and when this act is internalized in Vygotskian fashion the product is a unique kind of cognitive representation that is not only intersubjective (involving both self and other), but also perspectival in the sense that the child understands that the same referent could have been indicated in some other way—the speaker could have chosen another linguistic symbol to indicate a different aspect of this entity (Tomasello, 1999).

2.2.3. Early Skills of Pattern-Finding

In addition to these precursors for children's understanding of the symbolic dimensions of linguistic communication, prelinguistic infants demonstrate some of the prerequisite skills necessary for an understanding of the grammatical dimensions of linguistic communication. If we define these prerequisites as a pattern-finding skill (categorization, broadly defined), it has long been recognized that human infants are experts from early in development in finding visual patterns (see Haith and Benson, 1997, for a review). But some more recent findings have extended this to the auditory domain, and in some surprising ways.

It has recently been discovered that prelinguistic infants are able to find patterns in sequentially presented auditory stimuli with amazing facility. Saffran, Aslin, and Newport (1996) exposed 8-month-olds to two minutes of synthesized speech consisting of four tri-syllabic nonsense "words." For

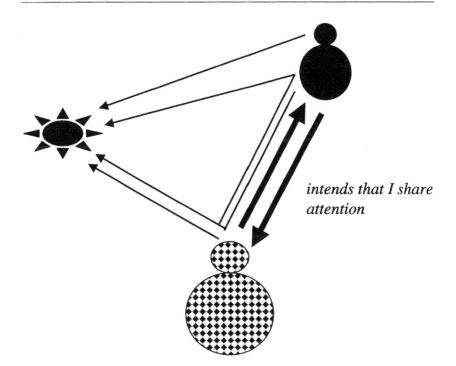

*intends that I share
attention*

Figure 2.2. Structure of a linguistic symbol. Each person can use it to intend (thick lines) that the partner follow her attention (thin lines) to some external entity, that is, to share attention to it.

example, infants would hear *bidakupadotigolabubidakutupiropadoti* . . . They were then exposed to two new streams of synthesized speech simultaneously (one presented to the left and one to the right) to see which they preferred to listen to (as indicated by the direction they turned their head). One of these streams contained "words" from the original (such as *tupiro* and *golabu*), whereas the other contained the same syllables but in a different order (so that there were no "words" from the original). Infants preferred to look toward the speech stream containing the "words" they had originally heard. The only cue in this experiment indicating "words" was that in the original and in one test stream the constituent syllables always occurred together (that is, the transition probabilities were equal to 1.0), whereas in the other test stream syllables occurred together randomly (that is, they never occurred together in the original; transition probabilities were equal to 0). There were no other cues such as intonation or pauses or the like to indicate "word" boundaries.

Subsequent studies have shown that infants can find patterns even when the syllables from the original speech stream and the test speech stream are not the same. Marcus et al. (1999) found that 7-month-olds exposed repeatedly over a three-minute period to tri-syllabic nonsense "words" with the pattern ABB (such as *wididi, delili*) preferred in subsequent testing to look toward the speech stream containing other "words" having this same ABB pattern even though the specific syllables involved were totally new (such as *bapopo*). Gomez and Gerken (1999) found very similar results with 12-month-olds. These results indicate that prelinguistic infants are able to find patterns in auditory stimuli of an abstract nature, which would seem to be a necessary (although not sufficient) skill in the learning of abstract grammatical patterns in linguistic stimuli.

Two other sets of studies help to place these results into perspective. First, infants can find patterns of this same type in nonlinguistic tone sequences and even in visually presented sequences (Saffran et al., 1999; Kirkham, Slemmer, and Johnson, 2002). These pattern-finding skills are thus not specifically linguistic. Second, when nonhuman primates (specifically, tamarin monkeys) are tested in these same procedures, they show these same abilities (Ramus et al., 2000; Newport, Aslin, and Hauser, 2001; Hauser, Weiss, and Marcus, in press). These pattern-finding skills are thus not uniquely human, and so probably express very deep-seated skills of primate vocal-auditory processing. So it is important to remember that 7- and 8-month-old infants who are finding all of these patterns in auditory and visual stimuli in experiments do not process the grammatical constructions of real language—consisting of meaningful symbols—in either comprehension or production. Their pattern-finding skills are thus not sufficient by themselves for dealing with real grammatical constructions used for communication—because the infants do not comprehend the symbolic dimension of those constructions.

And so, what we have is an amazing set of necessary cognitive skills—namely, the statistical learning of concrete and abstract auditory patterns—that are ready to be put to use in constructing the grammatical dimensions of language, once children's ability to understand linguistic symbols comes on-line in the months surrounding their first birthdays. And interestingly, once language acquisition begins in earnest children use their pattern-finding skills on the functional (or meaning) side of things as well. That is, to learn the conventional use of a particular word the child not only must discern across instances that it is the same phonological form (the easiest, limiting case of pattern-finding) but also must see patterns in the way adults use a particular form communicatively across different usage events. This functional pattern-finding ranges from seeing similarities in the different referents to which a word like *ball* might be applied to seeing similarities in the different relationships indicated by the many different uses of the word *for.*

2.3. Children's First Utterances

Intention-reading, broadly construed, is thus the foundational social-cognitive skill underlying children's comprehension of the symbolic dimensions of linguistic communication. Children begin to understand the linguistic symbols produced by adults when they are able to participate with adults in joint attentional frames and then, within that common ground, to understand their specific communicative intentions as expressed in an utterance. The ability to coordinate this intention-reading with social learning skills (creating cultural learning skills, including role reversal imitation) enables children to begin to acquire for themselves conventional linguistic symbols and a number of symbolically constituted gestures as well. With their skills in finding both concrete and abstract patterns in auditory sequences, once children have begun to acquire linguistic symbols they are also ready to begin relatively quickly to acquire more complex and abstract linguistic constructions. The motivational bases for all of this would seem to be specific to uniquely human social and cultural activities; in particular, the motivation would seem to emanate from (1) a desire to communicate with other persons, and (2) a desire to be like other persons (that is, to imitate them).

Children's first active uses of linguistic symbols take place within the common ground of joint attentional frames, and include both gestural and linguistic means. Most 1-year-olds produce a number of different kinds of gestures as well as some conventional linguistic symbols, and these two forms of communication are often coordinated in single utterances. Children of this age produce their gestural and linguistic utterances for both imperative motives, to get the adult to do something with respect to an object or event, and declarative motives, to get adults simply to share attention with them to some external event or entity (Bates, Camaioni, and Volterra, 1975). They also begin to make attempts to learn different kinds of symbols for expressing both aspects of their communicative intention that are already shared with their listener in the joint attentional frame (such as pronouns, demonstratives, some pointing) and aspects of their communicative intention that concern things outside that frame, which must be more specifically indicated (for example, with nouns and verbs).

2.3.1. Early Gestures

Human infants produce three main types of gesture: ritualizations, deictic gestures, and symbolic gestures. The first of these is not symbolic, the third is symbolic, and the second may or may not be. The fact that gestures run the gamut from non-symbolic to symbolic—and emerge along with the first linguistic skills—is strong evidence that children's ability to communicate symbolically is not tied specifically to language but rather emanates from a more fundamental set of social-cognitive skills (Tomasello and Camaioni, 1997).

Ritualizations are gestures in which the infant simply employs an effective procedure for getting something done. For example, many infants from around the world learn to request being picked up by raising their arms over their heads while approaching an adult. This act is not symbolic, as becomes clear if we examine the learning processes involved. Most likely, infants do not learn this gesture by imitating other infants but rather in a more direct way (Locke, 1978). For instance, the infant first attempts to crawl up the adult's body, or reaches for the adult's arm, or grabs at the adult's waist; that is, she engages in an activity designed to bring about the desired result physically. The adult understands what the infant wants and so responds accordingly. On a future occasion, the adult sees the infant approach and prepare for this same activity—her arms begin to go up—and so responds appropriately to these very first signs (the infant's "intention movement" in ethological terminology; Tinbergen, 1951). The infant, for her part, notices that as soon as she raises her arms the adult springs into action, and so she learns that just the initial part of the sequence is sufficient to obtain the desired result. She then begins to produce just the first part of the sequence, the "arms up" (often in a stylized version; Bates, 1979), in order to obtain the desired result not physically but socially and communicatively through adult assistance.

This learning process is essentially the one by which nonhuman primates learn their gestures (Tomasello, 1996). Because it does not involve understanding communicative intentions or cultural (imitative) learning of any sort, it does not create a shared communicative symbol. Indeed, it is very likely that if some other very small infant were to approach our signaling infant with his arms raised, our infant would not know what he wanted. She would not know that he was using "the same" gesture as she; she would know the gesture from the producer's side only. Ritualized gestures are thus not symbolic because the gesturer is not attempting to influence the attention of the other with some mutually understood communicative act (toward sharing attention or any other end), but only to achieve some concrete result using a behavior that originally was designed to be physically efficacious.

The second type of gestures is deictics, which are designed to direct adult attention to outside entities. The prototypes are showing (as in holding up an object to the adult) and pointing. Infant pointing has not been studied in great detail, but several important facts about how infants learn and use pointing gestures are known.

The most important fact is that, unlike most ritualizations that only involve a signaler and an interactant dyadically, pointing is generally triadic; there is some third entity involved. But this does not automatically mean that the infant is pointing in order to induce the adult to share attention with her on that third entity. Indeed, for some infants pointing is just another ritualization. For example, many infants use arm and index finger extension to orient their own attention to things. If an adult were to respond to this by attending to the same thing and then share excitement with the infant by smiling and talking to her, then this kind of pointing might also become ritualized—as a kind of request for increased social interaction with the adult (Moore and D'Etremont, 2001). In this scenario it would be possible for an infant to point for others while still not understanding the function of other persons' pointing, and indeed a number of empirical studies have found just such a dissociation in many infants (production but not comprehension of pointing)—as well as the reverse dissociation in which they visually follow adult pointing but do not themselves point (comprehension but not production; Franco and Butterworth, 1996; Carpenter, Nagell, and Tomasello, 1998). Infants who learn to point via ritualization, therefore, understand their gesture just as their "arms up" gesture: as a procedure for getting something done, not as an invitation to share attention using a mutually understood communicative symbol.

The alternative is that the infant sees an adult pointing for her and comprehends that the adult is attempting to induce her to share attention to something, and then imitatively learns that when she has the same goal she can use the same means, with roles reversed, thus creating an intersubjective symbolic act for sharing attention. It is crucial that in this learning process the infant is not just mimicking adults' sticking out their fingers; she is truly understanding and attempting to reproduce the adult's intentionally communicative act, including both means and end. It is crucial because a bi-directional symbol can only be created when the child first understands the intentions behind the adult's communicative act, and then identifies with those intentions herself as she produces the "same" means for the "same" end.

Empirically we do not know whether infants learn to point via ritualization or imitative learning or whether some infants learn in one way (especially prior to their first birthdays) and some learn in the other. And it may even happen that an infant who learns to point via ritualization later comes to comprehend adult pointing in a new way, and so comes to a new understanding of her own pointing and its equivalence to the adult version (Franco and Butterworth, 1996). Interestingly, Petitto (1988) has documented an important difference between the "natural" gestures of deaf children and their truly linguistic signs in American Sign Language (ASL). Most deaf children learn to point "naturally," but they also learn to point in ASL as symbols in this linguistic system (for example, for *me* and *you*). Deaf children differentiate these two types of pointing in several ways right from the beginning; for example, they sometimes make reversal errors with *me* and *you* as ASL symbols. These children thus seem to learn both an indexical or deictic form of pointing, as other children do, and also a symbolic form of pointing for ASL—most likely learned imitatively from observation of others using the ASL pointing symbol.

It is also of crucial theoretical significance that human infants point for others not just for imperative motives—to get help with something—but also for declarative motives such as simply wishing to share attention with them. Declarative pointing (and showing) may thus be the purest expression of the uniquely human social-cognitive motivation to share attention with others. Indeed, the lack of declarative pointing in the second year of life is a key diagnostic criterion for children with autism (Baron-Cohen, 1995).

The third kind of infant gestures is symbolic (sometimes called referential) gestures (Acredolo and Goodwyn, 1988; Pizzuto and Volterra, 2000). These are communicative acts that are associated with a referent either metonymically or iconically. Examples include such things as sniffing for a flower, panting for a dog, holding arms out for an airplane, raising arms for big things, and blowing for hot things. It is possible that some of these may be acquired via ritualization—the child performs a behavior spontaneously and the adult reacts in some positive way—but it is much more likely that in most cases infants are learning these symbolic gestures via imitation. That is, they are learning exactly as some infants learn to point symbolically via imitative learning or use linguistic symbols: by first understanding an adult's communicative intention in using the gesture and then engaging in role reversal imitation to use the gesture herself when she has "the same" communicative intention.

One interesting question concerning symbolic gestures is the role of iconicity. When the child holds out her arms like an airplane or pants like a dog, is she mimicking some aspect of the physical or behavioral properties of the object, or has she just learned from an adult a gesture that is as arbitrarily related to its referent as a linguistic symbol? There is not so much research relevant to this question, but it seems likely that the iconicity in such cases is in the eyes of the adult only and plays very little role in acquisition. Evidence for this interpretation is: (1) in the earliest stages, deaf children learning sign language are not helped by the iconicity of many sign language signs (Bonvillian, Garber, and Dell, 1997); (2) early in the second year, human infants can learn arbitrary gestures used referentially (like human object names) as easily as they learn words (Namy and Waxman, 1998); and (3) in experiments, 18-month-olds are unable to use iconicity to understand an adult's specific communicative intention (Tomasello, Striano, and Rochat, 1999). Symbolic gestures are thus very likely the same as spoken symbols in being learned via imitation of adults and in being only conventionally connected to their intended referents.

Thus, although human infants vocalize and babble from soon after birth, it is gestures that for many children seem to be the first carriers of their communicative intentions. And it is gestures that seem to pave the way to early language—at least from a functional point of view. In a study of the emergence of language in 12 Italian-speaking children, Iverson, Capirci, and Caselli (1994) found that virtually all the infants gestured frequently with adults, and that the function of children's gestures changed—from the primary carriers of communicative intent to a more supplementary function—as they began to acquire some conventional linguistic symbols (see also Marcos, 1991). Interestingly, in a comprehension experiment, Morford and Goldin-Meadow (1992) found that 1- and 2-year-old children could understand gestures in combination with speech, both when they were referentially redundant and when the gesture provided unique information (see also Golinkoff, 1983, on the interaction of speech and gesture in the early "negotiation of meaning" between infant and adult). Similarly, Harris, Barlow-Brown, and Chasin (1995) found a very strong correlation between children's tendency to point and their tendency to use object names. The research of Goodwyn and Acredolo (1993) also provides support for this position, as they found strong correlations between children's use of symbolic gestures before language and their early linguistic skills.

The importance and robustness of gesture as a communicative device are evidenced by the fact that even young blind children gesture while communicating (Iverson and Goldin-Meadow, 1998). And of course gesture remains a crucial aspect of human communication throughout childhood and even into adulthood (McNeill, 1992; Goldin-Meadow, 1997).

From this point of view, the existence of fully grammaticized sign languages and their ready acquisition by deaf children is not surprising. With respect to very early language in particular, it is interesting that deaf children acquiring a signed language do so on the same general timetable as hearing children learning a vocal language—thus demonstrating something of the robustness of the symbolic dimensions of human linguistic competence.

2.3.2. Early Holophrases

Most Western middle-class children begin producing conventional linguistic symbols in utterances in the months following their first birthdays. By the time they begin doing this, they typically have been communicating with other people gesturally and vocally for some months. Children's first linguistic expressions are learned and used in the context of these prior forms of nonlinguistic communication and for the same basic motives— declarative and imperative—and children soon learn to ask things interrogatively as well. There is typically a distinctive intonational pattern for each of these three types of speech act (declarative, imperative, interrogative). Children's first declarative utterances are sometimes about shared, topical referents and sometimes aimed at focusing the listener's attention on something new (typically assessed only from their own egocentric point of view; Greenfield and Smith, 1976).

At this early age the communicative functions of children's single-word utterances are an integral aspect of their reality for the child, and initially these functions (for example, imperative or interrogative) may not be well differentiated from the more referential aspects of the utterance (Ninio, 1992, 1993). That is to say, children's early one-word utterances may be thought of as "holophrases" that convey a holistic, undifferentiated communicative intention, most often the same communicative intention as that of the adult expressions from which they were learned (Barrett, 1982; Ninio, 1992). Many of children's early holophrases are relatively idiosyncratic, and their uses can change and evolve over time in a somewhat unstable manner. For example, Tomasello (1992a) reported the following holophrases for his daughter early in her language development:

- *Rockin:* First used while rocking in the rocking chair, then as a request to do so, and then as a name for the object.
- *Phone:* First used in response to hearing the telephone ring, then as she "talked" on the phone, then to point at and name the phone, and then when she wanted someone to pick her up so she could talk on the wall-phone (pointing to it).

- *Play-play:* First used as an accompaniment to her "playing" the piano, then to name the piano.
- *Towel:* First used as an accompaniment to her using a towel to clean up a spill, then to name the towel.
- *Steps:* First used as an accompaniment to her climbing or descending stairs (never to name the object).
- *Bath:* First used as an accompaniment to preparations for bath, then as she bathed her baby doll (never to name the object).
- *Game:* First used for others and then for herself playing with a baseball and baseball glove (never to name objects).
- *Make:* First used in block play to request that a structure be built, usually so that she could knock it down (and make a "mess").
- *Mess:* First used for the result of knocking down blocks, then when she wanted to knock them down.

In addition, however, some of children's holophrases are a bit more conventional and stable. Children speaking all the languages of the world often talk about such salient scenes of experience as the existence-nonexistence-recurrence of people and objects, the exchange-possession of objects, the movement-location of people and objects, various states and changes of states of objects, and the physical and mental activities of people (Brown, 1973). Thus, combining basic speech act motives and salient scenes of experience, young children of linguistic communities from around the world tend to use their earliest productive language to do such things as:

- request or indicate the existence of objects (for example, by naming them with a requestive or neutral intonation);
- request or describe the recurrence of objects or events (*more, again, another*);
- request or describe dynamic events involving objects (as described by *up, down, on, off, in, out, open, close*);
- request or describe the actions of people *(eat, kick, ride, draw)*;
- comment on the location of objects and people *(here, outside)*;
- ask some basic questions *(Whats-that? Where-go?)*;
- attribute a property to an object *(pretty, wet)*; and
- use performatives to mark specific social events and situations *(hi, bye, thank you, no)*.

An important issue for later language development is what parts of adult expressions children choose for their initial holophrases. The answer presumably lies in the specific language they are learning and the kinds of discourse in which they participate with adults, including the perceptual salience of particular words and phrases in adults' speech (Slobin, 1985a). In English, most beginning language learners acquire a number of so-called relational words such as *more, gone, up, down, on,* and *off,* presumably because adults use these words in salient ways to talk about salient events (Bloom, Tinker, and Margulis, 1993; McCune, 1992). Many of these words are verb particles in adult English, and so the child at some point must learn to talk about the same events with phrasal verbs such as *pick up, get down, put on,* and *take off.* In Korean and Mandarin Chinese, in contrast, children learn fully adult verbs from the onset of language development because these verbs are most salient in adult speech to them (parallel to an English verb like *remove* for clothing; Choi and Gopnik, 1996; Gopnik and Choi, 1995; Tardif, 1996). When they begin with an adult verb as a holophrase, children must then at some point learn, at least for some discourse purposes, to fill in linguistically the nominal participants involved in the scene (as in *Remove shirt!*). Children in all languages also learn object labels for some events, such as *Bike!* as a request to ride a bicycle or *Birdie* as a comment on a passing flight, which means that they still need to learn to linguistically express the activity involved *(Ride bike! or See birdie).* The point is that children may begin talking about different scenes in different ways initially, and these ontogenetic starting points frame the subsequent task in particular ways.

In addition, most children begin language acquisition by learning some unparsed adult expressions as holophrases—such expressions as *I-wanna-do-it, Lemme-see,* and *Where-the-bottle.* The prevalence of this pattern in the early combinatorial speech of English-speaking children has been documented by Pine and Lieven (1993), who found that almost all children have at least some of these so-called frozen phrases in their early speech. This is especially true of some children, especially later-born children who observe siblings (Barton and Tomasello, 1994; Bates, Bretherton, and Snyder, 1988). In these cases there is different syntactic work to do if the child is to extract productive linguistic elements that can be used appropriately in other utterances, in other linguistic contexts, in the future. For this the child must engage in a process of segmentation, with regard not only to the speech stream but also to the communicative intentions involved—so as to determine which components of the speech stream go with which components of the underlying communicative intention.

As a nonlinguistic example, we may imagine that a child sees an adult use a stapler and understands that his goal is to staple together two pieces of paper. In some cases, the child may understand also that the sub-goal/function of placing the papers inside the stapler's jaws is to align them with the stapling mechanism inside the stapler, and that the sub-goal/function of pressing down on the stapler is to eject the staple through the two papers—with both of these sub-functions being in the service of the overall goal of attaching the two sheets of paper. The child does not need to understand all of this to mimic an adult stapling papers with the same stapler over and over again (an analogy: the child can say *There-ya-go* over and over again without understanding its internal constituents). But to the extent that the child does not understand these sub-functions, she will be lost when she encounters a new stapler in which the sub-functions are effected by a different means, for example, one whose stapling mechanism does not require pressing down but rather squeezing. Extracting a functionally coherent unit from an intentional action sequence—whether in action or language—means identifying sub-functions (sub-goals) in some larger whole.

This segmenting of (communicative) intentions is used by English-speaking children to learn some kinds of linguistic elements (for example, extracting unstressed prepositions such as *of* from such phrases as *piece-of-ice* and *scared-of-that;* Tomasello, 1987), but in languages that are less isolating than English (for example, polysynthetic languages such as many Eskimo languages) the whole-to-parts pattern of acquisition, requiring the segmenting of communicative intentions to extract meaningful elements, is the normal case. For example, in Inuktitut many early utterances are word-sentences such as *Taartaulirtunga,* meaning "Something is in my way," or *Tuqutaulangasivungaa!* meaning "I'm going to get killed!" (Allen, 1996)—which obviously require some segmenting to extract the productive elements involved. In any event, the general principle is that young children come equipped to move in either direction—part to whole or whole to parts—in learning to linguistically partition experiential scenes and indicate their constituents with different linguistic elements in multi-unit expressions and constructions. All children probably use both processes to some extent in different aspects of language acquisition.

Thus, from soon after their first birthdays infants learn to communicate symbolically about the important scenes in their lives using conventional linguistic expressions. Most often their utterances reflect salient components of fully formed utterances that adults use in those scenes. Functionally speaking, children's early one-unit utterances are entire semantic-pragmatic packages—holophrastic expressions—that express a single relatively coherent, yet undifferentiated, communicative intention. Why children begin with only one-unit expressions—either individual words or holistic expressions—is not known at this time. But it is presumably the case that in many instances they initially only attend to limited parts of adult utterances, or can only process one linguistic unit at a time. The degree to which children productively control communicative functions as expressed by intonations separately from linguistic forms—so that they can hear an expression used for one function with one intonation but use it themselves creatively for another function with another intonation—is also unknown. However, there is some evidence from a single diary study that children's earliest holophrases are mostly tied to a single intonational contour for some months (Galligan, 1987), providing further evidence for their undifferentiated nature.

Many accounts of early language development describe the process as one in which children first acquire words and then combine them, perhaps via rules, into sentences. This is basically a structural point of view, and it is aimed at languages like English, which are very isolating, not at languages like Inuktitut. From a more functional point of view, children are hearing and producing whole utterances, and their task is to break down an utterance into its constituent parts and so to understand what functional role is being played by each of those parts in the utterance as a whole. When they produce holophrases, children have simply assigned the function of the utterance to a single linguistic unit (perhaps with an associated intonation contour), and so in the future they will have to attend to other linguistic units in similar utterances and in this way fill out their linguistic expression to fit the adult-like conventions.

2.4. Summary

Adopting the usage-based perspective from the first chapter, I have proposed in this chapter some specific hypotheses about the phylogenetic and ontogenetic origins of language. First, the symbolic dimensions of language derive from a uniquely human biological adaptation for things cultural. This adaptation may be characterized as the ability to understand that other persons have intentional and mental states like one's own—which leads, quite naturally, to a desire to manipulate those intentional and mental states via social conventions. Second, the grammatical dimensions of language derive from people's uses of linguistic symbols in patterned ways for purposes of interpersonal communication, as these are played out repeatedly over historical time. In the evolution of human languages, various kinds of primate-wide pattern-finding and categorization skills—in combination with such things as pragmatic inferencing and automatization—worked over historical time in processes of grammaticalization and syntacticization to create in different linguistic communities a variety of different types of grammatical constructions. There was no biological adaptation for grammar.

The evolutionary adaptation for understanding others as intentional agents like the self becomes manifest in human ontogeny today at around

9–12 months of age. It enables human infants to engage with other persons in a variety of new ways, and it enables them for the first time to understand the communicative intentions of other persons as embodied in acts of symbolic communication, that is, in utterances. More specifically, at around their first birthdays infants become able to:

- establish with adults various *joint attentional frames* that create a common intersubjective ground for communication;
- within these frames, *understand communicative intentions* as they are expressed in utterances; and
- engage in *role reversal imitation* to acquire symbolic conventions first used toward them in these frames.

Language emerges in human children in the months following the first birthday—and not before—because this is when these fundamental skills of intention-reading are solidly in place.

Children's first symbolic productions are various kinds of gestures and linguistic holophrases and expressions that are often coordinated with one another in the same utterance. Children's gestures come in different forms —ritualizations, deictics, and symbolic gestures—which reflect rather directly the intention-reading and social learning processes involved. The existence of symbolic gestures, sometimes prior to linguistic communication, demonstrates that human symbolic capacities are not confined only to language. But linguistic symbols, which are perspectival in a way that symbolic gestures are not, go beyond symbolic gestures in requiring especially sophisticated skills of intention-reading and perspective-taking.

In learning a language children could in principle memorize utterances in the contexts in which adults use them, and then reproduce those utterances in those contexts as needed—without internal analysis. They do this in some cases *(Hello, Thank-you, See-ya-later)*. But most often they attempt to analyze the utterances they hear and partition them into constituents both structurally and functionally. That is, they use their already existing skills of categorization and statistical learning on the utterances they experience to begin moving down the road of grammatical development. In this process children do two things simultaneously. First, they extract from utterances and expressions such small things as words, morphemes, and phrases by identifying the communicative job these elements are doing in the utterance or expression as a whole. Second, they see patterns across utterances, or parts of utterances, with "similar" structure and function, which enables them to create more or less abstract categories and constructions. These are the two faces of grammar: smaller elements and larger patterns. In producing utterances, children may then use their constructional patterns as templates within which they insert previously extracted words, morphemes, and phrases—often within functional restrictions—to produce creative and yet conventional utterances. The main point—to presage a coming theme—is thus that learning words and learning grammar are really all a part of the same developmental process.

THREE

Words

The question "What is a word really?" is analogous to
"What is a piece in chess?"

—LUDWIG WITTGENSTEIN

WORD LEARNING is often characterized as a kind of mini–linguistics lesson, similar to vocabulary lessons in a foreign language classroom, in which adults point to and name objects for children. In this pointing-and-naming game, the process seems relatively simple. The child only has to associate the word she is currently hearing with the thing she is currently seeing. Another popular metaphor is that children "map" words onto things (or perhaps concepts of things).

Unfortunately, this game is not representative of the vast majority of word-learning situations that children encounter in their daily lives. First, adults in many cultures do not stop what they are doing to name things for children at all. These children experience basically all words in the ongoing flow of social interaction and discourse in which adults produce many different types of words in many different types of utterances— virtually none of which present new words isolated from other words while at the same time the adult is explicitly designating some entity with pointing or some other gesture. Second, even the most pedagogically conscious Western middle-class parents seldom play the pointing-and-naming game with words other than object labels; parents do not say to their children "Look! Giving" or "Look! Of." This means that the child must learn many, perhaps most, words from more complex interactive situations in which determining the adult's intended referent for some novel word is much less straightforward. Third, even in the pointing-and-naming game, things are not as simple as they first appear. When someone holds up a toy car and names it for a child, how is the child to know whether the adult is saying something like *car* or *toy* or *Volkswagen*? Or even worse, how is the child to know that the adult is naming the object at all—as opposed to designating one of its parts or properties, or its owner or some action it is about to engage in?

Despite these difficulties, children around the world learn new words on a daily basis—several per day once the process really gets started. This is the miracle of word learning. Some theorists believe that the feat is so miraculous that children could not accomplish it without some special help, in the form of some special word learning constraints or principles that they bring to the word learning process. Another view—and the one that will be adopted here—is that children's skills of joint attention, intention reading, and cultural learning, as explicated in the previous chapter, provide them with the "special help" they need. At the beginning, children use these skills almost exclusively to determine the adult's communicative intentions in using a novel word in a particular context. But as they learn more and more language—both other words and some grammatical constructions—they are able to use their understanding of this known language to help them to determine the communicative intentions behind much of the new language they hear.

I thus adopt in this chapter the so-called social-pragmatic theory of word learning, in which children's ability to read the intentions and communicative intentions of other persons is central. Other factors are integral to the process as well: the ability to segment speech and the ability to conceptualize entities, to name just two important prerequisites. And linguistic factors also contribute importantly as well, and may even in some cases be necessary, to the learning process—especially for words that are defined mainly in contrast to other words (*lend* as opposed to *give*) and for words that typically take much of their meaning from the surrounding linguistic context *(get, of)*. But the current proposal is that the glue that holds all of these factors together is always the child's attempts to understand the communicative intentions of other persons as she interacts with them socially and linguistically.

3.1. Early Words and Their Uses

The vast majority of research on children's word learning has focused on content words such as nouns and verbs (and sometimes adjectives), with so-called function words typically being studied under the aegis of grammar and being basically ignored in theories of word learning. But the fact that children manage to master the form and function of so many different kinds of words—that do so many different kinds of communicative jobs—is, or should be, crucially important for theories of word learning (see Wittgenstein's, 1955, analogy between a linguistic vocabulary and a tool-box containing everything from hammers and saws to pencils and rulers). In the account of word learning presented here I will, following tradition, focus on the acquisition of content words (open-class words such as nouns and verbs), but will also attempt to place these in the context of the wider range of lexical items that young children acquire—many of which will be further discussed, also following tradition, in later chapters concerned with grammatical issues (for example, closed-class words such as articles, modal auxiliaries, and pronouns in Chapter 6). A complete theory of word learning should account for children's acquisition of all these word types, ideally within the framework of a single, coherent set of learning and cognitive processes.

3.1.1. First Words

The first words that children learn and use include exemplars from almost all of the major parts of speech from adult language: proper nouns, common nouns, pronouns, verbs, adjectives, adverbs, prepositions, and so forth. The main exceptions to this are some minor parts of speech that are low in salience both phonologically and semantically, such as articles, conjunctions, and auxiliary verbs. But virtually no one believes that adult part-of-speech categories are relevant to children just beginning to learn language; children are simply learning a collection of individual communicative conventions for regulating their social interactions with adults. Some investigators have therefore grouped children's early words into categories that seem more relevant for them, but even in this case without proposing that these categories are real for young children. The best-known scheme is Nelson's (1973; see Gopnik, 1988, for a similar grouping), which includes:

- General nominals: *apple, shoe.*
- Specific nominals: *Sarah, Mommy.*
- Action words: *throw, dance.*
- Personal-social words: *bye-bye, thank you.*
- Modifiers: *cold, wet.*
- Functors: *of, and.*

It nevertheless turns out that across many of the world's languages children initially seem to learn adult nouns more readily than adult verbs and other types of words, as first documented by Gentner (1982). This is a striking finding because across different languages nouns, verbs, and other words are used in very different ways. Thus, some languages would seem to be more noun-friendly because all clauses must have nominals (ensuring the relative high frequency of nouns), and nouns are often especially salient in the speech stream (they occur in utterance-final position, with stress, etc.). Other languages would seem to be more verb-friendly since many clauses consist of verbs only with no nominals (for example, when Chinese speakers indicate an ongoing event such as a boy kissing a girl, they quite often say only the equivalent of *Kiss*), and verbs are often more salient than nouns in the speech stream. Most critically, in basically all languages individual verbs—and many other relational words and function words—occur with higher token frequency in the language children hear than do nouns (since many relations and actions such as coming and going recur in the child's experience regularly, across many different situations, whereas particular objects such as ducks and flowers are mostly experienced irregularly). Nevertheless, children quite often, if not always, learn more nouns early in development than other types of words.

The claim that the so-called noun bias is universal has not gone unchallenged, however. A number of researchers have claimed that the hypothesis does not hold for particular languages, for example, Korean (Choi and Gopnik, 1995), Chinese (Tardif, 1996), and Tzotzill (de León, 2000). These are all very verb-friendly languages, and when spontaneous speech samples are taken the children quite often use more verbs than nouns early in development. The problem is that because children use each of their verbs more frequently than they use each of their nouns, spontaneous speech samples tend to underestimate children's noun vocabularies—since the probability that a child will use any particular noun in one hour of sampling is not very high. For this reason, Caselli, Casadio, and Bates (1999) used a parent interview measure to estimate the vocabularies of English-speaking children and Italian-speaking children, reasoning that this measure would be less sensitive to sampling issues. Italian has some of the properties of a verb-friendly language (e.g., verbs occur quite often at the ends of utterances in child directed speech) and so might be expected to show a verb advantage. But it did it not, and indeed Italian children show almost as strong a noun advantage as American children. Tardif, Gelman, and Xu (1999) addressed this issue directly by measuring Chinese children's vocabularies in both ways (spontaneous sample and parent interview), and the verb advantage for these children mostly disappeared with the interview measure. Surprisingly, there has been very little experimental work on this issue, but the studies that exist show that with similar numbers of exemplars children tend to learn novel nouns more easily than novel verbs (Goldin-Meadow, Seligman, and Gelman, 1976; Childers and Tomasello, in press).

Gentner (1982) provided a plausible explanation for the developmental priority of nouns: the Natural Partitions hypothesis. In brief, her hypothesis was that the nouns children learn early in development are prototypically used to refer to concrete objects, and concrete objects are more easily individuated from their environmental surroundings than are states, actions, processes, and attributes. Concrete objects are spatially bounded entities, perceptible at a glance, whereas actions and events have more fluid temporal boundaries, and these are defined in different ways for different verbs (*cleaning* is over when things are clean, but *running* and *smiling* have no such clearly defined endpoints). Verbs also vary in basic parameters such as whether causation is an essential semantic element (*die* versus *kill*).

Gentner and Boroditsky (2001) elaborated on this explanation, as depicted in Figure 3.1. The argument is that nouns and other open-class words show relative cognitive dominance, in that their primary function is to denote perceptible entities in the world, whereas relational words (especially closed-class items) mostly serve to provide linguistic connections among the more referential, open-class words. Indeed, most relational words have determinant meanings only in the context of nouns or other referential terms: the words *the* and *and* do not really indicate things in the world in the same way as *the ball* or *Jill and Jack*. Relational terms are thus more linguistically dominant, in the sense that they take their meaning partially from other linguistic items in the context. Verbs are somewhere in the middle of this continuum since they rely on their arguments *(He kicked the ball)* to denote a referential situation fully—leading Langacker (1987a) to say that nouns are more conceptually autonomous, whereas verbs are more conceptually dependent. As one piece of evidence for this view, Gentner and Boroditsky (2001) cite the study of Gillette et al. (1999), who found that when viewing a videotape of adult-child interactions with the sound off—so that none of the discourse contexts for key words could be heard—adults had much more difficulty inferring the verb an adult was using as opposed to the noun she was using.

While the general outlines of this explanation are not in dispute, it is almost certainly the case that other factors are at work as well. This is suggested by three additional sets of facts. First, most children learn many different kinds of words early in development—regardless of relative frequencies—thus demonstrating that they can, in the appropriate conditions, individuate many different kinds of referents in the world. And quite often the first words children learn are not nouns but personal-social words such as *hello, goodbye, please, no,* and *thank you* (e.g., Gopnik, 1988; Bloom, Tinker, and Margulis, 1993; Caselli et al., 1995). Because these words are performatives, and not referential at all, they are largely ignored in discussions of children's first words. (Interestingly, despite their lack of concrete reference, these words are not in any obvious way linguistically dominant, and so are presumably individuated mostly on the basis

◄── cognitive dominance				linguistic dominance ──►	
◄── open class					closed class ──►

proper names	concrete nouns	kinship terms and other relational systems	verbs	spatial prepositions	determiners conjunctions
Ida	*dog* *spoon*	*grandmother* *uncle*	*skate* *enter*	*on* *over*	*the* *and*

Figure 3.1. Division of dominance. From Gentner and Boroditsky (2001); reprinted with the permission of Cambridge University Press.

of perceptual experience—in this case, of social situations—which is, in a very broad sense, consistent with Gentner's latest hypothesis.) But the important point is that the nature of the referent involved cannot be the only factor determining whether children do or do not learn a word because they learn some words that lack a concrete referent.

Second, many of the nominals that children learn early in development—and that are counted when comparing their nouns to their verbs—do not really have as referents easily individuated concrete objects. Nelson, Hampson, and Shaw (1993) found that only about half of the specific nouns children use early in development are prototypical concrete objects, that is, basic-level object categories such as *dog* and *chair*—"things you can hold or bump into." Just as frequent were nominals that did not refer to such tangible things, words such as *breakfast, kitchen, plastic, kiss, lunch, light, park, doctor, night,* and *party.* From a conceptual point of view, the referents of these nouns would not seem to be more easily individuated than those of verbs and other relational words. Also interesting in this context are Nelson's (1995) observations of children's early acquisition of so-called dual-category words such as *brush, kiss, bite, drink, walk, hug, help,* and *call,* which can be used as either nouns or verbs. There is no evidence that the noun function is learned first, but rather the frequency and salience of adult use seem to be the most important factors.

Third, in an experimental study Tomasello and Akhtar (1995) found that 24-month-olds learn nouns and verbs equally well for ambiguous referential situations. In one study, all children saw an adult perform a novel and nameless action (target action) with a novel and nameless object (target object) on a special apparatus. Children in the "action highlighted" condition then watched as the adult prepared the apparatus so that the child could perform it again (by orienting the apparatus correctly for him). The adult then held out the object to the child and said "Your turn, Jason. Widgit!" while alternating her gaze between the child and the apparatus— as if requesting that the child perform the action. In the "object high-lighted" condition the experimenter did not prepare the apparatus for the child but simply held out the object to the child and said "Widgit, Jason! Your turn," while alternating her gaze between the child and the object (never looking at the apparatus at all). As determined by later testing, chil-dren in the "action highlighted" condition learned the new word for the target action, whereas children in the "object highlighted" condition learned the new word for the target object. A second study, using a similar method but a different set of cues, replicated this result. The important point here is that the pragmatics of the situation in which the child learns a new word structure the learning process, so much so that in some cases the ease with which referents are individuated is a secondary factor.

The fact that children can learn many different kinds of words early in development, and that in some conditions they learn other kinds of words as easily as concrete nouns, suggests a social-pragmatic modification to the Natural Partitions hypothesis. The modified hypothesis is that children learn words most readily in situations in which it is easiest to read the adult's communicative intentions. Thus, in the right situation they can learn event-type nouns such as *breakfast,* performatives such as *no,* and some verbs and other relational words. But concrete nouns, with percepti-ble referents, are often used in pragmatically simple situations, in which the adult's communicative intentions are especially clear—for example, in handling objects or pointing out new objects for shared inspection (al-though this has never been investigated systematically). Importantly, this hypothesis does not conflict with the Natural Partitions hypothesis, be-cause the cognitive dominance of nouns is one of the most important fac-tors making it easier for children to interpret utterances containing them. It is just that in the current view cognitive dominance (relative ease of indi-viduation) is only one of several factors that contribute to the relative ease with which children can read adult communicative intentions in utter-ances with novel words.

It would also be worth investigating whether nouns are used more often in linguistic contexts that are more well known to children, for example, in English, the various presentational constructions (*It's a X, There's a X,* and so on)—which are used almost exclusively with nouns (and there are no comparable linguistic frames for other types of words). There has been very little experimental research on the question of which words children find easiest to learn and the factors that determine this. Varying pragmatic contexts and linguistic contexts in presenting different types of novel words to young children would go a long way toward settling many of the outstanding issues.

3.1.2. Rates of Learning

During the first five years of language acquisition, young children average learning about one new word every one to two waking hours (depending on how such things as *dog* and *dogs* are counted). This is truly an amazing rate of learning. But the growth curve across this period is positively accelerating, with a much faster rate near the end of the preschool period. In fact, during the first year of language acquisition, age 1–2 years, children learn only about one new word per day, and at the very outset the rate is more like one word per week (Fenson et al., 1994).

Children's rates of learning in comprehension and production in English and Italian (based on the MacArthur Communicative Development Inventory, which is basically a parent interview; Fenson et al., 1994) are presented in Figure 3.2. The most obvious pattern to observe is that in both languages comprehension outstrips production by several orders of magnitude throughout early development (although it must be kept in mind that assessment procedures for comprehension and production are different; Tomasello and Mervis, 1994). Grouping the Italian words into four broad classes of word types, we get Figure 3.3. Here, the most obvious pattern to observe is that, after the very earliest phases, nouns predominate, especially beginning at around the 100-word mark. At 500–600 words (reached typically between the second and third birthdays), children's vocabularies in Italian and many European languages are about one-half nouns, about one-quarter verbs, and about one-quarter words of other types (grammatical function words, social-performative words, and so on).

Some researchers have claimed that at around 18 months of age many children have a "vocabulary burst," perhaps based on the Helen Keller insight "everything has a name." There is some research supporting the idea of a vocabulary burst at this age (e.g., Reznick and Goldfield, 1992; Mervis and Bertrand, 1995), which might indicate a change of process such as a "naming insight." But larger, more recent analyses have shown that this is simply a gradual increase in the rate of word learning, and that it only occurs in some children (Bates and Goodman, 1997). A number of theorists have therefore argued that there is no change of process at 18 months of age, but rather that the vocabulary burst reflects children becoming gradually more and more skillful at learning words (Bates and Goodman, 1997; P. Bloom, 2000). Indeed, there is not even an agreed-upon criterion for what constitutes a vocabulary "burst."

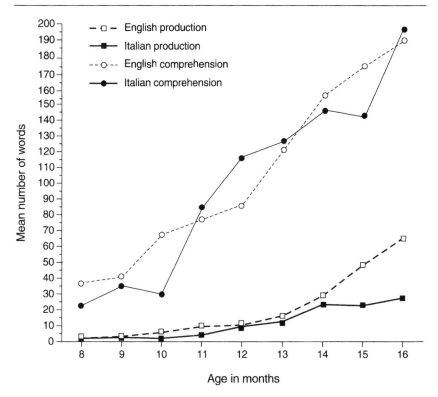

Figure 3.2. Growth of comprehension and production vocabulary from 8–16 months. From Caselli et al. (1995); reprinted with the permission of Elsevier Science.

Anisfeld et al. (1998) have shown that when children do accelerate in rate of word learning in the middle of the second year of life, the acceleration is often associated with the emergence of the first word combinations and grammar. This suggests a number of explanations for the increased rate other than some kind of new understanding about the relation of words to their referents. In particular, as children learn more language the utterances they hear include more familiar words, and so is easier for them to identify new words in the speech stream and also to identify the words' communicative functions in the utterance as a whole (see Section 3.2.3 below). It is also important to note that school-age children's vocabularies often grow at even faster rates, mainly because of literacy skills and productive morphological skills in deriving new words from known words in various ways (Clark, 1993). In general, investigation of older children's vocabularies shows an ever increasing ability to actively control all of the

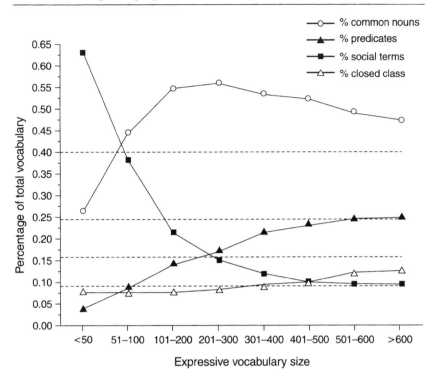

Figure 3.3. Vocabulary composition for Italian children from 18–30 months. From Caselli et al. (1995); reprinted with the permission of Elsevier Science.

possible derivational forms of a lexeme, and indeed much of the exponential growth of children's vocabularies during the school years may be attributed to this mastery of derivational processes (Anglin, 1993).

The overall picture thus seems to be that children learn words at ever increasing rates from age 1 year until the early teens, when a leveling off begins to occur (Bates and Goodman, 1997; Anglin, 1993).

3.1.3. Word Meanings

There have also been a number of attempts to characterize more precisely the nature of children's early word meanings. One important issue is the extent to which children's early words are truly symbolic, in the sense of being flexibly used across an array of appropriate referential situations. The problem is that some of children's early words seem bound to particular communicative situations; for example, a child might say *Bath* only when actually splashing in the tub and not to name bathtubs or comment on other children taking baths (Bates, 1976; Nelson, 1985). Although it is undeniable that some children use some of their early words in this event-bound way (see Barrett, 1986, and the examples from Tomasello, 1992a, in Chapter 2), systematic research has shown that that this phenomenon is not as widespread and pervasive as first believed (see Harris et al., 1988, for nouns; Vear and Ramos, 2001, for verbs). The fact is that children use the majority of their words fairly flexibly from the beginning. One possibility—currently unexplored—is that children's early event-bound words are simply those relatively few words that they have heard and attended to in only a single communicative context or with a single communicative purpose, with no opportunity (for whatever reason) to observe adult generalizations to other contexts.

Another important issue concerns how early word meanings are cognitively represented. Focusing on object labels (and some adjectives), the classic proposal is that of Clark (1973) to the effect that children's word meanings are cognitively represented as lists of perceptual features. In contrast, Nelson (1974) proposed that the "functional core" of an object label's meaning consisted of the child's understanding of what she could do with the object or what the object could do—with perceptual features being used simply to identify instances of the concept. Subsequent work has shown that both of these proposals have some validity. Thus, young children seem to show a fairly strong "shape bias" in identifying novel exemplars of a newly learned word. For example, if 2-year-olds are first taught that a novel object is a "gazzer" and then confronted with other objects that either look like the object or do the same thing, they most often identify as other gazzers the objects that look like the original (Jones and Smith, 2002). However, Kemler Nelson et al. (2000) taught 2-year-olds novel names for novel objects that had novel functions—functions that were related causally to perceptible aspects of the objects' physical structure—and then looked at how the children extended these names to new objects. They found that, given only minimal experience with the new objects, children generalized the names in accordance with the objects' functions. Their major conclusion was that "two-year-olds name by function when they can make sense of the relation between the appearances and functions of artifacts" (1271). When children rely on which of these methods of generalization is currently unknown.

Since these classic proposals of the 1970s, there has been very little work on how children cognitively represent the meanings of object labels and other nouns. But perhaps we might make some progress by following the lead of cognitive linguists, who are currently investigating word meanings from some novel theoretical perspectives, including the use of such theoretical entities as frame semantics, radial categories, and the like. For one thing, cognitive linguists highlight the importance of the various kinds of background cultural knowledge and categories that structure word meanings: a knuckle presupposes a finger, a pedestrian presupposes traffic, and a bachelor presupposes a culture in which marriage is expected. The meaning of many, if not most, words is thus not specifiable in isolation, but must be understood in the context of a larger set of cultural activities and entities (Fillmore, 1989; Langacker, 1987a; Lakoff, 1987). Cognitive linguists have also investigated the rampant polysemy characteristic of most common adult words—including metaphorical extensions—and they posit a number of different representational schemes (prototypes, radial categories, and so on) to account for this pattern of use. The finding is that most words, especially the common ones, require for their representation a structured network of interrelated word uses (for example, *run* as a physical activity, as the activity of operating machines, as the activity of operating a store, as the activity of standing for political office, and so on). These phenomena have scarcely been touched on in the literature on language development.

There has also been little recent work on the cognitive representations that underlie children's use of relational words and verbs. One exception is Pinker (1989), who used Jackendoff's (1990) model to characterize children's verb meanings in terms of adult verb semantics. Another exception is Tomasello (1992a), who attempted to specify early verb meanings more in terms of children's own nonlinguistic cognitive structures as determined by cognitive-developmental research in general (see also McCune-Nicolich, 1981). Invoking Piaget's (1952, 1954) theory of infant cognition, Tomasello proposed that the conceptualizations underlying early words for actions and events could be specified in terms of four basic conceptual elements: space, time, causality, and objects (and perhaps possession). Following Langacker (1987a), each of these dynamic words was seen as depicting a process that unfolded in a series of discrete sequential steps ("moments of attention" from a processing point of view), typically with an object changing location or state across this time (with perhaps the causal source of that motion integrally involved as well). The hypothesized conceptualizations underlying early language thus had the virtue of being things that young children could potentially construct from their own experience as they attempted to comprehend and use these words in communicating with adults. For example, a child's understanding of an act of giving may be depicted as a sequence of steps (see Figure 3.4) in which one person (P1) originally is co-located with or possesses an object (O), followed by a step in which someone else (P2) is co-located with or possesses that object, with a causal arrow connected to the first person indicating that she caused the transfer to happen.

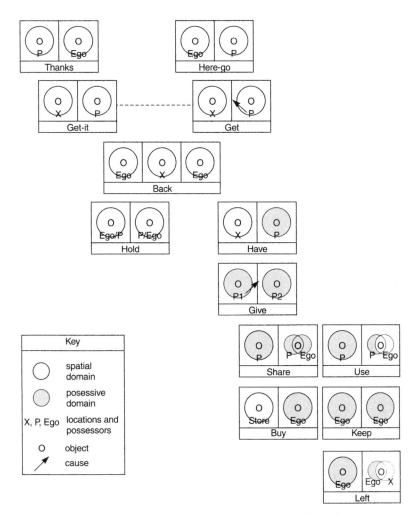

Figure 3.4. Conceptual situations underlying one child's use of words concerning the exchange and possession of objects. Each word is described by two "moments of attention" in an unfolding process (one panel for each moment of attention). For example, *get* is depicted as a first moment when O is in the spatial domain X (basically anywhere) followed by a second moment when O is in the spatial domain of person P. P causes this transfer (indicated by arrow). From Tomasello (1992a); reprinted with the permission of Cambridge University Press.

Some general hypotheses have been proposed to account for the order in which children learn their early verbs: (1) that children learn words for their own actions before they learn words for observed actions, and that when they do learn words for observed actions it is first for processes not involving intentional actions (Huttenlocher, Smiley, and Charney, 1983; Smiley and Huttenlocher, 1995); (2) that children learn words for simple, perceivable state changes before they learn words for more complex and abstract changes of state (Edwards and Goodwin, 1986); and (3) that from 3 years of age children have a bias toward verbs defined in terms of results (such as *to clean*) rather than in terms of the actions themselves (such as *to wipe;* Behrend, 1990; but see Forbes and Farrar, 1993). None of these hypotheses has overwhelming empirical support, and indeed to date there is no adequate explanation of the order in which children learn verbs (which seems to be variable across children), other than factors having to do with the frequency and saliency with which adults use particular verbs in speaking with children (Naigles and Hoff-Ginsberg, 1998).

In cross-linguistic analyses, the only word type other than nouns and verbs with any claim to universality (although it is controversial) is adjectives. As is well known, adjectives have some noun-like properties (relative time stability) and some verb-like properties (use as a predicate) (Givón, 1984). Also, because they denote properties that are most clearly identified with reference to commonalities across entities, adjectives often require language learners to compare across situations to extract the common property. Akhtar and Montague (1999) demonstrated experimentally that children as young as 2 years are able to do this in learning the appropriate use of a novel adjective.

In English, adjectives are used in a number of ways. Nelson (1976) identified three basic ways that children use words that adults would call adjectives: (1) as predications in utterances such as *This is big;* (2) as modifiers in utterances such as *The big boy hit me;* and (3) as classificatory modifiers in utterances such as *The baby moose* (where *baby* is most often a noun serving an adjectival function). Nelson found that 1- to 2-year-old children used different sets of specific words for these different functions. More than 80 percent of the predications they used involved temporary states of objects or animate beings (*It's broken, I'm hurt*). In contrast, most of their modificational uses of adjectives concerned time-stable descriptive properties *(Big doggie, Little kitty)* or evaluative properties *(Pretty flower, Bad boy)* from the beginning (see Saylor, 2000, for further evidence of this asymmetry). The classificatory adjectives, used to subdivide referent classes, consisted of animate types *(baby giraffe)* substance terms *(chocolate cookie),* and kind terms *(Panda bear)*—again, mostly nouns used in adjectival functions. Because for any given child there was little overlap in the specific words used in these three functions, Nelson proposed that young children do not have a single class of adjectives.

Prepositions and postpositions are words that serve to relate non-core arguments to the main clause of the utterance. In the early language of speakers of English and many other European languages, the most prominent prepositions are locatives. Johnston and Slobin (1979) investigated the ability of 2- to 5-year-old children to produce locative pre- or postpositions in English, Italian, and Serbo-Croatian. Using a standardized elicitation procedure, they found that children in all three languages first learned simple locatives such as *in, on, under,* and *beside* (see Wilcox and Palermo, 1975, for evidence that English-speaking children learn *in* and *on* before *under*). Only later did they learn more complex locatives involving either object-relative frames of reference (such as the front and back of a house) or deictic frames of reference (such as the left and right sides of a house, from the speaker's point of view). The linguistic complexity of the expressions used for these different functions in each language also accounted for a number of learning patterns. Tomasello (1987) found similar results for one English-speaking child's use of spatial prepositions early in development, and also found that salience in adult utterances (such as final position with stress) was important to the learning process. In addition, however, this child used other common English prepositions not involving concrete spatial relationships. For example, she learned the preposition *of* from such expressions as *piece of ice, piece of bread, scared of that,* and *scared of monsters.* The preposition *of* has much more varied uses than the spatial propositions, and children can learn it only by extracting it from larger expressions—with perhaps some subclassification of its many uses.

This same basic analysis applies to many other English words, some with semantically heavy functions and many others with more grammatical functions. For example, Levy and Nelson (1994), investigating early acquisition of temporal words like *because, tomorrow, today, morning, pretty soon, yesterday,* and *now,* found that children initially use these terms only in relatively formulaic phrases and for the same functions for which their parents use them. They thus hypothesized that in this case children's production of linguistic items precedes their comprehension, in the sense that their earliest uses do not display adult-like flexibility of usage. The early uses of these words thus serve specific discourse functions only, and a fully adult-like understanding awaits children's encounters with these words in a fuller range of functional contexts. Most investigations of children's acquisition of such things as auxiliary verbs, verb particles, articles, and adverbs also show that children's learning is much more discourse-specific than in the case of more contentful words such as nouns and verbs (see Chapter 6 for studies of various types of function words).

At the moment, the issue of how best to characterize children's early word meanings is unresolved. The current suggestion is that the field of child language acquisition could benefit greatly in this respect by attending to the work of cognitive linguists. For one thing, Langacker (1987a) and others use image-schematic diagrams, such as those in Figure 3.4, to depict iconically the conceptualizations underlying all kinds of word meanings. Barsalou (1999) argues and presents evidence that these kinds of perceptually based representations are a more adequate characterization of adult cognition than are the more commonly used abstract propositional representations (typically formulated in English words, as in feature lists). If cognitive-developmental research is used in constructing semantic primitives, iconic diagrams may thus provide more psychologically realistic representations of children's early word meanings. Second, cognitive linguists also provide analyses of the complex network of uses to which people put various words, including the different conceptual frames in which they occur. This process was referred to in Chapter 2 as pattern-finding in the communicative uses of a linguistic symbol. These uses can then be summarized as prototype and/or radial category representations. Again, in the developmental context these may be created using knowledge of children's cognitive development to help identify psychologically plausible interpretations of children's different word uses. This cognitive linguistics approach might possibly lead to a new and very productive line of research on children's early lexical semantics.

3.2. Processes of Word Learning

It is widely recognized that learning a word involves the cooperation of many different cognitive and social-cognitive processes (Golinkoff, Hirsh-Pasek, and Hollich, 1999). But these different processes play different roles, and they play them at different periods in development. In the current account, I will specify three types:

- *Prerequisite processes:* segmenting speech; conceptualizing referents.
- *Foundational processes:* joint attention; intention-reading; cultural learning.
- *Facilitative processes:* lexical contrast; linguistic context.

These begin to operate in human ontogeny in approximately this order, with prerequisite processes beginning to work prelinguistically, intention-reading processes jump-starting language into operation at 1 year of age, and linguistic processes providing a booster rocket that accelerates the pace of word learning exponentially during the preschool period. I will also discuss some processes of input and learning that operate, to some extent, at each of these periods.

3.2.1. Prerequisite Processes

Obviously before we can talk about children's understanding of how adults use particular phonological sequences to direct other people's attention to external phenomena, we must establish that children can indeed isolate particular phonological sequences and particular external phenomena.

PROCESSING SPEECH

When we hear someone speaking to us in a foreign language—or when an infant hears an adult speaking to her in any language—it is often extremely difficult to parse the utterance into its component words or other linguistic units. Thus, even when the infant understands the overall communicative intention of an utterance (for example, to fetch a toy), she may be unable to assign different components of that communicative intention to different segmental units such as words *(get, me, the, toy)* within the speech stream.

The cues children must use to segment speech in different languages are in some cases very different. Research by Werker and colleagues (summarized in Werker and Desjardins, 1995) has established that as infants approach their first birthdays they are so concentrated on the speech they hear around them that they are losing the ability to make speech discriminations that are made in other languages—and that they made earlier in infancy. Indeed, 1-year-old Japanese infants (like Japanese adults) have practically lost the ability to distinguish between the sounds English-speaking people hear as *ra* and *la,* and 1-year-old English infants (like English adults) have practically lost the ability to distinguish between the Mandarin sounds *ma* and *má* (with tone marking). During the first year of life human infants are "tuning up" to the speech discriminations and patterns of the language into which they are born.

In all languages the perceptual segmentation of utterances into words is accomplished by three basic mechanisms (Jusczyk, 1997). First, almost every language has a typical stress pattern associated with words. For example, in English the vast majority of two-syllable words have a stressed first syllable, as in *candle* or *doctor.* Second, each language has certain predictable sequences of sounds that often occur together and others that almost never do. For example, in English sequences of consonants such as *db* and *kt* virtually never occur together within words (so-called phonotactic constraints), and so hearing such a sequence in fluent speech may be used to infer a word boundary with a high probability. Third, infants may use distributional evidence on the level of whole words to segment fluent speech. For example, when someone hears *See the cat, My cat is pretty,* and *An old grey cat,* the word *cat* pops out as a coherent unit with some consistency across these utterances.

Experimental research using the preferential head-turning technique (infants turn their heads to listen to sounds they prefer to listen to—sometimes because they are bored with what they have been hearing) has found that by about 7 or 8 months of age infants in an English-speaking environment can segment words with the prototypical strong-weak stress pattern from fluent adult speech (e.g., Jusczyk and Aslin, 1995). A few months later infants begin to use other, mostly phonotactic cues to identify words with non-prototypical stress patterns (Jusczyk, Hohne, and Bauman, 1998). On the level of whole words, Jusczyk and Hohne (1997) visited 8-month-old infants ten times during a two-week period. On each visit they played audio recordings of the same three children's stories. Two weeks later, in the laboratory, infants preferred to listen to the words they had heard over similar words that had not been in the stories. However, Houston, Jusczyk, and Tager (1997) found that the recognition of specific words after 24 hours was much more difficult for infants if the words were spoken by a different person. They concluded that early in development infants' representations of words may be stored exemplars of previously heard words rather than abstract prototypes. This does not last long, however. Fernald et al. (1998) investigated the word-recognition skills of older infants, at 15 and 24 months of age. They found that the speed and efficiency of word recognition increased dramatically during this period. Although 15-month-olds did not orient to the correct picture indicated by a target word until after the entire word had been spoken, 24-month-olds shifted their gaze to the correct picture during the middle of the spoken word, anticipating the entire word on the basis of its initial syllable (see also Swingley, Pinto, and Fernald, 1999).

Segmenting words from speech in a particular language is obviously something an infant must learn to do. In their species-typical environments, other animals are not faced with this perceptual discrimination problem. And yet many household pets, perhaps especially dogs, learn to discriminate a number of words from one another (e.g., Warden and Warner, 1928)—although it is not clear if they are able to extract these from fluent speech. Especially impressive are the skills of the bonobo

Kanzi, who has learned to discriminate hundreds of English words, in most cases by hearing complete utterances of fluent speech (Shanker, Savage-Rumbaugh, and Taylor, 1999). It has also been shown that some mammals perceive phonemes categorically in much the same way as humans (Kuhl and Miller, 1975), and that some nonhuman primates discriminate utterances in the particular human language they hear around them from those in other languages (Ramus et al., 2000). Also, as reported in Chapter 2, Newport, Aslin, and Hauser (2001) and Hauser, Weiss, and Marcus (in press) found evidence of human-like pattern learning of auditory sequences in nonhuman primates. And so the empirical discovery is that the sound systems of human languages are adapted to general mammalian auditory perceptual capabilities more than the other way around—even though human beings can produce some species-unique sounds as well.

The adult-like production of speech takes much more time to develop, longer for some children than others. At early stages of language production some children actively avoid certain sounds, effectively ignoring words that contain them. Thus, Schwartz and Leonard (1983) attempted to teach 13- to 16-month-old children 16 novel words over several months, some words with phonological characteristics that had been previously evidenced in the child's production and some with characteristics that had not been previously evidenced in production. The major finding was that children more often produced the words that corresponded to their existing phonological capabilities and more often avoided those that did not. Also important is the metrical (rhythmic) properties of words. Gerken (1994) and Lewis, Antone, and Johnson (1999) found, using both naturalistic and experimental methods, that young children systematically alter their production of words so as to conform with metrical patterns they have already mastered. For example, many English-speaking children early in development prefer words with the typical strong-weak stress pattern (as in *table* or *napkin*) and avoid or change words with the opposite pattern (as in *surprise* or *remove*).

Of special interest from the current perspective, Vihman (1996) has proposed that young children have certain holistic phonological templates to which they assimilate their early words and even multi-word expressions, and that these are psychologically prior to any elementary so-called building blocks such as phonemes—which must be extracted from these larger structures (see also Behrens and Gut, in press). The process is thus from whole to parts. This proposal is especially interesting in the current context because in Chapter 4 the focus is on children's acquisition of syntactic templates that contain both a consistent prosodic contour and some consistent phonological material (specific words and phrases). In this case as well, one can see the acquisition of so-called building blocks, such as words, as a process of extraction from these holistic templates.

CONCEPTUALIZING REFERENTS

Human communication can work only if the people communicating share basic ways of perceiving and, to some degree, conceptualizing the world. Children come to the adult way of perceiving and conceptualizing the world partly by means of to the physical and perceptual equipment with which they are born, and partly through their own sensory-motor interactions with the world. According to Mandler (1992), language acquisition can begin in earnest only when infants progress from a direct perception of the world to conceptualizing it in more flexible and abstract ways. Mandler proposes that conceptualizations (mostly in the form of image schemas; see below) provide a level of representation intermediate between perception and language that enables children to begin to identify abstract word meanings. This process can be seen most clearly in children's emerging understanding of, and talk about, (1) objects and (2) events.

Human infants actively search for hidden objects from about 7 or 8 months of age (Piaget, 1954), but they show perceptual expectancies that hidden objects still exist even earlier (see Baillargeon, 1995, for a review). From a purely cognitive point of view, infants are ready to name particular objects quite early in infancy, and indeed there is some evidence that infants can associate some names with some people quite early (Jusczyk, 1997; although this is presumably not symbolic). But to really make progress in using words to indicate objects for other people, young children must begin to categorize objects into "kinds," because most nouns in a language are used to indicate such categories as *dog, ball, tree*, and so on. (Xu, Carey, and Welch, 1999). Gopnik and Meltzoff (1986) investigated the nonlinguistic categorizing abilities of beginning language learners (by noting which objects of an array they touched in sequence) and correlated this ability with their early use of common nouns, which should depend on this skill. They found that these 1-year-olds began to flexibly categorize objects and to flexibly use common nouns in close developmental synchrony, with the object categorization typically leading the way.

Conceptualizing events would seem, on the surface, to be more complicated. However, Piaget (1954) found that soon after infants searched for hidden objects they also tracked their visible and invisible displacements. Mandler (1992) reviewed a variety of lines of evidence that from before their first birthdays infants do not just perceive but also conceptualize the dynamic and relational aspects of their experience, involving such things as animate motion, caused motion, containment, and support. These are just as basic as object conceptualizations. Mandler posited that these more dynamic aspects of infant cognition are best characterized in terms of image schemas in which the commonalties across a number of specific dynamic experiences are extracted (Lakoff, 1987; Johnson, 1987). Evidence for this proposal is provided by a series of studies begun by McCune-Nicolich (1981) and pursued further by Gopnik and Meltzoff (1986) and Tomasello and Farrar (1984). The basic finding of all the studies is that young children only begin talking about such things as objects appearing, disappearing, reappearing, or being "gone" after they have begun to interact with objects nonlinguistically in ways that embody these concepts. Tomasello and Farrar (1986b) even provided experimental support in a training study in which they found that only children who could deal effectively with the invisible displacement of objects in a Piagetian object permanence task could learn, from extensive tutelage, words that indicated invisible movements.

It is also true that sometimes word learning actually leads and directs cognitive development. That is, as a result of attempts to learn the linguistic conventions used by those around them, young children sometimes come to conceptualize the world in ways that they would not have if they were not attempting to learn those conventions. Most important here is the work of Choi and Bowerman (1991), who found that very young children, still in their second year of life, come to conceptualize spatial relationships differently depending on the language they are learning. Thus, young English-speaking and Korean-speaking children conceptualize differently such basic spatial relations as containment *(in)* and support *(on)*—as evidenced by their behavior in preferential-looking studies—because English encodes these concepts with prepositions such as *in* and *on,* whereas Korean uses verbs that indicate such different kinds of spatial relationships as "tight fitting" and "loose fitting." Recently these investigators have extended these findings to other concepts and languages (Choi et al., 2001). A diagrammatic depiction of the cross-linguistic relationships is presented in Figure 3.5.

Language also influences conceptualization in some other ways, some of which will be reviewed in Chapter 7. For now the important point is that children must have some ability to conceptualize aspects of their perceptual experience in order to acquire linguistic conventions. But at the same time the process of acquiring linguistic conventions serves to focus children's attention on aspects of experience that they might otherwise not have focused on. The relation between children's language and cognition is a two-way street.

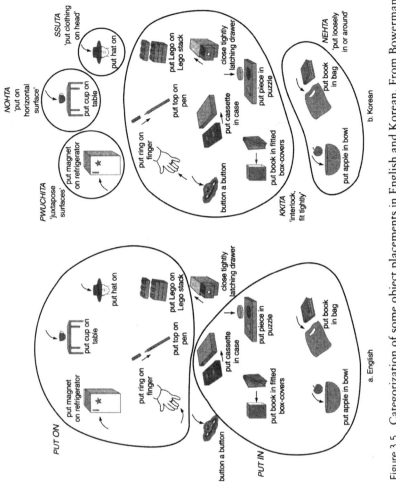

Figure 3.5. Categorization of some object placements in English and Korean. From Bowerman and Choi (2001); reprinted with the permission of Cambridge University Press.

3.2.2. Foundational Processes

As presaged in Chapter 2, in order to learn the conventional communicative significance of a linguistic item—to connect a segment of speech with a segment of communicative intention—the child has to engage in a dual-level social-cognitive process. She must first establish some form of common ground with an adult, in the context of a joint attentional frame, and then within this frame be able to read the adult's specific communicative intention in using a particular linguistic item—by both extracting its form and isolating its functional role within the adult's communicative intention as a whole. The establishment of common ground within a joint attentional frame is a dyadic affair, depending on both adult and child, whereas the intention-reading (and the resulting cultural learning) is mostly due to the child's own social-cognitive skills and efforts. There is research in support of the foundational role of both of these components of the process.

JOINT ATTENTION

Bruner (1983) argued and provided evidence that adult and child establishing common communicative ground is a *necessary* condition for the infant to break into the world of conventionalized communication known as language. Tomasello and Todd (1983) took the argument a step further by investigating the possibility that individual differences in the way mother-child dyads established and maintained joint attentional interactions might be related to individual differences in children's early language development. Observing six mother-infant dyads at monthly intervals from the infant's 12th to 18th month, they found a very high correlation between the amount of time infants spent in joint engagement with their mothers during the six observation periods and the size of the infants' vocabulary at the end of the study (see also Tomasello and Farrar, 1986a; Smith, Adamson, and Bakeman, 1988). A variation on this approach was reported by Tomasello, Mannle, and Kruger (1986), who investigated the relation between joint engagement and early language both in singleton children and in twins, who are known to be significantly delayed in early language development (see Tomasello, Mannle, and Barton, 1989, for a review). The main findings were that (1) the twin infants spent only one-tenth as much time in dyadic joint engagement with their mothers as the singleton infants, and (2) there was a very high correlation between time spent in joint engagement at 15 months of age and vocabulary size at both 15 and 21 months for both singletons and twins (see Tomasello, 1988, for a review of studies on joint attention and early language development).

More recently, Carpenter, Nagell, and Tomasello, (1998) found some similar relationships at an even earlier age, indeed as children were just beginning to learn and use language. They found that infants who spent more time in joint attentional engagement with their mothers at 12 months comprehended and produced more language at that age and in the months immediately following. They also found that mothers who followed into their 12-month-olds' attentional focus with words had children with larger comprehension vocabularies in the months immediately following (with relationships to language production showing up a bit later; see also Tomasello and Farrar, 1986a). When both of these variables were used together—the time spent in joint attentional engagement and the mother's tendency to "follow into" the child's attentional focus when she used referential language—over half of the variance in children's language comprehension and production was predicted at several points during the period from 12 to 15 months of age, with each variable accounting for significant amounts of unique variance. A number of measures of children's non-social cognitive development—mostly involving their knowledge of objects and space—emerged in an uncorrelated fashion with language and the other joint attentional activities, providing evidence that the correlation of joint attentional engagement and language was not just the result of some generalized developmental advance.

Experimental evidence for the facilitative role of joint attentional interactions is provided by Farrar, Freund, and Forbes (1993), who found that young children learn words much more rapidly in repetitive and scripted events with adults than in less predictable event sequences. An interesting twist on this story is that some children at an early age, and all children at later ages, learn new pieces of language from observing third parties talking to one another—outside the prototypical joint attentional frame between adult and language-learning child (e.g., Brown, 2001). In this case, the process of understanding different roles in this frame and substituting participants for one another is still the same (as in more prototypical cases of role reversal imitation); it is just that in this case the child is not one of the original participants in the linguistic interchange. Learning language in this way has not been studied in enough detail to reveal how children accomplish this feat, or if it creates special difficulties (or special opportunities) for them early in development (but see Akhtar, Jipson, and Callanan, 2001; Oshima-Takane, 1999).

Importantly, it has also been found that individual differences in the nonlinguistic joint attentional abilities of children with autism are systematically related to their ability to learn new linguistic symbols. A number of studies have found that these two sets of skills are related to each other in autistic children in the same way they are related in normal children (Loveland and Landry, 1986; Mundy, Sigman, and Kasari, 1990; Rollins and Snow, 1998; see Sigman and Capps, 1997, for reviews). More recently Siller and Sigman (2002) have even found that autistic children's non-linguistic joint attentional skills during early childhood are extremely strong predictors of their linguistic skills many years later in adolescence.

Together, these studies on joint attention and early language clearly demonstrate that being able to segment speech and to conceptualize the world are by themselves not adequate for acquiring a linguistic convention. The child must also be exposed to that convention in the context of a social interaction in which she and the adult find some way to share attention—or perhaps she discerns shared attention between other persons from the outside. Even within a joint attentional frame, however, it is still not a given that the child will be able to infer the adult's specific communicative intention in using a specific piece of language. We must therefore look at the process in a bit more detail.

INTENTION-READING

Reading communicative intentions seems to work a bit differently for object words and action words. First, with respect to object words, a number of observational and experimental studies have found that word learning is easier when adults name new objects for young children by following into their already established focus of attention, as opposed to using the new language to direct their attention to something else (Tomasello and Farrar, 1986a; Dunham, Dunham, and Curwin, 1993; Akhtar, Dunham, and Dunham, 1991; Carpenter, Akhtar, and Tomasello, 1998). But this does not mean that the child is a passive participant in the word learning process. Subsequent studies have shown that when there is a discrepancy between the adult's and the child's focus of attention—when young children hear a novel word in situations in which their focus of attention differs from that of an adult they nevertheless are able to do the extra work to determine the adult's referential intentions, almost never assuming that the new word is being used for whatever is their own current focus of attention irrespective of what the adult is attempting to do (Baldwin, 1991, 1993a, 1993b). In all cases of word learning children make active attempts to understand adult communicative intentions; it is just that in some situations they have to work a little harder at it.

The point is made most clearly in a series of studies by Tomasello and colleagues in which young children had to discern the adult's communicative intentions in using a new word in some fairly complicated social-interactive situations. In Baldwin's studies, the 18-month-olds had to shift their attention to what the adult was focused on visually in order to learn the new word. In the studies of Tomasello and colleagues, children had to use a variety of more complicated social-pragmatic cues. In the case of learning new object labels, the three relevant studies can be summarized as follows:

- In the context of a finding game, an adult announced her intentions to "find the toma" and then searched in a row of buckets, all containing novel objects. Sometimes she found it in the first bucket searched. Sometimes, however, she searched longer, rejecting unwanted objects by scowling at them and replacing them in their buckets until she found the one she wanted. Children 18 and 24 months old learned the new word for the object the adult intended to find (indicated by a smile and termination of search) regardless of how many objects were rejected during the search (Tomasello and Barton, 1994; Tomasello, Strosberg, and Akhtar, 1996).
- Also in the context of a finding game, an adult had the child find four different objects in four different hiding places, one of which was a very distinctive toy barn. Once the child had learned which objects went with which places, the adult announced her intention to "find the gazzer." She then went to the toy barn, but it turned out to be "locked." She frowned at the barn and then proceeded to another hiding place, saying "Lets see what else we can find," and taking out an object with a smile. Later, 18- and 24-month-olds demonstrated that they had learned "gazzer" for the object they knew the experimenter had wanted in the barn even though they had not seen the object after they heard the new word, and even though the adult had frowned at the barn and smiled at a distractor object (Akhtar and Tomasello, 1996; Tomasello, Strosberg, and Akhtar, 1996).
- A child, her mother, and an experimenter played together with three novel objects. The mother then left the room. A fourth object was bought out and the child and experimenter played with it, noting the mother's absence. When the mother returned, she looked at the four objects together and exclaimed "Oh look! A modi! A modi!" Understanding that the mother would not be excited about the objects she had already played with, but that she might well be excited about the object she was seeing for the first time, 24-month-olds learned the new word for the object the mother had not seen previously (Akhtar, Carpenter, and Tomasello, 1996).

These studies make two important points. First, no account in terms of simple association will work. In classic associationistic accounts, word and referent should occur in relatively close spatial-temporal contiguity. But that is clearly not the case in these studies: in the first two studies distractor objects are experienced in closer spatial-temporal contiguity with the new words than are target objects; in the third study, both distractors and the target are present when the new word is said. And so, not only do young children not need adults to stop other activities and name objects for them, they do not even need the adult to say the word while they are paying attention to the object; they are able to discern the adult's focus of attention in much more complicated situations (see Jaswal and Markman, 2001, for more on children's abilities to infer referents of nouns in non-ostensive contexts).

The second point is that children could not, in these studies, be relying on any one cue or small set of cues. The direction of the adult's visual gaze was not diagnostic of her referential intentions in any of the studies (as it was in Baldwin, 1991, 1993a, 1993b). In the first two studies, the child had to first understand that she and the adult were playing a finding game. Giving this intentional understanding (and a few details of the game), the child could then infer in the first study that when the adult frowned at an object, that was not the one she was seeking, and when she smiled at an object, that was the one she was seeking. But then in the second study the adult frowned while she was trying unsuccessfully to open the toy barn to "find the gazzer," so in this case the frown meant frustration at not being able to obtain the toy from inside the barn—which was the target of her referential intentions. The main point is that the adult's specific behaviors such as a smile or a frown were not sufficient by themselves to indicate for the child the adult's intended referent. In the third study, the adult did not single out any of the objects behaviorally, so the child had to infer which object was the target of the adult's referential intentions by determining which object was new to the adult, and thus likely to elicit enthusiasm. At 18–24 months children can read the communicative intentions of adults, and so learn new object labels from them, in a variety of fairly complex, non-ostensive situations.

Learning a new verb presents young children with some of the same and also some different challenges. For example, the actions and changes of state to which verbs refer are mostly transient. This means that, unlike the case of object labels, the referential situation in the case of verbs is quite often not perceptually available to the child when the word is uttered, nor can it be located by visual or other perceptual inspection of the immediate context. Tomasello (1992a) in fact found that a number of his subject's early verbs were never modeled when the action was perceptually present, but rather as the adult was requesting an action of the child ("Move!"), checking her intentions ("Do you want to go?"), commenting on a completed action ("I broke it"), and so forth. Indeed, Tomasello and Kruger (1992) found that children learn verbs best in impending-action situations (including requests), next in completed-action situations, and worst in on-going-action situations. Ambalu, Chiat, and Pring (1997) extended this finding by showing that movement verbs like *roll* and *spin* were learned best in impending-action situations but result verbs like *clean* and *fix* were learned best when the event was completed before the model was given. Gillette et al. (1999) invoked this temporal dislocation between word and referent as a major factor helping to explain why adults find it difficult to infer the verb an adult is using (as opposed to nouns) when viewing a videotape of adult-child interactions with the sound off.

An additional difficulty, as Talmy (1985) and Gentner (1982) have pointed out, is that a verb may be defined in many and diverse ways, for example, by the manner of motion *(to float)*, the instrument involved *(to hammer)*, the result achieved *(to empty)*, the action performed *(to wave)*, and so on, depending on the particular language involved. And there are other elements, such as the causative, that may or may not be a part of a verb's meaning (compare *kill* and *die;* see Bowerman, 1982). The "packaging problem"—deciding which aspects of a situation are relevant for a new word's meaning—seems much more difficult for verbs than for object labels, both for any given word and in terms of regularities across words that the child might learn to exploit at some point (Tomasello, 1995b). Thus, although children learn early in their language development that when adults use words to refer to objects they are usually naming the whole object (Golinkoff, Mervis, and Hirsh-Pasek, 1994), there would seem to be no analogous generalizations about verbs to help narrow the packaging options.

Tomasello and colleagues performed two studies with verbs, analogous to those with nouns, that, although they do not address all these problems, demonstrate at least some of the complexities involved.

· An adult set up a script with a child in which a novel action was performed always and only with a particular toy character (Big Bird always appeared on a swing, and other character-action pairings were demonstrated as well). She then picked up Big Bird and announced "Let's meek Big Bird," but the swing was nowhere to be found, so the action was not performed. Later, using a different character, 24-month-olds demonstrated their understanding of the new verb even though they had never seen the referent action performed after the novel verb was introduced (Akhtar and Tomasello, 1996).

· An adult announced her intention to "dax Mickey Mouse" and then performed one action accidentally ("Woops!") and another intentionally ("There!")—or sometimes in reverse order. Twenty-four-month-old children learned the word for the intentional not the accidental action regardless of which came first in the sequence (Tomasello and Barton, 1994).

In addition, two further studies looked at the kinds of cues children use to differentiate adult acts of reference to objects and actions. These studies demonstrate with special clarity that children are using a variety of kinds of cues to read adult referential intentions, evidencing a very deep and flexible understanding of adult intentional action.

- An adult introduced the child to a curved pipe, down which objects could be thrown. In one condition she first threw a novel object down, then threw another, and then announced "Now, modi" as she threw a third novel object. In this condition 24-month-olds thought *modi* was the name of that object. In another condition the adult took out a novel object and first did one thing with it, and then another thing, and then announced "Now, modi" as she threw it down the pipe. In this condition children thought *modi* was the name of the action of throwing objects down a pipe. In each case the child assumed the adult was talking about the entity, either object or action, that was new in the communicative situation (Tomasello and Akhtar, 1995).
- An adult played a merry-go-round game with a child several times. They then did something else. Then the adult returned to the merry-go-round. In one condition she readied the merry-go-round for play, then held out a novel object to the child while alternating gaze between child and merry-go-round, saying "Widgit, Jason." In this case, the 24-month-olds thought *widgit* was a request for them to use the new object with the merry-go-round. In the other condition the adult did not ready the merry-go-round for play and did not gaze at it, but instead held out the novel object while alternating gaze between child and object, and said "Jason, widget." In this case, the children thought *widgit* was the name of the object (Tomasello and Akhtar, 1995).

And so learning to read adult intentions when they use a novel verb would seem to include even more difficult factors than when nouns are involved. In particular, in line with the thinking of Gentner and of Gleitman and Fisher (see below), it is very likely that learning verbs is more dependent than learning nouns on the child's understanding of the surrounding linguistic context.

All these studies concerning joint attention and intention-reading concern how, in a particular situation, a child might discern which object or action an adult is referring to with a new word. They do not address the additional problem of how a child infers the meaning of a new word more generally, in the sense of determining the range of referents to which it applies. For both nouns and verbs, more information is needed to distinguish the extension (meaning) of a word from that of other semantically related words. And so, for example, when the child in an experiment picks out an object for the *dax,* we still do not know what other things she might also be willing to call a *dax* (all things of a certain shape, all things that roll, and so on); that is, we do not know either the intension or the extension of her understanding of the word's conventional use. For this, other information—such as that supplied by lexical contrast and by linguistic context—is needed.

3.2.3. Facilitating Processes

As children learn more and more language, they are able to use it to help them to isolate new words in the speech stream as well as to identify the particular aspect of the overall communicative intention that a new word is intended to indicate. This happens in two main ways: children can contrast new words with known words that might have been used in their stead (the adult says *moose* instead of *deer* for a deer-like animal, indicating some difference); and children can use the surrounding linguistic context to make inferences about meaning (the adult says *Give me the blicket,* and so a blicket must be an object). Both of these processes are best seen in the context of children's attempts to read adult communicative intentions.

LEXICAL CONTRAST

For over a century, linguists have noted that there is strong pressure against synonyms in a language, and consequently that, for the most part, every word in a language expresses a unique meaning. Thus, even the words *cop* and *policeman* differ in their connotations. But the deeper point is that words contrast in meaning with one another and so closely related words—words in the same "semantic field"—are in fact inter-defined. The meaning of *morose* is something a little different from *sad* and is not quite *depressed* either. In a language that did not have a word equivalent to *morose* the word equivalent to *depressed* might extend to cover a wider range of contexts. Clark (1983, 1993) in particular has demonstrated that young children use lexical contrast to help them home in on the adult way of using words. Markman (1989, 1992) has proposed the strongest version of the hypothesis, claiming that early in development young children that the meanings of words do not just contrast but are in fact mutually exclusive.

Lexical contrast plays an important role in children's word learning, both (1) in providing another source of information to complement the child's intention-reading in the immediate communicative context and (2) in providing crucial information about a word's ultimate extension. In terms of benefits in the immediate situation, children are helped in learning, for example, proper names and superordinate category terms when they know ahead of time the basic level name of some objects. According to Markman (1989), children who know that a particular entity is a *dog* are in a better position to comprehend the precise meaning of the word *animal* or the name *Rover* when used to refer to a dog—since the most natural referent is blocked by mutual exclusivity (see Hall, 1991). However, a number of researchers have provided evidence that young children can use different words for the same entities if they have information that the speaker intends to take a different perspective on those entities. Mervis, Golinkoff, and Bertrand (1994) and Deak and Maratsos (1998), among others, have demonstrated that young children will accept more than one word for a given entity. Especially impressive is the study of Clark and Svaib (1997) who engaged in discourse with 2- and 3-year-olds about a book of pictures. In the course of a single brief session, they were able to elicit from these children—by varying discourse context—different words for the exact same referent (such as *cat* and *animal* or *man* and *sailor*). Clark (1997) takes this as evidence that children have a many-perspectives understanding of language and that they do not follow strict mutual exclusivity, but only lexical contrast.

In addition to helping children learn such things as proper names and superordinate category terms, lexical contrast helps them identify intended referents in the immediate situation in other ways. In an effect first observed by Carey and Bartlett (1978), children often use a kind of process of elimination to learn novel words. For example, Markman and Wachtel (1988) showed preschool children two objects, one familiar and one novel (such as a spoon and a whisk), and said "Show me the fendle." Most children gave them the whisk in this situation, presumably because they knew that under ordinary circumstances the adult would call the spoon a "spoon," and so on this occasion she must intend this novel term to refer to the novel object. Markman and Wachtel also found that when a novel word was used when only a familiar object, such as a spoon, was present, children often inferred that the novel word was intended to indicate an object part—again, use of a novel word to refer to the spoon *qua* spoon was unlikely. Children behave in these ways in these situations because they know that the different words that adults use are usually intended to indicate different entities (see Golinkoff, Hirsh-Pasek, and Hollich, 1995, and Merriman, Marazita, and Jarvis, 1995, for this effect with verbs; Woodward and Markman, 1997, and P. Bloom, 2000, for reviews of similar studies).

Lexical contrast is also of crucial importance in helping children to specify the meanings of words more precisely over time. For example, many young children overextend words such as *dog* to cover all four-legged furry animals. One way they home in on the adult extension of this word is by hearing many four-legged furry animals called by other names such as *horse* and *cow.* An adult illustration comes from the reporting of the Gulf War, in which citizens were often told that on a given day the American military had flown X number of bombing "sorties." In the context, virtually everyone knew what this meant generally. But if asked more specific questions—To qualify as a sortie does the plane have to return to the location from which it took off? Must a certain type or number of planes or a certain type or number of bombs be involved? Can the point of origin be an aircraft carrier? Can a tank go on a sortie over land?—most people would display their ignorance of the conventional meaning of this term in military parlance. But if we learned other related terms, such as *bombing mission, bombing run,* and *bombing raid,* our understanding of *bombing sortie* would become more precise. Although the process has not been studied in much detail, being able to contrast word meanings with one another in this way almost certainly facilitates children's acquisition of new words, particularly words that are spin-offs of more conceptually basic situations (see Tomasello, Mannle, and Werdenschlag, 1988, for one example).

Following this reasoning, Tomasello (1992a) argued that his daughter could only have learned the verb *share*—which she used to request objects from others while forfeiting any claim of ownership—if she already knew the verbs *give* and *have* which were used to request objects in more generic situations, sometimes with an ownership claim. Indeed, the ownership component of the verb *have* only arose as a result of its being contrasted with the later-learned word *share.* The point is that the details of the use of these more specific terms are understood by the child as she first encounters them only in contrast to the generic terms that the speaker might have used but did not. Why did Mother say I could not *have* it but I could *share* it? Why did she call this thing that looks to me like a dog a *cow*? Clark's (1987, 1988) argument is that the principle that all words contrast with one another in meaning in some way is really a principle of rational human behavior along the lines of "If someone is using *this* word, rather than *that* word in the current situation, there must be a reason for it." The child then examines the current situation to see if she can discover what distinguishes, for example, the current situation about which the adult said *share* from the more common situation in which both she and the adult normally say *give* or *have.*

Interestingly, young children also use evidence about contrast in interpreting other kinds of adult communicative behavior. Diesendruck and Markson (2002) found that when an adult told a 3-year-old a fact about an object ("My uncle gave me this"), and then asked for an object using another fact ("Give me the one my dog likes to play with") children systematically avoided the original object. Children's broad application of contrast suggests that it is not just a linguistic principle but rather a more general pragmatic principle for interpreting communicative behavior. The important theoretical point is that lexical contrast is a natural outgrowth of children's attempts to understand adult communicative intentions, in the context of their understanding that people have many symbolic options for construing the immediate situation in whatever way they wish for their immediate communicative purpose, and that they make these choices for pragmatic reasons.

LINGUISTIC CONTEXT

Children's learning of a new word can also be facilitated—and perhaps in some cases enabled—by the linguistic context within which it is embedded in a particular utterance and across utterances. As argued above, children are always attempting to understand the entire communicative intention of the adult's entire utterance, and as they are attempting to identify at the same time the communicative intention of various components, some understanding of this whole is crucial.

Brown (1957) made the point in a very simple study. He showed 3- and 4-year-olds a picture of an unusual action performed on an unusual substance with an unusual object. He then told one group of children "In this picture you can see sibbing" (verb condition); told another group of children "In this picture you can see a sib" (count noun condition); and told a third group of children "In this picture you can see some sib" (mass noun condition). Each child then saw three pictures depicting a similar action, a similar object, or a similar substance, and was then asked—depending on the original experimental condition—to "Show me another picture of sibbing/a sib/some sib." Children tended to choose the picture that accorded with the linguistic form they had heard.

Subsequent research has shown that the process is perhaps a bit different for nouns than for verbs. For nouns, Katz, Baker, and McNamara (1974), Gelman and Taylor (1984), and Littschwager and Markman (1993) showed that even 2-year-old children could distinguish count nouns from proper names if they were introduced to a novel object as "This is a/the zav" versus "This is Zav." Soja (1992) replicated and extended Brown's (1957) finding concerning count and mass nouns by showing children a pile of a clay-like substance and encouraging them to focus on the substance by saying either "Here is some zav" or "Here is a zav" (see also McPherson, 1991; Bloom, 1994). However, children clearly do not need these syntactic cues to make the relevant distinctions, as many languages in the world (the majority) do not have articles (e.g., see Imai and Haryu, 2001). And even for English-speaking children, Soja, Carey, and Spelke (1991) found that young children treated words that referred to objects differently from words that referred to substances even when those words were presented in syntactically neutral form.

For verbs, a much stronger claim has been made. In particular, Gleitman (1990) has claimed that syntax plays an essential role in verb learning. The basic idea is that there is a strong correspondence between certain action/state concepts and the way they are expressed in language. Thus, all things being equal, a language should express the concept of giving (or a close equivalent) in an utterance containing three semantic roles expressed in nominals: the giver, the receiver, and the thing given. Similarly, the concept of thinking (or a close equivalent) should take as its complement a full proposition (as in *He thinks she's crazy*). Ultimately, many verbs are distinguished by a unique range of syntactic contexts (*see* can take either a direct object, as in *He sees it,* or a sentential complement, as in *He sees that she's lost*). Gleitman believes that these correspondences do not need to be learned by the child, but rather are at least to some degree part of the child's innate endowment that enables her to acquire language. (It could hardly be otherwise in this theory because if children use syntax to learn initial verb meanings, before they know much language, they must have some access to syntactic knowledge from the outset.)

Much of the empirical work of Gleitman and colleagues has focused on showing that in their speech to children adults differentiate verbs from one another by producing them in different ranges of syntactic contexts (e.g., Fisher, Gleitman, and Gleitman, 1991; Lederer, Gleitman, and Gleitman, 1995; Naigles and Hoff-Ginsberg, 1995). More recently, in a set of naturalistic observations, Naigles and Hoff-Ginsberg (1998) found that verbs that were used in more diverse sentence frames by mothers were also used in more diverse ways by their children (see also DeVilliers, 1985). Using a preferential-looking experimental paradigm, Naigles (1990) found that 2-year-olds matched the two utterances "The duck is glorping the bunny" and "The bunny and the duck are glorping" with their appropriate pictures (one depicting the duck doing something to the bunny and the other depicting the two participants engaged in the same parallel action). This is taken to indicate that they know the two syntactic frames involved in an abstract way. Similarly, Naigles (1996) found that young children could use multiple syntactic frames from adult language to distinguish contact from causative actions (see also Naigles and Kako, 1993). Using an act-out task, Naigles, Gleitman, and Gleitman (1993) found that when presented with utterances in which verb semantics and syntax conflicted, young children often went with the syntax (but see Akhtar and Tomasello, 1997: 964).

There is no question that children use linguistic context to help them learn the meanings of new verbs (e.g., see Behrend, Harris, and Cartwright, 1995, on children's use of verb inflections to infer verb meanings). But there are two major issues. One is whether this effect derives from the meaning of the rest of the utterance, or whether it derives more narrowly from the utterance's form (syntax, narrowly defined). For example, children in the Naigles (1990) study might very well have been using the word *and*, rather than syntax per se, as an indicator of the parallel action picture (this is also true of many of the stimuli in Naigles, Gleitman, and Gleitman, 1993). Fisher (1996) argues that children use a variety of sources of information from the surrounding utterance to learn the meaning of a new word. Some of these are quite mundane; for example, if the child hears *I'm tamming now* as the adult strikes her hand against the desk, the child can infer that the action being referred to by *tamming* is not one that changes the state of the object acted upon because the desk is not even mentioned. Along similar lines, Goldberg (1995) argues that since constructions have meaning, it is really the meaning of the construction that is the top-down component of "syntactic bootstrapping," not any abstract syntax-lexicon correspondences. The general point is thus that the linguistic contexts that help children to learn verb meanings may be working solely on the semantic level, in this sense that the child is determining the meaning of the utterance as a whole and then partitioning out those parts due to particular lexical items.

The second issue is the age at which children can use different aspects of the linguistic context to help them acquire new words. Age is important because in many cases researchers have hypothesized that the child makes inferences about the meaning of a new word from the syntactic form of the utterance in which it appears. But this can only work if the child begins with the syntax of the particular language she is learning—universal grammar will not tell the child the particularities of English grammar, for example, which are necessary in cases such as articles signaling count nouns or a certain range of syntactic frames signaling a particular English verb. By 3 or 4 years of age, everyone agrees, children have learned enough syntax to use it to acquire new words. But 2-year-olds are another story, and indeed each instance must be investigated separately. If 2-year-olds are not very good at using abstract syntactic constructions to infer word meanings, this lends credence to the hypothesis that children take some time to create the abstractions that they will later use to make top-down inferences about specific word meanings (see Chapter 4). Again, however, if children are simply segmenting the communicative intentions of an utterance semantically to learn a new word, then there is no reason why this cannot be an important part of the word learning process from the beginning.

Finally, there is one set of observations that is particularly informative in illustrating the role of linguistic context, including syntax, in helping children to learn the meanings of new words. Nelson (1995) identified a number of words in children's early vocabularies that could be used as either nouns or verbs. These so-called dual-category words included such common things as *bite, kiss, drink, brush, walk, hug, help,* and *call.* Many children use some of these words for both functions, often in referential situations that would seem to be identical (*Give me a hug/kiss* versus *Hug/Kiss me; Help/Call your sister* versus *Give your sister some help/a call*). In these cases (whose prevalence is unknown), it is hard to imagine how children could learn the two different uses of the same phonological sequence to indicate similar referential situations if they were not using as a major source of information its semantic/syntactic role in a larger utterance. Once again, then, we are led to a picture of word learning in which the child is determining the meaning of the utterance as a whole and then partitioning out those parts due to particular lexical items.

There is thus no doubt that linguistic context is an important, in some cases essential, factor in children's word learning. Indeed, one plausible explanation for the dramatic increase in the pace of children's word learning in the middle preschool period is that by that time each utterance they hear is more comprehensible to them—in terms of both the words they already know and the syntactic constructions involved—so that any new word must play a highly constrained role in the communicative intention of the utterance as a whole (as in *She puds that things can only get worse,* in which *pud* presumably indicates a psychological state of some sort). Linguistic contrast and context together thus provide very powerful hints and constraints—within the context of the child's attempts to read adult communicative intentions—that enable preschool children to acquire new words at the prodigious rate that they do.

3.2.4. Quantitative Factors of Input and Learning

To learn a piece of language children have to hear it. The conditions under which they hear it and the number of times they hear it are important factors in whether they do indeed learn it. Perhaps especially difficult is the process of getting started, before infants have any other language to help them isolate either the form or the function of a specific word or phrase. Interestingly, it seems that beginning language learners often do manage to find exactly the kind of language they need in the speech of their parents. Both Ninio (1993) and Brent and Siskind (2000) found that many of children's earliest words—up to 60 percent—are words that their parent has used relatively often as single-word utterances, things such as people's names, interjections, performatives, and some object and action words. Also relevant is the classic research of Peters (1983) and Slobin (1985a), who both observed that young children seem to be especially sensitive to words and phrases that are highly salient in the speech stream perceptually—by being stressed and/or in salient sentence positions (beginning or end). Attaching this salient word to the adult's entire communicative intention then leads to the acquisition of a holophrase.

A variety of studies have shown that after children have started learning words in earnest the amount of language they hear is a very good predictor of their vocabulary development. Representative studies are Huttenlocher, Hedges, and Duncan (1991); Hart and Risley (1995); Naigles and Hoff-Ginsberg (1998). Because these correlations might result from some more general factor (for example, parents who are skillful with language both talk a lot and have children who are skillful with language—with no direct causal link between the two) an especially important study is that of Pearson et al. (1997). They found a very strong relation in bilingual children between amount of exposure to each language and vocabulary size in that language. In combination, these studies are thus persuasive that hearing relatively large amounts of language facilitates vocabulary development.

But in these naturalistic studies there is no linking of information about precisely how often and in what ways children hear particular words, and how this affects their word learning. Indeed, the most natural interpretation is clearly false. That is, it is not the case that the more often a child hears a particular word, the quicker she learns it. As just two examples, the words *the* and *a* are among the most frequent words that young children hear, but they do not learn these words particularly early—for many obvious reasons. What is needed to complement these naturalistic findings are experiments in which children are exposed to new words under controlled conditions with a pre-set number of exposures. There is some such research, but surprisingly little.

The most robust finding of experimental studies is that comprehension precedes production. When Goldin-Meadow, Seligman, and Gelman (1976) asked 2-year-olds to comprehend or produce common words in an experimental setting, the children comprehended about 2–3 times as many words as they produced. Similarly, Childers and Tomasello (in press) found that with a similar number of exposures to nonce words 2-year-old children's comprehension was almost always better than their production. Exploring comprehension further, Carey and Bartlett (1978) found that many 3- and 4-year-olds could comprehend a novel word used for a novel object after only a single exposure, and many retained this comprehension up to six weeks later. Markson and Bloom (1997) found that over 80 percent of 2-year-olds comprehended a novel object label one week after having heard it just a few times (and over 80 percent of 3- and 4-year-olds after one month) (see also Heibeck and Markman, 1987; Rice, 1990). And Woodward, Markman, and Fitzsimmons (1994) found that even 13-month-old infants comprehended a new word at above-chance levels after 24 hours, given only a single training session with nine exposures to the novel word.

There is much less research on the quantitative dimensions of how children learn to produce novel words. Nelson and Bonvillian (1978) found that after only a few exposures to a novel label for a novel object, 2½-year-olds could produce that label appropriately more than half the time in the same session (depending on several other factors). But this may depend on children hearing only one new word in a session. Kuczaj (1987) reported that children in this same age range learned to produce, on average, fewer than 1 of 10 novel words presented to them on a single day when tested 24 hours later. In the only study to systematically investigate precisely how many exposures are needed to learn a novel word productively, Schwartz and Terrell (1983) found that children between 12 and 18 months took, on average, 10–12 exposures to a novel word to be able to produce it appropriately. These children eventually acquired about 35 percent of a group of 16 novel words presented to them over a ten-week period in from 10 to 20 exposures.

Another interesting issue is the spacing/timing of models. Schwartz and Terrell (1983) reported a very surprising additional finding from their study. They presented children with novel words on one of two schedules during their ten weekly sessions. On one schedule they exposed children to a novel word only once per session. On the other schedule they exposed children to a novel word twice per session. What they found was that children took approximately the same number of sessions (6–8) to learn to produce the new word in both conditions, meaning that they learned the less frequently presented words with about half as many exposures as the more frequently presented words (approximately 7 versus 12). A similar finding is reported by Childers and Tomasello (in press). They taught children novel words by giving them either 4 or 8 models, with these models distributed across days in various ways, for example, at the extreme, 1 model per day for 4 days versus 8 models all on the same day. The very strong finding was that children learned to produce both nouns and verbs better in distributed (over 4 days) than in massed (all in one day) exposures no matter the frequency; for example, 1 model per day for 4 days was better than 8 models all on the same day. In all conditions, retention was as good after one week as in immediate testing.

These findings on the timing of models may be interpreted in the context of the well-known findings in studies of animal and human learning that, given an equal number of exposures, distributed (or spaced) practice at a skill is almost always superior to massed practice. This finding holds for many skills for many species and has been replicated hundreds of times (see Dempster, 1996, for a review). These quantitative findings thus suggest that general learning processes are at work in word learning. In support of this claim, Markson and Bloom (1997; see also Markson, 1999) compared the learning of words to the learning of verbal and nonverbal facts. They taught some 3- and 4-year-olds the name of a particular novel object, "a koba"; they taught others that "This toy comes from a place called Koba" (a particular object); they taught others that "My uncle gave me this" (a particular object); and they taught still others that "This goes on here" (a sticker on a particular novel object). They found that in all of the conditions with verbally presented information, including word learning, children learned equally well quantitatively, both immediately and after week-long and month-long delays. Markson and Bloom interpreted these results as demonstrating that children can learn verbally presented facts about objects with the same number of exposures with which they learn object names, implying that at least some learning principles are general across linguistic and nonlinguistic domains.

Finally, an interesting quantitative issue concerning production is which of their words children use most often in spontaneous speech. Table 3.1 lists the words that one child at around her second birthday used most often in her everyday speech with her mother. As can be seen, for this child, who was mostly speaking in short two- to four-word utterances, various kinds of function words predominate. There are four conversational devices; three pronouns or proper names that refer to the child herself or her mother; nine pronouns, demonstratives, or articles having to do with object reference; six prolocatives or spatial propositions; two very generic verbs *(want, go)*; and several other words. There are no nouns in this list; the most frequently used noun for this child was *baby,* which was ranked number 56 in terms of frequency of use. Interestingly, these 25 words, which represent less than 2 percent of this child's vocabulary, account for about 45 percent of all the words she says in terms of token frequency. What this list and these facts demonstrate is that as soon as just a small amount of grammar begins, young children's utterances are peppered with a relatively small number of high-frequency lexical items such as certain pronouns and function words with highly recurrent discourse functions— with the more well-known nouns and verbs, which are typically thought of as the prototypical items in young children's vocabularies, used relatively infrequently as their specific referents occur in the child's experience at only irregular intervals.

Table 3.1   One child's 25 most frequently used words at age 2;0.

Reference	*Movement and location*
it	where's
one	here
that	there
the	on
a	down
this	go
it's	
that's	*Desire and prohibition*
my	want
	more
People	don't
I	
Mummy	*Conversational devices*
you	yeah
	no
	oh
	and

3.3. Theories of Word Learning

To account for the facts of word learning so far presented, as well as some others, there are three basic theories of children's lexical development. The first is that word learning is nothing special; children learn words by garden-variety associative learning. The second is that word learning is very special; so special that to learn a word children must utilize *a priori* word learning constraints or principles. The third, social-pragmatic theory is that word learning is somewhat special. Children do not need specialized word learning constraints or principles, but associative learning is not by itself sufficient. What is needed is a special form of social learning involving intention-reading, that is, cultural learning.

3.3.1. Learning Theory

Most people think it died with Behaviorism, but associative learning theory lives on. Smith (2000) has argued that the essence of word learning is associating sounds with salient aspects of perceptual experience. In support of this view, she has demonstrated in several experiments that children often assume that the meaning of a novel word is the most "salient" aspect of the current nonlinguistic context. For example, in an attempt to provide an associationistic explanation for the findings of Akhtar, Carpenter, and Tomasello (1996), Samuelson and Smith (1998) presented 2-year-olds with three objects, one at a time, each of which they dropped down a chute. The experimenter and child then moved to a special location where they played with a fourth object. They then moved back to the original location and (after a brief distraction) looked at all four objects inside a box, and the experimenter said "There's a gazzer in there." On the basis of this experience, most of the children thought the gazzer was the one they had played with at the special location. Samuelson and Smith argued that the children were associating the novel word, *gazzer*, with the most salient possible referent in this situation.

But two recent studies suggest a different interpretation of this result. First, in a direct replication and extension of this study, Diesendruck et al. (in press) reasoned that salience in this situation—as in all word learning situations—was determined by children's social-pragmatic inferences. To illustrate this, they compared a situation similar to that of Samuelson and Smith with another situation in which the experimenter accidentally dropped an object so that it rolled over to the same special location (where the experimenter and the child then played with it). They predicted that in this situation children would not infer that the experimenter's subsequent reference to the gazzer was aimed at the object played with in the special location because in this experimental condition there was no good pragmatic reason for the adult to be singling out this object—since it ended up in the new location only accidentally, and so was not treated in any special way intentionally. And this is exactly what they found. Children did not think there was anything special about the accidentally dropped object, and so they did not preferentially assign the novel label to it. The point is that in both studies—Samuelson and Smith and Diesendruck et al.—an object was made more salient, if salience is thought of as an objective property of an entity. Therefore, from Samuelson and Smith's point of view the children should have singled out the object played with in the special location in both studies. But children were not blindly drawn to the "salient" object in the Diesendruck et al. study because the accidentally dropped object was not especially salient from an intentional point of view. The most plausible interpretation of these findings is thus that in both studies the children were actively attempting to determine the adult's communicative intentions when she used the new word.

The second study is that of Moore, Angelopoulos, and Bennett (1999). They directly pitted objective salience against a relevant social cue (adult gaze direction). In the key experimental condition, an adult looked at and labeled one toy ("Look! A modi!") while another toy was made objectively more salient (by being lit up) at the same time. The salience did capture the children's attention (they looked over at the toy that was lit up), but this salience did not determine their pragmatic inferences about the meaning of the new word. In a subsequent comprehension test in which they were asked to retrieve the modi, 24-month-olds consistently chose the object that the adult had been looking at instead of the one that had been lit up (and that indeed had captured their attention at the moment the new word was said). So, at least by 24 months of age, gaze direction as an indication of adult attention and communicative intentions wins out over "objective salience" in this type of word learning situation.

An even deeper problem with garden-variety learning theory as an account of word learning is that the theory does not even acknowledge that linguistic symbols are special. The theory implicitly holds that a linguistic symbol is simply a sound (or possibly a hand sign) that "stands for" something in the world. What it means for one thing to stand for another is never really addressed. But if we look at children's earliest comprehension and production of real-live linguistic utterances, we see that there is something very special going on. The child encounters an adult making funny noises at her. To make sense of this odd behavior she must attempt to determine the purpose for which that person is making these funny noises. Once she determines that the adult is making these funny noises in an attempt to communicate with her, she still must determine precisely what the adult is attempting to communicate with some particular word. That is to say, the child must determine, first, the adult's overall communicative intention and, then, the particular way or ways that the new word is contributing to that communicative intention. This complex set of cognitive and social-cognitive processes is not accurately described by the simple term "association."

Relatedly and finally, learning theory has no concrete proposal for why language acquisition begins when it does at around 1 year of age. Human infants are very good at associative learning from very early in ontogeny, as demonstrated by the research of Haith, Rovee-Collier, and many others (see Haith and Benson, 1997, for a review). And so, as argued in Chapter 2, if association were all that was involved, language development should begin in early infancy. But it does not, and so we may assume that some additional factor or factors come on-line later, specifically at around 1 year of age.

3.3.2. Constraints and Principles

A second approach to word learning is the so-called constraints approach (e.g., Markman, 1989, 1992). In this approach the problem of word learning is formulated in terms of Quine's (1960) famous parable of a native who utters the expression "Gavagai!" and "shows" a foreigner the intended referent by pointing to a salient event as it unfolds: a rabbit running past. The problem is that since there is no shared context between interactants for this expression, there is basically no way that the foreigner can know whether the native's novel expression is being used to refer to the activity, to the rabbit, to some part of the rabbit's body, to the color of the rabbit's fur, or to any of an infinite number of things. This problem of referential indeterminacy—first explored in depth by Wittgenstein (1955)—is thus a kind of poverty-of-the-stimulus problem: children would seem to need additional information, over and above a perceived sound pattern and a perceived external scene, to learn the conventional communicative significance of a linguistic symbol. To solve this problem, constraints theorists have posited the existence of certain *a priori* constraints and/or principles that children bring to the word learning situation. These constraints and principles "limit the hypothesis space" so that the child is given a head start in solving the problem of referential indeterminacy in particular cases. The constraints approach thus emphasizes that the child needs *a priori*, specialized machinery to learn the linguistic conventions of those around her.

In Markman's (1989, 1992) account, young children first encounter language in possession of two especially important word learning constraints: (1) the Whole Object constraint, and (2) the Mutual Exclusivity constraint (a third is the Taxonomic assumption). The Whole Object constraint claims that, in the absence of direct evidence to the contrary, young children assume that a novel word is being used to refer to a whole object—not to one of the object's parts or properties or to an activity in which it is engaged. Children learn other kinds of words because the second constraint, Mutual Exclusivity, blocks the Whole Object constraint when children already have a name for an object. Thus, for example, if the child hears the word *modi* in association with an object whose name she already knows, she can assume that this new word is being used to refer to an object part, property, state, or action—although the theory does not specify how children determine precisely which of these other types of referents might be intended on a specific occasion. It is important to emphasize that the theory is not just that young children perceive the world in certain ways or find certain things especially salient, but rather that they assume *a priori* certain kinds of connections between language and the world.

While it is true that many children learning many of the world's languages acquire a disproportionately large number of adult nouns early in development, it is still the case that almost all children learning almost all languages learn other types of words early in development as well (and there are explanations for the priority of nouns other than the Whole Object constraint; see Section 3.1.1). Markman's theory assumes that these other words must all be learned in communicative situations involving objects for which the child already has a name (otherwise the Whole Object constraint would take charge). But this particular aspect of the theory has no empirical support, and indeed in the study of Tomasello and Akhtar (1995) 24-month-old children learned a new action word (verb) even when they did not know the name of the object engaged in the action. Young children's propensity to acquire nouns early in development thus very likely has some explanation other than an *a priori* Whole Object constraint. Children might learn many nouns early in development simply because whole, concrete objects are so salient and important in their social interactions with other persons, and so whole objects are often the focus of their social-pragmatic inferences—with no *a priori* connection to language. In terms of the Mutual Exclusivity assumption, studies by Mervis, Golinkoff, and Bertrand (1994), Deak and Maratsos (1998), and Clark and Svaib (1997) have demonstrated that from an early age young children will accept more than one word for a given entity if they understand that an adult is attempting to express different perspectives on that entity.

In partial recognition of the problems created by hard-and-fast word learning constraints, Golinkoff, Mervis, and Hirsh-Pasek (1994) proposed a number of word learning principles. Principles are "softer" than constraints and so may be violated more easily, and, at least in some accounts, they are not *a priori* but rather derived from children's word learning experiences. This is an important theoretical difference because this means that word learning principles cannot be used to solve Quine's problem of referential indeterminacy, at least not in the initial stages of word learning. Also, a main problem, once again, is that the theorists who espouse word learning principles have focused mainly on the learning of object labels to the neglect of other types of words, so that the proposed principles often work directly against the learning of word types other than object labels. A list of the major principles proposed (from Golinkoff, Mervis, and Hirsh-Pasek, 1994) and some of the other word types that would be hindered if they were actually employed is as follows:

- *Reference* ("Words map to objects, actions, attributes"): performatives such as *hi, bye, please,* and *thank you* are quite common in early language, and they are not referential.
- *Object scope* ("Words map to whole objects"): verbs, adjectives, prepositions, and many nonprototypical nouns like *breakfast, party,* and *park* are all quite common in early vocabularies, and they do not map to whole objects.
- *Extendability* ("Words extend to other referents"): proper nouns such as *Daddy, Jeffrey,* and *Mickey Mouse* are quite common in early vocabularies, and they do not extend to other referents at all.
- *Categorical scope* ("Words extend to basic-level categories"): proper nouns such as *Daddy* do not extend, and commonly occurring pro-

nouns such as *it, that,* and *she* extend to a wide range of objects well beyond basic-level categories.

And so not only would these particular word learning constraints and principles not help the child with words other than object labels, they would in fact be a positive hindrance to the learning of all these other word types.

Constraints theory and principles theory were created by looking at some facts about the learning of common nouns (that many children prefer object labels early in development, that they extend them routinely to novel objects, and so on), and then concocting a set of descriptive constraints that might account for these facts—with virtually no attention to other types of words. It is also a problem that constraints theory has not gone beyond an associationistic view of the symbolic relationship (it uses the metaphor of "mapping," instead of associating, word to world or concept, but the basic idea is the same), which is, as argued earlier, wholly inadequate to capture the distinctive quality of linguistic symbols.

Finally, like learning theory, constraints theory has no explanation for why language emerges when it does in human ontogeny—other than to stipulate that the constraints emerge when they do (perhaps maturationally), with no independent evidence of this other than the (circular) fact that language begins when it does. It would be much more satisfying to be able to connect children's word learning to other aspects of their cognitive and social-cognitive development in ways that would help to explain the age at which they begin to learn words.

3.3.3. Social-Pragmatic Theory

Like constraints theory, the social-pragmatic theory of word learning recognizes that garden-variety associative learning is not sufficient for the acquisition of linguistic symbols; the process must be constrained. But, in this view, posing the problem in terms of Quine's Gavagai parable—and then positing special word learning constraints to solve it—sets things up in the wrong way from the beginning (Bruner, 1983; Nelson, 1985; Tomasello, 1992b). That way of viewing things radically underestimates the informational richness of the social-interactive environment in which children learn language. In social-pragmatic theory, in contrast, the focus is on two inherently constraining aspects of the word learning process: (1) the structured social world into which children are born—full of scripts, routines, social games, and other patterned cultural interactions; and (2) children's social-cognitive capacities for tuning into and participating in this structured social world—especially joint attention and intention-reading (with the resulting cultural learning).

First, human children are born into worlds in which their caregivers have certain activities to perform on a regular basis, many involving the child directly. Some of these routines are fairly constant across cultures (such as nursing), while some are unique to particular cultures. Watson-Gegeo and Gegeo (1986), for example, report a "calling-out" routine engaged in regularly by Kwara'ae children and adults that is different from anything participated in by Western children. But Peters and Boggs (1986), in an analysis of adult-child routines from several societies, show that there are certain parallels between adult structuring of this routine and adult structuring of several routines common in Western middle-class culture. They speculate that the existence of some kinds of routines is virtually inevitable in human social life and that, although there may be important cultural differences in what routines are practiced, there may also be some underlying commonalities of process across cultures. And young children seem to learn almost all of their earliest language in cultural routines of one sort or another. Social interactional routines such as feeding, diaper changing, bathing, interactive games, book reading, car trips, and a host of other activities constitute the formats—joint attentional frames—within which children acquire their earliest linguistic symbols (Ratner and Bruner, 1978; Ninio and Bruner, 1978; Snow and Goldfield, 1983; for summaries see Bruner, 1983; Nelson, 1985). In general, if a child were born into a world in which the same event never recurred, the same object never appeared twice, and the adult never used the same language in the same context, it is difficult to see how that child—no matter her cognitive capabilities—could acquire a natural language.

Perhaps ironically, one of the most convincing demonstrations of the power of a structured cultural environment in the process of language acquisition does not involve human children at all because it involves, in effect, a comparison between being raised inside and outside a cultural context. The case is that of chimpanzees who have been taught to use human-like symbols. The first attempts to teach chimpanzees such skills relied on various associationistic training techniques. But when these pioneer chimpanzees were trained to point to the thing named, they could not then turn around and name the thing pointed to; when they were taught to name the thing pointed to, they could not point to the thing named. In contrast, apes such as the famous Kanzi, who were raised in a different way, did not show these limitations of language understanding and use. Savage-Rumbaugh (1990) reports that the crucial difference is that whereas the earlier chimpanzee students were "trained" to do certain things in certain situations, Kanzi was not trained at all. Rather, he was raised more naturally in a human-like cultural environment in which he was regularly included in highly structured cultural activities such as changing diapers, preparing food, going outdoors, taking a bath, blowing bubbles, riding in the car, looking at a book, and so on. Language was used by his caretakers in these situations in any way that seemed natural to them, and Kanzi learned symbols in these situations in seemingly human-like ways. This would seem to be a very convincing demonstration that routine cultural activities and events structure the language learner's experience in a way that is conducive to the acquisition of communicative conventions.

The second half of the equation concerns the social-cognitive abilities of young children that allow them to participate intersubjectively in these culturally constituted joint attentional frames. Participation with another person in cultural activities requires in most cases the ability to coordinate attention to the person with attention to the objects that person is interacting with, and even, in many cases, to take the perspective of that person on the object. As documented in Chapter 2, this coordination begins at around 9 months of age when infants begin to engage in a complex of behaviors and interactions with adults most often known as joint attention.

Within joint attentional frames, adults often make linguistic utterances in an attempt to exhort children to attend to certain aspects of the shared situation. In attempting to comply with these exhortations—that is, in attempting to comprehend the adult's communicative intention as expressed in the utterance—children use all kinds of interpretive strategies based on the pragmatic assumption that utterances are somehow *relevant* to the ongoing social interaction (Sperber and Wilson, 1986; Bruner, 1983; Bloom, 1993). In the social-pragmatic view, word learning does not consist in the child engaging in a reflective cognitive task in an attempt to make correct mappings of word to world, but rather it emerges naturally from situations in which children are engaged in social interactions in which they are attempting to understand and interpret adult communicative intentions as expressed in utterances (making sense; Nelson, 1985). Learning the communicative significance of an individual word consists in the child first discerning the adult's overall communicative intention in making the utterance, and then identifying the specific functional role this word is playing in the communicative intention as a whole. This is a process of intention-reading and extraction, not of association or constraint.

The most basic point that differentiates social-pragmatic theory from constraints theory is the recognition that human linguistic communication can take place only when there is some "common ground" (joint attentional frame) between speaker and listener, which sets the context for the reading of the specific communicative intentions behind a word or utterance. Thus, in Quine's "Gavagai!" situation, if, before hearing the novel word, the foreigner understood that she and her informant were searching for material to make a coat, she would be very unlikely to infer that the word was being used to refer to the running activity or the leg of the rabbit. If she knew they were searching for a particular pet rabbit with its own name, she would be very unlikely to interpret the word as a common noun for the class of rabbits. And on and on. In general, the shared intentional situation (joint attentional frame, common ground) constrains the interpretation of the speaker's communicative intentions from the outset—given, of course, a child and an adult capable of participating in shared intentional situations. Even Quine himself is very clear (1960: preface and 28) that the Gavagai situation is an unrealistic ("radical") situation, stripped of a shared culture, shared intentional situation, and other background cues to the native's communicative intent. But children do not learn language in such a vacuum; they learn it in the midst of meaningful social interactions in which they share common ground with their adult interlocutor (such as searching for material to make a coat), and this common ground then serves to "constrain the hypothesis space" without any dedicated, language-specific principles or constraints. In situations where there is no common ground—which happen all day every day in the lives of young children—children simply are not learning new words.

In the social-pragmatic view, then, children acquire linguistic symbols as a kind of by-product of social interaction with adults, in much the same way they learn many other cultural conventions (Tomasello, Kruger, and Ratner, 1993). The acquisition of linguistic symbols does not need external linguistic constraints in this theory because children are always participating in and experiencing particular social contexts, and it is these social contexts that serve to "constrain" the interpretive possibilities. The child who knows that his mother wishes him to put on his hat (she is holding it out to him and gesturing) assumes that her utterance is relevant to that intention, and this is what guides his interpretations of any novel word in the utterance. All of the philosophically possible hypotheses that Quine and others may create are simply not part of the child's experience in this particular social context—assuming of course that by the time language acquisition begins young children have a reasonably adult-like understanding of at least some aspects of the social activities in which they participate. Having complied with adult instructions to experience a situation in a particular way in a given instance, the child may then learn to produce the appropriate linguistic symbol herself (by role reversal imitation) when she wishes others to experience a situation in that same way—thus entering into the world of bi-directionally (intersubjectively) understood linguistic symbols (Tomasello, 1999).

Importantly, the social-pragmatic theory has a clear answer to the question of why language acquisition begins when it does. Language acquisition begins when it does because it depends on the ability to share attention with other human beings communicatively and so to form symbols, an ability that emerges near the end of the first year of life (Tomasello, 1995a; Carpenter, Nagell, and Tomasello, 1998; and see Chapter 2). This is not to deny that as a result of learning their first words children induce some word learning principles. One good example is the principle of contrast (see Section 3.2.3), a pragmatic principle that helps young children to specify word meanings more precisely. And of course as children learn more language they learn some principles of grammar (that *the* and *a* are used with count nouns, that sentential complements typically indicate mental verbs, and so on), and they use these linguistic contexts to "bootstrap" later word learning. The social-pragmatic theory thus does not deny the usefulness of some word learning principles; it simply emphasizes that the foundational skills of word learning are social-cognitive skills, and that all other participating skills—including any induced principles—are built on this foundation.

3.4. Summary

In this chapter I have adopted a social-pragmatic approach to word learning. As compared with other approaches, this approach has two important advantages. First, it connects the learning of words with many of children's other joint attentional and cultural learning activities in a way that demonstrates precisely what a linguistic symbol is, in comparison with other forms of simple association between sounds and experiences. Linguistics symbols are social conventions that may be used to manipulate the attentional and mental states of other people in a way that is different from, but still similar to, the way this is done with other joint attentional behaviors (such as nonlinguistic gesturing). Second, unlike any other theory, social-pragmatic theory explains why word learning begins when it does in the months immediately following the first birthday. The explanation is that word learning awaits the emergence of children's more fundamental social-cognitive skills of joint attention and intention-reading, on which it depends fundamentally. Social-pragmatic theory may also be used to explain the noun bias in early vocabularies by focusing on how easy or difficult it is to read adult communicative intentions as expressed in adult utterances in different situations.

In proposing factors involved in word learning, I have identified three types of factors, depending on their precise role. I have called joint attention and intention-reading *foundational* because they in essence define the symbolic dimensions of linguistic communication. But there are also factors that we may call *prerequisite*. Thus, in order to learn a word young children must be able to segment the speech stream into identifiable units, and they must be able to conceptualize different aspects of their experiential worlds. (In hypothesizing semantic representations for children's word meanings, it is important to keep in mind that these will be composed of elements from the child's own, not adults', conceptualizations.) In the beginning, these prerequisite and foundational skills are all that children have available to them; 1-year-olds do not have any constraints, principles, knowledge of syntactic context, or knowledge of paradigmatic contrast to rely on. As development proceeds, however, and "all the easy ones are taken," the job of word learning becomes both more complex and more powerful. Children learn to read adult communicative intentions in a wider variety of contexts, and they learn to use a wider range of informational sources that help them do this.

And so finally we must recognize other factors that are *facilitative* of the process of word learning. Most important among these are the linguistic factors of context and contrast. First, fairly early in their linguistic careers children begin to rely on their knowledge of the communicative significance of other words, and/or linguistic constructions, in the adult's utterance (that is, in the immediate linguistic context). This involves an understanding of the adult's overall communicative intention and a kind of blame-assignment procedure in which different components of this are assigned to different components of the utterance. For instance, suppose an adult asks the child something like *Do you want to glorp the modi?* To comprehend the new words, the child must understand something of the overall communicative intention (I am being asked if I want to do something to something) and what parts of this are already taken by the known words and constructions (and intonation)—and so what roles are left for the new words to play. Second, also fairly early in their linguistic careers children begin to use their knowledge of other words that might contrast paradigmatically in the adult utterance with one they do not know: Why did she say I could not *throw* it but I could *glorp* it? Contrast of this type would seem to be especially important in learning fine-grained distinctions among closely related words *(give, have, use, share)*. These two additional sources of linguistic information—one in the immediate linguistic context and one in the child's stored linguistic experience—are primarily responsible for the rapid pace of word learning during the late preschool years and beyond (that is, along with derivational morphology and literacy).

A very interesting finding that highlights the tight interrelation of children's different language acquisition skills is that lexical and grammatical development are highly intercorrelated. Anisfeld et al. (1998) found that children's early vocabularies begin to expand quite rapidly soon after the onset of grammatical speech, presumably indicating some synergistic interaction between the two. Additionally, Bates and her colleagues (Caselli,

Casadio, and Bates, 1999; summarized in Bates and Goodman, 1999) have found that only after children have vocabularies of several hundred words do they begin to produce in earnest grammatical speech. Moreover, they have found a very high positive correlation between children's lexical and grammatical skills at all points in early development.

There are a number of hypotheses that might explain these correlational findings. One is that children must have a certain number of words before they can understand a syntactic construction, and understanding more words helps in understanding more constructions. Another is that knowing linguistic constructions helps in learning words, in ways discussed above. A third—not incompatible with the other two—is that learning words and learning grammatical constructions are both part of the same overall process. Although a bit more complex, learning the communicative significance of a complex expression or construction shares many acquisition processes with learning the communicative significance of a single word. This parallel analysis for words and constructions is particularly apt if we consider words composed of multiple morphemes expressing a complex event or situation and its participants—even something relatively simple such as the Spanish *Dámelo!* (Give it to me!)—which is the normal case for many of the words in many of the world's more fusional languages (much more so than in isolating languages like English). Indeed, coming from the perspective of Polish, a highly inflected language, Dabrowska (2000) has called syntactic constructions simply "big words."

In any case, the processes of lexical and grammatical development are closely intertwined, and theories of child language acquisition would do well to begin to integrate their accounts of these different aspects of the process more closely. With this goal in mind, we can now turn to an investigation of the ways in which children acquire productive control of their first constructional patterns containing multiple words.

Early Syntactic Constructions

Our language can be seen as an ancient city: a maze of
little streets and squares, of old and new houses, and
of houses with additions from various periods; and this
surrounded by a multitude of new boroughs with
straight regular streets and uniform houses.

—LUDWIG WITTGENSTEIN

AT THE same time they are extracting words
from adult utterances, young children are also learning from these utterances more complex linguistic expressions and constructions as kind of
linguistic gestalts. Indeed, if one takes a usage-based view of language,
learning to use complex expressions and constructions shares a number of
fundamental processes with learning to use words. A child can learn to use
the English passive construction appropriately and productively, for example, only by witnessing events in the world and attempting to discern
speakers' communicative intention in referring to these events with a certain pattern of linguistic symbols (to communicate about an entity to
which something happens). Given that each language has its own lexical
and grammatical conventions, there is really no alternative to this basic
account of how children acquire linguistic symbols, be they words or more
complex constructions. But there is still the question of how concrete or
abstract these initial acquisitions are—whether they are based in specific
words and phrases or in abstract categories and principles—and this is indeed the central question in the study of children's early syntactic development. A brief history will clarify the issue and the current approach to it.

Using the linguistics of the 1950s (namely American structural linguistics), the first modern researchers of child language acquisition attempted
in the 1960s to identify the items and structures in children's language using exclusively the method of distributional analysis. They make basically
no assumptions about possible correspondences between child and adult
linguistic competence. The main finding was that many of children's earliest word combinations involved one constant word which could be freely

combined with any one of many variable words. Many of these lexically based patterns also seemed to show some consistencies, however, especially with respect to ordering, and so Braine (1963) formalized these patterns into a three-rule *pivot grammar* that was supposed to be what children used to generate their language:

1. P^1 + O (*More juice, More milk, There Daddy, There Joe*).
2. O + P^2 (*Juice gone, Mommy gone, Flowers pretty, Janie pretty*).
3. O + O (*Ball table, Mommy sock*—utterances without a pivot).

The main problem with formalized pivot grammar was that it was empirically inadequate since (1) children did not always use the same pivot in a consistent sequential position, (2) children sometimes combined two pivots, and (3) the O + O rule was essentially a wastebasket for noncanonical utterances (Bloom, 1971). It was also unclear in this account how young children could ever get from these purely child-like syntactic categories and rules to the more adult-like syntactic categories and rules that were being described by a number of emerging linguistic theories at that time.

The natural next attempt, therefore, was to apply the new adult linguistic models of the 1960s and 1970s to the data on child language acquisition. These attempts—which included several versions of transformational generative grammar, case grammar, generative semantics, and others—were reviewed and evaluated by Brown (1973). Brown's basic conclusion was that, while children's linguistic productions could be forced into any one of the models, none of them was totally satisfactory in accounting for all of the data. But the more fundamental problem was that there was really no evidence that children employed, or even needed, the adult-like linguistic categories and rules that were being attributed to them in these models. As one example, Bowerman (1973) surveyed the utterances produced by several children learning several languages and found that—on internal grounds—there was no reason to assume that the children used as a constituent of their utterances anything like Verb Phrase (VP = Verb + Complement), a crucial constituent of some adult models. The main point was that few if any of the phenomena of adult language that required the positing of VP as a coherent utterance constituent were present in the language of young children. Schlesinger (1971) made the same basic argument for the grammatical relations "subject" and "direct object." And there was a suspicion among many people who looked at languages across different cultures that no single formal grammar would be adequate to account for the variety of typological patterns observed (Slobin, 1973).

Returning to a more child-centered view, several theorists—including Brown (1973), Slobin (1970), Schlesinger (1971), Bloom (1973), and

Braine (1976)—suggested a more semantic-cognitive basis for children's early language: the so-called semantic relations approach. The basic observation in this case was that some of the fundamental syntactic relations apparent in children's early language correspond rather closely to some of the categories of sensory-motor cognition as outlined by Piaget (1952). For example, infants know nonlinguistically some things about the causal relations among agents, actions, and objects, and this knowledge might form the basis for a linguistic schema of the type Agent-Action-Object (and similarly for Possessor-Possessed, Object-Location, Object-Attribute, and so on). While this approach seemed to capture something of the spirit of early language—children mostly talk about a fairly delimited set of events, relations, and objects that correspond in some ways to Piagetian sensory-motor categories—it was also empirically inadequate, as many child utterances fit into none of the categories while others fit into several (and different investigators proposed different categories; Howe, 1976). Moreover, echoing the theoretical problems of pivot grammar, there were basically no serious theoretical proposals about how young children got from these semantically based categories to the more abstract syntactic categories of adults.

And so, swinging the pendulum back in the adult direction once again, in the 1980s a new group of theorists began to advocate a return to adult grammars, but in this case using some new formal models such as government and binding theory, lexical functional grammar, and the like (e.g., Baker and McCarthy, 1981; Hornstein and Lightfoot, 1981; Pinker, 1984). The general consensus was that proposing a discontinuity from child to adult language—as such things as pivot grammar and the semantic relations approach seemed to do—created insurmountable "logical" problems, that is to say, problems of learnability. These logical problems were thought by learnability theorists to be sufficient justification to make the "continuity assumption," namely, that children operate with the same basic linguistic categories and rules as adults (Pinker, 1984). This general point of view was strongly associated with linguistic nativism, in which all human beings possess the same basic linguistic competence, in the form of a universal grammar, throughout their lives (Chomsky, 1968, 1980a). The inadequacies of this approach soon became apparent as well (at least to more developmentally minded researchers), most fundamentally its inability to deal with the problems of cross-linguistic variation and developmental change—how children could "link" an abstract and unchanging universal grammar to the structures of a particular language, and why, if this was the process, children's language looked so different from adults' language. And again, there was no evidence that children actually use abstract adult-like categories—continuity was only an assumption.

It is thus fair to say that all the initial attempts to account for child language acquisition in terms of some kind of abstractions failed. They failed even though they included attempts based on

- the child making her own abstractions from adult utterances (pivot grammar);
- the child possessing adult abstractions from the beginning (as specified by one or another formal grammar); and
- the child starting with semantic-cognitive abstractions (the semantic relations approach).

Given all these failures, one obvious possibility is that young children begin with no linguistic abstractions at all, or with only a very limited set. What if instead of leaping at every opportunity to attribute to children abstract linguistic categories and constructions, researchers simply acknowledged the empirical fact that linguistic abstractions build up during ontogeny in a much slower and more piecemeal fashion than previously believed—and then adjusted their models accordingly? That is the strategy that will be pursued here.

On the face of it this approach seems to face the problem of You Can't Get There From Here—the downfall of earlier child-centered approaches such as pivot grammar and semantic relations—because adults clearly do work with a fairly wide range of linguistic abstractions. But the current approach is different from its progenitors in not sending children off initially in any wrong directions, making the wrong kinds of generalizations based on pivot grammar or semantic relations. Children make the right kinds of generalizations from the beginning, just slowly and unevenly—depending on input. Their early constructions are thus similar to adult constructions; it is just that they are simpler and more concrete, with fewer and weaker abstractions—because they are based on less linguistic experience. In combination with the previously described new developments in usage-based linguistics—comprehensive and rigorous yet still child-friendly models of the adult endpoint—and developmental psychology—more powerful models of child cognition and learning—this new approach makes it much easier than before to envisage how children might get from here (item-based constructions) to there (adult syntactic competence).

In this chapter, I attempt to describe, and to some degree explain, children's early multi-word syntactic constructions. The next chapter deals with children's later, more abstract syntactic constructions and lays out in more detail the basic theoretical approaches in the field. For now, the one piece of theory we need is this. Generative grammar approaches, whatever their specifics, predict that all of the particular linguistic items and structures that fall under a certain formal description should emerge at the same time in development and be applied productively across all lexical and grammatical items basically immediately. For example:

> Once a child is able to parse an utterance such as "Close the door!," he will be able to infer from the fact that the verb "close" in English precedes its complement "the door," that all verbs in English precede their complements. (Radford, 1990: 61)

In contrast, usage-based approaches expect children's learning to be more gradual, piecemeal, and lexically dependent—with the acquisition of particular linguistic structures depending heavily on the specific language to which a particular child is exposed, and with generalizations coming only after a fair amount of concrete linguistic material has been learned.

4.1. The Nature of Constructions

A basic unit of traditional linguistic analysis is the construction. Classically, one could talk about such things as the English passive construction, the German noun phrase construction, and so forth. Because the emphasis was on describing very general patterns, these constructions were almost always described in terms of abstract linguistic categories and rules such as Noun, Verb, Article + Noun, SVO, and so forth. The difference in modern-day usage-based approaches—especially construction grammar (Fillmore, 1989; Goldberg, 1995; Croft, 2001) and cognitive grammar (Langacker, 1987a, 1991)—is that the search is for all kinds of usage patterns, even those of only limited generality. Usage-based approaches therefore seek to account not just for "core grammar," as in most formal linguistic approaches, but for all kinds of linguistic items and structures—including idioms, irregular constructions, mixed constructions, and metaphorical extensions—all within one theoretical framework. Most importantly, usage-based theorists do not search for the most general abstractions possible in a corpus and automatically attribute them to the speaker. The level of abstraction at which the speaker is working in particular cases may or may not correspond to the most abstract level the linguist can find; it is in all cases an empirical question that most often needs psychological experimentation (priming experiments, experiments with nonce words, and so on).

4.1.1. Why Constructions Are Not Rules

As outlined in Chapter 1, formal linguistic approaches (including generative grammar) characterize natural languages in terms of formal languages, using as basic theoretical primitives meaningless algebraic rules and meaningful linguistic elements that serve as variables in the rules. But many contemporary linguists simply do not believe that the analogy between natural languages and formal languages is a particularly accurate or productive one—most importantly because it effaces the symbolic dimension of grammatical constructions. The alternative is to look at linguistic competence, not in terms of the possession of a formal grammar of semantically empty rules, but rather in terms of the mastery of a structured inventory of meaningful linguistic constructions.

Beginning at the beginning, for usage-based theorists the fundamental reality of language is people making utterances to one another on particular occasions of use. When people repeatedly use the same particular and concrete linguistic symbols to make utterances to one another in "similar" situations, what may emerge over time is a pattern of language use, schematized in the minds of users as one or another kind of linguistic category or construction. As opposed to linguistic rules conceived of as algebraic procedures for combining symbols that do not themselves contribute to meaning, linguistic categories and constructions are themselves meaningful linguistic symbols—since they are nothing other than the patterns in which meaningful linguistic symbols are used to communicate. Thus, the pattern X VERB*ed* Y *the* Z is a construction of English that signifies some kind of transfer of possession (either literal or metaphorical); the pattern *the* X signifies a "thing" (in the sense of Langacker, 1987b). There are no linguistic entities—lexical or syntactic—that are not symbolic in this way; all have communicative significance because they all derive directly from language use.

Usage-based linguists such as Langacker (1987a), Bybee (1995), Fillmore (1989), Goldberg (1995), and Croft (2001) thus recognize a continuum of meaningful linguistic constructions from morphemes to words to phrases to syntactic assemblies. These constructions are of different levels of complexity, but they are all meaningful in basically the same way. This is true regardless of whether they comprise concrete and particular items (as in words and idioms), more abstract classes of items (as in word classes and abstract constructions), or complex combinations of concrete and abstract pieces of language (such as mixed constructions). Thus, before they are 2 years old, many young children have in their linguistic inventories concrete words (such as *bird),* some bound morphemes of varying degrees of productivity (for example, plural *-s,* past tense *-ed,* but only with some words), frozen phrases (such as *I-wanna-do-it),* and a variety of item-based (mixed) constructions *(Where's-the X? X on-there; I-wanna X).* From a psycholinguistic point of view, children do not first learn words and then combine them into sentences via contentless syntactic "rules."

Rather, children learn simultaneously from adult utterances meaningful linguistic structures of many shapes and sizes and degrees of abstraction, and they then produce their own utterances on particular occasions of use by piecing together some of these many and variegated units in ways that express their immediate communicative intention.

The most important point is that constructions are nothing more or less than patterns of usage, which may therefore become relatively abstract if these patterns include many different kinds of specific linguistic symbols. But never are they empty rules devoid of semantic content or communicative function. In usage-based approaches, contentless rules, principles, parameters, constraints, features, and so forth are the formal devices of professional linguists; they simply do not exist in the minds of speakers of a natural language.

4.1.2. Utterances and Constructions

To explicate the nature of constructions more fully, we must begin with some terminological clarifications. The basic problem is that traditional linguistic analysis privileges words and rules, but these differ from each other on two dimensions simultaneously. Words are both simple and concrete whereas rules are both complex and abstract. To be clear, we must therefore unconfound these two dimensions. We will do so by referring to concrete pieces of language as either words (simple, such as *tree, run*) or expressions (complex, such as *How are you?*), and to linguistic abstractions as either categories (simple, such as N or NP) or constructions (complex, such as NP + V + NP). When we wish to be neutral with regard to the level of abstractness involved, we will use the terms *linguistic items* (simple) and *linguistic structures* (complex). The situation is actually a bit more complex than this, as one of the main arguments below will be that human beings master a number of linguistic structures that are complicated mixtures of concrete pieces of language and linguistic abstractions. But in any case, attempted clarity at the outset can only help, and so our initial working definitions of key terms may be summarized as shown in Figure 4.1.

A construction is prototypically a unit of language that comprises multiple linguistic elements used together for a relatively coherent communicative function, with sub-functions being performed by the elements as well. Consequently, constructions may vary in complexity depending on the number of elements involved and their interrelations. For example, the English regular plural construction (N + s) is relatively simple, whereas the passive construction (X *was* VERB*ed by* Y) is relatively complex. Independent of complexity, however, constructions may also vary in their

	Simple	Bold
Linguistic abstractions	Categories	Constructions
Concrete pieces of language	Words (morphemes)	Expressions (phrases)
Linguistic symbols (neutral re: abstraction)	Items	Structures

Figure 4.1. Terminology for talking about constructions at different levels of complexity and abstractness.

abstractness. Some constructions—indeed most of the well-studied constructions—are highly abstract, using various categories as their constitutive elements. For example, the very simple English regular plural construction and the more complex English passive construction are both highly (though not totally) abstract. To repeat, even these most abstract constructions are still symbolic, as they possess a coherent, if abstract, meaning in relative independence of the lexical items involved. Thus, in the utterance *Mary sneezed John the football,* our construal of the action is influenced more by the transfer-of-possession meaning of the ditransitive construction than it is by the verb *sneeze* (since sneezing is not normally construed as transferring possession; Goldberg, 1995). Similarly, we know that the nonce noun *gazzers* very likely indicates a plurality without even knowing what a gazzer is.

Importantly, however, some complex linguistic structures are not based on abstract categories, but rather on particular linguistic items (see especially the work in construction grammar, e.g., Fillmore, 1988, 1989; Fillmore, Kaye, and O'Conner, 1988; Croft, 2001). The limiting case is totally fixed expressions such as the idiom *How do you do?*—which is a structure of English with an idiosyncratic meaning that dissolves if any of the particular words is changed (one does not normally, with the same intended meaning, ask *How does she do?*). Other clear examples are such well-known idioms as *kick the bucket* and *spill the beans,* which have a little more flexibility and abstractness as different people may kick the bucket and they may do so in past, present, or future tense—but we cannot, with the same meaning, kick the pail or spill the peas. It turns out that, upon inspection, a major part of human linguistic competence—much more than previously believed—involves the mastery of all kinds of routine formulas, fixed and semi-fixed expressions, idioms, and frozen collocations. Indeed one of the distinguishing characteristics of native speakers of a language is their control of these semi-fixed expressions as fluent units with somewhat unpredictable meanings (Pawley and Syder, 1983; Wray and Perkins, 2000).

The theoretical problem for algebraic approaches such as generative grammar is what to do with these fixed and semi-fixed complex structures. They are complex and somewhat regular, and so they would seem to be a part of the grammar to be generated by rules. But as fixed expressions they would seem to be a part of the lexicon to be memorized like words. Chomsky's (1980a) approach to the issue is to simply draw a line in the sand. Idioms and idiosyncratic constructions are not part of core grammar, and so they are not subject to the principles of universal grammar. This approach has recently been characterized as the *words and rules approach* (also called the *dual mechanism approach*) by Pinker (1991, 1999) and Clahsen (1999), for whom the lexicon contains everything that must be learned by rote, while the grammar contains everything that can be subsumed under a rule and so is part of the generative, productive component of linguistic competence.* In line with the algebraic metaphor, every linguistic structure is either a rote-learned item (variable) or an instantiation of a productive rule (formula), with no provision for in-between cases.

The problem is that there are many in-between cases; Chomsky's line in the sand is not so easy to draw. There are three classes of difficult examples. First and most important are the many types of so-called mixed constructions, which have some components based on more regular rule-like patterns and some components based on more idiosyncratic conventions including particular words and/or morphemes. Consider the *let alone* construction:

I wouldn't live in New York, let alone Boston.
He wouldn't use a bicycle, let alone a car.
She wouldn't do calisthenics, let alone lift weights.

Fillmore, Kaye, and O'Conner (1988) have analyzed this construction in detail, highlighting its many idiosyncratic properties, not the least of which is the necessity of the construction-defining lexical item *let alone*— but acknowledging its canonical properties as well (for example, the initial clause is garden variety). One particularly difficult question is what exactly is the grammatical status of the clause after the comma *(let alone a car, let alone lift weights)*, since it would not seem to fit easily into any traditional grammatical categories. And so the problem is that this construc-

---

* We may refer to these approaches as "generative grammar lite" because they retain the flavor of the original but without all the fat (annoying formalisms).

tion is neither purely words nor purely rules (and its "rules" include both regular and irregular ones).

Another example of a mixed construction—what are sometimes referred to as "schematic idioms" (Nunberg, Sag, and Wasow, 1994)—is the *-er* construction:

> The bigger they are, the nicer they are.
> The more you try, the worse it gets.
> The faster I run, the behinder I get.

This construction is a bit more non-canonical than the *let alone* construction, as both of the two clauses are difficult to classify using classical grammatical techniques, although there are obvious canonical elements as well. The specific words and morphemes required here are also a bit less straightforward, with the initial *the* clearly required and with some kind of comparative term in each clause required as well (often but not always comparative adjectives ending in *-er*).

Another slightly odd mixed construction (of special complexity) is the "nominal extraposition" construction (Michaelis and Lambrecht, 1996):

> It's amazing the people you see here.
> It's ridiculous how much it costs.
> It's a joke the way they run that place.

Once more, there are obviously some general principles of English at work, but this construction also has some singular properties shared by no others in the language, including the mandatory presence of the initial *It's*.

A complex family of mixed constructions known as *there*-constructions (Lakoff, 1987) are especially common in early child language. In these constructions the NP subject follows the verb:

> There is my shoe.
> There are my shoes.

The construction is of course defined by the presence of the initial word *there,* but it makes a difference if *there* is functioning as a locative (as in the above examples) or as a so-called existential deictic *(There once was a man. . .)*—and both of these are different from similar constructions beginning with *It (It is my shoe; *It are my shoes).* In any case, the key question is: Are this construction and other mixed constructions memorized or generated by a rule? And is the rule specific to the construction or is it more general? Is it a part of core grammar?

A second class of constructions problematic for traditional analyses are constructions that are basically canonical, but that apply to a very limited range of linguistic items—so that in writing "rules" for them we must re-

spect their narrow scope. As just one example, in English we can say
things like:

> This hairdryer needs fixing.
> My house needs painting.

Note in this case that although *hairdryer* and *house* are the subjects of the
sentences they are the logical objects of the predicates *fixing* and *painting*,
which are expressed as participles. Virtually no other verbs besides *need*
work in this construction of the English language (some people will accept
the semantically similar verbs *require* and *want*). It would thus seem that
this construction, while basically canonical, is at the same time best described in lexically specific terms. And in some languages there are much
wider constructional patterns that still apply in very restricted ways; for
example, some languages organize constructions in one tense or person
ergatively but those in another tense or person accusatively (DeLancey,
1981; van Valin, 1992).

The third major class of constructions problematic for traditional analyses comprises those that are abstract and productive but idiosyncratic.
Consider the well-known "incredulity construction":

> Him be a doctor!
> My mother ride the train!
> Her wash the dishes!

This is an extremely productive construction; a native speaker of English
can generate examples virtually ad infinitum. It is also a totally abstract
construction, since most of these examples will share exactly zero morphemes, and so it would seem to be rule based. But this is also a highly idiosyncratic construction sharing little with other constructions of English.
While it is ordered in canonical SVO ordering, the S is in accusative case
(Him, Her) and the V is devoid of the normal agreement marker for third-
person subjects *(My mother ride,* not *rides).* (It is very likely that this construction is an historical relic—a salvaged part of some larger construction.) And so, which is it: rote-learned and in the lexicon, or rule-based
and in core grammar? The answer is that it is both and it is neither. It is
simply a construction of the English language that learners must acquire
by hearing exemplars and then generalize on the basis of a common pattern among those exemplars.

The impossibility of making a clear distinction between the core and the
periphery of linguistic structure is a genuine scientific discovery, and it has
far-reaching theoretical implications.* Most importantly in the current

---

* Even theorists from a generative grammar perspective have recently begun to recognize
the problem. For example, Jackendoff (1996) has noted the large number of idioms and

context, it presents major, perhaps insurmountable, difficulties for any acquisition theory that attempts to partition the linguistic universe cleanly into just two kinds of entities: rule-based and unruly. Instead, it suggests that language structure emerges from language use, and that a community of speakers may conventionalize from their language use all kinds of linguistic structures—from the more concrete to the more abstract, from the more regular to the more idiomatic, and with all kinds of mixed constructions as well. Adopting this perspective may require some rethinking of many traditional linguistic entities, and indeed a number of theorists are even moving toward the idea that so-called closed classes of grammatical words and morphemes (auxiliaries, prepositions, determiners, complementizers, and so on) do not really form coherent linguistic classes at all. People just learn to use the particular lexical items and grammatical morphemes individually *(must, the, that)*, and these typically number in the dozens for each so-called closed grammatical class of words/morphemes. And these morphemes do this in the context of larger constructions from which they typically derive much of their meaning. While the class names may be convenient for linguists, real language users may not operate with such classes at all (Cullicover, 1999).

If we take these points seriously, an important question for acquisition researchers becomes: If many, perhaps most, of the structures of a language (as embodied in various kinds of semi-fixed expressions, irregular formations, schematic idioms, and the like) may be acquired through "normal" processes of learning and abstraction—as they are in all theoretical accounts, including the words and rules of generative grammar lite—then why cannot the more regular and canonical aspects of a language be acquired in this same straightforward way? Why do we need a second set of mechanisms for core grammar over and above those used for learning other aspects of language structure?

4.1.3. Constructions and Grammar

In usage-based linguistics, the linguistic competence of mature speakers of a language is characterized not as a monolithic grammar—as in generative grammar—but rather as a "structured inventory of symbolic units" in the minds of its speakers (Langacker, 1987a; Croft, 2001). Exactly how these

unique collocations a language possesses and has basically posited that the lexicon is very much larger than we previously thought. Cullicover (1999) has examined a number of syntactic structures that have traditionally been described by abstract categories and rules, and has found that in case after case detailed analysis of the particular words and expressions involved reveals idiosyncrasies that cannot be accounted for with a general "one size fits all" abstract, algebraic description.

units are structured is currently not a settled question, and a number of different lines of investigation—including everything from psycholinguistic experiments to computational modeling—are being pursued in the quest for an answer. But at this point the majority view would seem to be that linguistic items and structures are organized in the minds of speakers in a complex, multi-dimensional network—with much variability in how richly particular linguistic units are connected to others. Langacker (1987a), Goldberg (1995), and Croft (2001) specify a number of kinds of links that linguistic units might possibly have with one another, including most importantly *instance links* (*Where's X?* is an instance of the *where*-question construction, and perhaps a *wh*-question construction more generally) and *part-whole links* (the passive construction has as one part the past participle construction). A hypothetical example—focused on some of the most abstract constructions of mature English speakers—is given in Figure 4.2. The question of how children's inventories match up with adults' is of course in all cases an empirical question.

Importantly, and radically, in usage-based approaches a given linguistic structure may exist psychologically for the speaker both as a concrete expression on its own—at the bottom of the structural hierarchy, as it were—and, at the same time, as an exemplar of some more abstract construction or constructions (Bybee, 1985, 1995; Langacker, 1987a, 2000). Thus, for most speakers of English, *I dunno* is a fixed expression with a single coherent meaning equivalent to a shrug of the shoulders. Its unitary status can be seen by the fact that the pronunciation involves many reduced elements, and indeed on some occasions the word *don't* can hardly be heard it all (Bybee and Scheibman, 1999). But speakers may also break down this expression into its constituent parts if the need arises. The phonological reductions involved in such cases result from general principles of automaticity in which repetition of a skill leads to smoother and less redundant movements in its execution (Schneider, 1999). It is also possible that parts of a construction may be automatized, and so unitized, while others are left variable, as in mixed constructions such as *Where's-the X?, I-wanna X, Lemme X, Gimme X, I'm-gonna X*. The main point from an acquisition point of view is that when a higher abstraction is made the lower-level, more concrete constructions and expressions do not necessarily go away but may remain available for use—especially if they are used frequently. And indeed, recent psycholinguistic research has shown that as adult speakers attempt to comprehend spoken language they quite often work at a very concrete, item-specific level (McRae, Ferretti, and Amyote, 1997).

In general, in usage-based models the token frequency of an expression in the language learner's experience tends to entrench that expression in

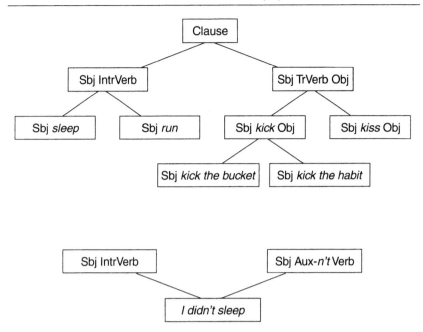

Figure 4.2. *Top:* A taxonomic hierarchy of clause types (instance links). *Bottom:* Multiple parents in a construction taxonomy (part-whole links). © William Croft, 2001. Reprinted from *Radical Construction Grammar: Syntactic Theory in Typological Perspective* by William Croft (2001), by permission of Oxford University Press.

terms of the concrete words and morphemes involved—enabling the user to access and fluently use the expression as a whole, as in *I dunno* (Langacker, 1988; Krug, 1998; Bybee and Scheibmann, 1999). However, the type frequency of a class of expressions (that is, the number of different forms in which the language learner experiences the expression or some element of the expression) determines the abstractness or schematicity of the resulting construction—which mainly (along with some other factors) underlies the creative possibilities, or productivity, of the construction, as in *Where's the X?* or *X got VERBed by Y* (Bybee, 1985, 1995). Together, token and type frequency—along with the cognitive processes of learning and categorization that they imply—explain the ways in which language users both (1) acquire the use of specific linguistic expressions in specific communicative contexts and (2) in some instances generalize these expressions to new contexts based on various kinds of type variations they hear, including everything from type variation in a single slot to type variation in all the constituents of a construction.

This usage-based principle—that people form constructions at different levels of abstraction and use them at different levels of abstraction as well—underlines the fact that what we are dealing with here is not formal linguistics but rather a kind of psycholinguistics. We do not simply describe linguistic constructions in the most abstract manner possible and then automatically assume that this is psychological reality (what Langacker, 1987a, calls the rule-list fallacy). Rather, we look for evidence in language use—distributional patterns, reduced pronunciation, performance in experiments introducing nonce linguistic forms, and so forth—for the actual level at which the speaker is operating psychologically. In general, we are not concerned with providing a set of algebraic rules that covers the data in the most elegant manner possible; we are concerned with how people use a natural language (see the papers in Tomasello, 1998a).

4.1.4. The Utterances Children Hear

To understand how children acquire a language we must know something about the language they hear—both in terms of specific utterances and in terms of the constructions these instantiate. There are two issues. The first concerns the role of so-called Motherese: the ways adults adjust their speech for young children and whether these adjustments are a necessary part of the acquisition process. The second issue is about the type and amount of language children hear ("input"), regardless of adult adjustments, and how this influences the language they acquire (and how they acquire it).

First, many Western middle-class adults speak to young children in some special ways, sometimes called Motherese. They often use a higher pitch and exaggerated intonation, they restrict the range of topics they talk about, and they are highly selective in the words and syntactic constructions they use. A number of studies have claimed that such adult speech adjustments facilitate children's language development (for classic studies see the papers in Snow and Ferguson, 1977; Galloway and Richards, 1994). But cross-linguistic research has demonstrated that these adjustments are not a necessary part of the process. Research in a variety of non-Western cultures has shown that many parents do not adjust their speech for young children to any great degree (e.g., see papers in Ochs and Schieffelin, 1986; Brown, 2001; de León, 2000). Moreover, in many of these cultures young children spend a large part of their day interacting not with adults but with siblings and peers (Lieven, 1994), and numerous studies have shown that preschool-age siblings and peers make very few adjustments for young language learners (see Barton and Tomasello,

1994, for a review). While the language development of children in these cultures has never been systematically documented quantitatively—and indeed it is possible that they do not acquire language as quickly as Western middle-class children—it is nevertheless clear that they become competent speakers of their mother tongues during early childhood. The overall conclusion is thus that special adjustments from adults are not necessary for children to acquire a language, although it is possible that these adjustments may in some cases speed up the process.

The second issue is whether the way individual parents speak to their children influences the children's language development. In this case we are less concerned with the fact that all normal children in all normal environments acquire language normally, and more concerned with the question of individual differences and, ultimately, process. Is children's early language a more or less direct reflection of the language they hear—which would imply that they are relatively conservative learners? Or do all children produce the same kinds of utterances at similar developmental periods no matter what they hear—implying the setting of a parameter or some other hookup to universal grammar on a relatively fixed maturational schedule?

Most of the early studies investigating this question used very global measures of the syntactic complexity—both the child-directed speech (CDS) children heard and their later language development, for example, mean length of utterance or total amount of speech (see Pine, 1994, for a review). Some studies also focused on particular linguistic structures, such as auxiliary fronted questions, noun phrases, and verb phrases. Thus, Newport, Gleitman, and Gleitman (1977) found correlations between (1) the way individual mothers used noun phrases and the number of inflections per noun phrase their children produced, and (2) the way mothers used auxiliary-fronted questions and the number of auxiliaries per verb phrase their children produced (see also Furrow, Nelson, and Benedict, 1979; Richards, 1990; Barnes et al., 1983; Hoff-Ginsberg, 1985). However, subsequent research identified many methodological and interpretive problems in looking for relationships between CDS and children's language development (e.g., Hoff-Ginsberg and Shatz, 1982; Gleitman, Newport, and Gleitman, 1984), leading to the consensus in the field that the findings are "mixed."

Virtually all of these studies investigated adults' and children's language on a relatively abstract level, that is, in terms of adult syntactic categories and constructions: noun phrases, verb phrases, and the like. In contrast, a few studies have investigated the particular grammatical words and phrases adults use and how these are related to what children learn. For instance, Theakston et al. (2001) found that the way children use particular English verbs (as either transitives, intransitives, or both) was strongly related to the way their mothers used those same particular verbs. Similarly, Pine et al. (submitted) found that whether children mark particular verbs for tense and agreement is related to the way they hear those same verbs used (marked in finite clauses or unmarked in non-finite clauses) by their mothers. Finally, Farrar (1990, 1992) found that children's acquisition of some particular grammatical morphemes in English (past tense -ed, plural -s, progressive -ing, and so on) was facilitated when mothers used these morphemes as immediate recasts of the child's utterances that were missing them. What these studies suggest is that there may be close links between the way adults use particular words, morphemes, and phrases in CDS and the way children learn those same words, morphemes, and phrases—much closer links than if syntactic constructions are defined in terms of abstract, adult-like syntactic categories and constructions.

The conclusion in the case of the issue of individual differences and the language acquisition process is thus that input does matter (see also Section 3.2.4). Children learn what they hear, and different children hear different things and in different quantities. What this suggests is that language acquisition is not just triggered by the linguistic environment, as proposed by generative grammarians, but rather the linguistic environment provides the raw materials out of which young children construct their linguistic inventories. The fact that most adults end up with fairly similar (though not identical) linguistic inventories does not negate the obvious fact that early in development children can only learn what they are exposed to. It is also useful in this context to note that when pattern-finding computer programs are given CDS as input, they are able to group together, by means of distributional analysis, linguistic items in a way that yields a number of word classes of a type that would seem to be psychologically realistic for young children (e.g., Redington, Chater, and Finch, 1998).

In light of these facts, we must start our investigation of children's syntactic development with a description of the types of utterances they hear. Surprisingly few studies have attempted to document the full range of linguistic expressions and constructions that children hear in their daily lives. The most comprehensive study is that of Wells (1983), who sampled the language that preschool children both heard and produced (using microphones attached to children's clothes) at regular intervals throughout the many activities of their day. The analyses conducted on these data, however, focused on only a small number of specific constructions.

In contrast, Cameron-Faulkner, Lieven, and Tomasello (in press) examined all of the CDS of 12 English-speaking mothers during samples of their linguistic interactions with their 2-year-old children. They first categorized each of the mothers' utterances in terms of very general constructional categories, resulting in the percentages displayed in Table 4.1 (which also includes a comparable analysis of Wells's data, which is important because those children were sampled in a wider variety of activities). The overall findings were as follows:

- children heard an estimated 5,000–7,000 utterances per day; of these,
- between one-quarter and one-third were questions;
- more than 20 percent were not full adult sentences, but rather were some kind of fragment or phrase (most often a noun phrase or prepositional phrase);
- about one-quarter were imperatives and utterances structured by the copula;
- only about 15 percent had the canonical SVO form (transitive utterances of various kinds) supposedly characteristic of the English language; and over 80 percent of the SVOs had a pronoun subject.

In a second analysis, these investigators looked at the specific words and phrases with which mothers initiated utterances in each of these general construction types, including such item-based frames as *Are you . . .* , *I'll . . .* , *It's . . .* , *Can you . . .* , *Here's . . .* , *Let's . . .* , *Look at . . .* , *What did . . . .* They found that more than half of all maternal utterances began with one of 52 highly frequent item-based frames (that is, frames used more than an estimated 40 times per day for more than half the children), mostly consisting of two words or morphemes. Further, more than 65 percent of all of the mothers' utterances began with one of just 156 item-based frames. And perhaps most surprising, approximately 45 percent of all maternal utterances began with one of just 17 words: *What* (8.6 percent), *That* (5.3 percent), *It* (4.2 percent), *You* (3.1 percent), *Are/Aren't* (3.0 percent), *Do/Does/Did/Don't* (2.9 percent), *I* (2.9 percent), *Is* (2.3 percent), *Shall* (2.1 percent), *A* (1.7 percent), *Can/Can't* (1.7 percent), *Where* (1.6 percent), *There* (1.5 percent), *Who* (1.4 percent), *Come* (1.0 percent), *Look* (1.0 percent), and *Let's* (1.0 percent). Interestingly, the children used many of these same item-based frames in their speech, in some cases at a rate that correlated highly with their own mother's frequency of use.

These results clearly demonstrate two things. First, spontaneous spoken speech, perhaps especially speech addressed to children, is not like written language and other formal modes of discourse. Consider the adult linguistic category "subject of a sentence." In their daily conversations, about 30 percent of the utterances children hear have no overt subject (imperatives, fragments), and another 30 percent or more have subjects that follow an auxiliary or main verb (questions). In addition, almost 15 percent have the

Table 4.1   Most general construction types mothers use in talking to their 2-year-old children.

	Current study		Wells (1983)	
Fragments		.20		.27
one word	.07		.08	
multi-word	.14		.19	
Questions		.32		.22
wh-	.16		.08	
yes/no	.15		.13	
Imperatives		.09		.14
Copulas		.15		.15
Subject-Predicate		.18		.18
transitives	.10		.09	
intransitives	.03		.02	
other	.05		.07	
Complex		.06		.05

Source: Cameron-Faulkner et al. (in press).

copula as the main verb, with many of these having the subject after the verb (in *here-* and *there-* presentational utterances, such as *There are my toys*). So children actually hear a prototypical English subject in only a relatively small proportion of the utterances directed at them (though this is still many hundreds per day). Moreover, even though it is usually claimed that English is a word-order language, the vast majority of subjects that children do hear are in the form of case-marked pronouns such as *I* and *he* (as contrasted with *me* and *him),* so they have case information as well. The methodological lesson is thus that that we can never presume to know what children are hearing on the basis of our "knowledge of English"; we must look empirically at what they actually are hearing.

The second main implication of these findings is that many, indeed the majority, of the utterances children hear are grounded in highly repetitive item-based frames that they experience dozens, in some cases hundreds, of times every day. Indeed, many of the more complex utterances children hear have as a major constituent some well-practiced item-based frame. This means that the more linguistically complicated and creative utterances that children comprehend and produce constitute only a small minority of their linguistic experience, and that in most cases these rest on the foundation of many highly frequent and relatively simple item-based utterance frames.

4.2. Early Constructional Islands

Children begin producing multi-word utterances at about 18–24 months of age. These utterances are cognitively grounded in their understanding of the various "scenes" that make up their social lives. A scene is a coherent conceptual package that contains an event or state of affairs along with one or more participants (Fillmore, 1977a, 1977b; Langacker, 1987a). By the time children begin to acquire language at 1 year of age they already are able to conceptualize any number of specific scenes from their daily lives, many of which are "manipulative activity scenes" such as someone pushing, pulling, or breaking an object; many of which are "figure-ground scenes" such as objects moving up, down, or into a container; and many of which are "possession scenes" such as getting, giving, or having an object (Slobin, 1985). As development proceeds children come to (1) partition these specific scenes into their various component elements, with different linguistic symbols indicating different components, and (2) use syntactic symbols such as word order and case marking to identify the roles these components are playing in the scene as a whole. At some later point they come to categorize these specific scenes into various classes of scenes that may be linguistically partitioned and marked in analogous ways.

Children's first multi-word utterances are socially grounded in their communicative goals, including both their speech act goals and the different perspectives they take on scenes in different communicative circumstances (Lambrecht, 1994). Thus, on different occasions children may have different communicative goals with respect to the same basic scene and so on one occasion ask a question about it, on another occasion request that someone make it happen, on another occasion simply report on its existence, and on another occasion socially mark its occurrence with some kind of performative. For example, for the scene of people leaving, the child might comment "Go-away," request that they "Go-away!" ask them "Where-go?" or tell them "Bye-bye"—depending on his or her communicative purposes. Moreover, children at some point come to understand that in different communicative circumstances scenes are most appropriately described from different points of view, depending on such things as the discourse topic previously established. For example, an event such as Daddy's breaking of the clock may be approached from the point of view of Daddy, as in *Daddy broke the clock,* or from the point of view of the clock, as in *The clock got broken* (see Clark, 1997).

The most direct linguistic counterparts to scenes are utterance-level constructions. An utterance-level construction is a relatively complete and coherent verbal expression associated in a relatively routinized manner with a complete and coherent communicative function (see Lakoff, 1978, on linguistic gestalts; Van Valin, 1993, on syntactic templates; Langacker, 1987a, on sentence schemas; Fillmore, Kaye, and O'Conner, 1988, and Goldberg, 1995, on verb-argument constructions). Utterance-level constructions provide language-learning children with preconstituted semantic-pragmatic packages that allow them to symbolize as whole intact units many of the experiential scenes of their lives—from various discourse perspectives and for various communicative purposes.

4.2.1. Word Combinations and Pivot Schemas

Children produce their earliest multi-word utterances to talk about many of the same kinds of things they talked about previously with their holophrases—since indeed many, though not all, early multi-word constructions may be traced back to earlier holophrases. From the point of view of linguistic form, the utterance-level constructions underlying these multi-word utterances come in three types: word combinations, pivot schemas, and item-based constructions.

First, beginning at around 18 months of age, many children combine two words or holophrases in situations in which both are relevant—with both words having roughly equivalent status. For example, a child has learned to name a ball and a table and then spies a ball on a table and says "Ball table." Utterances of this type include both "successive single-word utterances" (with a pause between them; Bloom, 1973) and "word combinations" or "expressions" (under a single intonational contour). The defining features of word combinations or expressions are that they partition the experiential scene into multiple symbolizable units—in a way that holophrases obviously (by definition) do not—and that they are totally concrete in the sense that they are comprised only of concrete pieces of language, not categories.

Beginning at around this same age, however, many of children's multi-word productions show a more systematic pattern. Often there is one word or phrase that seems to structure the utterance in the sense that it determines the speech act function of the utterance as a whole (often with help from an intonational contour), with the other linguistic item(s) simply filling in variable slot(s)—the first type of linguistic abstraction. Thus, in many of these early utterances one event-word is used with a wide variety of object labels *(More milk, More grapes, More juice)* or, more rarely, something like a pronoun or other general expression is the constant element *(I ____, or ____ it, or even It's ____ or Where's ____)*. Following Braine (1963), we may call these *pivot schemas*. Braine (1976) established that this is a widespread and productive strategy for children acquiring many of the world's languages. He identified many pivot schemas in the early language of children of five different language communities (see Table 4.2 for examples), sometimes including productive utterances never before heard from adults, for example, the famous "Allgone sticky" (Braine, 1971).

Tomasello et al. (1997) demonstrated more systematically that these pivot schemas are indeed productive in this way. They found that 22-month-old children who were taught a novel name for an object knew immediately how to combine this novel name with other pivot-type words already in their vocabulary. That is, when taught a novel object label as a single-word utterance ("Look! A wug!"), children were able to use that new object label in combination with their existing pivot-type words in utterances such as "Wug gone" or "More wug." This productivity suggests that young children can create linguistic categories at this early age, specifically categories corresponding to the types of linguistic items that can play particular roles in specific pivot schemas (such as "things that are gone," "things I want more of").

However, children at this age do not make generalizations across the various pivot schemas; each is a constructional island. Thus, Tomasello et al. (1997) also tested the idea that children who use pivot schemas can come to a new scene and already know how to partition it by means of a pivot word and some other word. But they found that children cannot do this. When taught a novel verb as a single-word utterance for a novel scene (for example, "Look! Meeking!" or "Look what she's doing to it. That's called meeking"), 22-month-olds were not then able to talk about the event in a more differentiated way that included reference to a participant in the event based on some generalized knowledge of how other events are partitioned in the English language (for example, they did not create a slot for the newly learned verb by saying "Ernie meeking!"). Apparently, in talking about a new event with a new event word, children follow the adult model rather closely; they do not create new ways of talking about it, other than to substitute participants for one another.

Pivot schemas do not have syntax. That is to say, whereas in many early pivot schemas there is a consistent ordering pattern of event-word and participant-word (such as *More* ____ or ____ *gone*), a consistent ordering pattern is not the same thing as a productive syntactic symbol used contrastively to indicate what role a word is playing in a larger combinatorial structure. If *Gone juice* does not mean something different from *Juice gone*, then the word order is not doing any significant syntactic work. The consistent ordering patterns in many pivot schemas are very likely direct reproductions of the ordering patterns children have heard most often in adult speech, with no communicative significance. This

Table 4.2 Some early pivot schemas used by children learning three languages.

Andrew (English)	Seppo (Finnish)		Tofi (Samoan)	
more car	setä tuu	man blows horn	alu lea!	go there
more cereal	setä polttaa	man burns	alu Usu lea	go Usu there
more cookie	setä tanssii	man dances	pa'u: pepe lalo	fall baby down
more fish			pa'u: pepe o sami	fall baby into sea
	pupu heittää	bunny throws		
no bed	pupu leikkii	bunny plays	tu'u lalo!	put down!
no down	pupu ajaa	bunny drives	lifo lalo!	set down!
no fix	pupu ajaa tuftuf	bunny drives train	mai lea!	bring there!
			mai mea lea!	bring thing there!
other bib	tipu kuti	chick tickles	mai lole pepe!	bring candy baby!
other bread	tipu pois	chick (geos) away		
other milk	tipu mamma	chick (eating) food	o nofo pepe	sits doll
			o nofo ia pepe	sits—emph—doll
boot off	pipi tuossa	sore there		
light off	tuossa kenkä	there shoe	pa'u: mea	fall thing
pants off	tuossa ammu	there cow	pa'u: teine	fall girl
			pa'u: lole	fall candy
see baby	mamma pois	(take) food away		
see pretty	kirja pois	(take) book away	'aumai isi!	bring other!
all broke	takki poin	(take) coat away	mai pepe!	bring baby!
all buttoned			mai lole!	bring candy!
all clean			ta'ita'i lima!	hold hand!
all done			si'isi'i pepe!	hold baby!
clock on there			si'isi'i tama!	hold boy!
up on there			si'isi'i teine!	hold girl!
hot in there				
milk in there			fia moe	want sleep
			fia moe lava	want sleep much
all done milk			fia moe pepe	want sleep baby
all done now				
all gone juice				

Source: Adapted from Braine (1976).

means that although young children are using their early pivot schemas to partition scenes conceptually with different words, they are not using syntactic symbols—such as word order or case marking—to indicate the different roles being played by different participants in that scene.

4.2.2. Item-Based Constructions

Item-based constructions go beyond pivot schemas in having syntactic marking as an integral part of the construction. The evidence that children have, from fairly early in development, such syntactically marked item-based constructions is solid. Most important are a number of comprehension experiments in which children barely 2 years of age respond appropriately to requests that they "Make the bunny push the horse" (reversible transitives) that depend crucially and exclusively on a knowledge of canonical English word order (e.g., DeVilliers and DeVilliers, 1973; Chapman and Miller, 1975; Roberts, 1983; Bates et al., 1984; Bates and MacWhinney, 1989). Successful comprehension of word order with familiar verbs is found at even younger ages if preferential looking techniques are used (Hirsh-Pasek and Golinkoff, 1991, 1996). In production as well, many children around their second birthdays are able to produce transitive utterances with familiar verbs that respect canonical English word-order marking (e.g., in the control conditions of Tomasello and Brooks, 1998, and similar studies reviewed in Tomasello, 2000b).

At the same time, there is abundant evidence from many studies of both comprehension and production that the syntactic marking in these item-based constructions is still verb specific, depending on how a child has heard a particular verb being used. Tomasello (1992a) found that almost all of his daughter's early multi-word utterances during her second year of life revolved around the specific verbs or predicative terms involved. This was referred to as the Verb Island hypothesis since each verb seemed like its own island of organization in an otherwise unorganized language system. The lexically specific pattern of this phase of combinatorial speech was evident in the patterns of participant roles with which individual verbs were used. Thus, during exactly the same developmental period some verbs were used in only one type of construction and that construction was quite simple *(Cut ____)*, whereas other verbs were used in more complex frames of several different types *(Draw ____, Draw ____ on ____, Draw ____ for ____, ____ draw on ____)*. Interestingly and importantly, within any given verb's development there was great continuity such that new uses of a given verb almost always replicated previous uses and then made one small addition or modification (such as the marking of tense or the adding of a new argument). In general, by far the best predictor of this child's use of a given verb on a given day was not her use of other verbs on that same day, but rather her use of that same verb on immediately preceding days.

The general explanation of such specificity would seem to be that for some experiential scenes the child was exposed to and attended to rich discourse involving multiple participant types and pragmatic functions for the associated verb, while for other activities she either was not exposed to or did not attend to talk about multiple participants and functions. This same pattern of verb-specific organization characterized this child's early use of syntactic symbols; for example, the instruments of some verbs were marked with the preposition *with,* while the instruments of other verbs were not (*Open it with this* versus *He hit me this*). What this means is that the child did not have a general semantic or syntactic category of "instrument," but rather she possessed more verb-specific categories such as "thing to open with" and "thing to draw with." And the same would be true of her other syntagmatic categories involving what adults would call agents, patients, recipients, locations, and so forth, which from the child's point of view were actually such scene-specific things as "kisser," "person kissed," "breaker," and "thing broken."

Using a combination of periodic sampling and maternal diaries, Lieven, Pine, and Baldwin (1997; see also Pine and Lieven, 1993; Pine, Lieven, and Rowland, 1998) found some very similar results in a sample of 12 English-speaking children from 1 to 3 years of age. In particular, they found that virtually all the children used most of their verbs and predicative terms in one and only one construction type early in language development—suggesting that their syntax was built around these particular lexical items. In fact, fully 92 percent of these children's earliest multiword utterances emanated from one of their first 25 lexically based patterns, which were different for each child. Along these same lines, Pine and Lieven (1997) found that when these children began to use the determiners *a* and *the* at 2–3 years of age, they did so with almost completely different sets of nominals (that is, there was almost no overlap in the sets of nouns used with the two determiners)—suggesting that the children at this age did not have any kind of abstract category of "determiner" that included both of these lexical items.

A number of systematic studies of children learning languages other than English have found very similar results. For example, Pizzuto and Caselli (1994) investigated the grammatical morphology used by three Italian-speaking children on their simple, finite, main verbs, from approximately 1½ to 3 years of age (see also Pizzuto and Caselli, 1992). Although there are six forms possible for each verb root (first-person singular, second-person singular, etc.), 47 percent of all verbs used by these children were used in one form only, and an additional 40 percent were used with two or three forms. Of the 13 percent of verbs that appeared in four or more forms, approximately half were highly frequent, highly irregular forms that could only be learned by rote. The clear implication is that Italian children do not master the whole verb paradigm for all their verbs at once, but rather they only master some endings with some verbs—and often different ones with different verbs. In a similar study of one child learning to speak Brazilian Portuguese at around 3 years of age, Rubino and Pine (1998) found a comparable pattern of results, including additional evidence that the verb forms this child used most consistently corresponded to those he had heard most frequently from adults. That is, this child produced adult-like subject-verb agreement patterns for the parts of the verb paradigm that appeared with high frequency in adult language (such as first-person singular), but much less consistent agreement patterns in low frequency parts of the paradigm (such as third-person plural). (Also see Serrat, 1997, for Catalan; Behrens, 1998, for Dutch; Allen, 1996, for Inuktitut; Gathercole, Sebastián, and Soto, 1999, for Spanish; and Stoll, 1998, for Russian.) Finally, in a study of six children learning Hebrew—a language typologically quite different from most European languages—Berman and Armon-Lotem (1995; see also Berman, 1982) found that their first 20 verb forms were almost all "rote-learned or morphologically unanalyzed" (37).

Similarly, in experimental studies, when children who are themselves producing many transitive utterances are taught a new verb in any one of many different constructions, they mostly cannot transfer their knowledge of word order from their existing item-based constructions to this new item until after their third birthdays—and this finding holds in comprehension as well (Tomasello, 2000b; see Section 4.3 for a review). These findings would seem to indicate that young children's early syntactic marking—at least with English word order—is only local, learned for different verbs on a one-by-one basis. What little evidence we have from nonce verb studies of case-marking languages (e.g., Berman, 1993; Wittek and Tomasello, submitted-a) is in general accord with this developmental pattern. This means that although there are real syntactic roles in item-based constructions, overtly marked syntactically, this marking is verb-specific, confined to various constructional islands. Following the conventions of Croft (2001), we may depict their structure as follows:

HIT-SUBJ's *hitting* HIT-OBJ
BREAK-SUBJ's *broken*

throw THROW-OBJ
SMILE-SUBJ's *smiling*

Note that here, and in the following representations, concrete pieces of language are in lower-case letters and italicized, whereas categories and

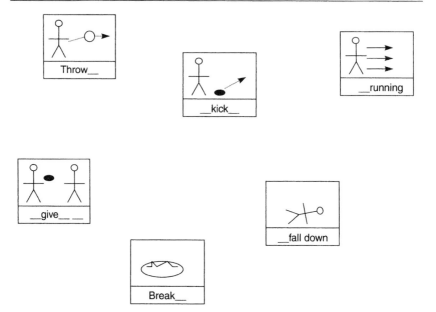

Figure 4.3. Some hypothetical item-based schemas of a 24-month-old child, each with a form (English words and slots) and a function (iconic depiction). In the verb island hypothesis the schemas are not structurally related, so no connections among them are depicted.

other abstractions are in upper-case letters. Designations such as HIT-SUBJ indicate the "subject" in the *hit*-construction, which may have special properties as compared with, for example, BREAK-SUBJ—their commonality only emerging with some higher level abstract constructions. Note that pivot schemas do not include designations such as SUBJ at all because there is no syntactic marking and so syntactic roles do not exist at that point—just slots.

The main point is that unlike in pivot schemas, in item-based constructions children use syntactic symbols such as morphology, adpositions, and word order to syntactically mark the roles participants are playing in these events, including generalized "slots" that include whole categories of entities as participants. But all of this is done on an item-specific basis, that is, the child does not generalize across scenes to syntactically mark similar participant roles in similar ways without having heard those participants used and marked in adult discourse for each verb specifically. This limited generality is presumably due to the difficulty of categorizing or schematizing entire scenes, including both the events and the participant roles involved, into more abstract constructions—especially given the many different kinds of utterances children hear and must sort through. Tomasello (1992a, 2000b) argued and presented evidence that up until age 2;6—and for many children until 3;0 or older—syntactic competence is best characterized as simply an inventory of independent verb island constructions that pair a scene of experience and an item-based construction, with no structural relationships among these constructional islands. Figure 4.3 depicts an hypothesized child's early constructional inventory graphically.

4.2.3. Verbs and Constructional Islands

Children's early item-based constructions come in many shapes and sizes, reflecting the diversity of both their own speech act goals and the speech act goals of their forebears in the culture who grammaticized the constructions they now have at their disposal. Tomasello (1992a), however, highlighted the special role played by early constructions that revolve around verbs. In this account, verb island constructions (as one special type of item-based construction) pave the way to more adult-like grammatical competence since so much of adult grammar, especially the more abstract parts, is centered around verbs and their arguments (Fillmore, 1988; Goldberg, 1995).

Recently, Goldberg and Sethuraman (manuscript) argued that all of the most basic verb-argument constructions of English have one or more basic verbs—usually a "light verb"—as their central sense. As one example, the various dative constructions in English have as their central sense utterances with the verb *give*, and Goldberg and Sethuraman provide some evidence from naturalistic data that many English-speaking children produce many of their early dative utterances with the single verb *give*. Ninio (1999) presented a related argument that children acquire their earliest constructions on the basis of one or two initial "pathbreaking" verbs—again usually basic, light verbs—which are used exclusively for some time, after which the acquisition of other verbs for use in that construction is much easier. Ninio provided evidence from children's acquisition of the basic transitive constructions of Hebrew. Although she did not address the dative constructions in particular, presumably she would predict that children first learn the ditransitive version of this construction with *give* and only later extend it to other semantically related verbs.

As simple and attractive as these proposals might be, a recent study by Campbell and Tomasello (2001) on the acquisition of the English dative constructions (to-dative, for-dative, ditransitive) found little support for either of them. First, the earliest verbs used in the ditransitive construction by the seven children of this study were: *give* (4), *show* (2), *bring, feed, send, read, get, make* (some children used more than one of these verbs in their initial recording). It is thus clear that not all children begin with *give* (and three of the four who do begin with *give* begin with another verb in the same month as well). Moreover, many of the other first verbs do not look very much like light verbs; *feed, send, show,* and *read* are fairly "heavy" verbs. The most likely explanation for children's choice of these particular verbs is that these are the verbs used most often by parents in talking to their children about activities that are salient for them (DeVilliers, 1985; Tomasello and Kruger, 1992; Naigles and Hoff-Ginsberg, 1998), and indeed there was evidence in this study to this effect. To the degree that *give* and other light verbs are used quite often, this is due to the fact that these verbs (by definition) are used widely and frequently in many different contexts.

Ninio's (1999) other claim is that a new construction is initially used by the child for some relatively extended period with the pathbreaking verb (in her study of transitives about one month) before it is used with any other verbs. From acquisition of the second verb on, the construction expands to new verbs quickly. Campbell and Tomasello (2001) did not find this in their study of the ditransitive construction. Overall, for this construction the finding was that only one of seven children fit the hypothesis of a period of several months with a pathbreaking verb followed by rapid extension to other verbs.

Recently, some other analyses and studies have called into question the hegemonic role of verbs in children's transition from more item-based to more abstract syntactic constructions (Lieven, Pine, and Rowland, 1998; Childers and Tomasello, 2001). Children may form constructions, and even generalize constructions, on the basis of different kinds of concrete linguistic material, for example, *I'm ____ing it, It's ____ing, It ____ed.* Nevertheless, the most abstract constructions characteristic of adult linguistic competence typically revolve around verbs in one way or another. And so it may still be true that although verbs do not provide the structuring element for all item-based constructions, they play an especially important, although not exclusive, role in the transition to more adult-like syntactic competence.

4.2.4. Processes of Schematization

From a usage-based perspective, word combinations, pivot schemas, and item-based constructions are things that children construct out of the language they hear around them using general cognitive and social-cognitive skills. It is thus important to establish that, at the necessary points in development, children have the skills they need to comprehend, learn, and produce each of these three types of early constructions.

First, to produce a word combination under a single intonation contour, children must be able to create a multiple-step procedure toward a single goal, assembled conceptually ahead of time (what Piaget, 1952, called "mental combinations"). They are able to do this in nonlinguistic behavior quite readily, from about 14–18 months of age in their own problem-solving, and they are also able to copy such sequences from the behavior of other persons at around this same age. Thus, Bauer (1996) found that 14-month-olds were quite skillful at imitatively learning both two- and three-step action sequences from adults—mostly involving the constructing of complex toy objects (such as a toy bell) that they saw adults assembling. Children were sensitive to the order of the steps involved as well. These would seem to be the right skills at the right time for constructing word combinations.

With respect to input for word combinations, there is good evidence that 1-year-olds do not catch on immediately to the general principle of combinatoriality involved in a way that transfers across specific words and expressions—without hearing specifically relevant discourse (as documented above). One especially important type of discourse may be so-called vertical structures (Scollon, 1973). Vertical structures occur in discourse when the child lexicalizes one aspect of the event and then the adult gives a reply that lexicalizes another aspect of the event (or vice versa). For example, the child might say "More!" and the adult reply "You want some *grapes?*" Or the adult might say "Do you want your *shoes?*" and the child reply "On!" The multi-word structure (for something like *More grapes* or *Shoes on*) thus only exists across the discourse turns of the two interlocutors; but the child registers them both in the conversation. Also important may be so-called replacement sequences in which the adult expands the child's utterance; for example, the child says "More!" and the adult says "Do you want *more grapes?*" Discourse sequences such as these may provide a kind of Vygotskian scaffolding in which children can see in the immediate context how to express their communicative intention more explicitly in a combinatorial way.

Second, the process by which pivot schemas are formed—as abstractions across individual word combinations—is presumably very similar to the way 1-year-olds form other kinds of sensory-motor schemas, including those learned through observation of others' behavior. Thus, Piaget (1952) reports that when infants repeatedly enact the same action on different objects they form a sensory-motor schema consisting of (1) what is general in all of the various actions, and (2) a kind of slot for the variable component. As one example, Brown and Kane (1988) taught 2-year-old children to use a certain kind of action with a particular object (say, to pull a stick) and then gave them transfer problems in which it was possible for them to use the same action but with a different object creatively (they learned to pull stick, pull rope, pull towel). Their skill at doing this demonstrates exactly the kind of cognitive ability needed to create a pivot schema across different utterances so as to yield something like *Pull X*. Such schemas, whether in behavior or in language, have some abstractness—in the slot designated by *X*—but they are mostly concrete in the sense that they are structured by a concrete piece of behavior. Forming such a schema is thus like laying overhead transparencies—each with a stored sequence such as an utterance printed on it—on top of one another. The repeated elements can be clearly recognized through the entire stack, but the variable elements are blurred because of their variability (Langacker's, 1987a). To repeat a point from earlier, the slot in a pivot-type schema is not a syntactic role because it is in no way syntactically marked—either by case marking or by a contrastive use of word order.

Forming the slot in pivot schemas is obviously a process of categorization. Classical views of categorization focus on the perceptual features of items in the world, but Nelson (1974, 1985, 1996; see also Mandler, 2000) has shown that early in development categories are formed on the basis of function. Thus, for a young child a ball is something one can act on in certain ways and that does certain things; its function derives from the role it plays in activities and events. Ultimately, if the child forms a generalized action or event schema with a variable slot for some class of items (such as *Throw X*), that slot and class of items are defined by their role in the schema—which is why Nelson calls them slot-filler categories. This means that in the case of pivot schemas such as *Throw X, X gone,* and *Want X,* the slot could be thought of as something like "throwable things," "things that are gone," "things I want more of," and so forth. This primacy of the schema in defining the slot leads to the kinds of coercion evidenced in creative uses of language in which an item is used in a schema that requires us to interpret it in an unusual way. For example, under communicative pressure a child might say "I'm juicing it" as she pours juice onto something, or "Where's-the swimming?" as she looks for a picture of a swimming activity in a book. This process of "functional coercion" is perhaps the major source of syntactic creativity in the language of 1- and 2-year-old children.

The input needed to create slots in pivot schemas (or any other syntactic constructions) has never been systematically studied. However, Tomasello et al. (1997) provided at least some evidence that the slots in pivot schemas are productive from very early in development (see above). But neither this study nor any other addressed the simple question of exactly what kinds of linguistic experience children must have in order to form a productive slot in a pivot schema. Presumably they do this on the basis of hearing repeated instances of highly similar utterances with the appropriate token and type variation: such things as *Throw ball, Throw paper,* and *Throw shoe.* But, to repeat, there are no studies. It is also not known whether different kinds of experience lead to slots with different properties, for example, based on different kinds of similarities of the objects involved. And we know nothing about the frequencies that might be required in different cases. All we know from experimental studies is that when 2- to 3-year-old children hear novel verbs, such as *baffing,* with dozens of different items in constant positions either immediately before or after the novel verb (such as *Baffing X, Baffing Y, Baffing Z)* they are able to create a productive slot in that position (e.g., Tomasello and Brooks, 1998; Brooks and Tomasello, 1999a; and others reviewed in Tomasello, 2000b).

Third and finally, it is not clear how young children learn about syntactically marking their utterance-level constructions, so creating item-based constructions. Essentially what they need to learn is that whereas some linguistic symbols are used for referring and predicating things about the world, others (including word order) are used for more grammatical functions. These functions are many and various, but they all share the property that they are parasitic on the symbols that actually carry the load of referring and predicating. Thus, with special reference to utterance-level constructions, an accusative case marker (or an immediate postverbal position) can function symbolically only if there is some referential expression to indicate the entity that is the object of some action; we may thus call syntactic markers second-order symbols (Tomasello, 1992). Although children do engage in nonlinguistic activities that have clear and generalized roles, there is really nothing in nonlinguistic activities that corresponds to such second-order symbols. (The closest might be the designation of participant roles in some forms of pretend play—but that is typically a much later developmental achievement.) Children presumably learn to deal with such symbols when they hear such things as, in English, *X is pushing Y* and then on another occasion *Y is pushing X,* each paired with its own real-world counterpart. From this, they begin to see that the verb island construction involving *push* is structured so that the "pusher" is in the preverbal position and "pushee" is in the postverbal position— regardless of the specific identity of that participant. The same would hold for a case-marking language such as German if the child heard something like *Der X schlägt den Y* (The X-nominative hits the Y-accusative) and then its opposite.

Interestingly, with respect to the linguistic experience necessary to construct an item-based construction, Bybee (1985, 1995) has proposed that in general the token frequency of an expression in the language learner's experience tends to entrench it as a single item of use with a coherent function. Thus, there is historical evidence that if one particular expression (that is, one particular string of words) becomes extremely frequent, it may become so fixed that it does not contribute to the generalizability of any abstract construction—presumably because its holistic meaning becomes so predominant that it begins to lose its internal constituency. Applied to child language, this would mean that, for instance, if a child heard or said "Gimme-that" enough times, this expression would become fixed as a unit (a holophrase) and so would not contribute to the generalizability of either the give-imperative construction (item-based) or the ditransitive construction (abstract). This might also mean that such high-frequency structures as *there*-constructions remain constructional islands because of their entrenchment and so do not interfere with the constructing of more "regular" categories and constructions (such as transitives and intransitives).

4.3. Marking Syntactic Roles

From a psycholinguistic point of view, utterance-level and other constructions comprise four and only four types of symbolic elements: words, morphological markers on words, word order, and intonation/prosody (Bates and MacWhinney, 1989). Of special importance for utterance-level constructions are the syntactic devices used for marking the participant roles (typically expressed as NPs) to indicate the basic "who-did-what-to-whom" of the utterance, what are sometimes called agent-patient relations. The two major devices that languages use for this purpose are (1) word order (of NPs) and (2) morphological marking (case and agreement marking).

The methodological situation for determining how young children understand word order and case marking is this. Spontaneous speech is of course the place to begin, but, as always with spontaneous speech, one can never be sure if the child has productive control of a particular linguistic device or if she is simply repeating what she has heard. And so of most importance in spontaneous speech are overgeneralization errors because they represent things that the child has not previously heard but must be producing creatively—presumably on the basis of some abstract category or construction. The other methodological option is experiments in which investigators control exactly what children do and do not hear, often using nonce verbs that children could never have heard before. In this case, we can be even more certain about precisely which aspects of an utterance children are and are not processing and in which ways, including the relevant aspects of word order and case marking.

4.3.1. Word Order

The systematic study of children's understanding of word order as a marker of agent-patient relations is confined almost exclusively to English. English is supposedly a language that marks its basic agent-patient relations via word order alone because there is no case marking on lexical NPs. But over three-quarters of the agent-patient utterances that English-speaking children hear contain pronoun subjects (see Section 4.1.4), most of which have unique forms for the subject version as opposed to the object version (*I* versus *me, she* versus *her,* and so on). In addition, agents in English and all other languages are overwhelmingly animate beings, and in some cases children can use this as a cue for comprehension as well. So in order to test young children's understanding of the syntactic function of canonical English word order, case-marked pronouns and animacy must be carefully controlled.

In their spontaneous speech young English-speaking children use canonical word order for most of their verbs, including transitive verbs, from very early in development (Braine, 1971; Brown, 1973; Bloom, 1992). And as reported above, in comprehension tasks children as young as 2 years of age respond appropriately to requests such as "Make the doggie bite the cat" (reversible transitives) that depend crucially and exclusively on a knowledge of canonical English word order (e.g., DeVilliers and DeVilliers, 1973). But if we do not know what children have and have not heard, adult-like production and comprehension are not diagnostic of the underlying processes and representations involved. Children might simply be reproducing the ordering of the particular words they have heard adults using (as in pivot schemas), or they might be marking agent-patient relations syntactically but only locally for that particular verb (as in item-based constructions), or they might be using these devices to mark these relations in a more abstract, verb-general way (as in abstract constructions; see Chapter 5).

English-speaking children's overgeneralization errors of most interest for the issue of the marking of agent-patient relations via word order are those involving the transitive SVO frame. This includes such things as *She falled me down* or *Don't giggle me* in which the child uses intransitive verbs in the SVO transitive frame productively. (Note that in both of these cases the intransitive version would be unergative, with *I* as subject.) Bowerman (1982, 1988) documented a number of such overgeneralizations in the speech of two English-speaking children, and Pinker (1989) compiled examples from other sources as well. The main result of interest is that these children produced very few of these types of overgeneralizations before about 3 years of age.

Production experiments focused on the marking of agent-patient relations by word order in English typically introduce young children to a novel verb in a syntactic construction such as an intransitive or passive and then see if they can later use that verb in the canonical SVO transitive construction. Cues to syntactic roles other than word order (such as animacy of the S and O participants, use of case-marked pronouns) are carefully controlled and/or monitored. Experiments of this type have clearly demonstrated that by 3½ or 4 years of age most English-speaking children can readily assimilate novel verbs to an abstract SVO schema that they bring to the experiment. For example, Maratsos et al. (1987) taught children from 4½ to 5½ years of age the novel verb *fud* for a novel transitive action (human operating a machine that transformed the shape of Play-Doh). Children were introduced to the novel verb in a series of intransitive sentence frames such as "The dough finally fudded," "It won't fud," and "The dough's fudding in the machine." They were then prompted with either neutral questions such as "What's happening?" or more biasing questions such as "What are you doing?" (which encourages a transitive response such as "I'm fudding the dough"). Although animacy cues could have been used in this experiment (human fuds inanimate dough), Pinker, Lebeaux, and Frost (1987) used a similar experimental design eliminating animacy cues. They introduced children to a novel verb in a passive construction, "The fork is being floosed by the pencil," and then asked them "What is the pencil doing?" to pull for an active, transitive response such as "It's floosing the fork." In both of these studies, the general finding was that the vast majority of children from 3½ to 8 years of age could produce a canonical transitive SVO utterance with the novel verb, even though they had never heard it used in that construction.

But the same is not true for younger children. Tomasello and Brooks (1998) exposed 2- to 3-year-olds to a novel verb used to refer to a highly transitive and novel action in which an agent was doing something to a patient. In the key condition the novel verb was used in an intransitive sentence frame such as "The sock is tamming" (to refer to a situation in which, for example, a bear was doing something that caused a sock to "tam"—similar to the verb *roll* or *spin*). Then, with novel characters performing the target action, the adult asked children "What is the doggie doing?" (when the dog was causing some new character to tam). Agent questions of this type encourage a transitive reply such as "He's tamming the car"—which would be creative since the child has heard this verb only in an intransitive sentence frame. Even though children could potentially have used animacy cues in this experiment, very few of them at either age produced a full transitive utterance with the novel verb. Importantly, as a control, children also heard another novel verb introduced in a transitive sentence frame, and in this case virtually all of them produced a transitive utterance—demonstrating that they could use a novel verb in an SVO construction when they had heard it used in that way. It is also important to note that it is not the case that young children are simply reluctant to use newly learned words in novel ways; when even younger children (22 months) are taught novel nouns, they use them quite freely in already established pivot schemas or item-based constructions (Tomasello et al., 1997).

The generality of this finding is demonstrated by a number of similar studies using different modeled constructions and measurement procedures. These studies have used children of many different ages and have tested for a variety of constructions (see Tomasello 2000b, for a review). Virtually all of the findings concern children's ability to produce a simple transitive SVO utterance after hearing a novel verb only in some *other* sentence frame (intransitive, passive, imperative, and so on). When all these findings are compiled and quantitatively compared, we see a continuous developmental progression in which children gradually become more productive with novel verbs in the transitive SVO construction during their third and fourth years of life and beyond, evidencing a growing understanding of the working of canonical English word order (see Figure 4.4). It should be noted that there are very few novel verb studies in languages other than English. The major exception is Berman (1993), who investigated young Hebrew-speaking children's ability to use an intransitively introduced novel verb in a canonical transitive construction—requiring them to creatively construct a special verb form (a type of causative marker on the formerly intransitive verb) as well as a special ordering of the other lexical items involved. She found a steady increase in novel transitive utterances over age very similar to that found in English-speaking children.

Finally, Akhtar (1999) used a different novel verb methodology to investigate young children's knowledge of English word-order conventions. An adult modeled novel verbs for novel transitive events for young children at ages 2;8, 3;6, and 4;4. One verb was modeled in canonical English SVO order ("Ernie meeking the car"), whereas two others were in non-canonical order, either SOV ("Ernie the cow tamming") or VSO ("Gopping Ernie the cow"). Children were then asked neutral questions such as "What's happening?" Almost all of the children at all three ages who heard the verb modeled in SVO order produced exclusively SVO utter-

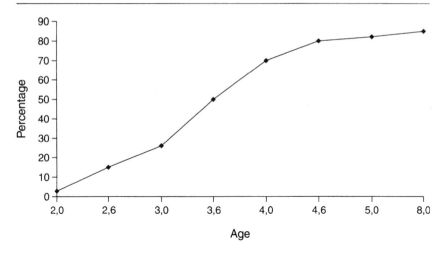

Figure 4.4. Percentage of children producing transitive utterances using novel verbs, by age. Adapted from Tomasello (2000b); reprinted with the permission of Elsevier Science.

ances with the novel verb. However, when they heard one of the non-canonical SOV or VSO forms, children behaved differently at different ages. In general, the older children used their verb-general knowledge of English transitivity to "correct" the non-canonical uses of the novel verbs to canonical SVO form. The younger children, in contrast, much more often matched the ordering pattern they had heard with the novel verb, no matter how bizarre that pattern sounded to adult ears. Interestingly, many of the younger children vacillated between imitation of the odd sentence patterns and "correction" of these patterns to canonical SVO order—indicating that they knew enough about English word-order patterns to discern that these were strange utterances, but not enough to overcome completely their tendency to imitatively learn and reproduce the basic structure of what the adult was saying with the novel verb. Abbot-Smith, Lieven, and Tomasello (2001) recently extended this methodology to younger ages (children at 2;4, using intransitives) and found that even fewer children (less than half as many as Akhtar's youngest children) corrected the adult's strange word order.

Perhaps surprisingly, young children also fail to show a verb-general understanding of canonical English word order in comprehension studies using novel verbs in which they must act out (with toys) a scene indicated by an SVO utterance. Thus, Akhtar and Tomasello (1997) exposed young children to many models of "This is called dacking" used to describe a canonical transitive action. They then, using novel characters, asked the children to "Make Cookie Monster dack Big Bird." All 10 of the children at 3;8 were excellent in this task, whereas only 3 of the 10 children at 2;9 were above chance—even though most did well on a control task using familiar verbs. In a second type of comprehension test, children just under 3 years of age first learned to act out a novel action on a novel apparatus with two toy characters, and then were introduced to the novel verb: the adult handed them two new characters and asked, while pushing the apparatus toward them, "Can you make X meek Y?" In this case children's only exposure to the novel verb was in a very natural transitive sentence frame used for an action they already knew how to perform. Since every child knew the names of the novel characters and on every trial attempted to make one of them act on the other in the appropriate way, the only question was which character should play which role. These under-3-year-olds were, as a group, at chance in this task, with only 3 of the 12 children performing above chance as individuals. Similar results, using a different comprehension methodology (a token placement task), were found by Bridges (1984). Using a comprehension methodology in which children had to point to the agent of an utterance—the main clue to which was word order, Fisher (1996) found positive results for children averaging 3;6 years of age (and Fisher, 2002, found somewhat weaker evidence for the same effect in children at 2;6).

Another technique used to assess children's comprehension of various linguistic items and structures is so-called preferential looking. In this technique, a child is shown two displays (often on two television screens) and hears a single utterance (through a centrally located loudspeaker) that describes only one of the pictures felicitously. The question is which picture the child will look at longer. The findings from studies using this method show some interesting things about young children's comprehension of verb semantics but not, as is sometimes suggested, about their comprehension of canonical English word order. The relevant studies are those using novel or very low frequency verbs, so we know that children have had no previous experience with them. In almost all of these studies the comparison is between transitives and intransitives. Thus, Naigles (1990) found that when they hear canonical SVO utterances English-speaking children from 2;1 preferred to look at one participant doing something to another (causative meaning) rather than two participants carrying out synchronous independent activities. She also found that children had the reverse preference when they heard an intransitive utterance. (See Hirsh-Pasek and Golinkoff, 1996; Bavin and Growcott, 2000; Bavin and Kidd, 2000; for related findings—and Tomasello and Abbot-Smith, 2002, for a critique).

With regard to the transitive SVO construction in particular, Naigles's study shows that in the preferential looking paradigm 2-year-olds know enough about the construction to know that it goes with asymmetrical activities (one participant acting on another) rather than symmetrical activities (two participants engaging in the same activity simultaneously). What the study does *not* show is understanding of word order. That is, it does not show that young children can connect the pre-verbal position with the agent (or subject) and the post-verbal position with the patient (or object) in a transitive utterance—which would be required for a full-blown representation of the transitive construction, and which is indeed required of children in both act-out comprehension tasks and novel verb production tasks. The only preferential looking study which attempted to examine this knowledge is by Fisher (2000). However, the sentences she gave children (1;9 and 2;2) had prepositional phrases that provided additional information ("The duck is gorping the bunny up and down"). Thus, the child merely had to interpret *bunny up and down* in order to "prefer" the picture in which the bunny (rather than the duck) was indeed moving up and down, without paying attention to the syntactic marking of verb arguments at all.

The overall conclusion is thus that in both production and comprehension the majority of English-speaking children do not fully understand word order as a productive syntactic device for marking agents and patients (subjects and objects) until after 3 years of age (although some minority of children understand it before, and some children may understand it weakly, in some limited contexts). In some cases, even the presence of animacy cues (agents were animate, patients inanimate) does not help. But, of course, most English-speaking children are hearing SVO utterances with one or more case-marked pronouns, and so we now turn to an investigation of their understanding of case marking.

4.3.2. Case and Agreement

In the 1960s and 1970s a number of investigators speculated that word order should be easier than case and agreement for children to learn as a syntactic device because canonical ordering is so fundamental to so many sensory-motor and cognitive activities (McNeill, 1966; Bruner, 1975; Braine, 1976; Pinker, 1981). However, cross-linguistic research has since exploded this "word order myth" (Weist, 1983). That is, cross-linguistic research has demonstrated that in their spontaneous speech, children learning many different languages—regardless of whether their language relies mainly on word order, case marking, or some combination of the two—generally conform to adult usage and appear to mark agent-patient

relations equally early and appropriately. Indeed, on the basis of his review, Slobin (1982) concluded that children learning languages that mark
agent-patient relations clearly and simply with morphological (case)
markers, such as Turkish, comprehend agent-patient syntax earlier than
children learning word-order languages such as English. In support of his
argument, Slobin cited the fact that some children learning case-marking
languages overgeneralize case markers in ways indicating productive control while they are still only 2 years old (Slobin, 1982; Slobin, 1985). In
comprehension experiments, it is clearly the case that children learning
morphologically rich languages, in which word order plays only a minor
role in indicating agent-patient relations, comprehend the syntactic marking of agent-patient relations as early or earlier than children learning
word-order languages such as English. Representative studies are reported
by Slobin and Bever (1982) for Turkish, Hakuta (1982) for Japanese, and
Weist (1983) for Polish (see Slobin, 1982, and Bates and MacWhinney,
1989, for reviews).

Interestingly in this regard, Dodson and Tomasello (1998) performed a
novel verb experiment with young English-speaking children—similar to
the novel verb production studies described in the previous section—in
which they introduced the novel verbs with pronouns, many of which are
case marked in English (*he* versus *him*). They found that the children did
somewhat better than their counterparts in studies in which they heard
only full noun phrases with no case marking, although the majority of
children still were not skillful before 3 years of age. In addition, Dodson
and Tomasello examined closely the individual utterances produced by
children under 2;6 in all existing novel verb studies, including the unpublished raw data of Braine et al. (1990). They found that virtually every token of a productive word combination by children in this age range had
the particular pronoun *I* or *me* as subject.

Theoretically, Slobin (1982) explains the developmental advantage of
morphology over word order in terms of the importance of "local cues."
The basic idea is that a case marker on a noun is easier to learn and use as
an indicator of agent-patient relations than is word order "because it applies to a particular noun and can be interpreted without taking the entire
sentence into account" (163). It is also worth noting that word order has
no phonological content per se, and so it may be an extremely ephemeral
cue for young children, whereas morphological markers give them some
concrete phonology on which to base a semantic-syntactic distinction. As
a test of this hypothesis, Wittek and Tomasello (submitted-a) performed a
novel verb experiment—one of the very few on a case-marking language—
using German. German is a case-marking language, but with the novelty
that case relations are encoded as markings on the determiners and adjec-

tives that are used along with nouns (only in some cases on the nouns themselves). The cue is thus more local than that of word-order languages (the marking is inside the NP), but perhaps not as local as that of the classic kinds of case-marking languages such as Turkish and Russian in which the marking is directly on the noun. Wittek and Tomasello gave children nonce nouns, for example, in a nominative case-marked form (*Der Doso dreht sich* = The doso is turning) and then tried in various ways to see if they could, in another sentence context, produce *doso* with an accusative (masculine) determiner (*Der Clown schiebt den Doso* = The clown is pushing the doso). Of central interest was how the German-speaking children's performance in this task would compare with English-speaking children's performance in similar nonce word tasks (in other studies) in which they had to demonstrate productive use of word order to mark agent-patient relations. In support of the Local Cues hypothesis, the basic finding was that the German children were more than twice as productive in marking agent-patient relations (with case-marked articles) as are English-speaking children using word order. (On the Local Cues hypothesis, see Bowerman, 1985; Weist and Konieczna, 1985.)

For English, most of the discussion of case marking has centered around pronoun case errors, as in *Me do it* and *Him going*. About 50 percent of English-speaking children make such errors, most typically at 2–4 years, with much variability across children. The most robust phenomenon is that children most often substitute accusative forms for nominative forms *(Me going)* but very seldom do the reverse *(He hit I)*. Tanz (1974) systematically documented this phenomenon and provided an explanation in terms of Slobin's (1973) operating principles. Most importantly, in English the objective form of the personal pronoun occurs in many different constructions (as direct object, as the object of a preposition, as the answer to question, and so on) whereas the nominative form is only used as subject of a sentence. The proposal is thus that children learn that the objective forms are promiscuous and so they generalize them quite widely, whereas they observe no evidence that the nominative forms can generalize at all. Tanz also notes that objective pronouns more often occur in the highly salient sentence-final position in English. In contrast to these findings for English, Kaper (1976) reported that Dutch-speaking children make pronominal case errors in both directions. In support of Tanz's first hypothesis, Kaper noted that in Dutch the objective and nominative forms of pronouns occur in roughly equal numbers of constructions, thus accounting for the presence of errors in both directions.

Another factor that almost certainly plays a role—although it has never been systematically studied—is the fact that English objective pronouns can occur as "subjects" in some constructions. For example:

Let her do it.
Make him drink it.
Help me find it.

It is thus possible that children hear these sequences but do not appreciate that the matrix verb *(let, make, help)* makes this a special construction in which the second verb is non-finite. There are basically no conventional constructions in English in which the nominative pronouns occur as direct objects. It is important to note, however, that this factor cannot be whole story because children make some errors that they almost certainly could not have heard from adults because their main verbs do not occur in these phrasal causative constructions with *let, make, help,* and so on. For example:

Me like it.
Her thinks so.
Him knows that.

These verbs are almost never used in phrasal causative constructions (very odd is *Help me like/think/know it*), and so these errors cannot be coming directly from children mimicking adult sequences out of context. At the moment there are no good explanations for these errors, although it is possible that when children retrieve a pronoun on some occasions (conditions unknown), they simply retrieve the form they command best.

Rispoli (1994, 1998) has proposed another theory. He notes again that the particular pronouns that English-speaking children most often overgeneralize are the objective forms *me* and *her* (and not the subjective forms *I* and *she*). But it turns out that children do make some nominative-for-objective case errors with other pronouns, especially *he* for *him* and *they* for *them*—as in *I ride he* and *And kill they.* Rispoli attributes these facts to the morphophonetic structure of the English personal pronoun paradigm:

I	she	he	they
me	her	him	them
my	her	his	their

It is easily seen that *he-him-his* and *they-them-their* each has a common phonetic core (*h-* and *th-*) whereas *I-me-my* and *she-her-her* do not. And indeed, the most frequent errors are ones in which children in these last two cases use the forms that have a common initial phoneme (*me-my* and *her-her*) to substitute for the odd-man-out (*I* and *she*), with the *her*-for-*she* error having the overall highest rate (because of the fact, according to Rispoli, that *her* occurs as both the objective and genitive form; the so-called double-cell effect). The overall idea is thus that children are making retrieval errors on the basis of both semantic and phonological factors.

Currently, there is no widely accepted explanation of children's pronoun case errors in English, and indeed it is likely that several factors are involved. Of most importance to resolve the issue in a theoretically interesting way is cross-linguistic research enabling the examination of pronoun paradigms with different morphophonemic and syntactic properties. In general, although more and more cross-linguistic data are being gathered daily on children's spontaneous speech, there are very few experimental studies in languages other than English. This means that we can never be sure about the productivity of the forms these children are using at different ages.

4.3.3. Cue Coalition and Competition

In all languages there are multiple potential cues indicating agent-patient relations. In many languages both word order and case marking are at least potentially available, even though one of them may most typically be used for other functions (for instance, in many morphologically rich languages word order is used primarily for pragmatic functions such as topicalization). In addition, in attempting to comprehend adult utterances children may attend to information that is not directly encoded in the language; for example, they may use animacy to infer that the most likely interpretation of an utterance containing the lexical items *man, ball,* and *kick* is that the man kicked the ball, regardless of how those items are syntactically combined.

In an extensive investigation of language acquisition in a number of languages, Slobin (reviewed in 1982) identified some of the different comprehension strategies that children use to establish agent-patient relations, depending on the types of problems their particular language presents to them. A central discovery of this research, as noted above, was that children can more easily master grammatical forms expressed in "local cues" such as bound morphology than forms expressed in more distributed cues such as word order and some forms of agreement. This accounts, for example, for the fact that Turkish-speaking children master the expression of agent-patient relations at a significantly earlier age than do English-speaking children. In addition, it turns out that Turkish is especially "child friendly," even among languages that rely heavily on local morphological cues. Slobin (1982) outlines 12 reasons why Turkish agent-patient relations are relatively easy to learn. An adaptation of that list (focusing on nominal morphology) is as follows. Turkish nominal grammatical morphemes are:

- postposed, syllabic, and stressed, which makes them perceptually more *salient;*
- obligatory and employ almost perfect one-to-one mapping of form to function (no fusional morphemes or homophones), which makes them more *predictable;*
- bound to the noun, rather than freestanding, which makes them more *local;* and
- invariably regular across different nominals and pronominals, which makes them readily *generalizable.*

All of these factors coalesce to make Turkish agent-patient relations especially easy to learn, and their identification is a major step in discovering the basic processes of language acquisition that are the employed by children in general.

A central methodological problem, however, is that in natural languages many of these cues go together naturally, and so it is difficult to evaluate their contributions separately. Therefore, Bates and MacWhinney (summarized in 1989) conducted extensive experimental investigations of the cues children use to comprehend agent-patient relations in a number of languages. The basic paradigm is to ask children to act out utterances using toy animals, with agent-patient relations indicated in different ways—sometimes in semi-grammatical utterances with conflicting cues. For example, an English-speaking child might be presented with the utterance "The spoon kicked the horse." In this case, the cue of word order is put in competition with the most likely real-world scenario in which animate beings more often kick inanimate things than the reverse. From an early age, English-speaking children make the spoon "kick" the toy horse, which simply shows the power of word order in English. Italian-speaking children, when presented with an equivalent utterance, ignore word order and make the horse kick the spoon. This is because word order is quite variable in Italian, and so, since there is no case marking (and in this example agreement is no help because both the horse and the spoon are third-person singular), semantic plausibility is the most reliable cue available. German-speaking children gradually learn to ignore both word order and semantic plausibility (animacy) and look for nominative and accusative marking on "the horse" and "the spoon" (Lindner, in press).

Table 4.3 provides a highly schematic summary of some of the findings of this research program, with special attention to children's ability to identify the initiator of the action when various cues are put into competition in the utterances they must act out. It can be seen in this table that in a number of languages children rely on cues that are different from those on which adults rely. Bates and MacWhinney's two major explanations for

Table 4.3   Order of importance of cues to actor assignment across languages.

English	
Adults	SVO > Animacy > Agreement > Stress
Under 5	SVO > Animacy > Stress > Agreement
Italian	
Adults	SV Agreement > Clitic agreement > Animacy > SVO
Under 7	Animacy > SVO > SV agreement > Clitic agreement
French	
Adults	SV agreement > Clitic agreement > Animacy > SVO
Under 6	SVO > Animacy (others not tested)
Dutch	
Adults	Case > SVO > Animacy
Under 10	SVO > Case > Animacy
Serbo-Croatian	
Adults	Case > Agreement > Animacy > SVO, VSO, SOV
Under 5	Animacy > Case > SVO, VSO, SOV > Agreement
Hungarian	
Adults	Case > SV agreement > Animacy > VO agreement
Under 3	Animacy > Case > SVO > Stress (agreement not tested)
Turkish	
Adults	Case > Animacy > Word order
Under 2	Case > Word order (animacy not tested)
Hebrew	
Adults	Case > Agreement > Order
Under 10	Case > Order > Agreement
Warlpiri	
Adults	Case > Animacy > Order
Under 5	Animacy > Case > Order

Source: Adapted from Bates and MacWhinney (1989).

these developmental changes are: (1) functional readiness, in the sense of the nature of the child's cognitive and linguistic skills at any given time, which determines what can be learned; and (2) various factors of cue validity and cue strength (basically the frequency and consistency with which children experience forms; see Section 5.4.3 for more on the competition model in general) that change as the child gains more linguistic experience (and thus more exposure to the less frequently occurring regular forms). In Chapter 5 we will look at additional factors—from grammatical complexity to cognitive complexity to perceptual salience to input frequency—that constitute the learning problem facing the child attempting to learn a particular construction in a particular language.

The research of Slobin and Bates and MacWhinney highlights, perhaps better than any other, that a language is a complex set of symbolic forms, with many sources of information about meaning which may in some instances conflict with one another. There is no way to tease apart these influences except in experiments. Even better would be competition-type experiments using various kinds of nonce words, which have never been done.

4.3.4. Learning Syntactic Symbols

In many ways learning to syntactically mark agent-patient relations in different constructions is the backbone of syntactic development; it provides the basic "who-did-what-to-whom" structure of the utterance. We might thus think of the use of word order and morphological marking to indicate agent-patient relations as the use of second-order or syntactic symbols—symbols for indicating other linguistic units' syntactic roles in the utterance as a whole.

Focusing on the most general verb-argument constructions of English—since, again, this is the only language in which there is an extensive experimental base—we may summarize the developmental progression of children's use of syntactic symbols by highlighting key characteristics of the types of constructions used at different periods:

- First are *holophrases,* in which children use a single linguistic symbol (often with a specific intonational contour) to express their communicative intentions about an entire experiential scene. No syntactic symbols are involved.
- Second are *pivot schemas* and other *word combinations* and *expressions* in which children use multiple words to express their communicative intentions, thus partitioning the experiential scene into at least two component parts. But again no syntactic symbols are involved.
- Third are *item-based constructions* (such as verb island constructions), in which children use syntactic marking such as word order or grammatical morphology to indicate explicitly some participant roles in scenes, but they do this differently for different item-based constructions (depending mainly on their linguistic experience with each of these).
- Finally are *abstract constructions,* to be dealt with in Chapter 5, in which children express their communicative intentions through utter-

ances that instantiate relatively abstract and adult-like linguistic constructions that syntactically mark participants for verb-general classes of constructions.

Table 4.4 provides an overview of these steps in English-speaking children's mastery of syntactic symbols and construction types.

The acquisition of other languages, although different in important ways, may also, to a first approximation, be described in this general way: first no explicit marking of syntactic relations, then local marking of syntax relations in constructional islands (whether they are marked with word order or grammatical morphology), then more construction-general marking but within limits. And the emphasis on limits is crucial because, as argued earlier, even many adult constructions are highly constrained, often in some relatively unpredictable ways. It is also important to emphasize that this account applies most directly to the most "regular" constructions that children are acquiring. English-speaking children, for instance, are also acquiring many quirky, idiosyncratic constructions that may not be generalized beyond the specific words and phrases that structure them. The list is virtually endless, including everything from pat phrases such as *Here-ya-go, I-dunno,* and *You're-welcome* to semi-productive but noncanonical constructions such as *there*-constructions.

4.4. Summary

The central question in the study of young children's early syntactic development is the nature of the underlying linguistic representations involved. In this chapter I have argued and presented evidence that in the initial stages—involving word combinations, pivot schemas, and item-based constructions—these representations are highly concrete, based around individual words and phrases with some open slots whose definition comes from those words and phrases (that is, in *Kick X*, X is simply the thing one kicks—a slot-filler category in the sense of Nelson, 1985). This pattern is at least partly a reflection of the adult language children hear, which quite often revolves around specific words and phrases as well. But it also very likely reflects the fact that children at this early age have not yet heard enough language to have made very deep generalizations. The generalizations they have made at this point have been made by a process of schematization, a type of pattern-finding that builds linguistic constructions around concrete pieces of language.

In the initial stages, then, children's linguistic competence is most accurately characterized not as "a grammar," but rather as an inventory of relatively isolated, item-based constructional islands. Development after

Table 4.4 Summary of construction types constituting children's early syntactic development and the characteristics in terms of which they are defined.

	Lexical partitioning of events/scenes	Syntactic marking of partici-pant roles in events/scenes	Categorization of events/scenes
Holophrases (12 months)	–	–	–
Pivot schemas (18 months)	+	–	–
Item-based constructions (24 months)	+	+	–
Abstract constructions (36+ months)	+	+	+

Source: From Tomasello and Brooks (1999). Reprinted with the permission of Psychology Press.

these initial stages, typically at 2–3 years of age, then proceeds gradually and in piecemeal fashion, with some constructions becoming abstract more rapidly than others—mainly depending on the type and token frequency with which children hear particular constructions, since this is what provides the raw material for the schematization process (see Chapters 5 and 8). Regardless of details, under no circumstances does this development look like an instantaneous setting of parameters in which all verbs and other lexical items immediately participate in a totally abstract construction. Contrary to Radford's example quoted at the beginning of this chapter, it is simply not the case that once a child is able to parse "Close the door" she knows that all verbs in English precede their complements.

The syntactic marking of agent-patient relations, the backbone of syntactic development, also begins locally with particular verbs in item-based constructions, that is, mainly in verb island constructions. The way this marking is done differs greatly in different languages, depending both on the specific kinds of cues used for this function—word order, case marking, agreement, or some combination of these—and on how these cues present themselves to the learner in terms of such factors as cue validity, cue reliability, and cue strength (as these are defined by the competition model). And so in addition to simple type and token frequencies, the language children hear is crucial with respect to the "messiness" of the data they have to work with—which in this case varies mainly as a function of the typology of the language to be learned. There are still many outstanding questions about how children cope with the messiness of the many cues involved in this process, and indeed a major finding of the research program of Bates and MacWhinney (1989) is that children often start off relying on different cues than adults. Studies using nonce verbs in a competition paradigm would help to answer many of these questions.

An important methodological note. It is a common practice in the study of child language acquisition to describe a child's utterance in terms of adult categories of one kind or another, and this is even done in some cases by researchers who otherwise take a more child-centered perspective. But until we do a thorough analysis of a given child's range of uses of all of her lexical items and constructions, we cannot know the nature of the representations underlying them (and experiments with nonce words would be even better). Thus, the first time we hear a child say something like "Wanna ride horsie," we cannot jump to the conclusion that she has mastered infinitival complements. Perhaps she just knows how to say "Wanna" plus the activity she wants, or perhaps it is a frozen holophrase, or perhaps it is something else. The nature of the linguistic representations that children are using to generate their utterances is in every case an empirical question, and it requires systematic investigation—not just assumptions (that is, not the continuity assumption).

Children build up the abstractness of their item-based constructions using their general skills of intention-reading and pattern-finding. They understand the communicative functions of utterances that embody various syntactic constructions, as well as some of their constituents, by reading the intentions of the speaker. They then find patterns across item-based constructions by schematizing and making analogies. Verb island constructions may play an especially important role because they provide the raw material with which children construct the most abstract constructions of their language, for example, argument structure constructions. We now turn to an account of these most abstract constructions and how children construct them.

Abstract Syntactic Constructions

On the whole grammar is not a tool of logical analysis;
grammar is busy with emphasis, focus, down-shifting,
and up-grading; it is a way of organizing information
and taking alternative points of view.

—WILLIAM LABOV

DURING the preschool years, English-speaking children begin to be productive with a variety of abstract utterance-level constructions, including such things as transitives, intransitives, ditransitives, attributives, passives, imperatives, reflexives, locatives, resultatives, causatives, and various kinds of question constructions. Many of these are so-called argument-structure constructions, and they are used to refer to experiential scenes of the most abstract kind, including such things as people acting on objects, objects changing state or location, people giving people things, people experiencing psychological states, objects or people being in a state, and things being acted upon (Goldberg, 1995). It is presumably the case that these abstract constructions represent children's generalizations across many dozen or more item-based constructions, especially in some cases verb island constructions. The major task of this chapter is to describe, and to some degree explain the emergence of, the abstract utterance-level constructions that English-speaking children first control—with some reference to similar constructions in other languages where there is sufficient research of the right kind.

In this context, two very important theoretical questions immediately present themselves. The first is the nature of the cognitive processes that enable young children to build up these abstract constructions. Perhaps because of the influence of linguistic nativism, there has been surprisingly little investigation of this issue in the acquisition literature. I will propose that to account for abstract constructions we must suppose that young children make analogies across whole utterances (structure alignment and mapping). Although the concept of analogy has a venerable history in historical linguistics, in developmental psycholinguistics it has almost no history as applied to syntax. And there is exciting new work on children's ability to deal with analogies in nonlinguistic domains that is directly relevant. Another important process in virtually all theories of syntactic development is distributional analysis, by means of which children group together into paradigmatic categories linguistic items that behave in the same way—where in most theories "behave in the same way" simply means that those items co-occur sequentially with similar items. I will propose a modified version of this process, calling it *functionally based distributional analysis,* in which the learner groups together into categories those linguistic items that function similarly—that is, consistently play similar communicative roles—in different utterances and constructions.

The second important question is how and why children make just the generalizations they do, and not some others that they might reasonably make from an adult point of view. In other words, how do children constrain their abstract constructions, so that they are applied only as widely as is conventional in the linguistic community, and not more widely? This question is fundamental to all theories of syntactic development, although generativists have spent the most time worrying about it. Generativists typically appeal to innate knowledge of universal grammar as the major source of constraint and argue that, without this constraint, usage-based theorists cannot curtail children's rampant tendency to generalize and overgeneralize. However, in recent years new data have emerged that suggest the importance, perhaps sufficiency, of three usage-based processes: (1) the entrenchment of constructions in conventional uses through repetition; (2) the preemption of generalizations by alternative constructions (contrast, competition); and (3) the formation of verb classes that enable children to predict the behavior of new verbs on the basis of their (mostly semantic) similarities to well-known verbs. Each of these processes plays its role at a different point in ontogeny, leading to a complex developmental dialectic between generalization and constraint.

The most important theories of syntactic development currently in the field are (1) theories based in formal linguistics, including most prominently varieties of generative grammar, and (2) theories based in one or another type of usage-based linguistics, including most prominently cognitive-functional linguistics and various types of connectionist modeling. I will argue that formal theories are insufficient, mainly because they have not yet solved the problems of cross-linguistic variability and developmental change. And I will argue in this chapter that while connectionist models are an extremely valuable tool, and are definitely on the right course in many ways, in their current state they are not sufficient to account for child language acquisition because they do not include in any significant way information about communicative intention or function. This prevents them from using both analogy, in the way it is very likely used by young children, and functionally based distributional analysis, which requires attention to the functioning of linguistic items in acts of communication. In the end, I will not be shy in arguing for a construction-based, usage-based theory of syntactic development that relies crucially on children's understanding of communicative intentions and function.

5.1. Abstract Constructions

The primary function of an abstract utterance-level construction is to focus the listener's attention on some aspect or portion of an experiential scene while backgrounding her attention to other aspects. Thus, the very same event may be described in many ways:

Fred broke the window
Fred broke the window with a rock
The rock broke the window
The window got broken
The window was broken by Fred
The window was broken by a rock
What Fred did was break the window
What got broken was the window
It was Fred that broke the window
It was the rock that broke the window
It was the window that Fred broke
It was the window that got broken

What determines the choice among constructions such as these on particular occasions of use is the speaker's assessment of the knowledge, expectations, and perspective of the listener as she is able to assess them in the current joint attentional frame—along with her own speech act goals. Thus, if our conversational topic is Fred, he is likely to be the subject when the speaker reports on the breaking of the window, whereas if we have just been talking about the window, it is likely to be the subject—triggering a different construction. Fisher, Gleitman, and Gleitman (1991) say that constructions serve as a "zoom lens" which the speaker uses to direct the listener's attention to a particular perspective on a scene; Langacker (1987a) speaks of constructions as forcing a certain "construal" of a situation; and Talmy (1996) describes the use of constructions to highlight certain aspects of a scene, at the expense of other aspects, as the "windowing of attention." And, in a point that will be elaborated later, it is indeed the construction itself, and not the particular lexical items involved, that mostly structures this construing or windowing.

The abstract constructions described below account for a large percentage of the utterances that young English-speaking children use habitually during the preschool years. These English constructions have many peculiarities relative to those of other languages, of course, but the empirical work necessary to give a comparable description of the constructions used in other languages—especially the experimental work—has yet to be done (but see the studies in Slobin, 1985b, 1992, 1997).

Before looking in more detail at specific construction types, we may give an overall accounting of the most general types of constructions children use from an adult perspective (that is, not attributing knowledge of these constructions to the child)—so that children's overall profile may be compared with that of their mothers (shown in Table 4.1). This is done in Table 5.1, which uses the same general categories as in the study of maternal child-directed speech (CDS) described in Section 4.1.4 (Cameron-Faulkner, Lieven, and Tomasello, in press). The analysis is based on data from the same 12 2-year-old children in that study (age 1;10 to 2;7; MLU 2.00 to 2.49, Brown Stage II), as they interacted with their mothers during the same sessions used for the analysis of CDS. As may be seen by comparing Tables 4.1 and 5.1, the main difference from the mothers is that the children do not ask nearly as many questions, and they use many more fragments, that is, utterances without a predicate.

Turning to a more child-centered perspective, we may now enumerate the most abstract constructions that English-speaking children use early in development. It should be said at the outset, however, that many of the constructions identified should actually be differentiated in a more fine-grained way (as families of sub-constructions), but again the empirical work that would make this possible has yet to be done. The central issue—as in the case of item-based constructions—is children's productivity. This is because producing creative yet canonical utterances in a verb-general manner implies that children are working with some kinds of abstract linguistic categories or constructions (not just item-based constructions). Without information about productivity, we simply do not know the nature of the underlying linguistic representations involved. Although some researchers have used an arbitrary criterion for establishing productivity in analyses of children's spontaneous speech (e.g., Brown's, 1973, criterion of 90 percent correct use of a grammatical structure in obligatory contexts), the fact is that the only solid evidence of productivity—and therefore of abstract linguistic representations—is overextensions in spontaneous speech (things the child has presumably never before heard) and

Table 5.1   Adult categorization of utterances 2-year-old children use in talking to their mothers (these are not child constructions).

Fragments		.69	N/NP (.39) = my finger
one word	.28		V/VP (.16) = nearly fell over
multi-word	.42		PP (.04) = on the blanket
Questions		.04	Wh = Where that go?
wh-	.04		Y/N = Are you writing?
yes/no	.003		
Imperatives		.03	Open it now.
Copulas		.07	That's Grandpa.
Subject-Predicate		.16	Tr = Mummy build a tower.
transitives	.09		Intr = I trip.
intransitives	.04		Oth = It make me sick.
other	.03		
Complex		.002	I want you sit there too.

Source: Compiled by Thea Cameron-Faulkner.

productivity in experiments in which the language children hear is carefully controlled.

5.1.1. Identificationals, Attributives, and Possessives

Among the earliest utterance-level constructions used by many English-speaking children are those that serve to identify an object or to attribute to it some property, including a possessor or simple location (Lieven, Pine, and Dresner Barnes, 1992). In adult language these would almost invariably require some form of the copula, *to be*, although children do not always supply it. Quite often these constructions revolve around one or a few specific words. Most common for the identification function are such things as:

It's a/the X
That's a/the X
This's a/the X

Most common for the attributive function are such things as:

Here's a/the X
There's a/the X
X's here
X's there

Most common for the possessive function are such things as:

(It's) X's ____
That's X's/my ____
This is X's/your ____

Clancy (2000) reports some very similar constructions for Korean-speaking children, and a perusal of the studies in Slobin's *Crosslinguistic Studies in Language Acquisition* volumes reveals many other languages in which these are frequently used child constructions for focusing attention on or attributing a property to an external entity.

The question of whether children make any generalizations across these item-based constructions has no answer at this time. Almost certainly they do not relate these constructions to other major constructions with full lexical verbs, such as transitives and intransitives, because these are not so closely related structurally in adult language (indeed they are very diverse structurally). There may be some relatively local generalizations within these constructions, for example, across *It's an X* and *That's an X* and also across *Here's the X* and *There's the X*—but not across these two pairs since only in *Here's an X* and *There's an X* constructions does the copula agree with the NP following it, as in *There are my toys* (see Lakoff, 1987, on the idiosyncratic behavior of these constructions in adult language). In all, such things as predicate nominal, predicate adjective, existential-there, and locative-there constructions—as they are most often called in traditional analyses—most likely remain constructional islands, of a sort, even in adult English.

5.1.2. Simple Transitives, Simple Intransitives, and Imperatives

The simple transitive construction in English is used for depicting a variety of scenes that differ greatly from one another. The prototype is a scene in which there are two participants and one somehow acts on the other. English-speaking children typically produce utterances of this type in their spontaneous speech early in language development for various physical and psychological activities that people perform on objects—everything from pushing to having to dropping to knowing. The schema is thus to some degree abstract and, in radical construction grammar representation (in which TRANS-SUBJ indicates "subject in a transitive construction") looks something like this:

TRANS-SUBJ TRANS-VERB TRANS-OBJ

The major verbs young children use in the transitive construction—including imperative uses—are presented in Table 5.2.

Table 5.2   Fifty most frequent verbs used in the English transitive construction, age 2–4.

Having objects	Moving or transforming objects	Acting on objects	Psychological activities
get	take	do	see
have	find	eat	like
want	put	play	say
need	bring	write	know
buy	drop	read	watch
keep		drink	tell
hold	make	draw	show
use	open	wash	mean
	fix	wear	hear
	break	catch	hurt
	cut	hit	try
	close	ride	love
		turn	thank
		throw	
		bite	
		push	
		touch	
		help	

Source: Compiled by Michael Israel using a sample of seven English-speaking children from the CHILDES database.

It is not clear, however, to what the extent young children understand their utterances of this type as exemplars of the same syntactic construction. Akhtar and Tomasello (1997) found that it was not until 3½ years of age that children began to use new verbs modeled for them as one-word utterances to produce and comprehend novel transitive sentences with appropriate word-order marking (see Section 4.3.1). Similar ages for productivity with this construction were reported by Braine and Brooks (1995), Maratsos et al. (1987), and Ingham (1993/94). It was also at around this age that Bowerman's (1982) children spontaneously said things such as "He falled me down," overgeneralizing the transitive construction to intransitive verbs.

The simple intransitive construction in English is also used for a wide variety of scenes. In this case the only commonality is that they involve a single participant and activity. The two main types of intransitives are the so-called unergatives, in which an actor does something (*John smiled*) and the so-called unaccusatives, in which something happens to something

(*The vase broke*). English-speaking children typically produce utterances of both these types early in language development, with unergatives such as *sleep* and *swim* predominating (unaccusatives occurring most often with the specific verbs *break* and *hurt*). At its most abstract the schema is simply:

INTR-SUBJ INTR-VERB

The major verbs young children use in the intransitive construction—including imperative uses—are presented in Table 5.3.

Again, the extent to which young children understand their utterances of this type as exemplars of the same syntactic construction is not entirely clear. Tomasello and Brooks (1998) gave young children a novel verb in a transitive construction and then encouraged them to use it intransitively (and vice versa). (The verb was from the fairly large class of English verbs that can be used in both constructions; specifically, it was a manner-of-motion verb on analogy with *roll, bounce, slide, spin, twirl,* and so on.) They found that by 2½ years of age the majority of children were able to use this novel verb productively in the intransitive construction. Children who were taught the novel verb in the intransitive construction had much more difficulty producing it in the transitive construction. This accords with other research on the transitive-intransitive alternation, which generally finds that children more often use an exclusively intransitive verb as a transitive than the reverse (Braine et al., 1990; Ingham, 1993; Maratsos et al., 1987; but see Lord, 1979). Bowerman's (1982) examples from her two daughters include "Don't giggle me," "Stay this open," and "I'll go it in there." Berman (1982, 1993) found a similar pattern for Hebrew, but Nomura and Shirai (1997) found the opposite pattern for a young Japanese child, who more often used transitives in the intransitive construction (see also Figueira, 1984, for Portuguese). The explanation given by Nomura and Shirai is that young Japanese children use intransitive verbs much more frequently than transitive verbs (see also Rispoli, 1987).

5.1.3. Ditransitives, Datives, and Benefactives

All languages of the world have utterance-level constructions for talking about the transfer of objects (and other things) between people (Newman, 1996). In English, there is a constellation of three related constructions for doing this: the *to*-dative, the *for*-dative (or benefactive), and the double-object dative (or ditransitive). The most abstract ditransitive form (exemplified in *He gave me a book*) is:

DITR-SUBJ DITR-VERB DITR-R DITR-O

Table 5.3   Fifty most frequent verbs used in the English intransitive construction, age 2–4.

Cause to move	Move or transform	Physical activities		Psychological activities
get	go	play	sleep	look
want	come	do	eat	see
have	goes	write	cry	know
	going	happen	walk	talk
	move	wait	turn	hurt
	stop	jump	swim	think
	put	ride	run	watch
		sit	fly	say
	break	help	rain	
	fall	dance	read	
	work	sing	drive	
	make	drink	win	
	fit		laugh	
	open			
	cut			

Source: Compiled by Michael Israel using a sample of seven English-speaking children from the CHILDES database.

This construction requires that DI-R be construed as a recipient. The prepositional form of the dative is:

DA-SUBJ DA-VERB DA-O *to* DA-L

This is exemplified in *I sent a package to Minneapolis,* and it does not have the restriction that the object of the preposition *to* be a recipient (it could be a simple location). Many verbs occur in both constructions (*give, bring, offer*), with the choice of which construction to use jointly affected by the semantic and discourse status of the participants (Erteschik-Shir, 1979). Most clearly, the prepositional form is appropriate when the recipient is new information and what is being transferred is known (compare the natural *Jody sent it to Julie* with the unnatural *Jody sent Julie it*). However, the selection of a construction is only partially determined by discourse because a great many English verbs occur only in the prepositional form (*choose, donate*) and a few occur only in the ditransitive (*cost, deny, fine*).

Most English-speaking children produce both ditransitive and prepositional forms of the dative in their spontaneous speech from fairly early in development, and some benefactives as well. Snyder and Stromswold (1997) argued and presented some evidence that children always acquire the double-object dative before they acquire the other two constructions. However, Campbell and Tomasello (2001) did not replicate this result (see also Tomasello, 1998c), but rather found variability across children. By 3 years of age children are at least occasionally using dative constructions in clearly innovative ways (such as "I'll brush him his hair"; "You put me just bread and butter"; Bowerman, 1978, 1988, 1990). Gropen et al. (1989) found that use of dative constructions with novel verbs could readily be elicited in children at age 5–6 years, seemingly expressing productive knowledge of the different semantic-pragmatic features of the ditransitive and prepositional dative constructions. The verbs with which the ditransitive and prepositional datives are most frequently used are presented in Table 5.4. In general the ditransitive and prepositional dative constructions are used with a delimited set of verbs, but the benefactive can be used quite widely with many different verbs—as, under the appropriate conditions, almost anything may be done for someone else's benefit.

5.1.4. Locatives, Resultatives, and Causatives

Beginning with their first words and pivot schemas, English-speaking children use a variety of locative words to express spatial relationships in utterance-level constructions. These include prepositions such as *X up, X down, X in, X out, on X, off X, over X,* and *under X,* and verb ? particle constructions such as *pick X up, wipe X off,* and *get X down.* Once children start producing more complex structures designating events with two or more participants, two-argument locative constructions are common. For Tomasello's (1992a) daughter these included such utterances as "Draw star on me" and "Peoples on there boat," which she produced at 20 months. By 3 years of age most children have sufficient flexibility with item-based constructions to talk explicitly about locative events with three participants, most often an agent causing a theme to move to some object-as-location (as in *He put the pen on the desk*).

The acquisition of three-argument locative constructions has been of major interest because a wide range of verbs occur in two distinct types of locative constructions that are associated with differentiated event perspectives (e.g., Brinkmann, 1995; Gropen et al., 1991a, 1991b; Levin and Rappaport Hovav, 1991; Rappaport and Levin, 1988). The "content as object" locatives are of the form *He cleared the dishes off the table* or *She loaded hay onto the wagon:*

LOC-SUBJ LOC-VERB LOC-OBJ *to/on/etc.* LOC

The "location as object" constructions are of the form *He cleared the table of dishes* or *She loaded the wagon with hay:*

Table 5.4   Twenty-five most frequent verbs used in the English ditransitive and/or prepositional dative constructions (including benefactive), age 2–4: number of children (out of seven) using a verb in one, both, or neither construction.

	Both	Ditransitive	Prep dative	Neither
get	6	0	1	0
give	6	1	0	0
make	6	0	1	0
show	6	1	0	0
read	5	0	2	0
bring	5	1	0	1
buy	2	3	1	1
take	1	1	4	1
tell	0	5	1	1
find	1	3	1	2
do	0	0	5	2
send	1	1	2	3
throw	1	1	2	3
call	0	4	0	3
fix	0	1	3	3
leave	0	1	3	3
open	0	0	4	3
want	0	0	4	3
ask	1	2	0	4
draw	1	1	1	4
feed	0	2	1	4
have	0	0	3	4
hold	0	0	3	4
put	0	0	3	4
say	0	0	3	4

Source: Campbell and Tomasello (2001). Reprinted with the permission of Cambridge University Press.

LOC-SUBJ LOC-VERB LOC *with/from/etc.* LOC-OBJ

The "content as object" constructions serve the discourse function of focusing attention on the participant that is changing location (dishes, hay) whereas the "location as object" constructions highlight the resultant change of state (the now-clean table, the now-loaded wagon). Bowerman (e.g., 1978, 1982, 1988) has amply documented that preschool-age children overgeneralize usage of these three-argument locative constructions by producing such novel utterances as "I spilled it of orange juice" and "She's gonna pinch it on my foot." Experimentally, Gropen et al. (1991a) have found that 3- to 4-year-olds will use novel verbs in both "content as object" and "location as object" constructions, and that they show some sensitivity to the different discourse perspectives involved (that is, they focus on the moving participant or the change of state).

The resultative construction (as in *He wiped the table clean*) is of the form:

RES-SUBJ RES-VERB RES-OBJ RES-ADJ

It is used, most typically, to indicate both an action and the result of that action. Although no experimental studies of the resultative construction have yet been conducted with novel verbs, the occurrence of novel resultatives in spontaneous speech attests to the productivity of the construction from sometime after the third birthday. In Bowerman's (1982) two daughters the following developmental progression was observed. At around 2 years of age the children learned various combinations of "causing verb + resulting effect" such as *pull + up* and *eat + all gone*. For the next year or so, each child accumulated an assortment of these forms which were used in an apparently adult-like manner. Subsequently each child, at some point after her third birthday, seemed to reorganize her knowledge of the independently learned patterns and extracted a more abstract schema. Evidence for this reorganization came from each child's production of a number of novel resultative utterances such as "And the monster would eat you in pieces" and "I'll capture his whole head off."

Causative notions may be expressed in English utterance-level constructions either lexically or phrasally. Lexical causatives are simply verbs with a causative meaning used in the transitive construction *(He killed the deer)*. Phrasal causatives are important because they supply an alternative for causativizing an intransitive verb that cannot be used transitively. Thus, if Bowerman's daughter had been skillful with phrasal causatives, instead of "Don't giggle me" she could have said "Don't make me giggle," and instead of "Stay this open" she could have said "Make this stay open." *Make* is the direct causation matrix verb in English, but an important related verb—and in fact the most frequent such verb for young English learners—is *let*, as in *Let her do it, Let me help you*, and so forth. Another common matrix verb that follows this same pattern is *help*, as in *Help her get in there* or *Help him put on his shoes*. It is unknown whether young children see any common pattern among the utterances in which these three different matrix verbs are used, but their most abstract potential form would be:

CAUS-SUBJ *make/let/help* CAUS-R [CLAUSE]

5.1.5. Passives, Middles, and Reflexives

The English passive construction consists of a family of related constructions that change the perspective from the agent of a transitive action (relative to active voice constructions) to the patient and what happened to it. Thus, *Bill was shot by John* takes the perspective of Bill and what happened to him, rather than focusing on John's act of shooting (with the truncated passive *Bill was shot* serving to strengthen this perspective further). In addition to this general function of the passive, Budwig (1990) has shown that the *get* and *be* forms of the passive are themselves associated with distinct discourse perspectives. Thus, the prototypical *get* passive in *Spot got hit by a car* or *Jim got sick from the water* tends to be used when there is a negative consequence which occurs when an animate patient is adversely affected by an inanimate entity or a non-agent source. In contrast, the *be* passive construction in *The soup was heated on the stove* is used when there is a neutral outcome of an inanimate entity undergoing a change of state where the agent causing the change of state is unknown or irrelevant.

> PASS-SUBJ *get* VERB-*ed by* PASS-OBJ
> PASS-SUBJ *be* VERB-*ed by* PASS-OBJ

In general, actional transitive verbs can be used in passive constructions quite readily, whereas many stative verbs seem to fit less well *(She was loved by him)*. This was demonstrated experimentally by Sudhalter and Braine (1985), who found that preschoolers were much better at comprehending passive utterances containing actional verbs *(kick, cut, dress)* than they were at comprehending passive utterances containing experiential verbs *(love, see, forget)*.

English-speaking children typically do not produce full passives in their spontaneous speech until 4 or 5 years of age, although they produce truncated passives (often with *get*) and adjectival passives much earlier *(He got dunked, He got hurt)*. Israel, Johnson, and Brooks (2000) analyzed the development of children's use of the passive participle. They found that children tended to begin with stative participles *(Pumpkin stuck)*, then use some participles ambiguously between stative and active readings *(Do you want yours cut?*—meaning do you want it to undergo a cutting action or, alternatively, do you want to receive it already in a cut state), then finally use the active participles characteristic of the full passive *(The spinach was cooked by Mommy)*. Although passive utterances are infrequent in English-speaking children's spontaneous speech, a number of researchers have observed that older preschoolers occasionally create truncated passives with verbs that in adult English do not passivize ("It was bandaided," "He will be died and I won't have a brother anymore"), indicating some productivity with the construction (Clark, 1982; Bowerman, 1982, 1988).

Confirming this observation, Pinker, Lebeaux, and Frost (1987) found experimentally that with training 3- to 4-year-old English-speaking children were able to produce passive utterances with novel verbs; however, they did not report whether any of these utterances were full passives. In a similar training study, Brooks and Tomasello (1999a) found that English-speaking children could learn to produce full passive utterances. In just two 30-minute sessions, 90 percent of the children 3–3½ years of age learned to produce a full passive utterance with a nonce verb—specifically a *get*-passive with a *by* phrase (as in *The car got meeked by Big Bird*). Tomasello, Brooks, and Stern (1998) gave 3.0-year-olds rich discourse interactions containing truncated passives, passive questions, and *by* phrases—all of which added up to a full passive—but they never exposed the children to a full passive utterance as a whole. Other children were given only models of full passive utterances. It was found that only children who heard full passive utterances produced them, suggesting that children do not learn to produce full passives by creatively piecing together a truncated passive with an independently learned *by*-phrase; they learn them from models of full passives directly as wholes.

It is important to note that children acquiring certain non-Indo-European languages typically produce passive sentences quite early in development. This result has been obtained for children learning Inuktitut (Allen and Crago, 1996), K'iche' Mayan (Pye and Quixtan Poz, 1988), Sesotho (Demuth, 1989, 1990), and Zulu (Suzman, 1985). Allen and Crago (1996) report that a child at age 2;0–2;9 (as well as two slightly older children) learning Inuktitut produced both truncated and full passives quite regularly. Although a majority of these were with familiar actional verbs, children also produced passives with experiential predicates and several clearly innovative forms with verbs that do not passivize in adult Inuktitut. The reasons for this precocity relative to English-speaking children are hypothesized to include the facts that (1) Inuktitut passives are very common in child-directed speech, and (2) passive utterances are actually simpler than active voice constructions in Inuktitut because the passivized verb has to agree only with the subject, whereas the transitive verb has to agree with both subject and object.

There is very little research on English-speaking children's use of so-called middle voice constructions (medio-passives) such as *This bread cuts easily* or *This piano plays like a dream* (see Kemmer, 1993). The prototype of this construction involves an inanimate entity as subject, which is held responsible for the predicate (that is why the adverb is typically needed; *This bread cuts* and *This piano plays* by themselves are scarcely grammatical). Budwig, Stein, and O'Brien (2001) looked at a number of utterances of young children involving inanimate subjects, and found that the most frequent constructions of this type in young in English-speaking children's speech were such things as *This doesn't pour good*. Reflexives are also not common in English-speaking children's early language (or in adult English), although they do produce a few things such as *I hurt myself*. However, reflexives are quite common in the speech of young children learning languages in which these constructions are frequent in child-directed speech. For example, most Spanish-speaking youngsters hear and use quite early such things as *Se cayó* (It fell down), *Me siento* (I sit down), *Levántate* (Stand up!), and *Me lavo las manos* (I wash my hands). Kemmer (1993) argues that middles and reflexives are both used for events that are only weakly elaborated in the sense that although the form of the utterance is transitive, there are not two distinct participants conceptually (as in transitive-active clauses); the true agent is either irrelevant (the bread cuts easily no matter the agent) or is not differentiated from the patient since it is the same entity (he washes himself).

5.1.6. Questions

Questions, of course, are used primarily to seek information from an interlocutor. In many languages this is done quite simply through a characteristic intonation *(He bought a house?)* or by the replacement of a content word with a question word *(He bought a what?)*. Although both of these are possible in English, English also has two more common forms: *wh*-questions and yes/no questions. In the classic structural linguistic analysis, English questions are formed by subject-auxiliary inversion (sometimes with do-support) and *wh*- movement. These rules assume that the speaker has available a simple declarative linguistic representation, which she then transforms into a question by moving, rearranging, or inserting grammatical items. Thus, *John kicked the ball* becomes either *Did John kick the ball?* or *What did John kick?*

But this rule-based analysis is highly unlikely early in development for two main reasons. First, some English-speaking children learn some *wh*-question constructions before they learn any other word combinations. For instance, Tomasello's (1992a) daughter learned to ask where-questions ("Where's-the bottle?") and what-questions ("What's that?") as her first multi-word constructions. Second, everyone who has studied children's early questions has found that their earliest constructions are tied quite tightly to a small number of formulas. For example, in their classic analysis Klima and Bellugi (1966) suggested that almost all of the *wh*-questions of Adam, Eve, and Sarah emanated from two formulas: *What NP (doing)?* and *Where NP (going)?* Fletcher's (1985) subject produced almost all of her early questions with one of three formulas: *How do . . .,* *What are . . .,* and *Where is . . .* More recently, Dabrowska (2001) looked in detail at one child's earliest uses of *wh*-questions in English and found that 83 percent of her questions during her third year of life came from one of just 20 formulas such as *Where's THING? Where THING go? Can I ACT?* and *Is it PROPERTY?*

Importantly, this learning pattern is not confined to English, as Clancy's (1989) study of two Korean children also found that early *wh*-words initially occurred with only one or two verbs, for example, the equivalent of *What is . . ., What do . . ., How do . . ., Where is . . .,* and *Where go. . .* The most plausible explanation of these patterns is that young children do not create questions via transformation rules, but rather they learn them, like other constructions, as linguistic gestalts with a characteristic function, moving gradually from more item-based to more abstract constructions.

One phenomenon that bears on this issue is so-called inversion errors. English-speaking children sometimes invert the subject and auxiliary in *wh*-questions and sometimes not—leading to errors such as *Why they're not going?* A number of fairly complex and abstract rule-based accounts have been proposed to account for these errors, and, as usual, some researchers have claimed that children know the rules but apply them only optionally or inconsistently (e.g., Ingram and Tyack, 1979). However, in a more detailed analysis Rowland and Pine (2000) discovered the surprising fact that the child they studied from age 2 to age 4 consistently inverted or failed to invert particular *wh*-word–auxiliary combinations on an item-specific basis. He thus consistently said such incorrect things as *Why I can . . .? What she will . . .? What you can . . .?* —but at the same time he also said such correct things as *How did . . .? How do . . .? What do . . .?* In all, of the 46 particular *wh*-word—auxiliary pairs this child produced, 43 of them were produced either 100 percent correctly or 100 percent incorrectly (see also Erreich, 1984, who finds equal number of inversion errors in *wh*- and yes/no questions). Again, the picture is that children learn questions as a collection of item-based constructions, moving only gradually to more abstract representations.

Across many languages a similar order of acquisition of *wh*-questions is observed. Clancy (1989) reviewed data from five languages (English, German, Japanese, Korean, and Serbo-Croatian) and found evidence for the order (see also Vaidyanathan, 1988, on Tamil):

what/where < who < how/why < when

Clancy explains this consistent ordering in terms of both cognitive factors (for example, the complexity of causal concepts relative to simple spatial concepts) and the frequency with which and the ways in which adults use *wh*-questions in their discourse with the children.

5.1.7. Constructions as Linguistic Symbols

It is clear from these analyses that each of the various utterance-level constructions has associated with it a relatively coherent and consistent constructional meaning (or set of meanings). In the two main theoretical approaches to syntactic development this fact is recognized and accounted for in two different ways. From a strict generativist perspective there are no constructions, and if there were they would have no meaning. More reasonably, from the perspective of generative grammar lite, Pinker (1989) proposes that constructional meanings derive mainly from the meanings of the particular verbs involved. Thus, the verb *give* specifies three arguments—the giver, the gift, and the recipient—and so utterances with this verb have this meaning, and any similarity to utterances with the verb *send* derives totally from the fact that these verbs have similar meanings (transferring possession, broadly construed), not from their use in an independently meaningful ditransitive construction. The verbs *donate* and *say* cannot be used felicitously in the ditransitive construction because their meanings are subtly different from those of *give* and *send*. Because the syntax is determined by the meaning of the central lexical item, the verb, this is sometimes called the lexical rules approach.

One implication of this view is that a verb must have listed in the lexicon a different meaning for virtually every different construction in which it participates (with some productive generalizations across tightly defined classes). For example, while the prototypical meaning of *cough* involves only one participant, the cougher, we may say such things as *He coughed her his cold,* in which there are three core participants. In the lexical rules approach, in order to produce this utterance the child's lexicon must have as an entry a ditransitive meaning for the verb *cough*. Although this example is somewhat fanciful, it takes only a moment's reflection to see that we regularly use verbs in constructions that are not prototypical for them; for example, a simple transitive verb such as *kick* can also be used ditransitively to indicate transfer of possession: *She kicked him the pillow.* Goldberg (1995) argues that it is highly implausible that the lexicon works in the way required by the lexical rules approach; there are just too many unusual verb meanings that need to be attributed to particular verbs. Moreover and worse, the lexical rules approach is viciously circular: "It is claimed that *kick* has an n-argument sense on the basis of the fact that *kick* occurs with n complements; it is simultaneously argued that *kick* occurs with n complements because it has an n-argument sense" (Goldberg, 1995: 11).

The alternative is a construction grammar approach, in which constructions themselves are symbolic units with meaning (Fillmore, Kaye, and O'Conner, 1988; Goldberg, 1995; Croft, 2001). In this view, much of the creativity of language comes from fitting specific words into linguistic constructions that are non-prototypical for that word on a specific occasion of use, with no implication that this requires a corresponding permanent lexical entry for the verb involved. For example, *He smiled her the answer* requires an especially imaginative interpretation to make the verb fit the "transfer of possession" meaning of the construction, and this is not likely to be the result of a productive generalization of a lexical rule (since *smile* normally does not even involve movement). But this example makes salient a process that occurs routinely when we say such things as *He kicked her the ball* or *She threw him a party* or *He baked her a cake* (since *kick, throw*, and *bake* are not normally transfer verbs). The main point is that if we grant that constructions may have meaning of their own, in relative independence of the lexical items involved, then we do not need to populate the lexicon with all kinds of implausible meanings for each of the verbs we use in everyday life. The construction grammar approach in which constructions have meanings is therefore both much simpler and much more plausible than the lexical rules approach.

Interestingly and importantly, the fact that linguistic constructions have meaning of their own creates a top-down pressure on the interpretation of utterances. This is responsible for many derivational and metaphorical processes (either with or without special morphology) as lexical items usually used in one syntactic role are "coerced" into another in the context of a specific construction. For example:

- Properties and activities are treated as if they were objects *(Blue is my favorite color; Skiing is fun; Discovering the treasure was lucky)*.
- Objects and activities are treated as if they were properties (*His mousy voice shook me; His shaven head distracted her; His Nixonesque manner offended me*).
- Objects and properties are treated as if they were activities *(She chaired the meeting; He wet his pants; The paperboy porched the newspaper)*.

5.2. Constructing Constructions

In the usage-based approach, children construct their abstract linguistic representations out of their item-based constructions using general cognitive, social-cognitive, and learning skills—which act on the language they hear and produce. It is thus important that we attempt to see exactly how they could do this. Toward that end, I outline here some pattern-finding cognitive processes that would seem to be needed (there is very little relevant research) to construct abstract, utterance-level constructions, citing developmental research demonstrating that children exercise these skills at the appropriate ages in other domains of activity. The two pattern-finding skills I will focus on are: (1) analogy, including the creation of the most abstract syntactic roles such as subject and object; and (2) distributional analysis, including the creation of the most abstract paradigmatic categories such as noun and verb. In some cases, particular aspects of the language children hear, and the way they hear it, facilitate the acquisition process.

But before proceeding it will be useful to make explicit some aspects of Croft's (2001) "radical" version of construction grammar because it contains some important insights relevant to the question of how children create abstract linguistic constructions and categories. Croft's primary aim is to apply construction grammar systematically cross-linguistically. In doing this—and on the basis of a very deep analysis of the ways in which linguists actually attribute structure to novel languages—he concludes that not very much in the actual items and structures of natural languages is universal (although of course much having to do with cognitive structures and communicative functions is). For example, there would seem to be no universal syntactic categories (grammatical relations) of the type subject, direct object, and so forth. But Croft has an even more radical proposal. He claims that the whole notion of syntactic categories as free-floating linguistic entities is wrong-headed. Such things as subjects and direct objects only exist in constructions, and indeed the entities that go by these names are actually different entities when they are in different constructions.

For example, in all of the following examples *John* is traditionally thought of as subject:

John hit Bill.
John was struck by a car.
There is John.

But the properties of the subject in these three constructions (transitive, passive, and there-construction, respectively) are very different—John is either agent, patient, or located object—although there are some commonalities as well. Croft seeks to capture the construction-specific nature of these roles, along with their commonalities, by referring to the above examples as having, respectively, a transitive-subject, a passive-subject, and a there-construction-subject (the convention we have already adopted here). This way of conceptualizing and labeling syntactic relations allows us to account for both continuities and emergent abstractions in the lengthy process of children's syntactic development.

Another very important aspect of this analysis has crucial implications for how we conceive of the process by which children create linguistic abstractions of various sorts. Croft is very careful to call such things as "transitive-subject" syntactic roles, not grammatical relations, as is common in most theories (both formal and usage-based). This is because he wants to highlight again the fact that such things as subjects and direct objects take their definition from the role they play in larger linguistic constructions. Croft claims that the term *grammatical relations* is misleading because it implies that such things as subject are defined by their relations to other items in the construction, rather than, as in his analysis, by their role in the construction as a whole. Transitive-subject defines one role in a complex linguistic gestalt. What this means for theories of acquisition is that we must look at syntactic roles such as subject not as word-based categories or relations to be separately learned by distributional analysis or some other categorization process, but rather as roles that emerge naturally (and, in a sense, epiphenominally) from the abstraction process when children apply it across whole, utterance-level constructions. This can only be done by a complex process such as analogy, which takes into account multiple components simultaneously.

The situation is different with traditional parts of speech, such as noun or verb, sometimes called paradigmatic or lexical categories. Unlike syntactic roles, paradigmatic categories are not explicitly marked in language. That is, whereas such things as subject are symbolically indicated by word order or grammatical morphology in the construction, nouns and verbs have no explicit marking (despite the fact that they often have some morphology serving other functions, such as plural markers on nouns, that can be used to identify them). Consequently, the category cannot be organized around any specific linguistic symbol, but can only be based on commonalities in the way the members of the category function (in other words, on distribution). And this is another very large difference between syntactic roles and paradigmatic categories. Syntactic roles such as subject do not have specific linguistic items as members, whereas paradigmatic categories such as noun have specific items, such as *dog* and *tree,* as members of the category—once again suggesting that such things as subject are not categories whereas such things as noun are. These considerations suggest that paradigmatic categories such as noun and verb (and noun phrase and verb phrase) can only be formed during development by distributional analyses in which the child begins to see specific linguistic items that behave in the same way (in the current theory, functionally) as members of the same category. This is very different from the process of making analogies across constructions.

5.2.1. Analogy

The current hypothesis is that children begin to form abstract utterance-level constructions by creating analogies among utterances emanating from different item-based constructions. Analogy has a long and distinguished history in accounting for certain aspects of historical language change (e.g., see Trask, 1996), including everything from the creation of morphological paradigms to the regularization of families of syntactic constructions. Although MacWhinney (1978) used analogy to account for some facts in the development of children's morphophonological skills, and it is sometimes used to account for some processes in morphological development more generally (e.g., Bybee and Slobin, 1982), it has a scarcely ever been used in an attempt to account for children's syntactic development. Analogy has been criticized by some theorists as a vague concept because one still has to specify the dimensions of similarity (as one does in all forms of induction), but recent research has begun to make the concept much more explicit.

The process of analogy is very like the process of schematization, as discussed in Chapter 4; it is just that analogies are more abstract. Thus, whereas all instances of a particular item-based schema have at least one linguistic item in common (for example, the verb in a verb island schema), in totally abstract constructions (such as the English ditransitive construction) the instances need have no items in common. In terms of the overhead transparencies analogy used to elucidate schematization, we can say that when we make an abstract analogy between two or more structures by laying overhead transparencies on top of one another, we can discern no recognizable figures; it is all just blurs. So the question is: On what basis does the learner make the alignments among constituents necessary for an analogy among complex structures?

The answer is that the learner must have some understanding of the functional interrelationships that make up the two structures being aligned. In the most systematic research program on the topic, Gentner and colleagues (Gentner and Markman, 1995, 1997; Gentner and Medina, 1998) stress that the essence of analogy is the focus on relations. When an analogy is made, the objects involved are effaced; the only identity they retain is their role in the relational structure. Gentner and colleagues have much evidence that people, including young children, focus on relations quite naturally and so are able to make analogies quite readily. An example is as follows. People are asked to compare two pictures, one of a car towing a boat and one of a truck towing a car that is identical in appearance to the car in the other picture. After this simple similarity rating task, the experimenter points to the car in the first picture and asks the person to point to the best match in the second picture. People have no trouble ignoring the literal match of cars across the two pictures and choosing the truck. In essence, they identify in both pictures the "tow-er," or the agent, based on the role it is playing in the entire action depicted.

We can make the same point with a somewhat whimsical linguistic example. Consider the following two sequences of letters:

U R X

I M A B

Let us try to make an analogy. It is not easy because there is not much in common between the two strings; they even have different numbers of items. But what if we now translate them into English in a fanciful context. The situation is that we are role-playing with a child in a pretend game, and one role is to be a creature named X and another role is to be one of several honeybees. The above sequences now translate into "You are X" and "I am a bee." We can now see that these are both predicate nominative constructions, and they are analogous: *you* corresponds to *I* as the one to be anointed, *are* corresponds to *am* as the identifying relation, and *X* corresponds to the two-word phrase *a bee* as the new identity taken on. Such correspondences can only be made once we know the functions of the items and structures involved.

Gentner and colleagues also stress what they call the systematicity principle, that in the making of analogies structures are aligned as wholes, as "interconnected systems of relations." In the current context this simply means that learners align whole utterances or constructions, or significant parts thereof, and attempt to align all of the elements and relations in one comparison. In doing this, learners search for "one-to-one correspondence" among the elements involved and "parallel connectivity" in the relations involved. The learner thus makes an analogy between utterances (or constructions) by aligning the arguments one to one, and in making this alignment she is guided by the functional roles these elements play in the larger structure. For example, in aligning *The car is towing the boat* and *The truck is towing the car,* the learner does not begin to match elements on the basis of the literal similarity between the two *cars,* but aligns *the car* and *the truck* because they are doing the same job from the perspective of the functional interrelations involved. This analysis implies that an important part of making analogies across linguistic constructions is the meaning of the relational words, especially the verbs, involved—particularly in terms of such things as the spatial, temporal, and causal relations they encode. But there is basically no systematic research relevant to the question of how children might align verb meanings in making linguistic analogies across constructions.

Gentner and colleagues also have some specific proposals relevant to learning. For example, they propose that even though in some sense neutralized, the object elements that children experience in the slots of a structure can facilitate analogical processes. In particular, they propose that in addition to type variability in the slots, also important is consistency of the items in the slots (that is, a given item occurs only in one slot and not in others). When all kinds of items occur promiscuously in all of the slots in two potentially analogous relational structures, structure mapping is made more difficult (Gentner and Medina, 1998). For example, children find it even easier to make the analogy cited above if in the two pictures a car is towing a boat and a car is towing a trailer, so that the "tow-er" is identical in the two cases. This principle explains why children begin with item-based constructions. They find it easier to do structural alignments when more of the elements and relations are not just similar functionally but also similar, or even identical, perceptually. Children work their way up to the totally abstract analogies gradually. There are also some proposals from the morphological domain, that a certain number of exemplars is needed—a "critical mass"—before totally abstract analogies can be made (Marchman and Bates, 1994). But if this is true, the nature of this critical mass (for example, verb types versus verb tokens) is not known at this time; there is no research.

It is thus possible that abstract linguistic constructions are created by a structural alignment across different item-based constructions, or the utterances emanating from them. For example, some verb island constructions that children have with the verbs *give, tell, show, send,* and so forth, share a "transfer" meaning, and they appear in the form: NP1 + V + NP2 + NP3. In the indicated transfer, NP1 is the "giver," NP2 is the "receiver," and NP3 is the "gift." So the aligning must be done on the basis of *both* form and function: two utterances or constructions are analogous if a "good" structure mapping is found both on the level of linguistic form (even if these are only categorically indicated) and on the level of communicative function. This consideration is not really applicable in non-linguistic domains. It may also be that in many cases particular patterns of grammatical morphology in constructions (such as X *was* VERB*ed*)—which typically designate abstract relations of one sort or another—facilitate, or even enable, recognition of an utterance as instantiating a particular abstract construction.

The only experimental study of children's construction of an abstract linguistic construction (as tested by their ability to assimilate a nonce verb to it) was conducted by Childers and Tomasello (2001). In this training study, 2½-year-old English-speaking children heard several hundred transitive utterances, such as "He's kicking it," involving 16 different verbs across three separate sessions. Half the children learned new English verbs (and so increased their transitive verb vocabularies during training—toward a critical mass) whereas the other half heard only verbs they already knew. Within these groups, some children heard all of the utterances with full nouns as agent and patient, whereas others heard utterances with

both pronouns *(He's* VERB-*ing it)* and also full nouns as agent and patient. They were then tested to see if they could creatively produce a transitive utterance with a nonce verb. The main finding was that children were
best at generalizing the transitive construction to the nonce verb if they
had been trained with pronouns and nouns, regardless of the familiarity of
the trained verbs (and few children in a control condition generalized to
the novel verb at all). That is, the consistent pronoun frame *He's* VERB-
ing it (in combination with type variation in the form of nouns as well)
seemed to facilitate children's formation of a verb-general transitive construction to a greater degree than the learning of additional transitive
verbs with nouns alone, in the absence of such a stabilizing pronominal
frame.

The results of this study are consistent with Gentner's more general
analysis of the process of analogy in several ways. First, they show that
children can make generalizations, perhaps based on analogy, across different item-based constructions. Second and more specifically, they also
show that the material that goes in the slots, in this case NP slots, plays an
important role (see also Dodson and Tomasello, 1998). In English, the
pronoun *he* only goes in the preverbal position, and, although the pronoun *it* may occur in either position in spontaneous speech, it occurs most
frequently in postverbal position in child-directed speech, and indeed that
is the only position in which the children heard it during training. These
correspondences between processes in the creation of nonlinguistic analogies and in the creation of abstract linguistic constructions constitute impressive evidence that the process is basically the same in the two cases.
But there is still much that we do not know. For example, we know very
little about how many exemplars are needed. Childers and Tomasello used
16 different verbs in several hundred utterances, but Abbot-Smith et al.
(submitted) found similar learning with one-quarter of the examples. We
also do not know how similar those exemplars should be semantically
(mainly in terms of verbs semantics), the specific role of pronouns (since
Childers and Tomasello had no "pronoun only" condition), or whether
the timing of exemplars relative to one another plays some role as well.

As outlined above, in the process of making analogies across utterance-
level constructions, learners create certain kinds of abstract syntactic roles
(Croft, 2001). The most studied such role is the English "subject." Many
subjects of English utterances are semantically agents, and so for many
people agentive subjects are prototypical of the category. Schlesinger
(1988) proposed a theory of semantic assimilation in which children begin
with a category of agent and then assimilate to it the non-agentive subjects
that they hear in the speech around them. Pinker's (1984, 1989) theory of
semantic bootstrapping shares many features with this account, emphasiz-

ing that once children have used the notion of agent as a kind of anchor for the notion of subject, they can then recognize non-agentive subjects because these are marked syntactically in the same way as the agentive subjects they know (for example, with word order or case marking). The problem is that young children learn and use many utterances and constructions with non-agentive subjects from the very beginning of their linguistic careers—such things as *It broke, It's a tape recorder, I see it, He likes it, It opens here,* and *She got splashed* (see Budwig, Stein and O'Brien, 2001). Thus, semantic bootstrapping would seem to send children off on the wrong track early.

The English subject is a very specialized syntactic role that involves a number of different functions, many of which do not occur together in the same category in other languages. Bates and MacWhinney (1982) talk about the English subject as a coalition of agent and topic, but other analyses show that even this is too simple. In Keenan's (1976) famous account, cross-linguistically there are something like 30 features associated with categories that approximate the English subject. These may be grouped into two broad categories. First are coding properties: for example, the English subject normally comes before the verb, it normally triggers agreement with the verb (*The boy runs,* not *The boy run*), and when it is a pronoun it is a special (case-marked) form (*He hits,* not *Him hits*). Second are behavioral properties: the subject in English determines a number of structural properties of an utterance, for example, in *He hit him and left* the only one who could have left is the subject *He.* But in other languages there seems to be a subject-like category that consists of a different coalition of these features, the best known in this regard being some Philippine and Australian languages (Foley and van Valin, 1984; Dryer, 1997). Rispoli (1991) therefore argues that we should conceptualize the ontogeny of syntactic roles such as subject as a process of "mosaic acquisition" in which different underlying features are acquired gradually and at different times in language-specific ways.

The overall developmental course of English-speaking children's mastery of the syntactic role of subject best supports Rispoli's account. In their early language, children simply use individual verbs in the ways they have heard them being used, and so they are operating simply with verb-specific syntactic roles. Some of these are non-agentive, and they vary greatly in topicality. Children make some subject case errors—such as *Him go* or *Her do it*—and leave these behind only gradually (see Section 4.3.2). The kinds of cross-clausal control properties characteristic of adult English subjects are simply not present in children's early speech because there are no relevant utterances. In comprehension experiments, young children are notorious for identifying as subject the animate participant (if there is only one of these), or the first-mentioned participant, or the agent—which suggests something less abstract than an adult-like notion of subject (see Corrigan, 1988, for a review). The only experimental evidence that English-speaking children have mastered the notion of subject concerns children approaching school age. Using a training procedure, Braine et al. (1993) taught children to place a plastic token on the picture representing the subject of a spoken sentence—using many different kinds of subjects—and then looked to see if they could generalize to subjects in novel sentences of many different kinds. The first evidence that they could came at 5–6 years of age (see also Corrigan, 1988).

Following Croft (2001), one possible explanation for the late acquisition of English subject is that, in reality, each abstract construction such as transitive, intransitive, passive, and there-construction actually has its own subject. The generalized notion of the subject role in an utterance or construction—which children would have to have mastered to perform well in most of the experiments—represents the finding of a set of commonalities among these many and varied construction-specific subjects. That is, subject represents a syntactic role in something like a highly general Subject-Predicate construction at the most schematic level of the constructional hierarchy. Perhaps this developmental process is triggered in the end by the need to master constructions involving cross-clausal control as children approach school age. Importantly, in some languages this process does not take place at all—simply because the language does not contain anything as abstract as subject governing cross-clausal control and other such behavioral properties.

And so, to summarize, it would seem quite natural to suppose that if children are indeed learning utterance-level constructions as linguistic gestalts, they are also finding analogies among them. There is much evidence that they do this in nonlinguistic domains, and some evidence that they do it in the linguistic domain as well. To make abstract constructional analogies children must understand something of the functional interrelations among elements of the constructions involved. This is made easier when some of those elements are identical, in both form and function, and so children's earliest analogies are what we referred to earlier as schematization in which constructions are created around specific linguistic items. But later they are able to draw analogies with no specific items in common across constructions.

5.2.2. Functionally Based Distributional Analysis

The current hypothesis is that paradigmatic categories such as noun and verb are formed on the basis of functionally based distributional analysis.

That is, children form paradigmatic categories of linguistic items—either words or phrases—that play similar communicative roles in the utterances they hear around them. Thus, *pencil* and *pen* occur in many of the same linguistic contexts in utterances—they do many of the same kinds of things in combining with articles to make reference to an object, in indicating subjects and objects as syntactic roles, and so on—and so a language user will come to form a category containing these and similarly behaving words.

The prototypical paradigmatic linguistic categories, and the only ones that are even candidates for universal status, are nouns and verbs. The classic notional definitions—nouns indicate person, place, or thing; verbs indicate actions—clearly do not hold, as many nouns indicate actions or events *(party, discussion)* and many verbs indicate non-actional states of affairs that are sometime very difficult to distinguish from things indicated by adjectives (as in *be noisy, feel good,* which in different languages may be indicated by either a verb or an adjective). However, Maratsos (1982) points out that both nouns and verbs have characteristic small-scale combinatorial properties; for example, nouns occur with determiners and plural markers and verbs occur with tense and aspect markers. Although, as noted above, these markers can be used to recognize instances of the categories once they are formed, obviously the core notions underlying nouns and verbs are cognitively and communicatively much deeper. Evidence for this is the simple fact, noted by Maratsos himself, that some of the most prototypical nominals do not have the same small-scale combinatorial properties as others: pronouns and proper names do not occur with determiners or plural markers.

Langacker (1987b) has provided a functionally based account of nouns and verbs that goes much deeper than both simplistic notional definitions and purely formal properties. Langacker stresses that nouns and verbs are used not to refer to specific kinds of things but rather to invite the listener to construe something in a particular way in a particular communicative context. Thus, we may refer to the very same experience as either *exploding* or *an explosion,* depending on our communicative purposes. In general, nouns are used to construe experiences as "bounded entities" (like an explosion), whereas verbs are used to construe experiences as processes (like exploding). Hopper and Thompson (1984) contend further that the discourse functions of reference and predication provide the communicative reason for construing something as either a bounded entity, to which one may refer with a noun, or a process, which one may predicate with a verb. Importantly, it is these communicative functions that explain why nouns are associated with such things as determiners, whose primary function is to help the listener to locate a referent in actual or conceptual space, and verbs are associated with such things as tense markers, whose primary function is to help the listener to locate a process in actual or conceptual time (Langacker, 1991; and see Chapter 6). After an individual understands the functional basis of nouns and verbs, formal features such as determiners and tense markers may be used to identify further instances.

Relying on the notion of prototypical categories, Bates and Mac-Whinney (1979, 1982) proposed that early nouns are anchored in the concept of a concrete object and early verbs are anchored in the concept of concrete action—and these are generalized to other referents only later (very similar to the hypothesis that subjects are originally anchored in agents). The problem is that young children use adult nouns from quite early in development to refer to all kinds of non-object entities (such as *breakfast, kitchen, kiss, lunch, light, park, doctor, night, party*), and they use many of their verbs to predicate non-actional states of affairs *(like, feel, want, stay, be;* Nelson, Hampson, and Shaw, 1993). Also problematic for accounts such as these, grounded in the reference of terms, is the fact that early in development children also learn many words that are used as both nouns and verbs, for example, *bite, kiss, drink, brush, walk, hug, help,* and *call* (Nelson, 1995). It is unclear how any theory that does not consider communicative function primary—in the sense of the communicative role a word plays in whole utterances—can account for the acquisition of these so-called dual-category words.

Instead, the developmental data support the view that children initially understand paradigmatic categories very locally and mosaically, in terms of the particular kinds of things particular words can and cannot do communicatively. Thus, with respect to nouns, Tomasello et al. (1997) found that when 22-month-olds were taught a novel name for a novel object in a syntactically neutral context ("Look! A wuggie") they immediately combined this new word with many predicative terms ("Hug wuggie," "Wuggie gone," and so on), indicating that they saw something in common between wuggies and the kinds of things one can hug or that can be gone (perhaps aided by the article *a*). Children of this same tender age also were able to indicate when they saw two "wuggies," even though they had never heard this word used as a plural. However, a very interesting fact helping to specify the processes involved is that these two productive achievements, in syntax and morphology, were very poorly correlated. The children who could productively combine *wuggie* with other words syntactically were not the same ones who could create a productive plural with this same word. This suggests that children are forming their paradigmatic categories for very local communicative purposes, in mosaic and piecemeal fashion, not for all of the many more abstract and interrelated functions that underlie these categories in adults. Exactly how these processes might apply to words that fit the adult category of noun less well (non-object common nouns, proper nouns, mass nouns) is not known at this time.

With respect to verbs, Akhtar and Tomasello (1997) did a similar study with slightly older 2- and 3-year-old children and found that, as with nouns, children became productive with novel verbs syntactically and morphologically in an uncorrelated fashion—again suggesting local, functionally specific, mosaically acquired, paradigmatic categories. Evidence from other languages also suggests that young children's paradigmatic categories develop in a gradual and piecemeal way as they attempt to assimilate to their more locally based categories the wider array of more abstract functions that underlie the adult version of the category (see Rispoli, 1991).

Overall, children's early paradigmatic categories are best explained in the same theoretical terms as their other cognitive categories. As noted above in the discussion of slot-filler categories in early pivot schemas, Nelson (1985, 1996) and Mandler (2000) have both argued that the essence of concepts lies in function; human beings group together things that behave in similar ways in events and activities. In the case of linguistic categories such as noun and verb, however, it is important to be clear that these are categories not of entities in the world (that is, not referents) but of pieces of language (words and phrases). When words and phrases are grouped together according to similarities in what they do communicatively—grounded in such functions as reference and predication—cognitively and linguistically coherent categories are the result. This is the essence of functionally based distributional analysis (see Tomasello, 1992a, for an earlier formulation). The data cited above demonstrate that children do this at first very locally, only later creating more broadly based and abstract paradigmatic categories. Interestingly, a number of studies of infant categorization show this same initial bias toward the local, with more broad-based, adult-like categories emerging only gradually (Quinn et al., 1996; Cohen, 1998; see Rakison and Oakes, in press, for a review).

It is also important that the formation of paradigmatic categories leads to processes of contrast within the resulting category. The consequence is a host of pragmatic inferences that follow from the fact that a speaker chooses one item from the paradigm as opposed to others she could have chosen to fill the same basic functional role in her utterance. Thus, for example, when a child hears a novel word (such as *lend*) in a context in which she would have expected to hear a more common one *(give)*, she is led to search for what distinguishes the current communicative situation from one that would have licensed the more normal expression (this is one application of the principle of contrast). In addition, this same process of paradigmatic category formation and contrast helps to account for the existence of morphological paradigms and some of the inferences (such as the force of zero marking) that can be made within them.

Finally, it is worth mentioning that after noun and verb, there are very few candidates for lexical categories present in all of the world's languages. Even within a language that is traditionally considered to have a number of clear categories, like English, in many cases the real situation is that traditional categories from Western linguistics are applied in something less than a thoughtful manner. Thoughtful and unprejudiced linguistic analyses reveal quite clearly, for example, that the things called adverbs in English do not really form a coherent category at all, nor do prepositions, nor do determiners, nor do conjunctions, nor do complementizers, and on and on. Perhaps the most interesting recent analysis is that of Cullicover (1999), who demonstrates with special clarity that many of the small closed classes of English are not really classes at all, but merely loose collections of individual lexical items, each of which has its own behavioral profile. The items in these collections are all called by the same name (preposition, complementizer) by tradition and convenience only.

5.2.3. Input, Frequency, and Complexity

Although, to repeat yet again, there is very little specific research, Figure 5.1 details the kinds of utterances that children would need to hear and the kinds of cognitive processes that they would need to engage in in order to form each of the different kinds of constructions already identified: concrete expression (word combination), pivot schema, item-based construction, abstract construction (with syntactic roles), and paradigmatic category. The hypothesized sets of utterances are based on the simple principle that in order to form an abstraction type variation is needed. But the truth is there is so little research, with a special dearth of experimental research, that we do not know for certain that type variation is even necessary (and indeed in some areas of developmental research children leap to make generalizations on the basis of a single exemplar; see K. Nelson, 1986). The hypothesized cognitive skills include such things as categorization, schematization, analogy, and distributional analysis.

Presumably, an important factor in all of this is simply the frequency with which children hear a linguistic construction. An interesting example is the passive construction (or its close equivalent cross-linguistically). Children acquiring English typically do not produce full passive sentences (with a *by* phrase) until 4 or 5 years of age, although they sometimes produce truncated passives earlier (Harris and Flora, 1982). One possible reason for the relatively late acquisition of the full passive in English is that it

Structure	Cognitive Process	Input
Expression	• Segmenting communicative intentions (perhaps) • Reproducing sequences	I wanna see it I wanna see it I wanna see it
Pivot schema	• Schema formation • Slot-filler category	Throw ball Throw can Throw pillow
Item-based construction	• Second-order symbols	John hugs Mary Mary hugs John
Abstract construction (and syntactic roles)	• Analogy	X hugs Y A kisses B M kicks N
Paradigmatic category	• Categorization (via distributional analysis)	a X, the Xs, Eat a X a Y, the Ys, Eat a Y a Z, the Zs, Eat a Z

Figure 5.1. Some of the requisite cognitive processes and experienced language necessary for constructing the main types of child constructions.

is a complex construction, containing several additional linguistic elements relative to active voice constructions (verbal morphology and a *by* phrase). Another possible reason is that it is not a frequent construction in children's early linguistic experience; Gordon and Chafetz (1990) estimate that English-speaking children hear a full passive in only 1 of every 20,000 adult utterances directed to them (1 in every 1,000 utterances for truncated passives). Interestingly, as reported above, children acquiring some other (mostly non-European) languages, such as Inuktitut, K'iche' Mayan, Sesotho, and Zulu, learn to produce passives quite early in development. In some of these languages the passive construction is marked in ways as complex as in English. The main difference would seem to be that in these languages passives are used more frequently and saliently in adult speech to young children.

Evidence for this proposal is provided by the experimental study of Brooks and Tomasello (1999a), who found that after two 30-minute sessions of extra exposure to full passive utterances in meaningful discourse contexts, 90 percent of English-speaking children between 3 and 3½ years of age could produce a full passive utterance with a nonce verb—approximately one to two years earlier than normal. Other experimental studies have demonstrated the key role of frequency in some other constructions. For example, in a classic study Nelson (1977) gave one group of children extra exposure to the English yes/no question construction and another group extra exposure to complex verb phrase constructions (with auxiliaries, and so on). Each group learned the construction to which they were given extra exposure at a significantly earlier age than would normally be the case (and than the other experimental group). It is important that in both of these experimental studies these complex constructions were modeled for children in meaningful discourse contexts, often in replies to children's utterances on the same topic—thus maximizing the possibility of children's comprehension. Another piece of interesting evidence is the finding that bilingual children tend to overgeneralize syntactic structures from the language they hear most frequently and know best to the one they hear least frequently and know less well, rather than in the opposite direction (Döpke, 1998).

Another obvious factor in what children learn and when they learn it is complexity of linguistic structure—in interaction with their existing perceptual, cognitive, and linguistic skills, of course—what Bates and MacWhinney (1989) call "functional readiness." Thus, a 1-year-old child cannot even repeat, much less imitatively learn, an utterance with a relative clause, whereas she might be able to learn a simpler construction. There is much traditional linguistic work on child language acquisition that looks at the order in which children learn certain structures and infers from this linguistic complexity. But such inferences can never be validly made solely on the basis of order of acquisition, that is, without some information about the relative frequencies with which children hear the constructions in question. Input frequency and structural complexity interact in complex ways in the developmental process.

5.3. Constraining Constructions

Importantly, there must be some constraints on children's linguistic abstractions, and this is a problem for both of the major theories of child language acquisition. Classically, a major problem for generative theories is that as the rules and principles are made more elegant and powerful through theoretical analyses, they become so abstract that they generate too large a set of grammatical utterances; and so constraints (such as the subjacency constraint) must be posited to restore empirical accuracy. In usage-based theories children are abstracting as they learn, but they cannot do this indiscriminately; they must make just those generalizations that are conventional in the language they are learning. It is thus clear that any serious theory of syntactic development, whatever its basic assumptions, must address the question of why children make the generalizations they do and not others.

Importantly in this context, both generative and usage-based theories predict that children will mostly use language the way adults do—either because they both have an innate universal grammar or because children copy adults. In the generative view children should really not make errors unless they get wrong some of the particulars of the particular language they are learning (thus disrupting linking to universal grammar), or unless some performance factors interfere with their competence. In the usage-based view, children mostly begin as conservative learners and gradually build up abstractions, so we should expect few overgeneralization errors early; such errors should begin only after a certain age—in the domain of syntax perhaps age 3 or so because that is when children show productivity in nonce verb experiments. At the moment there does not exist a data base establishing the developmental histories of different kinds of syntactic overgeneralization errors that would enable us to choose between these two theories on this point.

5.3.1. Over-Generativity and Negative Evidence

We may illustrate the basic problem with so-called dative alternation constructions. The situation is this. Some verbs can felicitously appear in both ditransitive and prepositional dative constructions, but others cannot:

He gave/sent/bequeathed/donated his books to the library.
He gave/sent/bequeathed/*donated the library his books.

Why should the other three verbs be felicitous in both constructions, but *donate* be felicitous only in the prepositional dative? The three verbs have very similar meanings, and so it would seem likely that they should all behave the same. Another example is:

She said/told something to her mother.
She *said/told her mother something.

Again, the meanings of the verbs are very close, and so the difference of behavior seems unprincipled and unpredictable (Bowerman, 1988, 1996). Similar alternations are the causative alternation *(I rolled the ball; The ball rolled)* and the locative alternation *(I sprayed paint on the wall;*

I sprayed the wall with paint)—both of which also apply only to limited sets of verbs.

One solution is quite simple. Perhaps children only learn verbs for the constructions in which they have heard them. Given the evidence reviewed in Chapter 4, this is very likely the case at the earliest stages of development. But it is not true later in development, especially in the 3- to 5-year age period. Children at this age overgeneralize with some regularity, as documented most systematically by Bowerman (1982, 1988; see Pinker, 1989, for a summary of evidence). As reported above, her two children produced things like "Don't giggle me" (at age 3;0) and "I said her no" (at 3;1). It is thus not the case that children are totally conservative throughout development, and so this cannot be the whole answer.

A second solution is also quite simple. It is possible that when children make overgeneralization errors adults correct them, and so children's overgeneralization tendencies are constrained by the linguistic environment. But in fact adults do not explicitly correct children's utterances for grammatical correctness (Brown and Hanlon, 1970). Adults, at least Western middle-class adults, do respond differently to well-formed and ill-formed child utterances, however. For example, they continue conversing to well-formed utterances but they revise or recast ill-formed utterances (e.g., Farrar, 1992; Bohannon and Stanowicz, 1988). But most theorists do not consider this kind of indirect feedback sufficient to constrain children's overgeneralization tendencies, as it is far from consistent. It is also not clear that this type of feedback is available to all children learning all languages. Nevertheless, it is still possible that linguistic feedback from adults may play some role—although neither a necessary nor a sufficient role—in constraining children's overgeneralization tendencies.

Given the inadequacy of both of these simple solutions, generativists have taken a different tack. The basic strategy is to let universal grammar constrain children, which means that they should make no overgeneralization errors at all. But to provide such constraint universal grammar must make some contact with the specific verbs and constructions involved, and this involves detailed learning about how specific verb meanings connect to specific syntactic structures (Pinker, 1989). For example, a verb can be used felicitously with both the English transitive and intransitive constructions if it denotes "manner of locomotion" (*walk* and *drive* as in *I walked the dog at midnight* or *I walked all day* and *I drove my car to New York* or *I drove all day*), but not if it denotes a "motion in a lexically specified direction" (*come* and *fall* as in *He came her to school* or *She falled him down*). Because learning these things requires some time, effort, and exposure, children make some errors—not because they have induced an incorrect syntactic construction, but only because they are in the process of getting their verb meanings right and so linking in the right way to universal grammar.

To account for this process Pinker (1989) hypothesized the existence of innate lexical rules, such as semantic classes of verbs, and innate linking rules incorporating these semantic subclasses of verbs (see Section 5.4.1). Given these, the process requires only that (1) children hear in the input some verbs alternating; (2) they hear other verbs in only one construction, but on the basis of semantic similarity to the verb that was heard to alternate, they assume that these also alternate; and (3) they learn the correct meanings for all their verbs. When these three conditions are met, the connection between lexical representations and surface form should be constrained in the appropriate way. In this account, overgeneralization errors are due to the fact that children do not yet have their verb meanings right, and so they are sometimes forced into one-shot innovations in particular circumstances (performance errors) that do not reflect their underlying grammatical knowledge (or affect it either).

5.3.2. Entrenchment, Preemption, and Verb Classes

From a more usage-based perspective, two factors involved in syntactic constraint have been most widely discussed: entrenchment and preemption (see Clark, 1987; Braine and Brooks, 1995; Goldberg, 1995; Bates and MacWhinney, 1989). First, the more frequently children hear a verb used in a particular construction (the more firmly its usage is entrenched), the less likely they will be to extend that verb to any novel construction with which they have not heard it used. Second, if children hear a verb used in a linguistic construction that serves the same communicative function as some possible generalization, they may infer that the generalization is not conventional—the heard construction preempts the generalization. For example, if a child hears *He made the rabbit disappear,* when she might have expected *He disappeared the rabbit,* she may infer that *disappear* does not occur in a simple transitive construction—since the adult seems to be going to some lengths to avoid using it in that way (the periphrastic causative being a more marked construction). In many cases, of course, entrenchment and preemption may work together, as a verb that is highly entrenched in one usage is not used in some other linguistic context but an alternative is used instead. This leads to the more general idea of a competition among forms as argued by Bates and MacWhinney (1989).

There is evidence from two recent studies that both of these factors play a role in the constraining process, as do semantic subclasses of verbs (and there is even some evidence for the two neglected factors of childhood conservativeness and adult feedback)—but they may do this to differing degrees at different developmental periods. First, Brooks et al. (1999) investigated the role of entrenchment in constraining children's overgeneralization tendencies. In an experimental study, they modeled the use of a number of fixed-transitivity English verbs for children from 3;5 to 8;0 years—verbs such as *disappear* that are exclusively intransitive and verbs such as *hit* that are exclusively transitive. There were four pairs of verbs, one member of each pair typically learned early by children and typically used often by adults (and so presumably more entrenched) and the other member of each pair typically learned later by children and typically used less frequently by adults (less entrenched). The four pairs were *come-arrive, take-remove, hit-strike,* and *disappear-vanish* (the first member of each pair being more entrenched). The finding was that, in the face of adult questions attempting to induce them to overgeneralize, children of all ages were less likely to overgeneralize the strongly entrenched verbs than the weakly entrenched verbs; that is, they were more likely to produce *I arrived it* than *I comed it*. It would thus seem that young children are less likely to overgeneralize relatively highly entrenched verbs.

One piece of evidence contrary to this conclusion is provided by the observations of Bowerman (1988, 1996). She reports that her two daughters produced many overgeneralizations for some early light verbs that should be highly entrenched, such as *go* and *come*. The problem, however, is that precisely because children use these light verbs so frequently—many times more often than heavier, more contentful verbs—they have many more opportunities to overgeneralize them. It is thus difficult to know if these verbs are overgeneralized more often than other verbs on a proportional basis. It is also possible that verb meaning is an important factor, and that these light verbs overgeneralize more readily than heavier verbs. These are questions for future research.

Second, there is also experimental evidence for the constraining role of both preemption and semantic classes of verbs (à la Pinker). Brooks and Tomasello (1999b) taught novel verbs to children 2;6, 4;6, and 7;0 years of age in either a transitive or an intransitive construction. They then attempted to induce children to generalize these novel verbs to the other construction (as in the causative alternation). Some of these verbs conformed to Pinker's (1989) semantic criteria governing verb classes (verbs similar in meaning to *break* or *roll* that alternate), and some did not (verbs similar in meaning to *hit* or *enter* that do not alternate). Additionally, in some cases experimenters attempted to preempt generalizations by offering children alternative ways of using the new verb. For example, for children who heard *The ball is tamming,* experimenters gave them the possibility of answering *What's the boy doing?* with *He's making the ball tam*—which gave them an alternative to saying *He's tamming the ball* (which in the cases of some verbs would have been infelicitous). In brief, the study found that both of these factors were effective in constraining children's generalization tendencies, but only from age 4;6. That is, children from 4;6 showed a tendency to generalize or not generalize a verb in line with its membership in one of the key semantic subclasses of verbs, and they were less likely to generalize a verb to a novel construction if the adult offered them a preempting alternative construction. But younger children were not affected by either of these factors.

These findings, particularly with regard to preemption, provide an explanation for why adult recasts of child utterances are so effective in promoting syntactic growth—as demonstrated correlationally by Farrar (1990, 1992) and experimentally by Saxton (Saxton et al., 1998; Saxton, 2000). The basic idea is that an adult recast gives the child both a positive exemplar of how adults say things—thus contributing to the entrenchment of the conventional adult form—and a preemption of the child's just-said infelicitous structure. For example, we can imagine the following sequence:

Child: She giggled me.
Adult: Oh! She made you giggle, did she?

The child thus gets an alternative possible means of expression in immediate juxtaposition with her non-conventional construction, which enables a clear comparison of the key aspects of the two utterances. As argued extensively by K. E. Nelson (e.g., 1986), even just one or a few experiences of this kind might be more effective in promoting learning than many correct exemplars given at the wrong time.

These studies demonstrate that the most often discussed constraining influences on syntactic constructions emerge only gradually in development during the preschool years. In line with children's early conservative tendencies, entrenchment works early as particular item-based constructions become either more or less entrenched depending on usage. This is the only factor at work for some time, as children do not have many alternative constructions to effect preemption, and they have not yet had time to learn semantic subclasses of verbs. Preemption and semantic subclasses begin to work later, perhaps not until 4;6 or so, as children learn more about the conventional uses of verbs and about all of the alternative linguistic constructions at their disposal in different communicative circumstances. Thus, just as utterance-level constructions become more abstract only gradually and in piecemeal fashion, so also are they constrained only gradually and in piecemeal fashion.

Combining these findings on constraints with the findings concerning the gradually increasing abstractness of children's syntactic constructions, we may create a hypothetical developmental scenario for processes of both generalization and constraint. Figure 5.2 illustrates this scenario, with three exclusively intransitive verbs very similar in meaning: *laugh, giggle,* and *chortle.* The hypothesis is that the intransitive verb *laugh* is not likely to be overgeneralized to the transitive construction because it is learned early and entrenched through frequent use as an intransitive verb only. *Chortle* is also not likely to be overgeneralized but for a different reason. Even though it is not highly entrenched, it is typically learned only after the child has begun to form verb subclasses (and *chortle* belongs to one that cannot be used in the transitive construction) and only after the child has also learned preempting alternative constructions (such as *That made me chortle with glee,* preserving its intransitive status). In contrast, *giggle* is more likely to be overgeneralized because it is not so entrenched as *laugh* and it is learned before the child has formed verb subclasses or learned many alternative constructions that might (as in the case of *chortle*) preempt an overgeneralization. That is, *giggle* may be a verb that is learned in a highly vulnerable window of developmental time.

And so, the familiar theoretical alternatives in this case are once again: (1) children possess innate syntactic knowledge that mostly solves the developmental problem (in this case innate lexical rules and linking rules—with performance errors accounting for overgeneralizations); and (2) children solve the problem gradually through general learning and cognitive processes. In the usage-based view we do not need to posit the existence of innate constraints in order to constrain the process. In terms of evidence, the experimental data suggest that a number of usage-based factors, especially entrenchment and competition (preemption), play roles in constraining children's generalizations with syntactic constructions. And over time children make generalizations about which semantic classes of verbs can be generalized to which kinds of constructions, allowing them to use newly learned verbs felicitously on the basis of very little direct experience with those verbs. Whether these three factors are together sufficient is a question for future research. Of most urgent need is a systematic description of children's syntactic overgeneralization errors with various constructions over developmental time.

5.4. Theories of Syntactic Development

As is well known, there are two basic theoretical approaches to children's syntactic development. The first includes all of those approaches that posit an innate universal grammar—dictating some kind of dual process model in which words, fixed expressions, and quirky constructions are all acquired by "normal" learning processes, whereas acquisition of the more

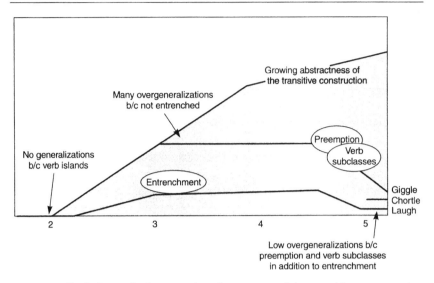

Figure 5.2. Shaded area depicts growing abstractness of the transitive construction (as in Figure 4.4). Other specifications designate constraints on the tendency to overgeneralize inappropriate verbs to this construction. Adapted from Tomasello (2000b); reprinted with the permission of Elsevier Science.

regular aspects of language is somehow guided by the innate universal grammar. The second paradigm includes all those approaches that posit only a single set of cognitive, social-cognitive, and learning processes to account for the acquisition of all types of linguistic items and structures, from simple to complex, from concrete to abstract, with all kinds of mixed constructions thrown in for good measure. In this section I outline, very briefly, the major approaches within each of these two paradigms—ending with a construction grammar account that identifies some of the major properties of linguistic constructions that need to be accounted for in a theory of syntactic development.

5.4.1. Principles and Parameters

Positing an innate universal grammar creates two major problems. The first derives from the fact of linguistic diversity. The problem is how any given child, learning any given language, can link the abstract categories of the innate universal grammar to the particulars of the particular language she is learning. The second derives from the fact of developmental change. The problem in this case is how to account for changes in children's language over time, given that the innate universal grammar itself does not change across development (the continuity assumption).

The major theoretical move to deal with linguistic diversity in generative linguistics is the theory of principles and parameters (Chomsky, 1981). In this view, universal grammar anticipates all possible cross-linguistic variation by setting out ahead of time a delimited number of parameters each with a delimited number of possible values (for example, phrasal organization: either head first, as in the Spanish *la casa grande,* or head last, as in the English *the big house*). It should be noted, however, that parameters are defined very differently by different investigators, and there is no agreed-upon level of analysis—or even an agreed-upon list of best exemplars (other than, perhaps, head direction and pro-drop). This is most clearly revealed by asking the question: Precisely how many parameters are there? Fodor (2001: 734) answers: "It might turn out that there are 20 parameters or 30 or 100 and more . . . On one recent estimate . . . there would be at least 32 parameters controlling the landing site for verb movement, perhaps multiplied by the number of possible verb forms (finite/infinitive/past participle, etc.)."

The more fundamental problem is the problem of linking. Such critical components of parameters as "head" (as in the head-direction parameter) do not come with identifying tags on them in particular languages; they share no perceptual features in common across languages and so their means of identification cannot be specified in the universal grammar. In a recent discussion on "setting syntactic parameters," for example, Fodor (2001: 761, 765) presents the problem this way:

> It would have been more convenient for children if natural language parameters were all concerned with surface facts . . . Instead . . . the relation between word strings and their parametric generators is opaque at best.
>
> . . . For UG [universal grammar] to be truly helpful, it should supply innate sentence structures *and* fix their relation to surface words strings . . . As long as there is substantial crosslinguistic variation with respect to how innately defined structure is overtly lexicalized, there will be ambiguities of string-to-structure alignment.

Setting a parameter thus encounters the basic problem of linking, a problem which Atkinson (1996: 473–474), in particular, criticizes his fellow generativists for not addressing. As one specific example, Mazuka (1996) analyzed how children might set the hypothesized head-direction parameter.

> Setting a Head Direction parameter by analyzing the syntactic structure of the input involves a paradox. The Head Direction parameter is supposed to

determine the order in which the head and complement should appear in the language the child is acquiring. But, for a child to set this parameter, she must first find out which units are the heads and the complements in the sentence she hears. If her linguistic skills are sophisticated enough to know which are heads and complements, she will also know which order they came in. If she already knows which order the head and the complements come in a sentence, there is no need to set the parameter. (24–25)

The hard part is thus recognizing "heads" and "complements" in a particular language, and this difficulty is logically prior to any act of parameter setting. To set the head-direction parameter in universal grammar, a language learner must first be able to recognize heads in the specific language she is learning; once this fundamental linking problem is accomplished the parameter setting is trivial, indeed superfluous.

The only theory attempting to address this problem is Pinker's (1984, 1987, 1989) theory of semantic bootstrapping. Pinker proposed the following: (1) a list of key syntactic categories innately given to all human beings, (2) a list of key experiential categories innately given to all human beings, and (3) a set of innate linking rules to connect the two. In the case of "subject of a sentence," as one instance, the process would work like this. "Subject" is innately linked to "agent of an action," or, if there is no agent, to such things as "experiencer," "theme," or "goal" (the so-called linking hierarchy). Consequently, if the child saw a dog bite a man and heard someone say "The dog bit the man," she would know on the basis of her general causal cognition that the dog is the agent of the action; her innate linking rule would then connect agent to subject. Because she notices the linguistic form associated with the subject, the child can also now recognize future exemplars of "sentence subject" on the basis of this form alone (say a particular word-order configuration or a particular case marker), even if they are not agents. Thus, the English-speaking child will eventually have to deal with experiential subjects that are not agents (as in *John saw Mary*) and even passive sentences in which subjects are not agents and agents are not subjects.

However, in the specific case of "sentence subject" it is almost certain that Pinker's proposal is not correct. First of all, on general theoretical grounds it has been known for some time that in ergative languages the notion of "subject" does not operate as it does in English and other accusative languages, and so a direct connection to "agent" is not possible. Moreover, even if there were some solution to this problem, many languages are what is called split ergative: some of their constructions are ergative while others are accusative based on such things as person (first and second person are accusatively structured whereas third person is ergatively structured) or tense (present-future is accusatively structured whereas past is ergatively structured; DeLancey, 1981; van Valin, 1992). In general terms, Slobin (1997) has made a persuasive case that there is much too much variability across languages—not to mention historical change within languages—for any static and innate look-up table to function in the way it would need to in order to solve the problem of linking (see also Braine, 1992).

The empirical problem with Pinker's proposal is that at least two naturalistic analyses of early child language have failed to find any evidence for innate linking rules. First, Lieven, Pine, and Baldwin (1997) analyzed the first sentences of 12 English-speaking children and found that many early subjects came from such unremarkable utterances such as *I like it, Maria have it, I see it,* and *It has a hole* in which there is no agent of an action at all (see also Pye et al., 1994). More strongly still, Bowerman (1990, 1997) found that it happens with some regularity in early child language that the subject hierarchy is violated totally, that is, arguments that are further down the linking hierarchy end up as subjects—as in the utterance "Pete hurt by car" (patient = subject, agent = oblique) reported by Tomasello (1992a) for a child at 1;8. In general, children learning English and many other languages use many non-agentive subjects early in development—everything from *It hurts* to *It's a tape recorder* to *He fell-down*—with basically no special advantage for agent subjects (Budwig, Stein, and O'Brien, 2001). And so, not only do innate linking rules run into difficulties cross-linguistically, they also make wrong predictions for the order of acquisition of some structures within a language. And there are no other syntactic roles or grammatical relations—that is, other than sentence subject—for which there is any detailed analysis or supportive evidence at all.

The second major problem for generativist theories of language acquisition is developmental change. The problem is that, by hypothesis, universal grammar does not change ontogenetically. On the basis of its nativist assumptions, generative grammarians make the continuity assumption:

> In the absence of compelling evidence to the contrary, the child's grammatical rules should be drawn from the same basic rule types, and be composed of primitive symbols from the same class, as the grammatical rules attributed to adults in standard linguistic investigations. (Pinker, 1984: 7)

This means that once the child has set some parameter of universal grammar, however that might be accomplished, her language should immediately look adult-like with respect to that parameter. To repeat our earlier example:

> Once a child is able to parse an utterance such as "Close the door!," he will be able to infer from the fact that the verb "close" in English precedes its

complement "the door," that all verbs in English precede their complements. (Radford, 1990: 61)

The prediction is thus for quick and across-the-board development of structures of a certain type once a parameter has been set (for example, the head-direction parameter specifying that all verbs precede their complements in English). But this manifestly does not happen in children's spontaneous production, where changes seem to occur piecemeal in association with particular linguistic items and item-based constructions. And it is also not consistent with their behavior in experiments of both production and comprehension, as reviewed in Chapter 4. Generativists have attempted to deal with this discrepancy between theory and fact in one of three basic ways: (1) by invoking hypothesized performance factors that mask children's underlying adult-like competence and parametric consistency; (2) by proposing that universal grammar does indeed change developmentally, as some parts mature before others; and (3) proposing that the linking process requires much learning of the particularities of the particular language being learned. None of these moves is fully adequate, but for different reasons.

First, the main problem in the case of performance limitations is that there has never been any serious attempt to actually measure and assess them directly, and so they are simply invoked whenever they are convenient. There have been strenuous objections to this practice from generativists (e.g., Roeper, 1996: 417) and non-generativists (e.g., Sampson, 1997) alike. The one partial exception to this neglect is Valian (1991). She specifically predicted that young children should produce more intransitive than transitive utterances, since intransitives are shorter, and that their alternating verbs (those that could be used in either way) should be used more often intransitively—since intransitives fit more easily into children's performance limitations. She found that indeed there was an increase in children's use of transitive verbs over the third year of life, and there was also an increase in children's use of the transitive form of alternating verbs. (But note that even here performance factors are not specifically and independently measured.)

In a more recent study, however, Theakston et al., (2001) examined Valian's claims in more detail by looking not just at children's verb classes but at individual verbs. In particular, they looked at 2-year-old children's use of particular transitive (such as *hit*), intransitive (such as *go*), and alternating (such as *break*) verbs. The main findings were that (1) children mostly used particular verbs as either transitives or intransitives only, suggesting that they were not making a choice between the two on the basis of performance factors; (2) children did not use alternating verbs more often as intransitives than as transitives; and (3) the way children used particular verbs was very well predicted by the way their mothers used those same verbs. These findings provide no evidence that young children's production of transitive and intransitive utterances is affected by performance limitations. In addition to this naturalistic study, as reviewed in Chapter 4, a number of experiments using nonce verbs have employed control procedures that have ruled out, for all practical purposes, performance limitations as a viable explanation for children's inability to demonstrate adultlike generativity with these novel verbs (see Tomasello, 2000b, for a review).

Second, maturation has been used, like performance limitations, as basically an unconstrained "fudge factor." The basic problem is that any time new acquisition data arise it may be invoked without any consultation of genetic research or any independent assessment of this causal factor at all—a procedure severely criticized by Braine (1994), Tomasello (1995c), Sampson (1997), and others. And again there are experimental data that are not compatible with the hypothesis. These mainly include studies finding that children who use a particular construction in their spontaneous speech (such as the simple transitive)—presumably indicating the maturation of certain underlying parameters in universal grammar—still do not generalize this same construction to newly learned verbs in experiments (and this is not due to a general inability to generalize newly learned linguistic structures; again, see Chapter 4 and Tomasello, 2000b).

Finally, some generativists have recently begun to accommodate the developmental facts by positing that children must have a certain amount of linguistic experience with their own language before they can set a parameter in universal grammar. In some generativist accounts, in order to begin to participate in a productive system of generative grammar the child must hear each of her lexical items in each of its appropriate syntactic contexts (see Hyams, 1994, for a proposal very near to this). The problem is that although this theory can explain the data—in the same way as a more usage-based account—it is at the cost of the whole point of a generative account, which classically posits that human beings possess and use linguistic abstractions early in ontogeny and independent of specific linguistic experiences other than a minimal triggering event. In all, this account basically leaves universal grammar with nothing to do. In the words of Mazuka (1996: 317; see also Meisel, 1995): "The strength of the grammatical parameter setting approach is that children can set a grammatical parameter with minimal data. . . . If children must somehow learn to combine words correctly first, and then set [for example] the Head Direction parameter by generalizing from the data, it will nullify the basic motivation for the parameter setting approach to language acquisition."

Because of its fundamental inability to deal either with cross-linguistic variation or with developmental change, our conclusion for the moment must be that the theory of principles and parameters currently has very little to offer serious students of child language acquisition.

5.4.2. Basic Child Grammar

Coming from a very different theoretical perspective, Slobin (1985a) proposed that young children's pre-linguistic cognition is organized into a small number of basic experiential scenes. Following Fillmore's (1977a, 1977b) proposals on the everyday interactional scenes and frames that structure human language, Slobin proposed that much of children's early language is structured by (1) the manipulative activity scene in which an animate agent causes a change of state in an inanimate patient, and (2) the figure-ground scene in which a person or object moves along some spatial path. Following the lead of Talmy (e.g., 1985, 1988), Slobin further proposed that certain of the concepts in these scenes were designated innately to be especially conducive to grammatical rather than to lexical expression. (Note that what is innate here are not any linguistic categories or constructions, per se, but rather certain nonlinguistic concepts and their amenability to expression in certain kinds of linguistic constructions.) Grammatical development then consisted of children learning how their particular language encoded these privileged concepts.

Drawing on his extensive cross-linguistic work, Slobin (1973, 1985a) also attempted to account for such things as the order of acquisition and ease of acquisition of particular linguistic structures in particular languages. To do this, he had to assess the cognitive and linguistic complexity of particular linguistic structures. In addition, he needed to posit some cognitive operating principles that reflected children's processing tendencies, including such things as (to simplify): (1) pay attention to the ends of words, (2) pay attention to stressed syllables, (3) note frequency of use, and (4) compare utterances heard with those you would produce in the same situation. Generally, with some adjustments, these operating principles have held up very well as heuristics in cross-linguistic investigations.

However, the basic proposal of innate notions innately biased toward grammatical expression has not held up so well. Slobin (1997) has provided a trenchant critique of his own earlier theory. He argues that despite some overall commonalities, different languages grammaticize things differently, and there is simply no way that the human genome can be pre-adapted for this. He gives numerous examples of morphemes that are grammatical in one language but lexical in another. For instance, in English noun classifiers are words, as in *a piece of paper* or *a glass of water,* whereas in Mandarin noun classifiers are gender-like markers on the noun. In some cases, morphemes for a particular set of notions can be both lexical and grammatical within the same language (Mayan motion verbs and directionals). In general, even when languages grammaticize the "same" notion in something close to the same way, the details are often very different in terms of exactly what the grammatical item designates. Slobin's overall conclusion on the possibility of a universal connection between function and form is thus: "To be sure, all of these examples are consistent with a *collection* of 'grammatically relevant notions'—definiteness, negation, manipulability, agent vs. experiencer—but there are too many packagings of such semantic and pragmatic characteristics to build in all of the possible packages in advance or to rank them in terms of 'naturalness' or 'accessibility'" (1997: 301).

And so, the idea that there is some innate universal grammar containing a look-up table of form-function correspondences (Pinker's innate linking rules) is extremely unlikely, and so is Slobin's milder claim that certain cognitive notions are innately and universally biased toward grammatical expression.

5.4.3. The Competition Model and Connectionism

If there are no universal, innate correspondences between particular communicative functions and particular linguistic forms, then children must learn these correspondences. This means that a theory of language acquisition need specify *a priori* only a single set of general learning processes with which to learn everything about a language, including these correspondences. And it does not need to worry about how to link all this with some hypothetical underlying entity such as universal grammar.

The most well-worked-out model along these lines is the competition model (Bates and MacWhinney, 1987, 1989). Although complex in practice, the basic idea of the model is embodied in four simple principles:

- The basic learning problem is to directly map linguistic forms to their conventional communicative functions.
- Particular form-function mappings vary in such things as their cue availability (is the form there when you needed it?) and cue reliability (does the form invariably indicate the same function?).
- As new communicative functions come into being (either historically or ontogenetically), there is competition among forms for their expression in the language.
- Distributional analysis of form-form correspondences, along with processes of categorization, leads to the emergence of new linguistic categories.

The competition model has been used in the widest and deepest research program of cross-linguistic experimental research to date. In general, the model has been highly successful in accounting for cross-linguistic patterns of sentence comprehension by both children and adults, as the papers collected in the volume edited by Bates and MacWhinney (1989) strongly attest. Most of the work (outlined in Section 4.3.3) has focused on young children's and adults' comprehension of agent-patient relations in experimentally presented sentences in which cues such as word order, agreement, and case role marking are put into direct competition. The outcome has been the discovery of the actual cues that people use in different languages to process their most basic syntactic structures. No other model has been put to the empirical test as much as the competition model, and thus no other model has yielded such a rich set of empirical discoveries about specific processing patterns in specific languages.

Criticisms of the competition model have mostly focused on its lack of a substantive linguistic theory to provide a detailed description of the adult endpoint toward which children are working. Indeed, Rispoli (1991) points out a number of ways in which the model assumes a kind of "theory neutral" linguistic description (involving, for example, subjects, agents, and topics as the structures whose cues children are attempting to use)—when it would be more consistent with the spirit of the model to leave open the nature of the structures that will eventually emerge in the acquisition in particular languages. Most importantly, the competition model is really a model of language comprehension and not so much a model of language learning. Thus, the experiments demonstrate which cues children and adults are using at different developmental periods, but it does not really provide an account of how they learn to use those cues in the first place.

Recently a number of connectionist models have been proposed that are similar in spirit to the competition model and that do focus directly on processes of learning. The majority of these concern morphology, and so they will be examined in Chapter 6. In terms of syntax, of special note is the model of Elman (1993, 2000). In this model a computer program's task is to predict which word will follow as it processes incoming input. Using this criterion, Elman showed that if built in a certain way (as a simple recurrent network) the model could predict next words quite well, even when the input contained complex syntactic structures such as relative clauses. Interestingly for developmental theories, however, this only worked if the network first learned simple sentences and then proceeded to the more complex ones. Initially this was accomplished by humans controlling the input, but in later work it was shown that the same effect resulted from limiting the working memory of the program, which effectively filtered out early in the process structures that were too difficult for the program to learn.

Models such as this are clearly not models of the way children acquire a language, most importantly because they do not provide an account that includes communicative function or meaning. This is of course a basic problem in its own right in terms of psychological plausibility, but, further, it means that connectionist models cannot make use of either of the two major pattern-finding cognitive skills outlined in this chapter. Thus, without some understanding of communicative function, analogies cannot be made—at least, not of the kind that are needed to, for example, create abstract utterance-level constructions. And without an understanding of communicative function, the only kinds of distributional analyses that can be done are those focusing solely on surface form—for instance, which elements occur next to which other elements—and not functionally based distributional analyses that group together into paradigmatic categories linguistic elements that do the same communicative job. Whether these are only failings of the current instantiations of connectionist models, or whether they are in principle limitations of these models, is a question for future research. One promising direction is a model by Chang (in press) that seems to generalize to novel linguistic material more readily than previous models, at least partly because it incorporates some constructional meanings.

In any case, what connectionist models have done is to provide existence proofs that the language children hear contains many patterns that can be extracted even on the basis of form alone. In combination with the findings of Saffran et al. (1997) and others that human infants are powerful pattern extractors on the basis of form alone (see Section 2.2.3), models such as Elman's and others make it quite plausible that young children can learn complex syntactic patterns from natural language input, especially since young children have additional learning tools to help them in this process.

5.4.4. Construction Grammar

Construed in a broad way, construction grammar is a version of cognitive-functional linguistics as practiced by researchers such as Lakoff (1987), Fillmore (1989), Goldberg (1995), and Croft (2001), and there are also many commonalities with the work of Langacker (1987a, 1991), who relies heavily on what he calls constructional schemas. The two central tenets of the theory are: (1) linguistic constructions are symbolic units with their own holistic properties, including symbolic significance of their own; and (2) much of human linguistic competence is best characterized in terms of concrete linguistic expressions and constructions that are continuous with but different from the more regular and abstract constructions typically studied in more formal approaches.

In terms of acquisition, Slobin (1985a) drew on some basic construction grammar principles in positing, as noted above, that much of children's language is organized holistically by complex scenes (such as the manipulative activity scene) and the constructions that symbolize them (that is, basic child grammar). Goldberg (1995) used construction grammar explicitly to argue that some of the most popular lexicalist approaches to grammar (such as that of Pinker, 1989; see section 5.1.7) were implausible as compared with an approach in which abstract constructions have their own independent meanings. Finally, Tomasello and Brooks (1999) followed Slobin and Goldberg in emphasizing the developmental importance of holistically organized constructions with independent meanings. But they also emphasized the item-based nature of much of children's early language much more than these other two researchers. They stressed that (1) initially children's constructions are based totally on particular words and phrases (not abstract categories) tied fairly closely to the language they hear; (2) linguistic abstractions (categories and constructions) develop continuously and relatively slowly; and (3) there are asynchronies in the developmental trajectories of different categories and constructions within a given child, even those that would be structurally similar from a formal linguistic point of view. They also emphasized the important point that this view, like the generative view, predicts that children will not make so many errors in early language, when they are mostly learning to produce concrete linguistic expressions that they have heard adults use, but that as development proceeds, children find patterns that are not conventional in the language they are learning and so make some errors.

One limitation is that none of these construction grammar accounts has focused to any large extent on the specific psycholinguistic processes by which children construct constructions and produce utterances from their inventories of linguistic items and structures. What is needed are some usage-based principles of learning and production to complement construction-based accounts of linguistic structure. This book is meant to remedy this situation by supplying a dynamic, psychological component to the construction grammar approach. Thus, much of the book is aimed at establishing the kinds of cognitive and social-cognitive processes by means of which children acquire different kinds of constructions and organize them into some kind of structured inventory and use them to produce creative yet canonical utterances. The proposal is that to do these things children use various skills of intention-reading and pattern-finding on the language they hear around them, as outlined in the previous chapters—along with some skills of language production. These skills will be summarized and to some degree integrated into a coherent account in Chapter 8.

5.5. Summary

In this chapter I have attempted to account for children's acquisition of the most abstract constructions of their language. These constructions serve to package information in a way that "windows attention" in a particular manner, that is, that takes a particular perspective on some type of scene and its participants. In their abstract form these constructions accomplish this in a gestalt fashion, as whole constructions and not as a function of any particular lexical items involved. This construction grammar perspective provides a more plausible account of the interaction between the concrete and the abstract in language development—because it focuses on abstractions across whole utterances—than does a lexical rules approach in which all depends on the meaning of the particular verbs involved (Goldberg, 1995). The lexical rules approach would seem to be better adapted to children's verb island constructions and other item-based constructions—which are defined by particular verbs or other words—than to their totally abstract constructions.

The process by which children construct these abstract constructions has been little studied. The current proposal is that they do this using the pattern-finding skill of analogy, which basically categorizes together complex wholes on the basis of commonalities in their relational structures. It is very important to emphasize that abstract analogies—for example between two structures that have no elements in common—can only be drawn if children use their intention-reading skills to discern the function of those elements in the larger structure. It is only by doing this that children may align the elements that correspond to one another—the elements that do the same communicative job—across the two structures (such as the elements that are serving as "tow-ers" in two different pictures of vehicles towing each other). Indeed, in the current account (following Croft, 2001) syntactic roles such as the English subject or transitive-subject or their equivalents in other languages are simply emergent phenomena in this analogy-making process, based on commonalities the child sees in the communicative functions of certain slots in certain item-based constructions.

The process of distributional analysis, by means of which young children construct paradigmatic categories such as noun and verb, also requires understanding the communicative function of various linguistic elements as they appear in utterances. For this reason I have stressed that the process should be called functionally based distributional analysis. The empirical fact that children master some of these functions before others within an adult-like category is crucially important here. For example, young children learn to put plurals on "nouns" independently of learning to use "nouns" productively in argument slots, and likewise for "verbs" concerning the marking of tense and syntactic combination. The best model to describe this process is Rispoli's (1991) model of "mosaic acquisition" in which some of the functions of an adult-like paradigmatic category are learned before others and in relative independence. This is obviously a usage-based process of determining functions first locally and only later more globally.

A crucial question for any usage-based theory of syntactic development—as well as any other kind of theory—is how children constrain their growing abstractions. How do they learn to make just the generalizations that are conventional in their language and not others? This is also a question for which there is shockingly little research; we do not even have good descriptions of the nature of and frequency of children's syntactic overgeneralization errors. But the research that does exist suggests that children's growing abstractions are constrained by a number of conspiring forces, which operate at different points in development. Constraints are not needed early in development, when children are very conservative learners and the language they hear and say is becoming entrenched in conventional uses. But as they learn more language children form classes of verbs and other words that behave similarly in some contexts, and then generalize to new contexts within this categorical constraint (Pinker, 1989). They do not seem to use this categorical constraint, however, until they are over 4 years of age. In addition, as children learn more constructions these block or preempt potential generalizations of others. Together these three usage-based processes—entrenchment, verb classes, and preemption—provide a good starting point for further research on this very difficult question.

In the review of theories of syntactic development in this chapter I concluded, not surprisingly, that the principles-and-parameters approach has little to offer at this stage. The theory is saddled with an hypothesized universal grammar that seems to be doing very little except creating difficult problems such as how to deal with cross-linguistic diversity (the linking problem) and developmental change (the continuity problem). Connectionism is obviously an approach much more in the spirit of the current usage-based approach, but it needs to incorporate into its models some account of communicative intentions and function before it can provide a psychologically realistic theory of child language acquisition. Construction grammar accounts have so far provided very little in the direction of the precise acquisition processes children use to construct their constructions, and so it is the burden of this book as a whole to try to remedy that situation by detailing the usage-based processes involved—those involving intention-reading, those involving pattern-finding, and those, as is the case most often, involving both.

It is important to stress in all of this theoretical debate that regardless of whether or not there is a universal grammar, children must still learn the individual linguistic items and constructions of the language into which they are born, and this requires them to master many and various concrete pieces of language and to make some straightforward abstractions across them. To repeat: this must happen regardless of one's theory. The question is whether we need in addition an innate universal grammar, along with a second set of acquisition processes to link up to it, and what functions this extra factor might serve.

SIX

Nominal and Clausal Constructions

Think of the tools in a tool-box: there is a hammer, pliers, a saw, a screw-driver, a rule, a glue-pot, glue, nails, and screws. The functions of words are as diverse as the functions of these objects ... Of course, what confuses us is the uniform appearance of words when we hear them spoken ... For their application is not presented to us so clearly.

—LUDWIG WITTGENSTEIN

ACROSS the languages of the world utterance-level constructions are constituted by two major types of sub-constructions: nominals and clauses.* Actually, in real discourse, nominals and clauses are often used alone as full utterances, which is one strong piece of evidence for their reality as functionally coherent and independent constructions. Thus, when someone is asked "Who is that over there?" a reasonable utterance in response is the nominal "Bill" or "My father," and when someone is asked further "What is he doing?" a reasonable utterance in response is the clause "Sleeping" or "Playing tennis." Of course many utterances are constituted by some combination of nominals and clauses: "My father is playing tennis."

Nominals are used by people to make reference to "things." In many theories, the prototype is concrete objects (people, places, and things). But it is well known that nominals may be used to refer to basically any kind of entity at all, real or imagined. Thus, when the need arises, there are ways of construing actions, properties, and relationships as if they were things, on analogy with concrete objects. For example, we may say such things as *Skiing promotes good health, That blue looks awful in my painting,* and *Bigger is better.* Indeed, there are some languages that do not really have a clear-cut class of concrete nouns specialized for the single func-

---

* The terminology here can be confusing because it differs among different theories and even schools within theories. To simplify, I will use the term *nominal* to refer indiscriminately to what are normally called nouns and noun phrases. I will use the term *clause* to refer indiscriminately to what are normally called clauses, verb phrases, and verbal complexes (specifying further in some cases where it is critical).

tion of reference, such as *dog* and *tree,* but rather they have a single class composed of words that can be used as either nouns or verbs depending on whether they are used in nominals or clauses—similar to English words such as *cut (I cut the bread, There's a cut on my finger)* and *hammer (I'm hammering in this nail with my hammer).* Langacker (1987b) notes that the discourse function of identifying the participants in events and states of affairs requires language users to construe whatever they wish to talk about as a "thing," so it can be referred to, no matter its "true" ontological status. And the major characteristic of a "thing" is that it is bounded, often spatially but sometimes only conceptually (as in *The disappointment lasted all night*) in a time-stable manner (Givón, 1979).

Clauses (verb phrases) are used for a variety of discourse purposes, sometimes referred to together (though somewhat misleadingly) as predication. Clauses are about events that unfold in time, or else states that remain the same over some discernible span of time. They are thus used for less time-stable entities than are nominals (Givón, 1979). In the analysis of Hopper and Thompson (1984, 1985) the structure of predication derives from the fact that in discourse human beings regularly and often report on events and states of affairs, or else request that some event or state of affairs be brought about. As in the case of nominals, a clausal construction can also force a construal, although it is sometimes difficult to construe a word normally used to refer to a thing as a process. But still, we can understand such utterances as *The newspaper boy porched the newspaper* or *The dog treed the cat.* Langacker (1987a) points out that one of the main functions of the copula, in languages that have it, is to be able to predicate using what are normally nouns and adjectives, as in *He is a man* or *He is pretty* (so-called predicate nominal or predicate adjective constructions).

To understand how nominals and clauses work in general, it is useful to return to the diagram introduced in Chapter 2, with a few twists (see Figure 6.1). In choosing a conventional linguistic expression to symbolize some referential event, a speaker makes contact in various ways with the joint attentional frame that she shares with her listener in the current usage event. Some of these types of contact are more listener based, as the speaker takes into account the listener's knowledge, expectations, and perspective in formulating her utterance. For example, she might choose a pronoun over a noun + determiner as a nominal construction to refer to an object that she and the speaker are currently focused on jointly. Also, in English, she must make some reference to the time of the referential event relative to now (the time of the usage event). Other types of contact with the joint attentional frame are more speaker based. For example, the speaker may make clear to the listener—either obligatorily or voluntarily for various reasons—her own goals and attitude with respect to the refer-

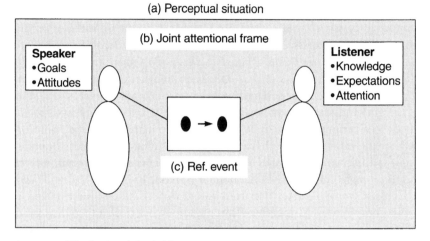

Figure 6.1. The basic adult-child communicative situation, as in Figure 2.1—but with some specifics of the speaker attitudes and listener perspective that determine how utterance is grounded in the joint attentional frame.

ential event. Thus, she may express that she wants the event to happen, that it might happen, that she heard it happened, that she's not sure if it is happening, that it did not happen, that it ought to happen, that she wishes it would happen, and so forth—which are normally expressed within the confines of the clause (verbal complex).

Because of all these functions, nominal and clausal constructions quite often, though not always, are composed of multiple morphemes and/or words. Although the specifics differ greatly in different languages, nominals often have as internal constituents various functors such as articles *(a, the)*, possessives *(his, my)*, quantifiers *(some, many)*, and classifiers such as gender markers. Many of these assist listeners in the process of determining the specific reference of a nominal, while others assist listeners in the process of tracking a referent across clauses in discourse.* Children learn and use nominals in their very earliest holophrastic language, but true skill with nominals comes very slowly because successfully identifying referents for different listeners in different discourse contexts requires sophisticated skills of perspective-taking (theory of mind). Although again with much cross-linguistic variability, clauses typically contain mor-

---

* Nominal morphology can do other things as well, of course, including especially marking case and agreement to indicate the nominal's relation to other constituents in the utterance. But these are utterance-level functions, discussed in Chapter 4; here we focus on nominal morphology whose main function is to "ground" the nominal in the joint attentional frame.

phemes or words indicating such things as tense, aspect, modality, negation, evidentiality, and social intimacy. And again, although children begin learning and using clauses relatively early in development, the mastery of complex clauses takes much time, as they are both cognitively complex, in the sense of containing many interrelated components, and pragmatically complex, in the sense of having complex relations to the current joint attentional frame. Perhaps of special difficulty are the functors in clauses that depend on later-developing cognitive and social-cognitive skills involving the understanding of temporal, causal, conditional, deontic, epistemic, and other kinds of complex physical and psychological relations.

Many functions within nominals and clauses occur repeatedly in the utterances of a given language, and so over historical time the symbols for these have become grammaticized into grammatical morphemes, often bound to a noun or verb. As documented in Chapter 4, grammatical morphemes serve as "local cues," and so children often find them easier to learn from a functional point of view than more distributed cues such as word order or agreement. But, paradoxically, grammatical morphology also presents special difficulties for language learners, as most clearly evidenced by the struggles of many second-language learners and children with specific language impairment. At least some of these difficulties arise from the facts that (1) grammatical morphemes are often not perceptually salient (unstressed and in linguistically embedded positions), and (2) grammatical morphemes are often plurifunctional—the same form is used for multiple functions, often confounded in single instances of use—requiring many comparisons across different utterances to isolate specific functions. For these and other reasons, grammatical morphology has recently become a focal point for comparing different theories of language acquisition, crystallizing a number of different issues concerning the degree to which children's linguistic competence may be acquired via a single set, versus two different sets, of learning and developmental mechanisms.

6.1. Reference and Nominals

Speakers do whatever they need to do in order to get listeners to share attention with them to some referent or referents. Their linguistic tools for doing this are the conventional nominal constructions of their language (sometimes in combination with deictic gestures such as pointing). But they must choose among these constructions in a particular usage event on the basis of the exigencies of the communicative situation at hand. Of most importance for this choice is the speaker's assessment of the knowledge and expectations of the listener at any given moment, an assessment based on their currently shared perceptual situation and on their previously shared experience, especially in the immediately preceding discourse context. In the terminology of Langacker (1991), speakers must "ground" their conventional act of reference in the current speech situation involving particular persons in a particular usage event. In the terminology of pragmatic theorists, speakers must assess the cognitive availability (accessibility, topicality, givenness) of the referent for the listener (Givón, 1993; Ariel, 1988; Gundel, Hedberg, and Zacharski, 1993).

Within the context of a general "availability hierarchy"—ranging from things the speaker assumes are in the listener's current focus of attention to completely novel referents—we may distinguish in children's language three main construction types for identifying referents for listeners: (1) deictic words (and gestures); (2) pronouns and proper names; and (3) noun phrases containing a common noun plus some determiner(s). Children use each of these devices in a rudimentary fashion in their earliest language, but adult-like mastery requires in all three cases extensive learning over several years.

6.1.1. Deictics

Even before they learn any language, young children are able to direct the attention of others to outside objects. They do this mainly gesturally, most often by pointing (see Chapter 2). From soon after their first birthdays, infants begin to carefully monitor the attentional status of the adult as they gesture, often making sure they secure her attention on themselves before gesturing and then checking back afterwards to make sure the adult has followed the pointing gesture successfully (Franco and Butterworth, 1996). There is no evidence in these early gestures, however, that infants are monitoring how much and what kind of information their listener needs. Thus, O'Neill (1996) found that it was not until after they were 2 years old that children pointed differently depending on whether their mother had or had not witnessed a hiding event (that is, that they took their mother's knowledge into account).

Obviously, pointing gestures may be used only when the referent (or its location) is perceptually available in the immediate nonlinguistic context. Linguistically, 1-year-olds often use demonstratives, such as the English *this* or *that,* in a similar manner (and demonstratives of one type or another seem to be universal in the world's languages; Diessel, 1999). However, at least from an adult point of view, these words also involve a perspectival component—relative distance from speaker. The word *this* is typically used for referents closer to the speaker, either physically or psychologically, whereas the word *that* is typically used for referents further away. It is highly unlikely that 1-year-olds systematically select either *this* or *that* depending on a referent's physical or psychological distance from the listener. In fact, a number of studies have found that young children struggle with this distinction until well into the preschool years. For example, in two well-known sets of comprehension experiments (Clark and Sengul, 1978; Tanz, 1980), an adult sat across a table from the child— with one toy closer to her and one toy closer to the child—and asked for "this" or "that" toy (without pointing). In general, children were not very skillful in taking the adult's point of view in this task until they were almost 4 years old (they were of course better when the adult sat beside them so that distance was the same for speaker and listener). Children were no better with either of the deictic pairs *here* and *there* and *come* and *go*.

In an experimental examination of 3-year-olds' production of *this* and *that*, Garton (1983) also found a general lack of discrimination on the basis of distance. However, she also observed that when children used the word *this* to indicate an object for an adult they most often picked up and handled the object, whereas when they used the word *that* they most often pointed to the object or offered it to the adult. Garton's interpretation is that 3-year-olds are just beginning to master a rudimentary contrastive system, beginning with themselves as central reference point. The perspectival component—the ability to comprehend these terms from the point of view of the speaker when it is different from that of the self— awaits further development after age 4.

One explanation for the late development of children's understanding of these basic demonstrative terms might be that young children most often experience adults using *this* and *that* along with a pointing gesture. Consequently, in learning *this* and *that* children might segment the adult's communicative intention inappropriately. That is, they might assume that *this* and *that* are used to indicate objects (indiscriminately) and that the distance component of the overall communicative intention is carried by the point. Support for this interpretation was provided by Tfouni and Klatzky (1983), who found, not surprisingly, that 3-year-olds were much better in an experimental task when the adult also pointed to the thing she wanted.

The other well-studied deictic pair is *I/me* and *you*. This pair is also perspectival, but in a very different way. Unlike the case of *this* and *that* in which the very same object may be indicated with either word depending on where the speaker is standing, with *I/me* and *you* the perspective shift is absolute—I am always I and you are always you—with the actual person indicated depending on who is speaking. This absoluteness should mean that *I/me* and *you* are easier to learn than *this* and *that* (although perhaps more difficult than "normal" words), and indeed they are. But it also means that when children make errors with these terms the errors are especially salient. Such mistakes are typically called pronoun reversal errors, as, for instance, when the child reaches up to a parent and requests "Pick you up" (meaning "Pick me up").

The first-person pronouns *I* and *me* are among the first words of many English-speaking (and other) children, and the second-person pronoun *you* is relatively early as well (Nelson, 1973; Fenson et al., 1994). Most children make few if any reversal errors with these terms. Reliable figures are not easily available, but an indirect estimate based on data reported by Dale and Crain-Thoreson (1993) would be 20 percent of the population. Another important fact from this same source is that children who do make pronoun reversal errors do so only about 20 percent of the time, although some children pass through periods in which they reverse very consistently (Oshima-Takane, 1992). By far the most frequent error is substituting *you* for *I/me* (as in asking the adult to "Pick you up"), which occurs about four times more often than substituting *I/me* for *you* (Dale and Crain-Thoreson, 1993).

It is unlikely that young children are confused about who is who cognitively; after all, in most cases they use proper names for the same people quite accurately. More likely is the hypothesis that they are confused about how these special words work; what we may call pragmatic confusion. The confusion may result either from children's immature social-cognitive skills (poor skills of perspective-taking) or from the unique pattern of adult-child discourse associated with these terms. Evidence for the role of perspective-taking comes from a study by Loveland (1984), who measured 2-year-olds' ability to take the perspective of others in a series of social games (such as turning a picture around so that others could see it) as well as their ability to use first- and second-person pronouns accurately. She found an almost perfect correlation between the two skills, and corroborated this relationship in a follow-up longitudinal study. With respect to discourse, Oshima-Takane (1988, 1999) hypothesized that first- and second-person personal pronouns should present less confusion to children who have siblings because these children are able to experience adult-child discourse from an outsider's perspective (for example, they can see parents referring to the sibling as *you*, as well as the sibling calling the parent *you*), as a complement to their own direct discourse with adults. In a series of naturalistic studies, experimental studies, and computational models, Oshima-Takane (see 1999, for a review) has amassed very strong evidence that additional (outside) perspectives on the operation of first- and second-person pronouns—for example, by observing sibling-adult discourse—significantly facilitates the acquisition of these terms. Oshima-Takane and Benaroya (1989) presented evidence that autistic children, who are reported to make pronoun reversal errors especially often, attend less well to the speech of others when they themselves are outside the discourse.

A second important factor may be a child's tendency toward imitation, or more accurately, mimicry. If children simply mimic what adults say to them (such as "Shall I pick you up?"), then they will make some pronoun reversal errors. The simplest version of this hypothesis, however, is obviously not true. In a case study, Oshima-Takane (1992) found that relatively few of the child's reversal errors were immediate repetitions of something the adult had just said. In addition, Dale and Crain-Thoreson (1993) found no overall difference in the tendency of reversing and non-reversing children (in all of their discourse with adults) to engage in immediate repetitions. However, if imitation is conceived more broadly, it turns out that many reversal errors result from the child reproducing an unanalyzed chunk of adult speech (perhaps heard days before). This pattern was reported by Loveland (1984) and Dale and Crain-Thoreson (1993), who found that 52 percent of the reversal errors in their sample were either immediate repetitions of the adult or the production of unanalyzed chunks. One interesting hypothesis arising from this analysis is that the relatively high proportion of autistic children who make pronoun reversal errors may result from the combination of a relatively strong tendency to mimic and poor perspective-taking skills—both well-known characteristics of these children (see Sigman and Capps, 1997, for a review).

One important and robust fact that is not easily explained by either pragmatic confusion or imitation is that children who do make pronoun reversal errors do so only some of the time. But it is possible that imitation is frequency dependent. Thus, continued hearing of the word *you* to refer to the child herself entrenches that reference and interferes with her other knowledge about how this word is used. (This might also explain why children use *you* inappropriately more often than *I* or *me*, since *you* is much more frequent in speech to children than *I* or *me*; Lieven, Pine, and Baldwin, 1997). At least some support for this hypothesis is provided by Dale and Crain-Thoreson (1993) who found that children made twice as many reversal errors when the utterance they were attempting to produce was especially complex. They hypothesized that when children's production capabilities are strained they often resort to imitating chunks of adult speech, or perhaps make other sorts of performance errors such as repeating as a referential term the one they have heard most often in the past. It is also relevant that these researchers found, surprisingly, an overall higher percentage of children making pronoun errors in a sample of precocious language learners than would be expected in a more typical sample. They hypothesized that these might be "risk-taking" children who attempt to produce sentences that stretch their production capabilities more often than other children. Alternatively, these younger children might be more cognitively immature (for example, in perspective-taking) than children who learn these words on a more normal timetable.

The acquisition and use of deictic nominals thus shows an interesting interaction between the role of children's social-cognitive development and the nature of the input available to them. Children cannot understand words requiring a deictic shift until they have learned, in some rudimentary way, to take the perspective of other people (Loveland, 1993). But then, the range of uses they experience makes it either easier or harder for them to begin zeroing in on more adult-like usage. For example, some difficulties with learning first- and second-person pronouns are at least partially alleviated if children experience additional discourse from an external perspective (Oshima-Takane, 1999). The demonstratives *this* and *that,* in contrast, present the problem that it is never quite clear which part of the communicative intention is being conveyed by these words per se and which part is being played by the gestures that almost invariably accompany them. It thus takes many years to segment accurately adults' communicative intentions when using these terms. The specifics of how children do this have yet to be spelled out.

6.1.2. Pronouns and Proper Names

Among children's earliest words are quite often names for parents, siblings, pets, or friends (Nelson, 1973). A relatively simple referential strategy for young children, therefore, is simply to use a proper name. In adult usage, proper names are used when speaker and listener are both familiar with an individual (including specific people, pets, and places) and know that they share such familiarity. Of course 1-year-olds very likely are not actively making such assessments of common knowledge but rather simply using proper names for individuals whose name they know, regardless of listener.

How children learn proper names is not as straightforward as it might seem, since proper names are used to indicate single individuals, whereas other referential terms (without determiners) typically indicate only categories. Hall and colleagues (summarized in Hall, 1999) have found that preschoolers use a variety of cues to determine when a novel word is a proper name rather than a common noun. Most importantly, preschool children expect a proper name to refer to only one individual, and so if they hear a novel word used without a determiner for single individuals they will assume it is a proper name. And by this relatively late age they also expect that certain kinds of things can receive proper names (such as people and animals) but not others (such as inanimate objects). In the analysis of Katz, Baker, and McNamara (1974), for animate entities young children first learn to individuate specific individuals (with proper names) whereas for inanimate entities they first learn to individuate categories of individuals (with common nouns). The limitation of this research from an acquisition point of view, however, is that it deals with older children who already know something about proper names; they are simply tested to see how they deal with a newly introduced one. There is only one study of how young children at the very earliest stages of language acquisition, when they are learning their first proper names and common nouns, comprehend differences in the way these two kinds of nominals work referentially. Birch and Bloom (2002) found that 2- to 4-year-olds correctly identified a person whom an experimenter called Jessie as the one they had seen her interact with—as opposed to one she had not interacted with previously.

Pronouns are, with respect to referential range, the opposite of proper names. Pronouns are used to refer not to one individual but to a wide array of entities, even unknown entities. What distinguishes the entities that are picked out by a pronoun is not anything about them as entities, but only their "givenness" in the current perceptual and discourse context. Indeed, Gundel, Hedberg, and Zacharski (1993) argue that pronouns are used for the most available (or given) referents in the discourse context, that is to say, the potential referents that the speaker believes are most available for the listener. In this account, stressed pronouns are used for referents that the speaker believes are already activated for the listener ("in current awareness"), and unstressed pronouns are used for referents that are not only activated but also in focus ("at the current center of attention"). The stronger of these two criteria ("current center of attention") is the same one these theorists use to justify null reference (for example, when someone responds to the question "What is your sister doing?" with the utterance "Swimming"). Pragmatic assessments of this type obviously require some skills of social cognition on the part of the speaker as she assesses the specific knowledge states of a specific listener on a specific occasion—which might seem to be problematic for children before the age of 4 or 5, who are notoriously poor at assessing the knowledge states of other persons.

Virtually no acquisition studies have investigated the communicative conditions in which young children choose to use a pronoun as opposed to a noun or some other referring expression. Given our almost total ignorance, at least five hypotheses are possible. One is that young children simply use the same referring expression as the adult with whom they are conversing in the immediate situation; if the adult refers to an object by name the child will also, whereas if the adult uses a pronoun the child will use a pronoun. A second possibility is that young children follow the principle of mutual exclusivity, and so they use an object's name if they know it, but use a pronoun if they do not know the name. A third possibility is that children find the lexical retrieval of pronouns easier than that of nouns (since one can simply retrieve the same pronoun for many different entities), and so they use pronouns whenever production of a noun is especially difficult (as when the noun is a very long word; see Gerken, 1991; Levinsky and Gerken, 1995, for a related hypothesis). The fourth and fifth possibilities involve children taking account of the knowledge states of the listener before choosing a referring expression—either on the basis of the perceptual situation (for example, the listener is looking at the referent) or on the basis of discourse factors (for example, the listener just heard the referent mentioned).

Campbell, Brooks and Tomasello (2000) attempted to test each of these five hypotheses experimentally with 2½- and 3½-year-old children. They found that the children did *not* use pronouns differentially (1) when the adult modeled either a pronoun or a noun for the target object, (2) when the adult either did or did not witness a target event, or (3) when they needed to use unfamiliar and difficult nouns as opposed to familiar and easy ones. The finding was that the children used pronouns differently mainly depending on the immediately preceding discourse of the experimenter, in particular whether they had been asked a specific question such as "What did X do?" (eliciting "He . . ." or a null reference) or a general question such as "What happened?" (eliciting "The boy. . . ."). This was the only effective factor observed in the study. Wittek and Tomasello (submitted-b) replicated and extended these results by finding that 2- and 3-year-old children did not use pronouns and nouns differentially depending on whether the referential object was (1) alone and in view, (2) on a shelf in view along with other objects (so that pointing and pronouns were not effective in singling out the target object), or (3) out of view (another situation in which pointing and pronouns should not be effective). Again, however, they found that the immediately preceding discourse had a strong effect on children's choice of nouns, pronouns, or null reference. These findings thus suggest that young children's referential choices rely much more heavily on the just-previous utterances of interlocutors—presumably as evidence of the current knowledge states of these others—than on what those interlocutors have or have not just experienced perceptually.

An interesting additional finding that reveals something about slightly older children's understanding of pronouns and how they work is reported by Tomasello, Anselmi, and Farrar (1984/85). In this study, an adult requested clarification of a randomly selected set of 2- to 4-year-olds' referential expressions in an otherwise normal discourse interaction. The finding was that when the children attempted to clarify their referential expression using a pronoun, they supplemented their utterance with a gesture more often than when they attempted to clarify their referential expression using a noun. This difference presumably indicates preschool children's understanding that pronouns cannot accomplish an effective act of reference without some supplemental indication of the intended referent (such as a gesture) in situations in which shared knowledge by speaker and listener cannot be assumed. It should be noted that the major cue available to children in this study was adult discourse indicating that the child's original attempt at reference was unsatisfactory.

Finally, there is a literature investigating young children's understanding of the so-called binding principles. The basic issue in this literature is the conditions under which young children understand that two nominals in the same utterance are being used to refer to the same entity in the world. The ways languages do this turn out to be fairly complex and interact in interesting ways with the constituent structure of utterances. It thus happens that, in English, in the utterance *Beside him, Bill saw a snake* the initial *him* can be either Bill or someone else. But in the utterance *He wanted to drive Bill's car* the initial *he* cannot be Bill. Most of the research on these issues is conducted in the generative grammar paradigm, and the basic finding is that children master these subtle principles of co-reference only very slowly, with some aspects taking well into the school years (see O'Grady, 1997, for a review). Although no developmental research has been done on issues of co-reference from a cognitive-functional (usage-based) point of view, the theoretical account of van Hoek (1997, 2002), focusing on so-called conceptual reference points, would provide an interesting starting point for such an investigation.

6.1.3. Nouns and Determiners

The other major referential strategy of young children is the use of a full noun phrase containing some kind of common noun and some kind of determiner(s). Unlike pronouns and proper names, full noun phrases do not assume—at least not to the same degree—shared knowledge between speaker and listener. In addition, they employ a more analytic technique of reference than either of these other two types of nominals, typically (though not always) using multiple words to indicate the intended referent. Thus, prototypical noun phrases comprise two separately indicated sub-functions: a common noun (*boy, yard, party*) is used to indicate a category of things, and a determiner (*a, the, my*) is used to help the listener to specify an individual member of that category.

The prototypical common noun is a count noun such as *dog, tree,* or *man.* These words only specify a category of individuals and require some further specifications to pick out an individual member of the category—*the dog, my dog, a big dog, that dog, the dog that bit me.* In English there are some kinds of nouns that are not used with determiners in this same way, however. These are mass nouns such as *rice, wax,* and *hair.* While these can be used with some determiners in some circumstances, they most often are not, or else they are used with a special determiner such as *some* (and not normally with plurals). In the analysis of Langacker (1987b; see also Wierzbicka, 1985), the main issue is whether the entity being indicated by the noun is undifferentiated internally. He illustrates this point by using a count noun as if it were a mass noun in a special context, for example, *The termite is having desk for breakfast.* Here, *desk* is being construed not as an individual entity with four legs and a flat writing surface, but as a homogeneous substance. Although there are many more subtleties and complexities to this distinction, the important point for current purposes is simply that young children begin to distinguish reliably between count and mass nouns—and their prototypical uses with or without determiners—at some point during their third year of life (McPherson, 1991). Relatedly, during this same age range, young children begin to understand and make generic references to whole classes of entities, rather than individuals, using common nouns (typically as plurals), as in *Tigers are mean, Skateboards are fun, Birds make nests* (Pappas and Gelman, 1998).

Of special interest here is children's early understanding and use of common nouns and determiners in a single act of reference. Children produce such noun phrases in their very earliest multi-word speech, sometimes as whole utterances (saying "A clown" when asked "What is that?" or "My blanket" when asked "What do you want?"). The determiners used in these early utterances fall mainly into three categories. The first is demonstratives, as in *this ball* or *that cookie.* As noted in Section 6.1.1, these are often used deictically with pointing, but their perspectival aspect (distance from speaker) is not mastered for several years. The second category is possessives, as in *my shoes* or *Maria's bike.* These are also used quite early in language development, and they are of special importance because they seem to be used quite accurately from the beginning (see, e.g., Tomasello, 1998c). This early mastery of possessive noun phrases means that all the trouble children have with other kinds of noun phrases, involving such things as demonstratives and definite and indefinite articles (see below), are not due to general difficulties with forming a phrase consisting of a common noun plus a determiner. Their difficulties must come from somewhere else, presumably the additional perspectival and/or pragmatic dimensions that must be mastered for appropriate use of these other types of determiners in noun phrases.

The determiners that have been studied most extensively in English acquisition are the definite and indefinite articles, *the* and *a*. Appropriate use of these is notoriously difficult for second-language learners of English, especially for those coming from languages that do not have articles at all (Japanese, Russian). Although textbook accounts quite often present these words as contrasting alternatives, the fact is that each of them has a wide range of uses, some of which are quite unrelated to one another. Indeed, the historical situation is that across many languages the definite determiner derives from a demonstrative—a mainly deictic function—whereas the indefinite determiner derives from the number word for *one*, a very different function. In English, the definite determiner was grammaticized from a demonstrative many generations before the indefinite determiner was grammaticized from the number word for *one* (Trask, 1996).

Naturalistic observation of English-speaking children's use of the definite and indefinite articles supports this initial separation of functions. Children's first uses of these words, at around their second birthdays, is mostly bound up with the larger item-based constructions in which they occur. In these constructions, they occur almost always immediately after either a verb or a preposition. Thus, Pine and Lieven (1997) found that 56 percent of children's earliest utterances containing articles (before age 2;6) derived from one of three constructional frames. These were different for different children, but they mostly came from the following sets:

- *Definites:* Where's the X, In/on the X, There's the X
- *Indefinites:* That's a X, A X, Get a X, Want a X

Interestingly, concerning the nouns involved, Pine and Martindale (1996) found that only about 10 percent of children's nouns that occurred with articles at age 2;1 occurred with both articles; the figure was more like 20 percent at age 2;6, with the majority of children at both ages having exactly zero nouns with which they used both articles. (By comparison, in the mothers' speech to these children, the percentages were two to three times greater.) These findings provide general support for the idea that children's early uses of the definite and indefinite articles are not closely related (Karmiloff-Smith, 1979), and thus that these two words do not form a contrastive pair from within the same grammatical category (contra Valian, 1991).

But there are some contexts in which the definite and indefinite articles may be used contrastively, and it is these that have been the focus of most developmental research. Children have to overcome two main difficulties to use English articles appropriately. The first difficulty is that these words encode two different, but highly correlated, dimensions of the referential situation: specificity and givenness. On the one hand, the definite article *the* serves to pick out a specific entity, as in *I want the cookie* (that's in your hand), whereas the indefinite article *a* serves to pick out a non-specific entity, as in *I want a cookie* (any cookie). On the other hand, the definite article *the* is used when the speaker can assume that the referent is to some degree given (or available) for the listener, as in *I have the kite* (the one we just talked about), whereas the indefinite article *a* is used to introduce a new referent into the discourse situation even if that entity is definite, as in *I have a kite* (you'll find it upstairs). These two aspects—specificity and givenness—most often occur in a totally confounded manner, and indeed it is only in somewhat special uses that they are unconfounded. As we shall see, young children understand quite early in development that the definite article indicates a specific referent whereas the indefinite article indicates a non-specific referent. But they do not master the subtleties of the use of articles depending on current listener knowledge and attention—givenness, the perspectival component—until much later. Indeed, it may be that mastery of the specificity function gets in the way of children's discovery of the later-acquired perspectival function.

The second difficulty is that this second dimension of article use—taking into account listener perspective (givenness)—requires sophisticated social-cognitive skills. Much research in developmental psychology has demonstrated that the requisite perspective-taking skills are not well developed until 4 years of age (see Flavell, 1997, for a review). Unlike the case of the personal pronouns *I-you*, there are no studies that specifically correlate children's perspective-taking skills and their skills with definite and indefinite articles. But there is much relevant research to help sort out what children know about these words at what ages.

First, Brown's (1973) naturalistic observations have documented that by 3 years of age English-speaking children use the definite and indefinite articles quite flexibly and appropriately with respect to the specificity of the referent intended. However, Brown also notes that this spontaneous usage provides little evidence one way or the other for children's skills with the perspectival component, especially in the most demanding case in which the intended referent is known by the speaker but unknown to the listener (that is, where givenness is different for speaker and listener). This especially difficult case has been the target of a number of experimental investigations, and not surprisingly the general finding is that when young children have a referent they wish to introduce to someone for whom it is totally new in the discourse context, they tend to overuse the definite article (the egocentric error). For example, with no introductory comments whatsoever they might tell a friend "Tomorrow we'll buy the toy."

The first systematic investigation of English-speaking children's use of articles was reported by Maratsos (1976). Maratsos gave both comprehension and production tasks of various kinds to 3- and 4-year-olds. For example, in a storytelling task the child was introduced to a story about "a car and a boat" or about "some cars and boats." At the end of the story the adult asked the child about one car or boat. For stories containing only a single exemplar, the child should have used the definite article *the*, whereas for stories containing multiple exemplars, the child should have used the indefinite article *a*. Children were also given imitation tasks, which essentially consisted of stories with missing articles that the child was expected to fill in, and comprehension tasks, in which the child had to act either on "the X" or on "a X." Generalizing across these and other tasks, Maratsos concluded that whereas 3-year-olds did understand the contrast between definite and indefinite articles with respect to specificity (for example, they could use indefinite articles appropriately for referring to generic referents or to some unspecified member of a class), it was not until age 4;6 that they understood the contrast between definite and indefinite articles with respect to differences in the listener knowledge presupposed (givenness, perspective). Although she focused on a much wider variety of communicative functions and tested children across a much wider age range, Karmiloff-Smith's (1979) findings from a series of studies on French-speaking children's use of definite and indefinite articles are in general accord with these findings.

Emslie and Stevenson (1981) modified Maratsos's procedure somewhat to see if this would help 3- and 4-year-olds use articles in a manner sensitive to the perspective (knowledge and attention) of the listener. Most importantly, they had children tell a story from a set of pictures to another child sitting on the other side of a partition. In line with Maratsos they found that 3-year-olds used the articles consistently and appropriately with regard to specificity. With regard to perspective, the key task was one in which children were asked to narrate a story from a series of pictures to another child, and in the middle of the series a picture of a completely new and irrelevant object or person appeared—definitely requiring an indefinite article for its introduction ("And then a snake appeared in the grass . . ."). They found that only the 4-year-olds consistently used the indefinite article to introduce the novel referent for their unsuspecting listener. In the same vein, Garton (1983) found that in a similar experimental task children before their fourth birthdays did not use the definite and indefinite articles differentially for adults either wearing or not wearing a blindfold.

Interestingly for the question of children's understanding of givenness or perspective, Emslie and Stevenson (1981) noted that when children mentioned a referent in the same story for a second time, they tended to use,

212 Constructing a Language

appropriately, the definite article. However, this behavior is not diagnostic because the referent being mentioned for a second time is now given for both the child and her listener. Power and Dal Martello (1986) therefore had Italian-speaking 4- and 5-year-olds narrate the same story twice, each time for a different listener. But children again used more definite articles the second time they told the story, even though the listener was completely new to the story—again making the egocentric error.

The findings of the naturalistic and experimental studies are thus quite consistent and paint the following picture. Young children initially use articles in complementary (almost non-overlapping) distribution. They master the differential use of definite and indefinite articles with respect to referent specificity by 3 years of age, if not earlier, but they do not master the differential use of these words with respect to presupposed listener knowledge (givenness, perspective) until 4 years of age, if not later. This general ontogenetic pattern accords well both with other findings concerning children's acquisition of nominals—such as demonstratives and pronouns—and with the general pattern of their social-cognitive development in terms of perspective-taking skills.

A cautionary note, however, comes from a study by Thomas (1989). He found that adults acquiring English as a second language, especially those whose first language has no articles, show the same pattern of acquisition as young children. In particular, they master the specificity function first and continue to struggle with the perspectival function for some time, as evidenced by their continued making of the egocentric error (overuse of the definite article when the referent is new for the listener). This finding suggests that the real problem is not necessarily perspective-taking as a general cognitive skill that develops over early childhood, but rather the learning problems created by plurifunctionality, specifically, the fact that the use of English definite and indefinite articles contrasts on two dimensions simultaneously. For both young children and second-language learners the specificity function is for some reason more salient than the givenness function (see Cziko, 1986)—perhaps because of the general difficulty, for both children and adults, of taking another person's perspective. We may therefore say that in the case of both demonstrative and articles, a reasonable hypothesis is that learners' difficulties are a joint function of the social-cognitive difficulties they have with perspective taking and the learning difficulties presented by plurifunctional lexical items.

One final interesting finding is reported by Garton (1983; citing unpublished data). She found that children's use of definite and indefinite articles is strongly influenced by the particular question the adult asks the child at the critical moment in the task. For example, she reports a strong tendency for children to answer a question of the form *What did the truck knock over?* with a definite reference of the form *The horse,* even if there are multiple identical horses on the table. This result is reminiscent of the finding of Campbell, Brooks, and Tomasello (2000) that the most important factor in children's choice of a referential expression—focusing on the choice of noun, pronoun, or null—is the type of question asked. Thus, a key variable in the experimental studies of children's use of articles may be the nature of the presuppositions about the questioner's knowledge embodied in the question. The potential influence of this variable is not reported in a systematic fashion in all studies, and it may explain some of the discrepant findings in the literature, such as those of Warden (1976), who finds much older ages for English-speaking children's mastery of definite and indefinite articles.

6.2. Predication and Clauses

The *raison d'être* of many utterances is something "new" that the speaker wishes to point out to the listener. This new information is prototypically contained in a clause (verb phrase). A clause typically comprises symbolic elements indicating one or more participants in a scene (typically by some nominal construction) and some event or state of affairs in which these participate (typically in some verbal construction). All languages have both clauses containing one participant, intransitives, and clauses containing two participants, transitives (and often transitivizing or detransitivizing morphology that makes a verb into one or the other; see Hopper and Thompson, 1980, for the classic account). Interacting with transitivity to determine basic clause types is the meaning of the verb in terms of its inherent aspect (aktionsart). The most fundamental distinctions are among: (1) change of state verbs, which are used to indicate events directed toward some goal or end state (*break, die*); (2) activity verbs, which are used to indicate internally homogeneous events with no such directedness (*run, smile*); and (3) stative verbs, which indicate relatively enduring states (*be, have*).

An integral part of clauses as well is their grounding in the current speech event. Just as nominals are grounded in space, in the sense that they help the listener to "locate" the intended referent, clauses are grounded in time to help the listener identify which particular event is being indicated (Langacker, 1991). This is typically done in two ways that work together. The internal temporal contour of a clause is designated by some marking of its grammatical aspect (for example, progressive aspect marks ongoingness, as in *X is smiling*), while the external placement of the event along a time line, grounded in the speech moment, is designated by some marker of its tense (such as past tense) (Comrie, 1976). These work together in narrative discourse to enable such temporal juggling as *While I was Xing, she Yed*. In addition, and importantly, many clauses contain some indication of the speaker's attitude toward the event or state of affairs. For example, in English people frequently mark their attitude through the use of modal auxiliaries such as *may, can, can't, won't, should, might, must, could,* and *would*—and other languages mark such things as how the speaker came to know what she is saying, so-called evidentiality. All of this works together—with some grammatical morphemes in some languages being plurifunctional in the extreme—in what is called tense-aspect-modality (TAM) marking. TAM marking may be done either with freestanding words or with grammatical morphology, depending on exactly which of these things in a given language has been grammaticized, and to what degree.

6.2.1. Early Verbs and Argument Structure

English-speaking children learn their first verbs—typically in the months preceding their second birthdays—for changes of state, for activities, and for states, with no discernible developmental advantage for any of these. The prototypical situation in the case of change of state verbs is a transformation defined in terms of relatively abstract relational elements. Thus, early-acquired verbs such as *get, find, stop, break, open,* and *fall-down* indicate a class of conceptual situations whose only commonality is some pattern of spatial-temporal-causal relations (for example, "break" may occur for any object, in any of a variety of ways, involving different specific activities). The prototypical situation for activity verbs, in contrast, involves concrete and perceptible types of sensory-motor action. Thus, early acquired verbs such as *run, smile, jump, lick, draw, see,* and *catch* are not defined by abstract spatial-temporal-causal relations, but rather by the characteristic actions involved, defined in terms of specific objects and body parts moving in specific ways (sometimes involving specific objects). The prototypical situation for state verbs is something being in a state for some discernible length of time, often indicated in English in predicate adjective constructions such as *She's happy/nice/little/red*.

A number of hypotheses have been proposed about possible cognitive factors that might make some verbs more developmentally basic than others. First, Huttenlocher, Smiley, and Charney (1983) hypothesized that (1) words for movement and change (such as *off, out*) are acquired before words for intentional action (*get, push*); and (2) these later-acquired words for intentional action are used first for self actions and only later for the actions of others (see also Huttenlocher, Smiley, and Ratner, 1983; Smiley and Huttenlocher, 1995). These hypotheses are based on the idea that young children find it difficult to conceive of intentional action, especially that of others. However, in a diary study, Tomasello (1992a) found only mixed support for these hypotheses. In this study the child's earliest verbs were indeed words for movement and change (*more, gone,* and so on), but within the same early time frame she also learned intentional verbs such as *move, get, stay, push, stuck, catch, try, play, pee-pee, bite, hurt, cut,* and *draw.* She used many of these to comment on or request the actions of others; for example, she said that someone was "Crying" or that someone "Fall-down" or that someone needed to "Move" or "Get-it" for her (see Edwards and Goodwin, 1986, for similar findings).

Another obvious candidate for cognitive complexity is the number of participants involved in an event. Testing this hypothesis in the same diary study, Tomasello (1992a) found that the child's earliest verbs were about single entities acting or undergoing changes of state or being acted upon by the child herself. (The latter case refers to utterances of the type *Kick ball,* as the child kicked it herself—the proposal being that for these utterances the self is egocentrically presupposed and not a part of the underlying conceptualization.) Relating this to Huttenlocher's hypotheses, we may acknowledge that movement words are typically learned first, but this is only because they typically involve a single object. Contra Huttenlocher, intention words may be learned just as early if they involve a single participant or the self acting on a single object. Words for an external agent's intentional action on another object/person are learned later only because they involve two cognitively represented participants.

Bloom, Lightbown, and Hood (1975) proposed another hypothesis about the cognitive bases of early verbs: words are learned for dynamic events before static states. They presented evidence for this proposal from four children sampled periodically. Tomasello (1992a) provided further support with continuous diary data, most clearly for verbs within the same semantic domain (and especially for change of state verbs, since activity verbs do not normally have stative counterparts). For example, this child began very early with the global expression *move* as a request for object movement and only later learned *stuck* and *stay* for the absence of object movement. Similarly, she learned the dynamic possession verb *get* before the static possession verb *have.*

Putting these facts together, it would seem that young English-speaking children learn verbs first for dynamic events that involve only a single participant. The event may be either intentional or not, may be construed as either a change of state or an activity, and may involve either the child or another person. Around the second birthday children begin to learn more verbs that may be used to indicate static states of affairs and events involving two explicitly conceptualized participants.

A closely related issue is the nature of the nominals used as arguments of verbs in children's early utterances. DuBois (1987, in press) has demonstrated that adults in a number of languages show a very consistent pattern, what he calls preferred argument structure. The basic idea is that new information, expressed in lexical noun phrases, is typically introduced in either intransitive utterances (often in specialized presentational or existential constructions such as *There's this X . . .*) or else as the object of transitive utterances. It is very rare for the subject of a transitive utterance to carry new information expressed in a lexical noun phrase (see also Chafe, 1994, on the light subject constraint). Note that this means, typically, that there is only one lexical noun phrase per clause.

Clancy (1995, 2000) documented that 2-year-old children learning Korean follow this same pattern. In particular, she found that whereas the subjects of transitives were very rarely lexical noun phrases (13 percent), the subjects of intransitives and the objects of transitives were much more often lexical noun phrases (over 33 percent). The most common way in which new referents were introduced was in existential (intransitive) constructions, and thereafter the same referent was referred to either with a pronoun or with a zero (null reference). The prototypical transitive utterance had either the speaker or the listener as subject, normally with a first- or second-person pronoun, acting on an inanimate entity. Clancy argues that these transitive utterances are thus in a fundamental way iconic with the experience of the speaker and the listener, who remain constant in the situation but with changing objects and events across time. Allen and Schröder (2000) have confirmed this general pattern of preferred argument structure in the speech of 2-year-olds speaking Inuktitut, a highly polysynthetic language in which arguments are explicitly realized much less often overall.

Finally, it has been often noted that children speaking English and other languages quite often do not overtly express subjects in their early utterances. A number of explanations have been proposed. For example, some investigators have claimed that transitive utterances place inordinate processing demands on young children, especially at the beginning of utterances, and so they simply drop the subject (e.g., L. Bloom, 1970; Valian, 1991; P. Bloom, 1990). A related explanation is that subjects tend to appear in utterance positions that are prosodically and metrically weak, and so they get passed over in production (Gerken, 1990). It is also possible that it matters how often a child hears a particular verb with or without a subject. For example, in English children hear some verbs most often as imperatives (without a subject) and they use those same verbs in other constructions without subjects (for example, *put, make*—quite often with self as actor); this account has never been tested, but some suggestive evidence is provided in the study of Tomasello (1992a).

The major alternatives to these processing and input explanations are pragmatic accounts, closely related to the notion of preferred argument structure. Thus, Greenfield and Smith (1976) argued and presented evidence that from the beginning of language acquisition children overtly express only the most informative elements of an utterance and subjects are typically given information. More recently, in their work on preferred argument structure, both Allen and Schröder (2000) and Clancy (1993, 2000) have shown that pragmatic factors—essentially the degree to which the subject is given in the immediate perceptual and/or discourse situation—predict very well (although not 100 percent) when subjects will be left out. Allen (in press) emphasizes factors such as whether the referent is new to the discourse context, whether it is physically present, whether there are competing potential referents in the context, whether the referent is one of the speech participants or a third person or object, and whether the referent is an object of joint attention at the moment of the utterance.

None of these accounts has proven totally adequate to the task of predicting when children will and will not overtly express subjects in their utterances. But there is no reason to believe that null subjects result from only one factor. It seems likely that they result from the confluence of a number of factors on a given occasion of use. An important line of investigation to help solve this mystery, therefore, might focus on why children sometimes do not overtly express other kinds of arguments in their utterances. In one such investigation focused on the verb *eat* (with which the thing eaten is often not mentioned, as in *I already ate*), Rispoli (1992) found that the most important factors were discourse-pragmatic factors involving the grounding of the current utterance in the ongoing joint attentional frame.

6.2.2. Tense and Aspect

To ground their clauses in the current joint attentional frame, speakers must locate the symbolized state or event in time. Weist (1986), building on Smith (1980), proposes four stages in children's ability to linguistically indicate the temporal ordering of events using tense marking in an adult-like manner:

• *Age 1;6*: talk about events in the here and now only.
• *Age 1;6 to 3;0*: talk about the past and future.

- *Age 3;0 to 4;6*: begin to talk about past and future relative to a reference time other than now (typically indexed with adverbs such as *when*).
- *Age 4;6 and older*: talk about past and future relative to a reference time other than now using adult-like tensing system (typically verb morphology).

The problem with this neat account is that the linguistic indication of tense interacts in complex ways with the linguistic indication of aspect, and it does this differently in different languages. Aspect comes in two forms, both of which concern the way the temporal unfolding of the event is construed. In lexical aspect (or situational aspect), which concerns the meanings of verbs in clauses, the main distinction is between change of state and activity verbs (roughly, telic and atelic). Change of state verbs-in-clauses are used to refer to an event bounded by an endpoint (such as *swim the English Channel*), whereas activity verbs-in-clauses are used to refer to an event not so bounded *(swim around)*. In grammatical aspect (or viewpoint aspect), which concerns how one construes an event (be it telic or atelic), the most basic distinction is whether the event is viewed from the outside, as a completed whole (perfective), or from the inside as potentially incomplete (imperfective; Comrie, 1976). In English, this manifests itself in the difference between *He swam* (simple past; perfective), in which the activity is complete, and *He was swimming* (past progressive; imperfective), in which the activity is in process and incomplete at some reference time.

ASPECT AND PAST TENSE

The best-known hypothesis about children's ability to indicate temporal relations in their early language is the Aspect Before Tense hypothesis. Beginning with Antinucci and Miller (1976), Bronckardt and Sinclair (1973), and Bloom, Lifter, and Hafitz (1980)—studying Italian, French, and English, respectively—many researchers have noted that children tend to use past tense most often with change of state (telic) verbs and present tense (or present progressive) most often with activity (atelic) verbs. In the strongest version of the Aspect Before Tense hypothesis, Antinucci and Miller hypothesized that until about age 2;6 children use past tense only for changes of state in which the end state is still perceptually present, and indeed children at this age think that the past-tense marker actually indicates that an event is bounded (telic) and completed (perfective), rather than one that occurred in the past (independent of its telicity and perfectiveness). Thus, the first past-tense verbs are prototypically things like *dropped, spilled,* and *broke* in which all of these things are confounded.

Antinucci and Miller attributed this pattern of use to children's immature conception of time, and Bronckardt and Sinclair elaborated this view in a Piagetian framework. However, this strictly cognitive explanation is no longer held by anyone. This is because, first of all, even before their second birthdays many children do on some occasions clearly refer to past situations with activity verbs that have no current perceptual manifestations (Gerhardt, 1988; see Behrens, 2001a, for a review). Second, in a number of comprehension experiments in which children must choose the picture that best depicts a present-tense, past-tense, or future-tense utterance regardless of aspect, they perform well from a relatively early age (e.g., see Weist et al., 1984, 1997, for Polish-speaking children, and McShane and Whittaker, 1988, and Wagner, 2001, for English-speaking children). And third, a number of studies have shown that children and adults learning a second language use tense-aspect marking in the same biased way as young children, and they presumably are not cognitively immature (see below).

Nevertheless, it is a fact that in basically all languages that have been studied children much prefer to use the past tense for events construed as telic and perfective, such as *broke* and *made,* and they much prefer to use present tense (or progressive) for events construed as atelic and imperfective, such as *playing* and *riding.* Thus, it is relatively rare to hear a 1-year-old or a young 2-year-old saying things like *breaking* or *making, played* or *rode.* The languages for which this has been documented include English, Italian, French, Polish, Portuguese, German, Japanese, Mandarin Chinese, Hebrew, and Turkish (see Li and Shirai, 2000, for a review). Quantitatively, in a diary study Clark (1996) found that between the ages of 1;7 and 3;0 her son used the progressive *-ing* with activity verbs about 90 percent of the time and used the past tense *-ed* with the accomplishment subclass of change of state verbs about 60 percent of the time. Tomasello (1992a) found that an even higher percentage of *-ed* use occurred with change of state verbs in general.

It turns out that one major reason children show this pattern is quite straightforward: this is the pattern they hear in the language around them. In a longitudinal study of Turkish-speaking children, Aksu-Koç (1988, 1998) found that mothers tend to use tense and aspect markers with certain kinds of verbs in basically the same pattern as the children, although the children often show the pattern in more exaggerated form. Stephany (1981) and Shirai (1998) reported some evidence this same pattern for, respectively, Greek-speaking and Japanese-speaking mothers and children.

Shirai and Andersen (1995) reported the same result in an especially extensive study focused on three English-speaking children and their mothers. In a study of these same three children, Shirai (1994) reported the only correlations between specific mothers and their children in this linguistic domain. The study was designed to further test Brown's (1973) observation that the English progressive -ing is basically never used by young children (or adults) with totally stative verbs (like have and love). Shirai found that only one of the three children ever used the -ing ending with a totally stative verb with any substantial frequency (3.1 percent of her progressives). Most importantly, that child's mother was the only one of the mothers who showed this same use (3.6 percent of her progressives). This mother and child said comparatively unusual things like "You're being silly," "I'm having trouble," "I loving Georgie," and "My tummy's hurting."

All of these findings accord well with what Shirai and Andersen (1995) call the Distributional Bias hypothesis, namely, that the distribution of tense and aspect markers with particular classes of verbs in children's speech (as classified mainly by lexical aspect) follows the distribution the children hear in the language around them. Li and Shirai (2000) note that the distributional bias in adult speech to children—that is, the use of telics and perfectives with past tense and the use of atelics and imperfectives with present tense—has historical roots. In many languages past-tense and/or perfective markers derive historically from words indicating completive or resultative aspect, whereas imperfective, habitual (such as the English present tense), and stative marking quite often derive from progressive aspect. This pattern of grammaticalization is presumably evidence of a strong association in discourse over historical time of these two tense-aspect groupings (see Bybee, Perkins, and Pagliuca, 1994).

And so, once again what we see is an adult pattern in the use of grammatical words and morphemes that most often conflates and/or confounds distinctions that the child will need to segregate if she is to attain adult-like competence with these grammatical words and morphemes. Presumably to make all the appropriate distinctions in the current case, the child needs to hear and comprehend enough instances of activity verbs construed imperfectively in the past tense, change of state verbs construed in the progressive aspect, and all other possible combinations. Only wide and varied experience with many such patterns will provide the raw material necessary for the child to segment and sort out which components of a given verbal construction are being used to indicate which components of the temporal profile the speaker intends to indicate. As in the case of a nominal constructions with determiners—in which the child must sort out such things as referent specificity and listener perspective, which are often confounded—it is no surprise that it takes children many years to do this, and that it is easier to do in languages in which historical grammaticalization patterns have led to fewer conflations and confoundings of these types (Slobin, 1985, 1997).

FUTURE TENSE AND MODALITY

In many ways the future is more salient for young children than the past. From a very early age young children anticipate upcoming events and indicate this behaviorally and linguistically. But for children learning many languages the grammatical marking of futurity lags behind grammatical marking of the past. This does not seem to be due to some kind of performance or pragmatic factors influencing production only, as children—at least, English-speaking children—also comprehend grammatically encoded references to the future less well than those to the present and past. In two simple experiments, Herriot (1969) asked young children to choose the picture that best fit with an adult utterance. He had children choose between pictures depicting past, present, and future events, and he used past-, present-, and future-tensed utterances to describe them. The clear finding was that children struggled most with the future-tense utterances.

In a series of comprehension experiments, Harner (1976, 1981) compared preschool children's comprehension of grammatically encoded references to the immediate past and future (within minutes) to their comprehension of grammatically encoded references to the more remote past and future (previous or next day). What she found was an asymmetry hinted at by previous researchers such as Cromer (1971). Children comprehended grammatically encoded references to the past equally well whether it was the immediate past or the remote past. However, they comprehended grammatically encoded references to the immediate future much better than references to the remote future. This did not seem to be due to conceptual difficulties, as in a control condition these same children were perfectly capable of understanding references to the remote future when these were indicated by temporal adverbs in phrases such as *The day after today* and *The day after this day*.

Harner (1981) explained the observed asymmetry in terms of the rather uncertain status of the English future tense. Linguists such as Lyons (1968) contend that the English future as expressed by the auxiliary *will* is as much about modality as about futurity, and indeed the historical roots of this word in acts of willing is apparent. Harner's hypothesis was thus something parallel to the Aspect Before Tense hypothesis for the past tense; specifically, she contended that immediacy of impending action and uncertainty about it are crucial components of the child's interpretation of the English *will*-future. She therefore claimed that what is most important in sorting out which aspects of future situations are encoded by the auxiliary *will* is children's acquisition of other modal auxiliaries (such as *can, may, should, wanna, gonna, hafta*) that can be contrasted with it (perhaps especially *gonna,* which competes with *will* for future reference). Consistent with this interpretation (and inconsistent with a cognitive hypothesis concerning children's difficulties in conceptualizing the future), Kuczaj and Daly (1979) found that it is easier for children to comprehend hypothetical references in the future domain than in the past domain. In any case, the domains of futurity and modality are obviously closely intertwined, and this is reflected in the grammaticalization patterns in many languages (Bybee, Perkins, and Pagliuca, 1994) and in children's acquisition and usage as well.

This interrelation between futurity and modality is even evident in children's patterns of usage with the two most common future-tense terms in English: *will* and *gonna.* Gerhardt (1985; see also Gee and Savasir, 1985) examined six English-speaking children's uses of these two terms in play interactions between the ages of 3;2 and 4;2. She found that *will* occurred overwhelmingly (94 percent of the time) in utterances designed to effect some kind of interpersonal coordination, for example, offers ("If you want I'll help you now"), requests ("Will you give it to me?"), and compliance with requests ("OK. I'll do it"). In contrast, *gonna* occurred most often as a pronouncement of upcoming plans with only a minimal interpersonal dimension ("I'm gonna leave now"), only about half of which were ever carried out (as opposed to 90 percent for *will* utterances). Gerhardt and Savasir (1986) give a similar analysis of the English present tense, which, as is well known, does not simply indicate present activities (since this is normally done with the present progressive). These investigators found that most often 3-year-olds use the English present tense to implicitly refer to some norm, for example, "This goes in there," "Dollies sleep in houses," and "We put her shoes on" (so that she can go outside).

Gerhardt (1985) argues that children's understanding of the way modal and future terms are used to indicate all kinds of non-actual events and states of affairs (irrealis) is intimately bound up with the way these terms are used to regulate interpersonal interactions (modality). Further evidence for this view comes from a study by O'Neill and Atance (2000) concerning 2- to 5-year-old children's use of terms to express uncertainty. They found that children first used terms like *maybe, probably,* and *might* in connection with future intentions (and some ongoing events). They did not use these terms to express uncertainty with respect to future events per se until considerably later in development, after 3 years of age in most cases. And so, the major difficulty in learning future tense reference for many children—certainly those learning English—is the intimate relation between futurity and other forms of irrealis and modality.

DISPLACED TEMPORAL REFERENCE POINTS

Finally, of special difficulty are young children's attempts to learn and use constructions that require a reference time other than the current moment, and to mark past and future with respect to this remote reference point. This ability was investigated by Weist, Wysocka, and Lyytinen (1991) in a study of American, Polish, and Finnish children. These children were given a comprehension task in which they had to identify the appropriate picture when hearing utterances like "The boy had already started the fire when his friend arrived." These investigators found that children in all three languages (with a slightly different pattern for the Finnish children) were able to handle such complexities beginning at around age 4;6. They argue that this result is best explained by general cognitive developments in the understanding of time and in the ability to decenter from the here-and-now. Their conclusion is based not only on the fact that the age of acquisition was similar in three very different languages, which encode these complex tense relations in very different ways, but also on the fact that adult second-language learners of these and other languages (in spontaneous settings) show a different pattern of development. Adults learning a second language often learn both temporal words such as *when* and complex verb tenses such as the pluperfect to set remote reference times much more quickly than young children (Weist, Wysocka, and Lyytinen cite Meisel, 1987, and Buczowska, 1989).

Related to this are findings with the English present perfect, as exemplified in such utterances as *I have seen that before* and *He has been there before*. This verb form is notoriously ill-defined, with some controversies over its status as a tense or aspect marker and other controversies over its meaning—which is most often portrayed as "past time with current relevance" (Slobin, 1996). Weist (1986) argues that because of this dual allegiance to past and present, mastery of the English present perfect also requires some coordination of a remote reference time and current time. It is thus a relatively late acquisition for British English-speaking children, and even later for American English-speaking children—perhaps as late as 4 or 5 years of age, depending on one's criterion of mastery (Fletcher, 1981). However, interestingly, this form is used in Scottish English-speaking communities much more frequently than in other English-speaking communities, and perhaps with a clearer contrast to the simple past tense. The Scottish English-speaking children thus seem to acquire productive control over this form well before their British and American counterparts (Gathercole, 1986).

6.2.3. Modality and Negation

MODALITY

Modality has to do with the speaker's "attitude" toward the content of what she is saying, including such things as obligation, necessity, permission, volition, intention, ability, possibility, and certainty. Although such attitudes may sometimes be expressed in adjectives (*likely, necessary*), adverbs (*maybe, necessarily*), and other forms, it is the grammaticized forms that have received the most research attention. In many languages these take the form of utterance-level moods such as imperative, subjunctive, optative, and conditional. In English, the grammaticized forms comprise most importantly the modal auxiliary verbs such as *must, should, have to, got to, may, might, can,* and *could.* Syntactically, these verbs possess some characteristics of main verbs and some characteristics of auxiliary verbs, but as a class they are an extremely heterogeneous lot. Not even the most ardent nativists, who often argue for the existence of innate linguistic categories, believe that the English modal auxiliaries form a coherent syntactic class (Pinker, 1984). Children acquire them individually and piecemeal (Lieven, submitted).

Classically, the two basic categories of modality are deontic and epistemic. Deontic modality concerns actions and is "necessity based." The question is whether one ought to, has to, can, may, will, or wants to do something. According to Stephany (1993), this class of attitudes has its ontogenetic origins prelinguistically in imperatives, typically expressed through a demanding intonation. Epistemic modality, in contrast, concerns knowledge and is "possibility based." The question is whether something is, must, might, could, or should be the case. Historically, deontic modality typically emerges first, and then that same form often expands to epistemic uses as well (Fleischman, 1982; Traugott, 1989; Sweetser, 1990). For example, in English we may say that someone *must* do something, to indicate our attitude about that action, but this same modal verb may also be used to say that something *must* be the case, to indicate our relative epistemic certainty.

In ontogeny, deontic expressions also emerge before epistemic expressions, often by around the second birthday (Kuczaj and Maratsos, 1975; Bassano, 1996). Young children are very concerned with what they and others can, must, will, and want to do (Fletcher, 1985). In English, among the earliest modal expressions are the semi-grammaticized *wanna, gonna, hafta,* and *needta.* Gerhardt (1991) analyzes these as originating from no-tions of external compulsion *(hafta),* internal compulsion *(needta),* or in-ternal volition/intention *(wanna, gonna).* As noted in the previous section, both *will* and *gonna* as the major future tense markers in English are inti-mately bound up with the other modal expressions, as they express voli-tion and intention as much as futurity. Also important early on are *can, can't,* and *don't,* as requests about and expressions of permissions and wishes (and, to a lesser degree, ability). Similar notions are, for the most part, expressed in one way or another in most of the world's languages very early in language development.

The first epistemic attitudes to be expressed in English come out in the use of cognitive verbs in expressions such as *I think . . ., I guess . . ., I know . . ., I bet . . .,* and *I wish . . .,* typically around the third birthday (see Chapter 7). Use of the modal auxiliaries to say, for example, that some-thing *must* be the case or *should* be the case is a relatively late develop-ment for English-speaking children, typically not before the fourth birth-day (at least partially because children hear these very rarely; Stephany, 1993). In other languages, however, various kinds of epistemic modality are encoded in ways that children find more salient and easier to learn. For example, Korean has obligatory verbal suffixes that encode various epistemic distinctions. Choi (1991) found that the three children she stud-ied began to acquire these markers soon after their second birthdays: the marker for new information appeared first, then the marker for old infor-mation, then the marker for certainty, and finally the marker for indirectly acquired information. What this means, of course, is that children are cognitively capable of acquiring forms for making some epistemic distinc-tions fairly early, if these forms and their functions are of the right type (see also Aksu-Koç and Slobin, 1986, on Turkish).

As in many other domains of child language, however, experimental studies of comprehension—in which children do not get to choose what they will talk about but must talk about situations experimenters con-trive—indicate that it takes some years for children to master all the sub-tleties of modal expressions. Hirst and Weil (1982) assessed the ability of 3- to 6-year-old English-speaking children to make strength comparisons among different modal expressions. In the deontic domain, an experi-menter gave them instructions about how to manipulate a doll; in doing this she used the words *must, may,* and *should* ("You should hold it like this"). In the epistemic domain, an experimenter gave them instructions about where to find an object; in doing this she used the words *is, may, should,* and *must* ("It should be behind there"). In both domains, it was not until children were 5 to 6 years old that they could discriminate the different degrees of force indicated by these different terms. Noveck, Ho, and Sera (1996) basically replicated these results. Using a slightly different set of modal terms, chosen to be more familiar to younger children (and including negatives like "It can't be under the cup"), Byrnes and Duff (1989) found English-speaking children to be competent about one year earlier than this, at about 4 or 5. As might be expected, both of these studies found that children could most easily discriminate expressions that differed the most in strength. In a similar finding, Bascelli and Barbieri (2002) reported that it was not until they were 5 to 6 years old that Italian-speaking children clearly differentiated the different meanings of *dovere* (must) and *potere* (may). In the deontic domain this meant that they had trouble differentiating obligation from permission, while in the epistemic domain it meant that they had trouble differentiating certainty from possibility.

There are only two systematic studies of older children involving much subtler modal distinctions. First, Piéraut-Le Bonniec (1980) performed a series of experiments using a variety of modal terms (with children having to indicate which of two perceptible situations best fit the sentence they heard) and found that it was not until children were well into school-age that they discriminated different types of obligation and different types of certainty (*It may be in there, It must be in there, It should be in there, It can't be in there,* and so on). Second, Coates (1988) had children sort cards containing many different modal terms into piles of similar terms (including *must, have to, should, ought, will, shall, gonna, intend, could, can, able to, allowed to, may, might, possible,* and *probable*). She found that 8-year-olds had great difficulty in putting together similar terms and even 12-year-olds did not show adult-like competence.

NEGATION

Negation could be considered a modality, as it clearly reflects a speaker attitude. But it is normally treated separately, mainly because it serves so many different functions and comes in so many different forms.

From a functional point of view, Bloom (1970) distinguished three kinds of negation that emerge early in development: rejection (for example, *No!* to refuse an offered piece of food), nonexistence (*No juice* to comment on an empty bottle), and denial (*No* to answer a question). These three functions seem to emerge early in all languages that have been carefully studied, although some researchers have subdivided some of Bloom's categories and added others. For example, Vaidyanathan (1991) studied early negation in two children acquiring Tamil (one of the major languages of India). He added to the list the category prohibition *(Don't do that!)* and found that the functions emerged in the order: rejection, nonexistence, prohibition, and denial (see also Tam and Stokes, 2001, on Cantonese).

In the largest cross-linguistic study of the development of negation, Choi (1988) studied two English-speaking, five French-speaking, and four Korean-speaking children between the ages of 1;7 and 3;4. In order to account for all the different functions observed in these languages, she differentiated Bloom's three categories into nine categories. Her most general finding was that the functions of negation emerged in three phases:

- *Phase 1*: nonexistence, prohibition, rejection, failure *(It won't go)*.
- *Phase 2*: denial, inability *(I can't)*, epistemic negation *(I don't know)*.
- *Phase 3*: normative negation *(We don't do that)*, inferential negation *(Maybe not)*.

Although there were differences across the three languages, in general children had some competence in Phase 1 before their second birthday, competence in Phase 2 soon after their second birthday, and competence in Phase 3 in the months preceding their third birthday. Choi also documented in detail the forms used in each of the three languages, and these are displayed in Table 6.1.

It is always possible in studies of spontaneous speech that linguistic forms or functions are emerging in a particular order either because of the language children are hearing or because of the pragmatic functions that arise and need to be communicated about in the daily lives of young children. Therefore, Hummer, Wimmer, and Antes (1993; building on the work of Pea, 1982) used an elicitation task with the specific goal of investigating young children's understanding of denial. It is well known that young children in all languages often answer yes/no questions with *Yes* indiscriminately. This may be because they do not understand the notion of a proposition and its denial or it may be because they have simply learned that questions of this type need some kind of answer, and so they are employing a generic discourse strategy just to take their turn. To investigate these possibilities, Hummer, Wimmer, and Antes (1993) asked 48 German-speaking children from 1;1 to 2;7 a series of yes/no questions designed to be extremely simple; for example, they held up a picture of a dog and asked "Is this a cat?" They found that young 1-year-olds were basically clueless, with only 3 of 16 children producing a single *nein* response correctly (out of a possible four). In contrast, children at around 2;6 were very good, with 14 of 16 children answering correctly on either three or four questions. The children in the middle, at around 2;0, were more mixed, with no child answering correctly on all four questions, but with most children answering correctly two or three times, with a number of in-

Table 6.1   Development of forms and functions of negations in English, French, and Korean.

	Age	MLU	Nonexistence	Prohibition	Rejection
English	1;7–2;3	1.2–1.8	*allgone*		*no*
	2;1–2;10	1.8–1.9	*allgone* *no* N +	*no* *no* V	*no* *I don't want to* +
	2;5–3;6	2.9–3.6	*allgone* *no* N	*no* *don't* V *you can't* V	*no* *I don't want to*
French	1;11–2;7	1–1.9	*parti* *a plus*		*non* *pas là, pas ça*
	1;11–2;11	1.7–2.5	*parti* *y a pas*	*non* *pas* V	*non* *pas* X *je veux pas*
	2;5–3;6	2.5–3.5	*y a pas* *il y en a plus*	*non* V *pas*	*non* *pas ça* *ça va pas*
Korean	1;7–2;1	1–1.9	*epta*		*i(:)ng* + *an twae* +, *ani* +
	1;11–2;9	1.6–2.9	*epta*	*ani* + V-*ci ma* + *an twae*	*ani* *an* V +
	2;9–3;3	3.1–4.5	*epta*	*an twae* + V-*ci ma*	*ani* *an* V *sile*

Source: Adapted from Choi (1988). Reprinted with the permission of Cambridge University Press.

correct *yes* responses (and other responses) mixed in. Hummer, Wimmer, and Antes use these data to argue that the denial function of negation emerges only gradually from the earlier negation functions.

The syntactic forms of early negation are many and various, ranging from the simple *No!* (and its equivalent in other languages) to a variety of complex syntactic constructions—many of which can be seen in Table 6.1. Klima and Bellugi (1966; see also Brown, 1973) identified the syntactic phenomenon in children's early negation that has captured the most research attention. In a number of different languages an early form of syntactic negation involves placing a negative word or particle at the beginning of an utterance, even in constructions in which the negative word or particle should be internal. It is thus relatively common to observe things

Table 6.1 (continued)

Failure	Denial	Inability	Epistemic	Normative	Inferential
(it) can't + *not fit* *doesn't* V +	*no* *not* X	*(I) can't*	*I don't know*		
(it) can't *won't*	*no* *not* X AUX *n't*	*I can't*	*I don't know*	*can't*	*not* X AUX *n't*
non *pas ici*	*non* *pas* X	*pas arrive*	*(sais) pas*		
non *pas ça* *ça va pas*	*non* *pas* X	*je peux pas* *j'arrive pas*	*je sais pas*	*faut pas*	V *pas*
ani	*ani* N *ani* *an* V				
an twae	*ani* N *ani* *an* V	*mot* V	*molla*	*ninke ani*	*an* V

like "No Nathaniel a king," "No Mommy do it," and "No the sun is shining" (see McNeill and McNeill, 1968; Wode, 1977; on Japanese, German, and other languages). The claim of Klima and Bellugi and others has been that children are attempting to say what an adult would say with an utterance-internal *not*, for instance, "The sun is not shining," and utterances such as these are mistakes, child inventions, incorrect grammar. Bloom (1970) rejected this account, pointing out that many of these utterances are instances of a so-called anaphoric negation, on a model with a discourse sequence such as: (Mother) "Do you want an apple?" (Child) "No, I want a pear." The child is just not pausing after the word *no* in the same way as an adult. Wode (1977) hypothesized that children, in a sense, overextend this anaphoric negation illegitimately and thus produce utterances with inappropriate sentence external negation (see Park, 1979, for a different view).

However, examination of the discourse contexts of these utterances indicates that Bloom's analysis can only account for some utterances of this type. An interesting new analysis has thus recently been proposed by Drodz (1995). In this analysis, children are doing something similar to anaphoric negation, but importantly different as well. The claim is that children are essentially denying a proposition just put forth by their interlocutor, on analogy with an adult saying something like *No way the sun is shining*. This is so-called exclamatory negation. As evidence for his analysis Drodz cites the fact that sentence-external negation is actually quite rare (though highly noticeable) in children's speech, as is exclamatory negation. Moreover, in a new analysis of a number of English-speaking preschoolers' discourse with their mothers, it was found that almost all of children's sentence external negations served as objections and/or rectifications of the mother's immediately preceding utterance. Indeed, many of them actually incorporated the majority of the mother's previous utterance in the reply. An example of this echoic characteristic would be: (Mother) "The cat is on the mat." (Child) "No the cat is on the mat." Importantly, children's utterances with sentence-internal negation at this same (and immediately following) time are used for different functions, especially nonexistence and rejection, and are not typically echoic.

6.2.4. Integrating Constructions

One of the more difficult problems in adult linguistics is finding a unified account of how speakers integrate their tense-aspect-modality (TAM) marking with particular utterance-level constructions, since this marking is realized in different ways in different constructions. For example, yes/no questions in English begin with an auxiliary verb that carries such things as tense and agreement marking, whereas simple indicative utterances in the present or past tense carry tense and agreement on the lexical verb, which occurs after the subject. The traditional approach is to try to find a single abstract account explaining how language users do this across the board. Another possible approach is a radical construction grammar perspective in which TAM marking has some unity across utterance-level constructions but is also specified in different ways in these different constructions—and this is part of the definition of the construction (see Croft, 2001).

In theories of acquisition the issue is quite clear. Generative grammar accounts posit a functional category Inflectional Phrase (IP) that either is innately specified at birth or else matures at around the second birthday (e.g., Rice, Wexler, and Hershberger, 1998; Radford, 1990). The prediction is that all of the grammatical inflections that are part of IP, including those for tense and agreement, should emerge at the same time in development, and they should be immediately productive across all of the lexical items with which they are used. But when these predictions are specifically tested, they do not hold up. Wilson (in press) investigated this hypothesis in the spontaneous speech of five English-speaking children. He looked at their acquisition of three elements that instantiate IP: the copula *be,* the auxiliary *be,* and third-person singular agreement *(-s).* On the basis of this analysis, Wilson concluded that "for each child the relative pace of development of the three morphemes studied varies significantly, suggesting that these morphemes do not depend on a unitary underlying category" (from abstract). These findings are generally consistent with similar findings from investigators studying other languages that are much more richly inflected than English, such as Italian (Pizzuto and Caselli, 1992, 1994), Polish (Dabrowska, 2000), and Portuguese (Rubino and Pine, 1998). It is also important that when one very specific version of this theoretical approach—Schuetze and Wexler's (1996) agreement/tense omission model—is tested in a different way, by examining the errors that children do and do not make with tense and agreement, again the generative grammar predictions are not upheld (Pine et al., submitted).

On the other hand, no one has yet proposed a comprehensive account from a usage-based or construction grammar perspective of how children integrate TAM marking with their utterance-level constructions. But presumably such an account would focus, especially early in development, on the specific lexical and grammatical items involved as well as on the specific utterance-level constructions involved. For example, one proposal might be that children learn to do their TAM marking in yes/no questions basically independently of the way they do this in their other constructions—at least initially. Thus, children would first learn a few dozen pairings (and the kinds of things that follow them) of the following kind: *Are you, Shall we, Don't you, Did you, Is it, Have you, Can you.* Gradually, patterns would emerge from this piecemeal learning that would allow children to do their TAM marking productively in yes/no questions, even with novel verbs. But at the beginning there would not be generalizations from this marking to the TAM markings in other constructions. For example, in their *wh-*questions children would be learning such pairs as: *Where's, Where are, What's, What does, How can, How do, When can, Why does, Why is* (and the kinds of things that follow them). Whether and to what degree children make construction-general generalizations about TAM marking at older ages is at this point an open question.

The predictions of these two competing accounts of TAM marking are thus very clear, and what little empirical work there is at the moment seems to favor the usage-based approach in which children begin with item-specific and construction-specific learning. The one empirical study which favors a generative grammar account (Rice, Wexler, and Hershberger, 1998) reported that the average age of emergence of children's inflections in IP (as opposed to other inflections) were quite similar. But these investigators did not report data for individual children, and so it is impossible to tell how many, if any, individual children actually showed the predicted developmental synchrony.

6.3. Learning Morphology

The need to ground nominals and clauses in the ongoing speech event is present constantly. Although there are major differences among languages, these constant communicative pressures have led in many cases to the grammaticalization of forms for effecting these functions, and recurrent functions other than grounding may also lead to the creation of grammatical morphology (for example, plurals and case marking). From the point of view of learning and generalization, grammatical morphology displays a number of interesting properties. Among these is the fact that children sometimes overregularize grammatical morphemes, which has put them in the center of some major theoretical debates about the nature of cognitive representation in general. In addition, because they are often not very salient in the speech stream—and perhaps for other reasons such as their plurifunctionality in many cases—second-language learners and children with specific language impairment often have special problems with grammatical morphemes.

6.3.1. The English Past Tense

One of the most intriguing phenomena of child language acquisition is U-shaped developmental growth. That is, in some cases children seem to learn the conventional adult way of saying things early in development, but then become worse as they get older, saying such things as *mans, feets, comed, sticked,* and *putted*—returning only later to the conventional adult forms. The traditional interpretation of this developmental pattern is that early on children learn, for example, the past-tense form *came* by rote as an individual lexical item; later they learn to use the regular past-tense morpheme *-ed* and apply it whenever they want to refer to the past (sometimes inappropriately, as in *comed*); and finally, before school age, they learn that there are exceptions to the general rule and display adult-like competence (Kuczaj, 1977; Bowerman, 1982). U-shaped developmental growth is thus intriguing because it seems to signal changes in underlying linguistic representations and processes.

Perhaps ironically, given that English is a morphologically impoverished language, the grammatical morpheme that has been studied most intensively in this regard is the English past tense -ed. Children seem to overgeneralize the use of this morpheme relatively frequently (although exactly how frequently is a matter of debate; see below), at least partly because of the distribution of -ed in the language they hear. Of the 30 verbs that English-speaking children hear most frequently, 22 are irregular and do not take -ed to form the past tense (often they employ a stem change as in come-came and bring-brought—there are about a dozen subclasses; Bybee, 1995). The vast majority of tokens of past-tense verbs that children hear in English utterances are thus also irregular, by some estimates by a margin of 3 to 1 over regulars. Of the 30 verbs that English-speaking children hear next most frequently (ranks 31–60), 22 are regular, with verbs that take the regular -ed past tense outnumbering irregulars in speech to children by about 3 to 1. What this means is that children at the beginning have little evidence for the regular pattern, but as they learn more verbs evidence for the pattern becomes clearer and clearer. Children who overgeneralize the -ed past tense typically do so after they have learned about 100 verbs (Bybee and Slobin, 1982).

The largest and most systematic study of children's acquisition of the English past tense was conducted by Marcus et al. (1992). They examined written transcripts of 83 English-speaking preschool-aged children and found that overgeneralization errors were relatively rare proportionally (2.5 percent of irregular tokens produced had, inappropriately, the -ed), and that they occurred at this same low rate throughout the preschool period. Typically, for a given verb children produced the correct past-tense form before they produced the overgeneralized form, and they made the overgeneralization error least often with the irregular verbs they heard most often in parental speech. For a particular child's use of a particular verb, there was sometimes a relatively extended period (weeks to months) in which the correct form and the overgeneralized form coexisted.

Marcus et al. explain these results with one form of a dual process model. Children acquire the irregular forms by rote learning, but they acquire the regular forms by establishing a rule. Rote learning is subject to all the parameters of "normal" learning, such as the effects of frequency and similarity among exemplars; rule learning is impervious to these effects. (The existence of these different processes is supposed to be of great theoretical significance, since they confirm the existence of rule-based cognitive representations that are not subject to the "normal" laws of learning; Pinker, 1991, 1999). But the specifics of English past-tense acquisition clearly do not fit this neat picture; children sometimes misapply the rule (overgeneralize), even in some cases using both correct and incorrect forms during the same developmental period. Marcus et al. explain these anomalies by invoking in addition the principle of preemption (what they call the uniqueness principle or blocking) and some factors that affect its application. The basic idea is that the regular rule applies whenever it is not blocked (that is, it is a default rule). This means that when children have an irregular form (such as *sang*) it blocks application of the regular *-ed* rule, but when they do not have such a form they might reasonably produce *singed*. The problem with this account, of course, is the finding that children often use both the correct and overgeneralized forms at the same time. Marcus et al. deal with this empirical problem by hypothesizing that blocking sometimes does not work as it is supposed to, basically because of "performance errors." Lexical retrieval is probabilistic and frequency dependent; children sometimes have trouble retrieving infrequent irregular forms and so the rule gets applied simply because it is not properly blocked.

Recently, however, some aspects of this account have been called into question. Maratsos (2000) points out that the error rate reported by Marcus et al. (1992) was computed by pooling all verbs together, and consequently very high-frequency verbs statistically swamped out low-frequency verbs. Indeed, verbs that appeared infrequently for a given child (fewer than 10 times) were excluded from some analyses altogether. Thus, for example, one child produced 285 past tenses for the verb *say*, with a very low error rate of 1 percent. This same child, however, produced 40 different verbs fewer than 10 times each (155 tokens in all). The overgeneralization error rate for these individual verbs was 58 percent. But because of their low token frequency, all of these verbs together contributed less to the computation of the overall error rate than the verb *say* by itself. In addition, Maratsos points out that many individual verbs used by individual children are used in both correct and overgeneralized forms for a period of many months (in a few cases years), which could only happen in the rule-plus-blocking account if the child experienced persistent and long-lived retrieval problems of a type Marcus et al. do not discuss.

Maratsos' alternative account is based on the notion of competition—a weaker, frequency-based kind of preemption (see Section 5.3.2). In this account children can produce past-tense forms either by rote or by rule, and there may be a period in which they produce both for a given verb. The winner of the competition will be determined eventually by the form the child hears most often in the speech around her (and perhaps by other factors); that is, the most frequent form comes gradually to block the less frequent form, regardless of which is "regular" or "irregular." This is in contrast to the Marcus et al. account in which there is an asymmetry between regulars and irregulars—the regular does not even need to be heard a single time to "win," since it is a default—and the only role for frequency is as a performance factor that interferes with the normal mechanism.

6.3.2. The German Plural and Other "Defaults"

A number of researchers have pointed out that the English past tense is not representative of the way morphology works in the majority of cases in the majority of languages of the world, and it is thus a decidedly poor choice for comparing different theories of morphological acquisition. Although it does represent a relatively common pattern cross-linguistically, there are many other patterns that children have to learn as well, and many of these do not confound factors like the English past tense. Most importantly: (1) the English past tense has only one truly productive form (*-ed*, although with three allomorphs), with all the other patterns comprising only a few verbs and being relatively nonproductive; (2) the productive form is a suffix, which can be affixed to many different kinds of stems, whereas the irregular forms are typically stem changes, none of which has the potential to apply very widely (since they are so strongly phonologically conditioned: *sing-sang, ring-rang*); (3) the regular form *-ed* has a high type frequency (favoring rule formation), whereas each irregular form has a high token frequency (favoring rote learning). Two other morphological markers that have similar drawbacks are the English plural (Marcus, 1995) and the German past participle (Marcus et al., 1995), if frequency is counted correctly (see Bybee, 1995).

From a theoretical point of view, therefore, it has come to be recognized that an especially interesting case is the German plural. The plural in German can be marked by one of five suffixes *(-n, -e, -er, -ø, -s)*, some of which may also be accompanied by stem changes to produce eight different forms. Of crucial importance theoretically are the following facts: (1) many of the eight forms are relatively productive; (2) many of the eight forms operate by suffixation; and (3) the form that is least phonologically restricted *(-s)* is relatively infrequent but still applies in all kinds of "emergency" situations such as loan words from other languages, proper names, onomatopoeic words, and acronyms. Despite these obvious differences to the English past tense, Marcus et al. (1995) have claimed that the German plural works in an identical manner: there is one regular form, learned by rule, and many irregular forms, learned by rote. Even though it is relatively infrequent, the regular form is hypothesized to be *-s* because it applies in such a wide variety of phonological contexts (a so-called minority default). The German plural is thus especially important theoretically because one of the main claims of the dual process account is that type frequency (in this case the number of different nouns used with each ending) does not determine the regular rule; what determines the rule is only its default status (see, e.g., Clahsen, 1999).

In the dual process account, only the rule-based form -s should be truly productive for German-speaking children (although they may find local analogies among some of the irregular forms). But the facts of German acquisition do not bear this out. First, young children overgeneralize virtually all of their plural markers, and the most frequent overgeneralization is the form -n, not -s (Clahsen et al., 1992; Ewers, 1999; Köpcke, 1998). Second, the nouns to which children overgeneralize -s are not a default group, but rather they are a predictable subset of phonologically similar words (mainly those ending in liquid or nasal sounds; Köpcke, 1998; Behrens, 2001b). Third, in experiments with nonce nouns, adult German speakers most often use -n and in general supply plurals based on properties of the stem such as -n with monosyllabic feminine nouns or feminines ending in a schwa or -e with masculine monosyllabic nouns (Köpcke, 1988). Clahsen et al. (1992) attempted to deal with these inconsistencies by positing that young children initially surmise incorrectly that -n is the default plural before correcting themselves later. But there is no evidence for this proposal, and no one has proposed a process by which children could reset the rule (reassign default status) after it has been incorrectly assigned (Behrens and Tomasello, 1999). On the basis of her especially detailed and thorough analysis of one child's earliest overgeneralizations with the German plural, Behrens (2001b: 24) concludes:

> The proposed distinction between "regular" -s . . . and stored irregular forms does not capture the productivity of the German plural system . . . The child studied here quickly identifies the full set of German plural markers and overgeneralizes all of them . . . The overall low error rate in this period (3.2 percent) hides subgroup effects: some plural classes are virtually error free, others show peaks of up to 40 percent errors in a given biweekly period. Such variability in the error markers, and such selectivity in which nouns are affected by errors are incompatible with a blocking and retrieval process as proposed in the Dual Mechanism Model . . . Instead, the error patterns observed are compatible with standard analyses of the German plural system as well as learning accounts that predict that children will generalize based on the distributional properties of the target system.

An interesting additional case that has recently come to light is the Polish genitive. There are three genitive endings in Polish, and their distribution is conditioned by gender and, in the case of masculine nouns, by a host of semantic, morphological, and phonological factors. There is no single ending which functions as a default for the class of nouns as a whole or for masculine nouns, although feminine and neuter nouns can be considered to have a default. Thus, the Polish genitive allows us to compare the acquisition of two subsystems which have a default ending (like English past tense) and one which does not (like German plurals). Dabrowska (2001) examined transcripts from three Polish-speaking children to see if there were any differences in the way these children treated these endings, especially with regard to overgeneralizations. Overall, she found that the children acquired all three inflections very early, before age 2, and made few errors. Moreover, most errors involved overgeneralization not of any defaults but rather of the two "irregular" masculine endings (completely contrary to the predictions of the dual process model); and the more frequent of the two irregular endings was also overgeneralized more frequently. This finding is theoretically important because it represents a case in which children are not presented with a pattern of input suggesting any kind of default form, and yet they have no particular acquisition difficulties and they do not seem inclined to try to impose a default form.

6.3.3. Single Process and Dual Process Models

Perhaps surprisingly, the debate over how tiny children learn tiny morphological markers has taken on epic proportions in cognitive science in general. A little history explains why. As noted throughout this book, in classic structuralist accounts, language acquisition consists in the learning of meaningful words plus empty rules for inflecting and combining them. Rumelhart and McClelland (1986) attempted to undermine this view by creating a computer program (connectionist model) that seemed to learn the English past tense and that also, over time, seemed to successfully model the well-known U-shaped developmental pattern. It did this without instantiating any abstract rules; it worked only on exemplars and used basic learning principles sensitive to both frequency and similarity. The model was criticized for various shortcomings, especially the need for researchers to feed it exemplars in a particular way (Pinker and Prince, 1988), and other researchers then created improved models (e.g., Plunkett and Marchman, 1991, 1993).

The success of these revised models led their detractors to formulate the dual process view, in which children learn irregular morphology in a manner similar to that proposed by the connectionists, but regular morphology is different because it participates in some way in the innate and abstract rule system of universal grammar. Arguments for the dual process view thus focus on differences between the ways regular and irregular morphology are learned. Of central importance is the claim that the rule-based process is insensitive to all the factors that affect the learning and use of the items not participating in the rule. These include most importantly (1) frequency (the token frequency of a given morpheme and the type frequency of the morpheme in terms of the number of different items with which is used); and (2) semantic and phonological similarity among exemplars. In the dual process view, then, rule-based items are acquired in a manner totally insensitive to semantic and phonological similarity among items and to type and token frequency, whereas the learning of irregulars is sensitive to all of these factors. The hypothesized existence of these rule-based cognitive representations is thus taken as evidence that large parts of human cognition consist of abstract, formal representations, not connectionist networks involving no forms of cognitive representation at all (other than weighted nodes reflecting their history with individual exemplars). This is why the debate extends well beyond issues of child language acquisition.

The empirical problem is that the data of child language do not provide evidence for two separate processes, and the invocation of such things as performance factors and children misidentifying the default rule do not rectify matters adequately. Moreover, there is no satisfactory model of how children recognize the regular or default form in a morphological paradigm, given that no single cue or set of cues is invariably associated with it cross-linguistically (a morphological version of the linking problem; see Bybee, 1995; Behrens and Tomasello, 1999). Consequently, Bybee (1985, 1995) proposes a single process model. It accounts quite well not only for the data of child language acquisition but also for those of historical language change. The model shares much with connectionist models—most importantly in its rejection of the notion of symbolic rules that are immune to influences from normal learning processes—but it differs by positing that on the basis of their linguistic experience children build up abstract schemas that underlie their productivity. The nature of these schemas is always closely tied to the exemplars it embodies and the learning processes by which it was formed—but it is still abstract in a way not normally recognized in connectionist accounts. More specifically, the model posits that words enter the child's lexicon with a certain strength based on token frequency. High token frequency (strength) of an item (for example, *was* as a past tense) enables it to resist assimilation to any generalized schema. Words similar in semantic and/or phonological form cluster into schemas. The productivity of a schema is a function of (1) the similarity among its exemplars (such as in terms of semantic or phonological properties); and (2) its type frequency in terms of the number of different lexemes with which it has been used.

Thus, in Bybee's view, the German plural -*s* is a quite open schema in the sense of having relatively lax phonological restrictions, but it is not so productive because it is used with only a restricted set of nouns (that is, it has low type frequency). The German -*s* plural is thus a "default" morpheme, in the sense that it has few restrictions, but it has all of the earmarks of a learned schema—its productivity is conditioned by phonological similarity and type frequency—and none of the earmarks of abstract rules which are supposed to be immune to these factors. The English past tense -*ed* is an interestingly different case, as it not only is quite open phonologically and semantically but also is used with very high type frequency (and the irregulars do not impinge on it because they are very strong as individual lexical items owing to their high token frequency). These factors make it much more productive than morphemes such as the German -*s* plural that are used by default but with low type frequency, and so Bybee calls patterns of the English -*ed* type not just default but "regular."

Empirically, there is no evidence that morphemes of any type—default, regular, or otherwise—participate in anything other than normal processes of language learning. Theoretically, the Bybee model needs just one set of language learning processes, and thus has no need for an extra set of highly abstract, content-free abstract rules—nor, therefore, for extra blocking mechanisms to keep these abstract rules from applying too widely. It would thus seem that on both these grounds, the Bybee single process model—like the single process account of syntactic development—is to be preferred.

6.3.4. Morphology as "Weak Link"

In general, the acquisition of productive systems of grammatical morphology in natural languages is extremely difficult. According to Klein and Perdue (1997), most adult second-language learners, especially those learning in more natural settings outside the classroom, develop what these authors call the basic variety of a language. This consists of lexical items combined in syntactic constructions, but typically with only one morphological form of each word. Similarly, McWhorter (1998) argues and presents evidence that one of the distinguishing characteristics of pidgin and Creole languages (typically new languages created under unusual situations of language contact) is their relatively impoverished systems of grammatical morphology. It is also well known that one of the major diagnostic features of children with specific language impairment is their relatively poor mastery of the grammatical morphemes in their language (Leonard, 1998; Bishop, 1997). Finally, when perfectly competent adult speakers of a language are put under various kinds of processing pressure as they listen to a story—as when the spoken language describing the story is distorted by white noise or subjects must perform a distracting task while listening—what falls apart most readily in subsequent tests of retention is the grammatical morphology (Dick et al., 2001).

The basic reasons that grammatical morphology is an especially weak link in the language learning process are three. First, it is typically expressed in phonologically reduced, unstressed, monosyllabic bits in the interstices of utterances and constructions. Second, in some though by no means all cases, it carries very little concrete semantic weight, for example, the English third-person -s agreement marker is in most cases almost totally semantically redundant; and indeed research with children with specific language impairment has shown that greater semantic weight indeed facilitates children's acquisition of a grammatical morpheme (Leonard, 1998; Bishop, 1997). Third, as is apparent in many of the analyses of this chapter, many grammatical morphemes are plurifunctional in ways that make acquisition of the full range of uses in appropriate contexts extremely difficult. Perhaps for all of these reasons, Farrar (1990, 1992) found that children's acquisition of some particular grammatical morphemes in English (such as past tense -ed, plural -s, progressive -ing) was facilitated when mothers used these morphemes in immediate recasts of the child's utterances that were missing them. Recasts are well known to help children identify elements with low salience since they provide the child with an immediate comparison of her own immature utterance and the corresponding full adult form with full morphology (K. E. Nelson, 1986).

The acquisition of grammatical morphology thus presents something of a paradox. As was outlined in Chapter 4, grammatical morphemes quite often provide "local cues" that children find it relatively easy to relate to their functions—all other things being equal—since the morpheme occurs close to the place where it does its work. But with grammatical morphemes, all other things are seldom equal. Their acquisition is problematized by processing issues (lack of perceptual salience), semantic issues (lack of communicative weight), and plurifunctionality (low cue validity in the sense that they signal multiple functions, as in the English definite article signaling both semantic specificity and pragmatic givenness—not to mention cases such as German noun endings that signal all in one form case, gender, and number). The acquisition of grammatical morphology thus brings into focus many of the most basic processes of language acquisition, often in conflicting ways. Also, since only certain forms are grammaticized historically—typically ones that serve functions or bundles of functions that recur repeatedly—and since any morpheme that was simply too complex to learn would not last more than one generation, the acquisition of grammatical morphology should be an excellent locus for the study of the interaction between historical language change and child language acquisition.

6.4. Summary

In this chapter I have described some of the processes by means of which young children make reference to things in the world and predicate things about them. The main point is that in referring and predicating speakers must always make sure that the symbols and constructions they use are tailored, more or less precisely, to the communicative needs of their listener in the current joint attentional frame—mainly in terms of her current knowledge and expectations. Languages have many different kinds of conventional means for accomplishing these acts of communicative grounding. For reference, they have everything from dedicated words for the speaker, listener, or a mutually known third person (personal pronouns) to special grammatical morphemes (determiners) that in concert with a categorical term (common noun) assist listeners in identifying specific referents. For predication, they have special words or grammatical morphemes for indicating the temporal contour of events and when relative to now they have happened or will happen (aspect and tense) and other words or morphemes for indicating the speaker's attitude toward the predication (modality).

Because the communicative circumstances that require the use of these grounding devices recur frequently in a speech community, in many cases they become grammaticized over historical time. This keeps them close to home, so to speak, and they can be used as local cues, often attached to the linguistic element they are working in concert with. But grammaticalization often leads to weak, unstressed monosyllables that can, for some people in some circumstances, pose perceptual problems. In addition, some of these functions recur quite often in bundles and languages grammaticize the bundles. This creates learning problems since it requires that learners have a wide range of experiences of the right kind in order to tease apart the different functions confounded together in a single form—for example, the specificity and givenness functions of English determiners or the notorious confoundings of many languages' marking of tense and aspect. Children thus have to employ their pattern-finding skills in this case to find patterns in how the same linguistic item is used, and how similar linguistic items are used, across many instances of use across fairly long periods of developmental time. Moreover, since many of these functions have to do with rather subtle assessments of the listener's knowledge and expectations, young children, who are notoriously bad at such perspective taking, must sharpen their social-cognitive skills in order to acquire the appropriate uses of these forms.

The theoretical choices in accounting for the acquisition of grammatical morphology are essentially the same as for the acquisition of syntax. One group of researchers believes that learners possess a set of pristine, content-free rules, and so what they must do is to identify which elements of the language they are hearing go with which rules—and which go with no rules, thus leading to a dual process theory. Because these rules are too abstract and so overgenerate, these theorists must also posit constraints or blocking mechanisms to keep them reined in—and sometimes performance limitations to account for cases where the rules (or even the blocking mechanisms) are not applied as they should be. In contrast, I have argued here for a single-process, usage-based theory—most importantly because it accords better with the developmental facts of children's acquisition of morphology. It fits better with the way children acquire such things as the German plural and the Polish genitive, which do not conform to the neat pattern of the more studied English past tense, as well as with their acquisition of other grammatical morphemes. And in the only real test of whether there exists something like Inflectional Phrase that unites various inflections such as tense and agreement under a single functional category—as posited by modern generative grammar—Wilson (in press) found no positive evidence, but instead found evidence for the item-based learning of separate inflections. It thus seems most plausible that learners of morphology come to the learning situation with a single set of cognitive, social-cognitive, and learning skills that enable them both to read the communicative intentions of the other persons in context and to find patterns among all of the different utterances and constituents of utterances, including grammatical morphemes, that they hear over time. No additional theoretical machinery is needed.

Complex Constructions and Discourse

Today's syntax is yesterday's discourse.

—TALMY GIVÓN

ALL NATURAL languages have ways for talking about multiple related events and states of affairs. In the most straightforward cases, a speaker simply strings together different clauses across time, linking them with various kinds of appropriate connectors (or not). In other cases, the different clauses are more tightly interrelated and thus appear as constituents in a single complex construction under a single intonation contour, which in most cases is an historical grammaticalization (syntacticization) of discourse sequences in which specific types of clauses have recurred together repeatedly in the speech community. The linking of clauses—whether more loosely or more tightly—serves a variety of discourse functions, from expressing speaker attitudes about things (as in infinitival and sentential complements) to specifying referents in more detail (as in relative clauses) to indicating the spatial-temporal-causal interrelations among events (as in adverbial clauses).

The investigation of children's acquisition of complex constructions has, to date, been conducted mostly by formal linguists. Usage-based approaches have mainly been applied to earlier stages of development only. And indeed, many formal linguists believe that while usage-based approaches may be adequate for describing pivot schemas and other simple constructions, an adequate analysis of complex constructions requires the use of some heavier theoretical machinery, namely, some formal theory of grammar. But functional analyses of the adult use of complex constructions in spontaneous spoken discourse, as opposed to in writing, has revealed that their structure is not nearly so abstract and divorced from function as previously believed. Recent analyses of child language from this same functional, usage-based point of view have yielded some surprising new insights into these most syntactically interesting of constructions.

As children are acquiring the various constructions of their language, from simple to complex, they are at the same time learning how to use these constructions to communicate more effectively in extended conversational interactions with other people. Conversational and discourse skills are concerned not so much with the mastery of the grammaticized and conventional aspects of a language, but more with the mastery of strategies for using those constructions to manage the flow of information across turns in a developing conversational interaction. Skill at conversation involves such things as taking turns appropriately, managing the conversational topic effectively, and repairing a conversational interaction when it breaks down. Managing all this involves very sophisticated skills of intention-reading and perspective-taking, many of which do not fully develop until late in the preschool period.

As a special case, children also acquire skills of narrative discourse (and sometimes literacy) in which the immediate context in which a given utterance must be grounded is not the surrounding nonlinguistic context but rather the linguistic context formed by the rest of the narrative. Skill with narratives thus requires the mastery of a set of devices for providing coherence and cohesion across clauses in order to tell a good story, which in most cases means adapting previously mastered grounding devices for these new functions (raising again issues of plurifunctionality). An especially difficult and important component in this process is the introduction of new referents into the discourse, and the tracking of those referents across multiple clauses using various types of previously mastered nominal constructions in a way that helps the listener to build in her own mind a coherent and interesting narrative structure. Again this requires sophisticated skills of intention-reading and perspective-taking, many of which do not develop fully until the early school years and beyond.

7.1. Complex Constructions

In classic accounts such as that of Bowerman (1979), complex constructions are divided into those involving coordination, in which two independent clauses are linked in a more or less equal manner, and those involving subordination, in which one clause is used to modify or complement another (main) clause. However, the distinction between coordination and subordination is not so clear-cut in young children's spontaneous speech, as will be demonstrated below, and so a more helpful classification focuses on the function of the clauses relative to one another.

In the current brief overview of a complex research literature, we distinguish three (actually four) main ways in which young children use clauses with respect to one another. First, children use clauses to express psychological attitudes (first and mostly their own) toward events and states of affairs expressed in other clauses. The psychological attitudes they most often express are (1) intention/desire/compulsion *(want to V, try to V, have to V)* and (2) perception/belief *(think that P, know that P, see if P)*. Second, children use clauses to help identify referents (relative clauses). For example, a child may inform her mother, "That's the doggie that barks all the time," with the second clause (involving barking) serving to help specify (among other things) which doggie is intended. Third, children relate events to one another by expressing multiple clauses linked in particular ways, for example, *If X then Y, X because Y, X and then Y, X but Y*. The clauses in these cases are obviously more loosely linked than the cases in which the child expresses a psychological attitude about a state of affairs or specifies in more detail an intended referent. We will review research here on all of these types, distinguishing the two different types of psychological attitudes for a total of four types.

7.1.1. Infinitival Complement Constructions

In English in the last few hundred years a number of verbs have been grammaticalized into modal auxiliaries such as *may, can, might,* and *should* (Krug, 2000). These auxiliaries are distinguished from main verbs by several characteristics, but the most important are that they are not inflected for tense or person as are main verbs (*He kicks X;* but *He may V*) and that they are fronted in questions (*May he V?* but not *Kicks he X?*). As outlined in Chapter 6, English modal auxiliaries mainly concern speaker attitude and are classically subdivided into deontic uses indicating compulsion *(You must go)* and epistemic uses indicating relative certainty *(It must be raining)*.

There is another set of verbs in English that are not modal auxiliaries (they are inflected for tense and person, they are not fronted in questions) but that are very likely on their way in that direction historically. They also concern speaker attitudes—in most cases intention, volition, or compulsion—and they are used quite frequently by young children. The most common are *wanna V, hafta V, gotta V, needta V* (and perhaps *gonna V*), and they typically structure the earliest complex sentences that English-speaking children learn and use—typically emerging at around the second birthday. Gerhardt (1991) analyzes children's use of *wanna* as indicating "internal volition" or desire, their use of *hafta* (and *gotta*) as indicating "external compulsion" (often due to a social norm such as a rule), and *needta* as indicating "internal compulsion" (almost no choice because of an internal state). As noted in Chapter 6, *gonna* is quite often used less as a future marker than as an indication of the child's intention *(I'm gonna sock you)* and so is plausibly a member of this set of semi-auxiliary verbs as well. In some cases less grammaticized predicate adjectives also serve as matrix verbs, as in *be ready to* V or *be fun to* V or *had better* V.

In his classic study, Limber (1973) noted that children acquire these special semi-modal verbs each in its own way, with no indications that they see them as a class (similar to the modal auxiliaries; see Chapter 6). In a larger study, Bloom, Tackeff, and Lahey (1984) studied all utterances produced by five 2-year-old children that contained the word *to* followed by a verb complement. The most common matrix verbs in this construction are listed in Table 7.1. However, the forms *wanna* V, *hafta* V, *gotta* V, and *gonna* V accounted for almost all (95 percent) of the earliest uses early in the third year of life, each being used for some time in an item-specific manner. Bloom, Tackeff, and Lahey's most controversial claim was that for young children the word *to* is not a semantically empty infinitive marker for the second verb, but rather it is a meaningful morpheme that is simply one more use of the word *to*, similar to its other uses. As evidence for this claim (disputed by Hyams, 1984), they noted that each child learned these expressions at the same time she was learning *to* as a directional preposition. Moreover, they noted that all of these semi-modal expressions may be plausibly analyzed as containing a "direction toward" meaning (like *to*), and indeed historically in English the *to* in infinitives derives from the preposition *to* as used in purpose clauses (Haspelmath, 1989). One final finding was that it was very rare for the children to use these expressions with an intervening NP, that is, they almost never said things like "I need her to do it." When they did, it was only as they approached their third birthdays and in fairly formulaic expressions such as *I want you to* V. Interestingly, in a study of children learning Korean, a language in which these kinds of expressions obey a very different syntax (many different complementizers), Kim (1989) found some very similar results; that is, he found matrix verbs with similar meanings used in item-specific ways at similar ages.

Diessel (in press) reported the largest study to date of non-finite complement clauses. He studied a wider range of constructions—including such things as participial and *wh*-infinitive constructions—and he investigated four children up to 5 years of age in quantitative detail. The first finding is that over 95 percent of children's utterances with non-finite complement clauses contained to-infinitives, and these were the first to emerge as well. (The other 5 percent were such things as the participials *Start V-ing* and *Stop V-ing* and a very few *wh*-infinitives such as *I know what to do*.) Like Bloom et al. (1984), Diessel found that the first matrix verbs to appear

Table 7.1   Matrix forms that provided complement verb contexts for "to." Entries are listed in order of frequency for all children combined.

Intention (modals)	Inchoative	Invitative	Instructive	Negative
want	try	like	show how	forgot
go	time	supposed	know how	hard
have	ready	get	know what	used
got	about		know where	(too) far
	need		tell	long way
			ask	not nice
				wait

Source: Adapted from Bloom et al. (1989).

were *wanna, hafta,* and *gotta,* which emerged at about 2;3 and accounted for over 90 percent of all the to-infinitives over the course of the entire study. Initially the children used these in very formulaic ways. That is, almost all of the first to-infinitives they produced had as subjects the first-person pronoun *I,* were in present tense (assuming *gotta* as present tense), and were not negated—as in *I wanna play ball, I hafta do that,* and *I gotta go.* The constructions involved may thus be represented by, for example (leaving open the question of how a particular child at a particular point in development might understand the abstraction involved):

I *wanna* VERB PHRASE
I *hafta* VERB PHRASE
I *gotta* VERB PHRASE

The two other most frequent matrix verbs for to-infinitives were *like to* VERB and *try to* VERB (accounting for about 4 percent of to-infinitives). Diessel stresses that utterances with these kinds of formulaic matrix clauses followed by infinitives are not really expressing two full propositions. When the child says *I wanna play,* she is not talking about two acts—one of wanting and one of playing—but rather she is talking about her current attitude toward playing, much as when she uses a modal auxiliary (as in *I can play*).

From age 2 to age 5, these children's growing linguistic sophistication with this class of constructions was manifest in three main ways. First, their use of the semi-modals became less formulaic and more diverse, so that they now included third-person subjects ("Dolly wanna drink that") and negatives ("I don't like to do all this work"). Second, they learned a wider range of matrix verbs, including such things as *forget* ("I forgot to buy some soup") and *say* ("The doctor said to stay in bed all day"). Third, they learned more complex constructions with an NP between the two verbs. As in Bloom, Tackeff, and Lahey's study, these first emerged at around 2;6–3;0, and were dominated by four matrix verbs which accounted for 88 percent of all the utterances of this type. These were thus constructions of the type:

See SEE-OBJ VERB-*ing* (NP)
Want WANT-OBJ *to* VERB PHRASE
Watch WATCH-OBJ VERB-*ing* (NP)
Make MAKE-OBJ VERB PHRASE

After three years of age other matrix verbs representing a more diverse set of constructions emerged. And so, in general, Diessel found a developmental progression from constructions in which the matrix verb and main verb were more tightly integrated—utterances with the semi-modals *wanna, hafta,* and *gotta*—to those in which the two verbs were more distinct, as in the constructions with an intervening NP, and two full propositions were expressed.

The classic experimental studies of non-finite complements are those of C. Chomsky (1969), who investigated two relevant constructions in older children (5–10 years). First, she compared children's comprehension of utterances like *John told/persuaded/forced Bill to leave* (in which Bill leaves) to utterances like *John promised Bill to leave* (in which John leaves). Even the oldest children often misinterpreted utterances with *promise.* Chomsky's explanation was that children employ a "minimum distance principle" in which they assume that the subject of the second verb is the noun closest to it, which works for basically all verbs in English in this construction except *promise.* Maratsos (1974), however, provided evidence that young children do not use this principle, but rather they use a "semantic role principle" in which the semantics of the matrix verb plays a significant role. Thus, when children were given passive versions of some of Chomsky's sentences—such as *Bill was told by John to leave*—they did not make mistakes even though they violated the minimum distance principle (Bill leaves). They did not make mistakes because they understood the semantics of the verb *tell* (the recipient of the telling performs the action of the second verb); they apparently did not understand the unique semantics of the verb *promise* and/or they were misled by its disanalogy to all the other verbs used in this construction.

The other relevant construction studied by Chomsky (1969) is that represented by the utterance *The doll is easy to see,* in which the doll is the object of seeing. In most other utterances with a similar surface form the doll would be the agent of seeing, for example, in *The doll is eager to see.*

Again, children had difficulties with the unusual item, in this case until 8 years old. Kessel (1970) found similar results. However, Fabian-Kraus and Ammon (1980) criticized the methodology of these studies—specifically, when the adult places a blindfold on the doll's eyes and asks if she is "easy to see," it is a somewhat misleading situation. With a more child-friendly methodology, these investigators found almost perfect comprehension of the *easy to see/eager to see* contrast by 5-year-olds (and very good comprehension by many 4-year-olds).

7.1.2. Sentential Complement Constructions

Whereas many of the most common matrix verbs with infinitival complements are generally similar to deontic modals in their concern with purpose/intention/compulsion, many of the most common matrix verbs with sentential complements are similar to epistemic modals in their concern with certainty/perception/knowledge. But again, the matrix verbs in sentential complements—such things as *think, know, believe, see, say*—are not modal auxiliaries but tensed verbs. In addition, and in contrast to infinitival complements, the second clause in sentential complement constructions is a fully tensed clause with an overt subject (that is, a fully independent clause). The prototype, then, is utterances like *I know she's in there* and *I think I can do it*. Sentential complement constructions sometimes mark the second clause with the complementizer *that*, although this is rare in spontaneous spoken speech of all types. Also, in some cases other complementizers such as *if* and various *wh-* words are used, as in *I'll see if it flies* and *She knows where it is* (these are different in that the *wh-* word serves as an argument in the second clause).

Once again, the classic studies are by Limber (1973) and Bloom and colleagues (Bloom et al., 1989). In analyses of young English-speaking children's spontaneous speech, these investigators found that sentential complement constructions emerged later than infinitival complement constructions, typically between 2;6 and 3;0. They also found that the earliest verbs used in these constructions were a very delimited set, mainly *think, know, look,* and *see*. Shatz, Wellman, and Silber (1983) and Bartsch and Wellman (1995) analyzed a large corpus of utterances with these and similar psychological verbs and found that children's earliest uses did not depict psychological processes per se, but rather they were being used in formulaic phrases such as *ya' know* and *look-a-here* for discourse purposes (as in much adult language). DeVilliers (2000) notes that when children under 4 years of age are asked a question such as *What did the girl say she bought?*—in which there is a discrepancy between what she really bought and what she said she bought—they tend to respond with what she really bought, providing further evidence that they do not fully comprehend the construction.

The most comprehensive study to date of sentential complement constructions is that of Diessel and Tomasello (2001), who analyzed the development of finite complement clauses in the speech of seven English-speaking children aged 1;2 to 5;2 (a total of 2,807 utterances). Because their study included more children over a longer period of ontogeny than that of Bloom et al. (1989), they identified a much wider range of matrix verbs for children's sentential complement constructions (see Table 7.2). Nevertheless, the two studies are in general agreement about the most common matrix verbs at the earliest stages.

What Diessel and Tomasello found was that children's earliest sentential complement utterances did not really have the main clause/subordinate clause structure that comprises the textbook analysis of the adult version of this construction. The children's utterances did not really contain two propositions, one concerning, for example, an act of thinking and another concerning a state of affairs in the world. Instead, the children seemed to be using psychological verbs in very short and formulaic clauses such as *I think P, I know P,* and *See if P*—almost always to express their own attitude toward the contents of the other clause or else to draw another person's attention to the contents of the other clause. For example, one child's first 15 utterances containing the verb *think* were as follows (from age 3;1 to age 3;7):

I think I'm go in there
Think some toys over here too
I think he's gone
It's a crazy bone . . . I think
I think it's in here . . . Mommy
I think I don't know that one
Think it's in this
I think my daddy took it
And I think . . . we need dishes
I think I play jingle bells
Oh . . . I think it's a ball
I think it's in here
Think it's in there
I'm get my carriage . . . I think
I think that your hands are dirty

Note that in all cases the subject of the verb *think* is the first person *I* (sometimes not expressed). Note also that the verb *think* appears in invariant form: it is always in the present tense, it is not negated or inflected, and

Table 7.2   Matrix verbs that provided sentential complement contexts. Entries are listed in order of frequency for all children combined.

7 children	6 children	5 children	4 children	3 children	2 children	1 child
see	show	watch	hope	hear	forget	care
look	pretend	wonder	find	ask	happen	understand
think		remember		wish	read	write
know		mean		sing		pray
guess		bet		care		like
say						
tell						

Source: Adapted from Diessel and Tomasello (2001).

there are no modal auxiliaries. There is only one utterance containing the complementizer *that,* and in two instances the phrase *I think* actually occurs after the so-called subordinate clause. Indeed, what seems to be going on here is that this child is using the phrase *I think* (or just *think*) as a kind of parenthetical evidential marker indicating her own uncertainty with regard to the rest of the utterance. Thus in most cases the phrase *I think* could be replaced by an adverb such as *maybe* without affecting the meaning. All of these characteristics fit very well with the criteria set out by Thompson and Mulac (1991) for identifying "clausal operators," rather than fully propositional main verbs, in adult speech: the subject is either missing or in first/second person; the verb is active, present tense, without auxiliaries or other accoutrements; the matrix clause is shorter than the dependent clause and can occur in various positions; and there is no *that* complementizer. The prototype construction is thus such things as (with CLAUSE referring to any of a number of types of simple clauses, both finite and non-finite, including a list of verb island schemas):

> *I think* CLAUSE
> *See* CLAUSE
> *I bet* CLAUSE
> *Watch* CLAUSE

The pattern just documented is not confined to this child or this verb; all seven children showed this pattern early in development with all their complement-taking verbs of the *think-know* variety (also including *guess, bet, mean, wish, hope, remember*). What differed was how quickly different children began to diversify in their use of these kinds of matrix verbs in this construction. Figure 7.1 shows further developments for this child (Sarah) as well as those for one other child (Adam) for the verb *think.* It can be seen in this developmental pattern—especially when it is compared

Age	Sarah	Adam
>2;11		*I think* [2;11] (2)
3;0–3;11	*I think* [3;1] (26)	*I think* (7)
	(Do) you think [3;7] (2)	*Do you think* [3;3] (4)
		Does he think [3;3] (3)
		You don't think [3;5] (1)
		What do you think [3;5] (1)
		I don't think [3;8] (2)
4;0–5;0	*I think* (42)	*I think* (99)
	Do you think (3)	*Do you think* (5)
	I thought [4;1] (7)	*I don't think* (2)
	I'm thinking [4;2] (1)	*Why do you think* (2)
	They think [4;3] (1)	*What do you think* (1)
	What do you think [4;4] (1)	*One think* [4;6] (1)
	I don't think [4;8] (2)	*Paul think* [4;10] (10)
	I'll think [4;10] (1)	

Figure 7.1. "Main" clauses of S-complements including *think* at different ages for two children. Adapted from Diessel and Tomasello (2001).

with the emergence of other verbs for these same children—that children begin formulaically and only gradually come to express a full proposition with the matrix clause. Diessel and Tomasello thus conclude that English-speaking children's earliest utterances with *think* and *know* plus a proposition are not really exemplars of a sentential complement construction; they are much simpler constructions in which a proposition is modified by some marker of the child's epistemic attitude, in a manner very similar to the way they mark propositions with modal auxiliaries.

Although there are some interesting differences of detail, these children's utterances with *if* complements and *wh*- complements were also used in a very similar manner. In particular, children also typically began using these with very formulaic matrix clauses such as:

See if P, Let's see if P, Let me see if P, I'll see if P, I want to see if P
See what/where/how . . ., Look what/how . . ., Watch what/how . . .
I wonder what/where . . ., Guess what/who . . ., Know where/who/what . . .

The main exception to this pattern were the verbs *say, tell,* and *pretend,* which began in a much more differentiated way almost from the beginning. Even before 3 years of age children used these with a much more differentiated set of subjects, with verb morphology and modals, and with a much higher proportion of *that* complementizers. Presumably, a part of the explanation for this difference is that these verbs are semantically much heavier, referring less to attitudes and mental states and much more to overt behavior.

Diessel and Tomasello consider three main types of explanation for this overall pattern of results. First, as alluded to above, the use of formulaic epistemic clauses as matrix clauses in sentential complement utterances (typically with a first- or second-person pronoun as subject) is also quite common in informal adult speech (Thompson and Mulac, 1991). Consequently, much of what children are doing in the data reported above is using the lexically based expressions and constructions that they have heard adults using frequently. It then takes extra effort for them to discern other, less formulaic uses of these same and related expressions. Second, processing two full propositions—one referring to an act of thinking, for example, and one referring to a state of affairs in the world—is cognitively very complex. Thus, it stands to reason that children's earliest multi-clausal utterances should have one clause as a short and formulaic expression that puts minimal demands on working memory. Third, the use of psychological verbs such as *see*, *think*, and *know* involves children's understanding of the mental life of other people. As established by a large body of research, this understanding undergoes significant developments during the preschool years (especially between 4 and 5 years of age), and it is thus likely that 2-year-old children, regardless of their linguistic skills, are not really capable of understanding such things as *He thinks that P*. The fact that children are more skillful earlier with non-mentalistic verbs like *say* and *tell* provides support for the importance of this factor.

Finally, it should be noted that virtually all studies, including those looking at non-European languages (e.g., Kim, 1989), have found that infinitival complements, as described in the previous section, emerge before sentential complements. Presumably, an important factor in explaining this developmental ordering is the fact that infinitival complements typically deal with expressions of volition and intention, which are understood by 2-year-olds, whereas sentential complements more often deal with expressions of knowledge and belief, which are not understood until 4 years old.

7.1.3. Relative Clause Constructions

Relative clauses are not like complement clauses because they do not involve coordination with a main clause at all. Rather, relative clauses serve the very different function of specifying noun phrases in detail. Textbook descriptions focus on so-called restrictive relative clauses—such as *The dog that barked all night died this morning*—in which the relative clause serves to identify a noun by using presupposed information (both speaker and listener already know there was barking all night—that's why it can be used as identifying information). Because relative clauses are a part of a noun phrase argument, they are classically characterized as embedded clauses, and so they have attracted much research attention in both linguistics and developmental psycholinguistics.

The majority of relevant research in child language acquisition has been experimental studies of relative clause comprehension. The focus has been on the question of why children find it harder to interpret so-called center-embedded relative clauses, that is, in English, relative clauses that modify the subject rather than some other utterance constituent. For example, children find it harder to comprehend *The cow that jumped over the fence kissed the pig* than *The cow kissed the pig that jumped over the fence*—as assessed by an act-out task in which children must manipulate toy animals in a manner consistent with the adult utterance. There have been three major hypotheses proposed (with variants):

- *Non-Interruption hypothesis.* Children have trouble interpreting center-embedded relative clauses because they interrupt the processing of the main clause (Slobin, 1973).
- *Conjoined Clause hypothesis.* Children interpret all relative clauses as if they were simply other main clauses and so act them out as such (Tavakolian, 1981).
- *Parallel Function hypothesis.* Children tend to assign single syntactic roles to the NPs involved. This means that the only center-embedded relative clauses that should be difficult are those in which the same noun plays two different roles. Thus, children should have special difficulties with such things as *The cow that the horse kicked ran away,* since the cow was recipient of the kicking but actor of the running away. Utterances such as *The cow that kicked the horse ran away* should be easier since the cow is actor in both cases (Sheldon, 1974; see MacWhinney, 1999, for a similar hypothesis).

Because there are so many different kinds of relative clauses, especially in English but also in other languages, it should be possible to distinguish among these alternatives experimentally. However, a number of methodological difficulties have attended studies of this type (Correa, 1995a), and to date no resolution has been found. One very telling symptom of these difficulties is that many of the classic studies find no age effects—older children perform just as poorly as younger children—which suggests that perhaps the task is unnatural or confusing in some way. Correa (1995b) designed a new task that was more natural and found significant age effects between 3 and 6 years. On the basis of a number of considerations, including an analysis of children's pattern of errors, she concluded that the main problem for children in these tasks is simply keeping track of the many different characters and their activities. This conclusion is in general consistent with that of Clancy, Lee, and Zoh (1986) who found—in a study of English, Japanese, and Korean—that a number of different information processing demands in these comprehension experiments all affected children's performance in significant ways. Yet another reason is that children find it difficult to interpret center-embedded relative clauses is that they have very little experience with them; they do not hear them and they do not produce them. The subjects of English utterances tend overwhelmingly to be pronouns, proper names, or other highly topical NPs (Chafe, 1994), for which relative clauses are useless. In his study of four English-speaking children from 2 to 5 years of age, Diessel (in press) found that less than 1 percent of mothers' relative clauses in their child-directed speech modified the subject. Importantly, basically none of children's utterances with relative clauses during the early preschool period contained subject relatives.

There is very little work on children's use of relative clause constructions in their spontaneous speech. Limber (1973, 1976) and Menyuk (1969) discussed a few aspects of English-speaking children's early use of relative clauses, and Slobin (1982, 1986) compared children's acquisition of relative clauses in Turkish and Serbo-Croatian, identifying a number of processing factors that make acquisition especially difficult in Turkish. The largest study of children's acquisition of relative clauses is by Diessel and Tomasello (2000), who studied four English-speaking children between ages 1;9 and 5;2 in quantitative detail. They made a surprising discovery: virtually all of these children's earliest relative clauses were of the same general form, and this form was not the form typically described in textbooks. Examples would be:

Here's the toy that spins around.
That's the sugar that goes in there.

What is noteworthy here is (1) the main clause is a presentational construction (predicate nominal or closely related), basically introducing a new topic using a proform *(Here, That)* and the copula *(-'s)*; and (2) the information in the relative clause is not presupposed, as in textbook (restrictive) relative clauses, but rather is new information about the just-introduced referent. Indeed, Lambrecht (1988) and Fox and Thompson (1990) argue that these characteristics are so distinctive that we need to posit a "presentational relative construction," a unique utterance-level construction with its own information structure, pragmatics, and meaning. The construction is reasonably common in adult discourse, and indeed more than half of the relative clauses heard by the children in Diessel and Tomasello's study were presentational relatives.

By any reasonable analysis, presentational relatives do not involve an embedding of one clause in another, since the construction as a whole essentially has nothing other than normal topic-comment structure. The main clause involves the copula only and is not itself a true proposition, and the relative clause is not presupposed information but rather contains the new information the speaker wishes to convey. Typically, the main clause is highly formulaic, often involving the introducers *That, Here, There,* or *It* plus the copula. The prototype is thus utterances such as *That's the robot that fell off, Here's the one that melts, It's the boots Mandy gave me.* We might thus represent the construction(s) involved as follows:

It's the N *that* VERB PHRASE
Here's the N *that* VERB PHRASE
There's the N *that* VERB PHRASE

Whether or not these are united by some higher-level construction is at this point unclear.

Interestingly, these kinds of utterances were often preceded by exemplars of what Diessel and Tomasello (following Lambrecht, 1988) call the "presentational amalgam construction." Their status as instances of relative clause constructions is dubious, for certain, but they otherwise resemble in many respects presentational relatives. Some examples are:

That's doggy turn around.
This is my doggy cries.
That's a turtle swim.
Here's a mouse go sleep.
This is the fire engine go Woo-woo.

Quantitatively, Diessel and Tomasello established several important facts about children's early relative clauses. First, 75 percent of the earliest relative clauses produced by the children during their third year of life were exemplars of the presentational relative construction. Another 8 percent occurred in nominals used as whole utterances, for example, *Another picture I made.* Another 10 percent occurred in utterances using the verb *look* to introduce a new topic in a manner very similar to the presentational relative construction, as in, for example:

Look at all the chairs Peter's got.
Look at that train Ursula bought.
Look at that big truck going some place.

Given that the isolated nominals clearly do not involve one clause embedded in another, and given that the presentational relatives (including those with *look*) do not involve a classic embedding, fully 93 percent of the children's earliest relative clauses did not involve the embedding of one clause inside another but rather consisted of a single complex proposition. It is also noteworthy that more than two-thirds of all of the children's earliest relative clauses contained intransitive verbs, further constraining the number of event participants the child needed to keep track of.

Second, in children's later development presentational relatives and isolated nominals with relatives still played a major role—they constituted 37 percent and 23 percent, respectively, of all of the relative clauses produced at ages 4 to 5—but in general children became much more diverse in their usage. During this later period they came to produce much less formulaic main clauses, and their relative clauses modified nouns playing several different roles in the main clause. This general pattern of the early predominance of presentational relatives followed by more diverse use may also be seen in the data of Jisa and Kern (1998) on French-speaking children. However, Dasinger and Toupin (1994) note much variability in the kinds of relative clauses used across different languages. Thus, although presentational relatives are also used quite frequently by Spanish and Hebrew children, they are used less frequently in German and Turkish, where major discourse participants are usually introduced by means of other constructions. Systematic development research on these other languages is sorely needed.

In any case, focusing on the quantitative findings from English, we may propose four explanations for the developmental pattern observed in children's early use of relative clauses. First, children hear many presentational relatives from their parents, 54 percent of all parental relatives in the study of Diessel (in press). Second, the earliest relative clauses are built on children's highly practiced, formulaic, and item-based constructions of the type *There's the X, Here's the X, That's an X, It's an X.* Lieven, Pine, and Baldwin, (1997) document that these are among the earliest and most frequent constructions mastered by English-speaking children. Third, the topic-comment information structure of presentational relatives is also quite familiar to young children from a variety of their other constructions, and indeed the presentational main clause typically serves to focus attention on a referent perceptually present in the immediate context. Fourth, presentational relatives—perhaps especially those with intransitive relative clauses—simplify the processing requirements as much as possible by minimizing the number of participants involved, and, as argued above, do not even involve embedding of the classic variety.

7.1.4. Conjoined Clause Constructions

Infinitival complements, sentential complements, and relative clauses all represent constructions in which two clauses are relatively tightly integrated. There is another class of complex constructions in which two clauses are integrated much more loosely, typically with connectives such as *and, but, so, because, when,* and *if.* The loosest integration occurs in the coordination of two independent clauses, for example, in utterances such as:

> You do this, and I'll do that.
> She whistled loudly, but Fido didn't answer.

On the other end of the continuum are so-called adverbial clauses, which indicate such things as temporal, causal, and conditional relations between clauses. In adverbial constructions one of the clauses is not independent but in some sense depends on the other, as in utterances such as:

> I bought it *because* it was cheap.
> I'll turn it on *so* you can watch it.
> *When* you get there, you must call your mother.
> *If* you come early, you'll get a good seat.

Prototypically, an adverbial clause provides background or orienting information relative to the main clause, whereas in coordinate constructions both clauses provide foregrounded information.

Bloom and colleagues (1980) studied the coordinate and adverbial constructions (along with some others) of four English-speaking children from 2 to 3 years of age. They focused on the ages at which children learned to use the different connectives and the ways they learned to use them. Their results are summarized in Figure 7.2. In agreement with most other smaller-scale studies, they found that the connective *and* was the first to be learned by all of the children; and during the 2- to 3-year age period it was used for a variety of different functions, for example:

> *Additive:* Maybe you can carry that *and* I can carry this.
> *Temporal:* Jocelyn's going home *and* take her sweater off.
> *Causal:* She put a Band-Aid on her shoe *and* it maked it feel better.

The next connectives to be learned were *because, when, so, then, if,* and *but,* with some individual differences among children. In terms of func-

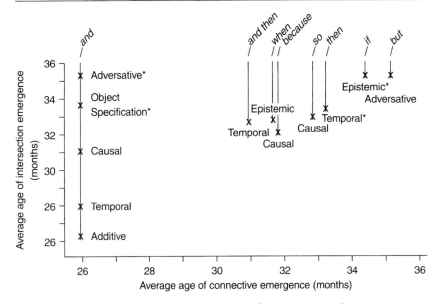

Figure 7.2. The development of the intersection of connectives with semantic relations. X marks intersections that were productive for only two of the four children. Adapted from Bloom et al. (1980); reprinted with the permission of Cambridge University Press.

tions (irrespective of which connectives expressed them) the observed order was:

additive < temporal < causal < adversative

General support for this ordering was also found in a study of Dutch-speaking children by Spooren and Sanders (submitted).

Once again, the most comprehensive and quantitatively detailed study of coordinate and adverbial constructions is that of Diessel (in press). He analyzed almost 5,000 utterances containing a coordinate or adverbial connective from five English-speaking children during the 2- to 5-year age period. In general agreement with Bloom et al. (1980), he found that the first connective to emerge at around 2;0 was *and,* and that it was used for a variety of functions. Perhaps surprisingly, this single connective accounted for over half of all of the utterances with connectives during the course of the study. Perhaps even more surprisingly, approximately 80 percent of all the utterances with *and* were single clauses, the connection being either to the adult's previous conversational turn or to an immediately preceding child utterance that was uttered independently, with its own intonation contour. For example:

Child: Nina has dolly sleeping.
Adult: The doll is sleeping too?
Child: *And* the man's sleeping on the big bed.

Child: Flipper's on TV yeah.
Child: *And* Shaggy's not on TV.

Later, of course, children used *and* as a connective between two clauses somewhat more frequently, although the use with isolated clauses predominated throughout; at 4 to 5 years of age, about 30 percent of the uses were as a clausal connective, with 70 percent introducing isolated clauses. Interestingly, Peterson and McCabe (1987) followed children's later uses of *and* (up to 9 years old) and found that it continued to be by far the most frequent connective used by children and that it was still used for a wide variety of semantic relationships even though new and more specific connectives were being learned during this time—with the prototypical use as a simple coordinating conjunction accounting for only about 20 percent of uses at all ages.

The next connectives to emerge were *because, so,* and *but.* The first two of these were used most often to indicate psychological causes or reasons for happenings in the world. *Because* was used initially to explain or justify something in response to an adult query or challenge, mainly in the form of the *why*-question. Of the first 15 utterances with *because* produced by each of these five children (total = 75), almost 90 percent were in response to adult *why*-questions, so that the vast majority of uses of *because* were for introducing isolated utterances, not for introducing dependent clauses in a complex construction.

Child: You can't have this.
Adult: Why?
Child: *Cause* I'm using it.

In contrast, *so* and *but* were used in a more self-initiative manner, typically to further expound on a previous utterance by either the child or an adult. About 70–80 percent of the earliest uses occurred in an isolated clause. For example:

Child: It opened.
Child: *So* the horsie could get out.

Adult: It's called the skin of the peanut.
Child: *But* this isn't the skin.

Later, both of these connectives were used more often to introduce dependent clauses in complex constructions—about 40 percent of all uses at age 5.

In addition to these early-learned and relatively frequently used connectives, Diessel (in press) tracked six other less frequently used connectives that were mostly not produced until after 3 years of age: *when, if, while, until, after,* and *before*. These connectives were not used very often in isolated clauses, but were used from the beginning as a connective of two clauses under a single intonation contour (over 80 percent of the time overall). In most of these cases the clause with the connective provided background or presupposed information, for example:

And we both sleep on the floor *when* we take naps.
It's gonna stay raining . . . *if* you put it down.
He bite the tongue *while* he was eating.
It's getting crowded *after* I put all the dollies in.

Interestingly, some of these connectives were also used on occasion in the initial clause, mostly in the 3- to 5-year age range, for example:

After it dries off . . . then you can make the bottom.
When it's got a flat tire . . . its need to go to the station.
If he takes all of them I'm gonna beat him up.

Diessel argues these initial adverbial clauses are late to appear because (1) they typically supply orienting information for the following clause, and young children are notoriously bad at providing orienting information for others (see below on narratives); and (2) normally one must know what is coming in the second clause before producing the first orienting clause, thus requiring the child to hold two full propositions in mind to make her utterance.

Diessel explains the order of emergence of all these different connectives in coordinate and adverbial constructions in terms of three factors. First, the connectives differ in terms of the complexity of their discourse functions, which means that some of them can only be acquired later. Second, the connectives differ in terms of the linguistic complexity of the constructions in which they appear; for example, utterance-initial adverbial clauses would seem to require fairly complex linguistic and processing skills. Third, inspection of the mothers' uses of these same connectives reveals, not surprisingly, that the ones the child uses earliest are, on the whole, the ones the mother uses most frequently. In addition, Kyratzis and Ervin-Tripp (1999) point out that many of these connectives actually have several very different discourse functions, and that adult-like mastery of this plurifunctionality takes many years.

As with other complex constructions, experimental studies of conjoined clause constructions have found that young children often do not show skills of comprehension that match their spontaneous productions. The best-known example is Clark's (1971) investigations of children's under-

262 Constructing a Language

standing of complex utterances with the connectives *before* and *after.* Into the school years children have problems in acting out with toy characters events that are described in such a way that the order of mention of the clauses is discrepant with the real order of events. Clark's hypothesis was that they do not know the full meaning of the terms *before* and *after.* However, French and Nelson (1985) argued and presented evidence that children are much better with these terms when the experimental materials are highly familiar to them (see also Silva, 1991). In addition, Slobin (1982) found that young Turkish-speaking children were much better with these terms, mainly because they occurred in simpler constructions involving "local cues" (see Chapter 4). Kawashima and Prideaux (1992) supported this contention by finding very similar performance in comprehension tasks by preschoolers who spoke Japanese, a language that also uses local cues to mark temporal relationships in complex constructions.

7.1.5. Two Theories

Table 7.3 presents a very rough overview of English-speaking children's acquisition of the major types of complex constructions. What can be clearly seen in this table is that children's earliest complex constructions form a very delimited set revolving around a relatively small number of lexical items and item-based constructions in the so-called matrix clauses (*I wanna, I gotta, I think, Look at, See, It's the,* and so forth). Children learn first those constructions they hear most frequently, and before 3 years of age it is very unlikely that they are embedding one proposition in another in any of these constructions. From a functional point of view, the earliest infinitival complements are like deontic modals (*hafta V* is like *must V*); sentential complements are like epistemic modals (*I think P* is like *Maybe P*); and presentational relative constructions are like simple utterance-level constructions (*There's the N that Vs* is like *This N Vs*). Children's later use of these constructions becomes much more varied and, in many cases, involves the embedding of one proposition in another.

There are a number of different generative grammar accounts of the acquisition of these complex constructions, but what is in common to all of them—based on an appeal to the continuity assumption—is an analysis utilizing highly abstract and adult-like categories. As just one example, Pinker (1984: 214–215) proposes the following procedure for the acquisition of complement-taking predicates:

> Whenever a predicate takes an argument which is itself a complete proposition, and when that proposition is represented in the tree without its subject by a phrasal category X:

Table 7.3 Overall pattern of development of English-speaking children's complex constructions.

	2;0–2;6	2;6–3;0	3;0+
Infinitival complements	wanna V, gonna V, hafta V, gotta V [95% of earliest]	see N V-ing, want N to V, watch N V-ing, make N V [88% of all of this type]	Heavier and more diverse set of matrix clauses
Sentential complements		think P, know P, see P, say P, look at P [80% of earliest]	Heavier and more diverse set of matrix clauses
Relative clauses		it's/there's/here's/that's the NP that . . . , the NP that . . . . [83% of earliest; 70% of total]	Heavier and more diverse set of main clauses
Conjoined clauses	P and Q	P and Q, P but Q, P cause Q, P so Q, P if Q, P when Q [92%]	If/when P, then Q (i.e., preposed clauses)

Source: Approximate percentages from Diessel (in press) or Bloom et al. (1980).

C1. Connect X as a sister of the predicate that contains the propositional argument.

C2. Create a lexical entry for the predicate, in which the propositional argument is encoded as the function X-COMP where X is the category label of the subjectless proposition.

C3. Add to the lexical entry of the complement-taking predicate the equation X-COMP's SUBJ = (FUNCTION), where (FUNCTION) is the grammatical function annotated to the matrix argument that is coindexed with the missing complement subject in the contextually inferred semantic representation . . .

C4. Add two equations to the lexical entry of the complement-taking verb. The first should have the form X-COMP's MORPH = å, where å is *inf*, *fin*, *perfpart* [perfect participle], etc., depending on the morphology of the embedded verb . . . The second should have the form X-COMP's CMPZR = ß, where ß is the word found in complementizer position (i.e., specifier of X′ in the complement).

In contrast to this totally abstract analysis, Diessel (in press) concludes that before 3 years of age children's skills with complex constructions are heavily item-based, with a gradual broadening and deepening of competence after this age. Thus, just looking at the infinitival and sentential complements, we might propose the following. Children are exposed to and acquire five main types of these constructions, with possible further subdivisions (following the classic account of Quirk et al., 1985). Given that they already know good bit of language before they begin to learn these constructions between 2 and 3 years of age, what they acquire initially are patterns that are complex mixtures of specific lexical items and some more abstract categories. Oversimplifying, a given child might learn something like the following (note that the categories depicted might actually be lists, or some mixture of lists and categories, or more concrete categories, or specific words, or whatever—the following is only intended to illustrate the kind of analysis intended):

Infinitival: NP   wanna/hafta/gotta   VERB
Participial: See/look at/remember   NP   VERB-*ing*
S-complement: NP   think/know/guess   that/ø   CLAUSE
If-complement: NP   see/tell/wonder   if   CLAUSE
Wh-complement: NP   see/look/know/   what/how/when   CLAUSE-gap

It should be noted that in the analyses of Hudson (1995) and Cullicover (1999) even adult competence must be specified to some degree lexically as well, because each of these constructions has some quirks associated with it depending on the particular complementizers and matrix verbs involved.

Diessel thus argues in the case of infinitival complements and sentential complements that although children's early productions appear to include two propositions, one embedded in the other, in actual fact the main clauses in all cases are more like clausal operators. The verbs in these main clauses virtually all have to do with the child's psychological attitudes or those she wishes to bring about in a second person—either intention/ volition or perception/cognition—and thus they function very much like modal auxiliaries. In the case of relative clauses, Diessel shows that the main clause functions simply to introduce a new topic/referent, and comes from a very small set of expressions with the copula or another light verb. The information structure in all three of these constructions is such that the new and interesting information appears in the supposedly subordinate clause. The development of these constructions after 3 years of age centers on children's acquisition of a broader range of types of main clauses, and on operating on these main clauses with modals, negatives, and so on, in a way that makes them into full propositions. Diessel calls this "clause expansion."

The conjoined clause constructions work slightly differently. The vast majority of them, especially before 3 years of age, derive from conversational replies (or follow-ups to an initial utterance) in which the first word is a connective such as *and, but,* or *because.* Gradually the child comes to put together both of these utterances with the connective between them. After 3 years of age, a major development is that children begin to learn connectives that function from the start to connect two clauses. Furthermore, at this age they also learn to use some adverbials (such as *if-* and *when*-clauses) to begin utterances, as orienting information for listeners— which demands a higher level of utterance planning. Overall, Diessel calls the process involved in the development of coordinate and adverbial constructions "clause integration."

Explaining the order of acquisition of complex constructions, both between and within broad categories, involves a number of potential factors. For example, children seem to learn infinitival complements before sentential complements. This could be because infinitival complements are more tightly integrated than sentential complements, because they deal more with intentions and less with beliefs (which are cognitively more difficult), because they are more useful (since expressing intentions and desires is so important for young children), and, not to be forgotten, because children hear them more often in their linguistic experience. As another example, at the outset children use mostly presentational relative clauses, and this could be because of cognitive complexity, linguistic complexity, familiarity with information structure, or frequency. It is crucially important that explanations of children's developing competence with complex constructions also take account of the fact that adult-like competence emerges only gradually as children master a wider range lexical material and come to terms with the plurifunctionality of some of the key function words involved.

Systematic investigations are sorely needed. The three most important outstanding issues concern (1) cross-linguistic comparisons, (2) comparisons between experimental and observational findings, and (3) the relation of input to acquisition. Thus, it would be very helpful to know if children's acquisition of complex constructions in other languages shows the same kinds of item-based patterns as the English, with the same kinds of frequency distributions. And discrepancies between observations of this process and experimental findings need to be resolved. At least part of the answer seems to be that in experiments children are typically confronted with instantiations of complex constructions drawn from adult usage, or even worse, from written language—and their skills are much too lexically dependent and context dependent to operate on this new and strange material. In terms of input, Huttenlocher et al. (in press) have recently found very impressive correlations between the number of utterances instantiating complex constructions that children hear—both at home and at school—and their acquisition of these same constructions in both production and comprehension. Experiments with nonce verbs—perhaps depicting Martians with novel psychological states—might also help to specify children's underlying linguistic representations in more detail, or perhaps sentence-repetition experiments in which children must repeat utterances instantiating constructions with which they have different amounts and/or types of experience.

7.2. Conversation and Narrative

The analysis of conjoined clauses illustrated how children can integrate linguistic structures across conversational turns. But when engaged in a conversation, the child focuses her attention not on the linguistic structures she and her partner are using but rather on the topic she is conversing about. The analysis of children's conversational skills, therefore, is mainly concerned with how immature language users manage information in conversation—how they establish and maintain conversational topics across turns—which is very different from a concern with their skills in building linguistic structures.

7.2.1. Topic Maintenance and Repair in Conversation

From soon after birth infants begin learning about turn-taking in social interaction (Trevarthen, 1979). By their first birthdays, infants can begin to both follow into and direct adult attention to outside objects. From about 18 months of age, young children can predicate things about some already established topic of shared attention, for example, pointing to a shoe and commenting to an adult "Mommy's" (Greenfield et al., 1985). At around 24 months of age, children are able to take a fully adult-like turn in a true conversation in which they linguistically specify in their turn both the topic of shared interest and the comment they wish to make about it, typically containing new information (Foster, 1986). In the current framework, we may say that things that are in the joint attentional frame are shared and therefore topical (or accessible in the terms of Gundel, Hedberg, and Zacharski, 1993, and Ariel, 1988), whereas things outside that frame are new and so take a special effort to be placed in focus linguistically.

In the beginning, children mostly make their assessments of which things are already in the joint attentional frame and which things are new only from their own egocentric point of view (Greenfield and Smith, 1976). As development proceeds, they learn to make reference to topics in various conventionally appropriate ways, given their assessment of the current joint attentional frame from a less egocentric perspective. And so, older children make sure to establish topics explicitly when needed by pointing or by using pronouns or definite NPs, before they attempt to focus the listener's attention more specifically. This gradual progression from nonlinguistic to linguistic means for establishing topics, and its coordination with the linguistic expression of new information in comments (from the listener's point of view), is depicted in Table 7.4.

At 2 years of age children produce about two-thirds of their utterances directly adjacent to an adult utterance (the other third coming after a long pause; Bloom, Rocissano, and Hood, 1976). However, many of these utterances are not semantically contingent on the adult's previous utterance; they are off the topic or else they are attempts to initiate a new topic. Indeed, children at this age answer only about one-third of the questions adults ask them (Pan and Snow, 1999). Children are also limited in their provision of full conversational turns, that is, turns including both some reference to the preceding topic and some new information. Bloom, Rocissano, and Hood found that 21 percent of the turns taken by 21-month-olds in conversations with their mothers were full conversational turns, with that number rising to 46 percent by 36 months of age.

When they do engage in a relatively extended conversation on a single topic, young 2-year-olds typically take only one or two turns per conversation (Foster, 1986; Tomasello and Mannle, 1985); this value doubles, or more, by 4 years of age (Barton and Tomasello, 1991). And much of this early conversation is dependent on a structured nonlinguistic situation as

Table 7.4   Developmental sequence of topic-comment coordination using gestures and language.

		Topic	Comment
0–9 months	Protoconversations	—	—
9–12 months	Joint attention	Nonlinguistic	—
12–18 months	Holophrase	Linguistic	—
18–24 months	One-word predication	Nonlinguistic	Linguistic
24+ months	True conversation	Linguistic	Linguistic

Source: Based on Tomasello (1988). Reprinted with the permission of Elsevier Science.

a kind of scaffolding. Thus, Lucariello and Nelson (1986) found that mother-child dyads engaged in significantly longer conversations when engaged in routine nonlinguistic interactions. Similarly, Conti-Ramsden and Friel-Patti (1987) found that the degree of "scriptedness" in the nonlinguistic interaction predicted the sophistication of 2-year-olds' conversational skills (see also Didow and Eckerman, 1996, 2001). In a series of experimental studies, Bachrach and Luszcz (1979, 1983) attempted to set a conversational topic with young children as they looked at pictures with them (for example, "Here's a story about a duck"). In general, the 3-year-olds were more influenced by the particularities of the picture than by the topic the adult tried to set, whereas the 5-year-olds attempted to stay on the adult's suggested topic as they described the pictures.

It is not always clear in children's early conversations how much they are holding up their side of the bargain versus how much parents are structuring the interaction for them. One way to investigate this question is to look at young children in interaction with other young children. In a variety of studies, it has been found that child-sibling and child-peer conversations are shorter and less coherent than child-adult conversations (Dunn and Shatz, 1989; see Barton and Tomasello, 1994, for a review). For example, Mannle, Barton and Tomasello (1992; see also Tomasello and Mannle, 1985), found that 2-year-olds' conversations with their mothers were two and one-half times longer than those with their 3- to 5-year-old siblings. This would seem to indicate that adult conversational skills play a large role in scaffolding the longer and more complex conversations in which young children participate.

A surprising additional finding, however, is that young children are quite skillful at joining ongoing conversations between other persons. Dunn and Shatz (1989) found that most of children's attempts to join an ongoing conversation between a parent and sibling were successful in the sense that the conversation continued on topic. Barton and Tomasello (1991) found this as well, and in addition they found that these three-way conversations were several times longer than the dyadic conversations that these same children engaged in with their mothers, with the children themselves taking three times as many turns. These investigators hypothesized that three-way conversations "take the pressure off" young children because in such conversations they do not need to take every other turn to ensure its continuation, but can wait and enter into the conversation whenever they feel competent. These findings support the view that young children comprehend and can deal effectively with linguistic interactions that do not include them directly (Akhtar, Jipson, and Callanan, 2001). This is important because in many cultures young children get less speech directed specifically to them than in Western middle-class culture (Ochs and Schieffelin, 1986), and so they must more often eavesdrop on other people's conversations and assert themselves by joining in.

As they approach school age, children take the listener's knowledge and perspective into account in much more sophisticated ways in conversation—for example, through the use of very subtle discourse particles such as *actually, in fact, although, just, still, nevertheless, on the other hand,* and *certainly* (Ervin-Tripp, 1996). However, this developmental process is extremely slow, as 10-year-olds use discourse particles of this type three times more often than 6-year-olds but still much less often than adults (Scott, 1984).

Another important indication of young children's conversational skills is their ability to repair a conversation when it has somehow derailed. Garvey (1977) found that 3- to 5-year-olds respond appropriately to a wide variety of requests for clarification from adults (which come at the rate of about one every five minutes in relatively focused conversational interactions; Mannle, Barton, and Tomasello, 1992). At 2 years of age, about half of children's unintelligible utterances (as judged by experimenters) are queried by adults (Snow et al., 1996). Gallagher (1977, 1981) and Wilcox and Webster (1980) investigated children from the very origins of their language development at 18 months of age, and found that from the beginning they can respond to adult queries such as *What?* or *Huh?* in specific ways, especially by repeating themselves (see also Marcos and Bernicot, 1994, on French-speaking children). Further along these lines, Anselmi, Tomasello, and Acunzo (1986) found that children just after their second birthdays responded differentially when the adult query was more generic *(Huh?)* than when it was more specific *(Put it where?).* In the latter case they responded, appropriately, by more often providing only the requested information (as opposed to repeating the whole utterance, for example). Overall, in this study children in the 2- to 4-year age period responded to requests for clarification at least somewhat appropriately about 85 percent of the time.

In a variation on this theme, Tomasello, Farrar, and Dines (1983) found that 2-year-old children reformulated their utterances differently when queried by their mother than when queried by an unfamiliar adult. For their mother, they more often repeated themselves (perhaps because they knew she was familiar with their speech and so she must not have heard the utterance well), whereas for the unfamiliar adult they more often reformulated their utterance (perhaps because they knew she was unfamiliar with their speech and therefore needed an additional formulation). This finding is important because it represents one of the earliest indications that young children are taking into account characteristics of (if not the specific knowledge and expectations of) their conversational partners in creating their conversational contributions. Another interesting study that underscores this mental dimension to the process is that of Schwe and Markman (1997), who found that 2-year-olds responded differently when adults failed to comply with their requests, as a function of their assessment of whether the adult did not understand their message or understood it but chose not to comply.

Children themselves do not request clarification very often. In one large-scale longitudinal study, Pan et al. (1996) found that virtually no 14-month-old children ever requested clarification of a parental utterance. By 20 months of age, almost one-third of the children requested clarification at least occasionally, and by 32 months virtually all the children did so with some regularity. Their clarification requests at these young ages are generally of the generic type—typically *Huh?* or *What?*—and do not show a detailed analysis of which part of the adult utterance caused their comprehension difficulties. Even at 7 years of age, when they are put into a difficult communicative situation (for example, on the telephone), children seldom ask for clarification in a manner that appears adequate to adults (Lloyd, 1991).

7.2.2. Narrative Discourse

At sometime around their second birthdays, young children begin to talk not just about ongoing events but also about past events, a transition sometimes characterized as moving from the here-and-now to the there-and-then (Sachs, 1983). This displacement of conversational topic in time and space is interesting in the first instance because of the progress it reveals in children's ability to cognitively, indeed symbolically, represent the world.

In addition, however, this displacement creates some fundamentally new communicative problems for the child. Most fundamentally, the child's linguistic communication until this point has relied heavily on the shared perceptual context between herself and her listener, enabling her to use pointing gestures and pronouns, for example, with little risk of misunderstanding. But when the child is recounting an event that happened yesterday at Grandma's, or last summer at Disney World, the normal perceptual support is missing and she must find new ways to ground her utterances with respect to her listener's perspective. In general, the child must learn the use more so-called endophoric devices for grounding her acts of reference and predication in already recounted parts of the narrative (as opposed to exophoric or deictic devices used to ground reference and predication in the immediate perceptual context). The problem is that many of these endophoric devices are none other than the exophoric devices the child has already been using for months or years for other functions.

For example, definite reference and pronouns *(the boy, he)* must somehow make contact with something the child has already said in the narrative if the listener, who was not there for the event, is to successfully identify the intended person (the pronoun and definite article in true narratives are thus anaphoric, not deictic). Also, telling stories involves a constant monitoring of (1) which aspects of the event should be foregrounded and emphasized (such as plot line) and which should be backgrounded and deemphasized (such as onlookers if they do not play a central role in the plot); and (2) what is given and what is new for the listener. These effects are achieved by a wide variety of devices, ranging from verb tense and aspect (plot line is most often conveyed with perfective tenses) to complex constructions (backgrounded information is often in one or another kind of subordinate clause). And indeed in many accounts it is the functional demands of narrative discourse that have led historically to some of the more complex aspects of linguistics structure (Hopper, 1997)—although quite often the child first learns the devices on the utterance level and then learns their use in narratives.

The more linguistically oriented studies of children's personal narratives have mainly focused on children's ability to relate a coherent and cohesive sequence of events, which typically requires some kinds of setting/orientation information in addition to plot line. The general finding across many studies is that children's earliest narratives between 2 and 3 years of age are sorely lacking in setting/orientation information. As an example, Peterson (1990) reports the following narrative from a child at age 2;3 (following talk about a tape recorder):

Child: He bite my leg.
Adult: What?
Child: Duck bite my leg.
Adult: The dog bit your leg. Oh, oh, the duck. Oh boy!
Child: Me go in the water.
Adult: You went in the water?
Child: Yeah. My leg.

The child is clearly relating a past event of great importance, but the topic comes out of nowhere—to the degree that the adult doesn't even know initially that a duck is the protagonist—and the child provides no information about when, where, or how the event took place. And it is likely that the actual sequence of the biting event and the leg-in-the-water event was the reverse of the order in which they are recounted by the child.

Children's personal narratives are, by definition, particular to individuals, which can make comparison across ages, groups, and languages difficult—as children have different events to relate. Therefore, some researchers have attempted to create comparability by having children narrate a standard set of events, typically in the form of a series of pictures. In general, the finding here is that young children struggle even more than in their personal narratives to craft a coherent narrative. For example, Berman and Slobin (1994) had young children in many different languages narrate a wordless picture book. The youngest children were 3-year-olds, and they were almost uniformly unsuccessful in providing a coherent narrative with a discernible beginning, middle, and end. These children used very few cohesive devices for keeping track of the participants and events across time, and they availed themselves of fewer of the expressive options in their language for taking different perspectives on events and packaging events into larger units for purposes of narrating. The older children were much more skillful. Berman and Slobin invoke three main dimensions of development that explain children's progress with narratives into the school years:

- They become better able *cognitively* to conceive of the full range of encodable perspectives that may be taken on a series of events—for example, as dynamic activities or static states.
- They become better able *communicatively* to assess the listener's perspective—including everything from the choice of a nominal to deciding what should be foregrounded and what should be backgrounded.
- They become more skillful *linguistically* with the full range of devices provided by their language for accomplishing their discourse goals—including such things as the use of past perfect forms (as in *had hidden*) and complex nominalizations (as in *the destruction of the city*).

In all of this, two of the most difficult tasks for young children in narrative discourse are (1) keeping track of specific referents as they participate in different events across time (and clauses), and (2) ordering events (and orientation information) in time. First, with respect to reference tracking, Peterson and Dodsworth (1991) found that children aged 2;0–3;6 most often employed pronominals *(she, it)* and demonstratives *(this, that one)* for repeated reference to the same discourse participant in their personal narratives. They also quite often repeated the same nominal, or a close synonym, across clauses for the same participant. After about 3 years of age children also used comparative reference *(another cat)*, nominal ellipsis *(There was a cat, or maybe two)*, and substitution *(Birthday parties? I went to one last week)*. Peterson (1990) looked more broadly at the kind of information children provided for unfamiliar listeners to help them identify precisely who was being talked about (and where the action took place) in their personal narratives. She found that young children, again aged 2;0–3;6, were very poor at this in general. Most often they used *we* without specifying who was involved (although the investigators assumed that it typically was the family) and omitted explicit reference to participants other than themselves. When they named others, they typically did so with a first name only and no further identifying information to help their unfamiliar listeners with the task of identification. There was an increase across this age in the amount of information children supplied about the spatial setting.

Bennett-Kastor (1983) took a more quantitative approach and examined a wider age range, from 2 to 5 years. The focus was on referents that were referred to in the narrative more than once. Table 7.5 provides a quantitative overview. The 2-, 3-, and 4-year-olds used about the same number of nominals per story (3.5), and they repeated mentioning them about the same number of times per story (4.5). But the 5-year-olds used about twice as many nominals as these younger children, and they mentioned each of them about 50 percent more often. The final two columns in Table 7.5 indicate, respectively, the number of clauses that intervened between repeated mentions of the same participant (clause gaps) and the number of clauses over which a given nominal spanned (clause span). Again the 5-year-olds look very different from the younger children. They only needed to touch base with a given participant about half as often as the younger children (double length of clause gaps) and that participant was continually mentioned, on average, across a span of more than three times as many clauses. In another set of analyses, it was found that 5-year-olds also can introduce new participants into the story, and weave them into the plot coherently, much later in the story than the younger children. Bennett-Kastor concludes that there is a great leap in children's skills with

Table 7.5   Noun phrase coherence values per story per age group.

Age	Number of NPs	Average mention per NP	Coherency value per mention	Coherency value per NP
2	3.67	4.55	1.16	5.27
3	3.50	3.86	0.88	3.38
4	3.57	4.92	1.06	5.20
5	7.20	6.39	2.19	14.00

Source: Based on Bennett-Kastor (1983).

nominals in narratives at around 5 years of age. At this age they begin to tell stories with more participants, with more events per participant, with denser structure (less frequent reiteration of the same nominal), and with later participant introductions.

Karmiloff-Smith (1986) proposed that until age 5 children keep track of referents mostly by employing the "thematic subject constraint," that is, they tend to establish a single character as central and make her the subject of each of the succeeding utterances in the narrative (without providing much in the way of explicit connectives). After 5 years of age, children develop more sophisticated discourse skills in which syntagmatic relations are established across many clauses. Unfortunately for language learners, many of the linguistic forms that are an integral part of these discourse skills are forms that children have already been using for some time for other communicative purposes. For example, *because* is first used by children only in conversation to answer *why*-questions (see above on conjoined clauses), and children must later learn to use it to connect information across clauses in narratives in a way that explains events for their listener. Karmiloff-Smith (1986) thus stresses that many of children's struggles with narratives derive from the plurifunctionality of the linguistic devices that must be mastered. Hickmann (1995) concurs and argues that skills with narrative discourse in general are late-developing in children speaking all of the languages that have been studied (mostly developing during the school years); claims to the contrary are simply based on researchers ignoring this plurifunctionality and attributing to children full knowledge of a form upon its first use in a single context.

In picture-elicited narratives children also show a relatively late mastery of the full range of devices their language offers for introducing and keeping track of referents across clauses. Summarizing several series of studies, Karmiloff-Smith (1986) argues that from 3 to 5 years of age children's pronouns and definite articles in narratives are actually functioning deictically. They are being used appropriately at the level of the individual utterance to indicate a referent, but different mentions in the same story are not endophorically related to one another. As an example, she offers a short narrative by a young child with many ambiguous uses of *he,* among other ambiguities:

> There's a little boy in red. He's walking along and he sees a balloon man and he gives him a green one and he walks off home and it flies away into the sky so he cries.

In contrast, children over 5 years of age are much better at avoiding such ambiguous references by grounding their nominals with respect one another endophorically, as can be seen most clearly in their self-corrections in telling part of the same story:

> . . . He meets a man selling balloons and he gives the boy . . . a man selling balloons who gives him a green balloon. He goes off really pleased.

Karmiloff-Smith also observes significant developments in children after 8 years of age, especially in their ability to appreciate the plurifunctionality characteristic of many, indeed most, referential terms. Similarly, Kail and Hickmann (1992) found that only 9-year-olds chose appropriately among the many referential terms available in French given experimental conditions in which listeners either did or did not share with them perceptual access to the stimulus materials. Cross-linguistic studies have found that even though there are many specific differences in the devices different languages provide for making reference in narratives (e.g., MacWhinney and Bates, 1978; Hickmann and Hendriks, 1999), endophoric coordination of acts of reference and appreciation of the plurifunctionality of referential devices are uniformly late acquisitions, and may even depend to some extent on the acquisition of literacy skills during early schooling (Hickmann, 1995).

Turning to the role of temporality in discourse narratives, the major fact is that in their earliest personal narratives, 2- and 3-year-old children provide very little information about time orientation in the sense of when an event happened relative to now. Indeed, Peterson (1990) observed that such time orientation in early narratives was "almost nonexistent." When they do provide such information it is typically with formulaic and not-well-understood terms such as *yesterday* or *last night,* often used indiscriminately for past time.

These early narratives also show very little internal temporal structuring, except that they most often follow the sequence of events as they actually happened. But the use of linguistic devices to modulate this iconic structuring is minimal, and often is simply redundant with the iconic ordering (Peterson and McCabe, 1991a, 1991b). The most common terms

are, in English, *and, and then, and so,* and *so,* which are present even in
the earliest narratives. Children's appropriate production and comprehension of more sophisticated temporal terms such as *before, after,* and *first*—
not to mention *while, during, until, since,* and so on—is notoriously poor
until well into the school years (see French and Nelson, 1985, for a review). Moreover, in a sensitive analysis of the range of uses to which children put some of these terms Levy and Nelson (1994) argue that temporal
language provides the paradigm case for "use before meaning," as children acquire temporal terms in relatively fixed formulas or in a restricted
range of discourse uses. In a study of the picture-elicited narratives of Ger-
man- and Turkish-speaking children, Aksu-Koç and von Stutterheim
(1994: 451) found that children before 5 years of age had much difficulty
coordinating sequence and simultaneity, and only the children older than
5 years were able to organize their speech along a narrative thread so that
they could "move from a mere juxtaposition of equally weighted pieces of
information to hierarchical structures in discourse." Once again for temporal ordering, the age of 5 years seems to mark a turning point in children's narrative skills, with further important developments continuing to
take place throughout the school years.

7.2.3. Thinking for Speaking

Some of the researchers who have investigated discourse and narrative
skills have speculated on the role of linguistic communication in children's
cognitive development more generally. Perhaps the most interesting proposal is that of Slobin (1996), who focuses not so much on possible long-
term effects of language on nonlinguistic cognition—the conventional
construal of the Whorfian hypothesis (linguistic determinism: language determines thought)—but rather on the different ways that different languages require young children to attend to things and to construe things
for purposes of formulating a linguistic utterance on-line: so-called thinking for speaking.

Illustrative of this perspective, Berman and Slobin (1994) found that
when children learning different languages are asked to tell a story based
on the same set of pictures, they end up conceptualizing the story in very
different ways. In "thinking for speaking" these children must learn to pay
attention to some things and to ignore others, and to construe (or perspectivize) things in one way rather than another, in accordance with
the linguistic conventions of the particular language they are learning—
especially those conventions involving obligatory grammatical marking.
For example, speakers of Spanish have more possible tense-aspect distinctions available to them than do speakers of English, and so young Spanish

children must pay attention to and choose among various temporal profiles in their narrative discourse in a more differentiated way than young English children. Slobin's studies have gone on to document a number of effects of language on the on-line process of conceptualization, for example, the ways languages influence how children attend to specific types of spatial, causal, and social relations, and perspectivize scenes (see Slobin, 1996, for a review).

More fundamentally, Nelson (1996) has proposed that a major change in the relation of language to thought takes place when children become skillful with narratives, at around 4 or 5 years of age. Young children before this age use language to direct and cajole, comment and question, request and exclaim, but they do not use it to represent the world explicitly—as they will later when they, for example, report on a trip to the beach in narrative discourse, complete with evaluative commentary about many aspects of the event. That is to say, before they can engage in narrative discourse 2- and 3-year-old children use language in the context of concrete activities, in effect letting those activities do much of the talking. But when older children report on some event in which they have previously participated, the only representational medium is language, and it does virtually all of the representational work.

> Language [at 2 and 3 years of age] is used in, as part of, and in conjunction with [cultural] activities, and not primarily as a medium of conveying knowledge from one person to another. Its primary use is pragmatic, not symbolic . . . Language uses in these shared activities help to mark them, to move them forward, but language is not initially used to *represent* them as such in the child's cognitive or communicative productions. (Nelson, 1996: 91)

In contrast, older children use language not just to participate in and influence events but also to depict them and comment on them for others.

A number of theorists have also proposed that discourse might play an important role in children's coming to have a "theory of mind," that is, coming to view other persons as mental agents who can have beliefs (including false beliefs) about the world (Harris, 1996; Tomasello, 1999). The basic idea is that to comprehend the communicative intentions of others children must in some sense simulate the perspective of other persons as they are expressing themselves linguistically, and so the back and forth of discourse involves the child in a constant shifting of perspectives from her own to that of others and back again. In general agreement with this hypothesis, Peterson and Siegal (1999) found that deaf children whose deaf parents were fluent users of a sign language in discourse were much faster to develop theory-of-mind skills than were deaf children whose hearing parents did not speak a sign language fluently.

One especially important form of discourse would seem to be disagreements and misunderstandings. Dunn (1988) has documented something of the wide range of disputes and conflicts, as well as cooperative interactions, in which children of the same family participate on a daily basis (see also Dunn, Brown, and Beardsall, 1991). Perhaps of special importance, siblings often have conflicting wants and needs as they both desire the same toy or wish to engage in the same activity at the same time. In addition to this conflict of goals or desires, they have conflicts involving beliefs as one expresses the view that X is the case, and the other disputes this and claims that Y is the case. Or, similarly, they have a clear difference of knowledge or beliefs as when one child makes a presupposition that the other does not hold in kind (such as the presupposition of shared knowledge in using *He* or *It*); or the same thing may happen in reverse as other persons make unwarranted presuppositions about knowledge and beliefs they share with the child. Supportive of this general view is the finding that Western middle-class children with siblings tend to understand other persons in terms of their mental states (false beliefs) at a younger age than children without siblings (Perner, Ruffman, and Leekam, 1994).

There is also another kind of discourse that may be important in children's coming to understand others as mental agents, and that is the process of communicative breakdown and repair (see above). As children begin to engage in discourse with adults in the 2- to 3-year age period, it happens with some regularity that someone does not understand what they say. Golinkoff (1993) documents some cases in which even very young infants engage in a process of what she calls "the negotiation of meaning" in which the child says something unintelligible, the adult guesses at its meaning, and the infant either accepts or rejects the interpretation. As children get older they experience both (1) misinterpretations, in which the adult interprets the child's utterance in a way that she did not intend, and (2) clarification requests, in which the child says something that the adult does not understand and so the adult asks for clarification. These kinds of discourse—which occur frequently for virtually all young children learning a natural language—lead the child to try to discern why the adult does not comprehend the utterance: perhaps she did not hear it, perhaps she is not familiar with this specific linguistic formulation, and so forth. Analysis of the cause of the breakdown then leads to the formulation of a strategy for repair. In all, it would seem that these kinds of misunderstandings and repairs are an extremely rich source of information about how one's own understanding of a linguistically expressed perspective on a situation may differ from that of others.

The other two main hypotheses about the relation of language and theory of mind are: (1) that the acquisition of mental state terms such as *see*, *want, think,* and *know* in some way facilitates or enables children to conceptualize others as having minds of their own (Bartsch and Wellman, 1985); and (2) that certain kinds of syntactic structures—specifically, the kind of embedded syntax (sentential complements) that goes along with many mental state terms (as in *I think she's here*)—either enables or facilitates a theory of mind by providing the necessary representational format for formulating propositions that refer to false beliefs (as in *I think the moon is made of green cheese*) (DeVilliers, 2000). Empirical research on the relationship between language and theory of mind has not progressed to a state where we can choose among all these different theoretical alternatives, but the research does seem to indicate fairly clearly that the acquisition of a language either facilitates or enables children's appreciation that other persons are psychological agents with their own mental lives (see also Tomasello and Rakoczy, in press).

7.3. Summary

Historically, complex syntactic constructions are tightened versions of looser discourse sequences. They have become tightened because similar discourse sequences are used repeatedly for common overall functions. Children, however, know none of this; they simply experience the modern syntactic construction and learn it for its modern function. Indeed, in many cases children learn first the historically later construction (or the historically later use of a construction) because it is currently more frequent in their discourse experience. For instance, the use of *I think* as a kind of evidential marker indicating speaker uncertainty almost certainly emerged historically later than the use of the verb *think* as a true matrix verb with a sentential complement indicating an act of thinking. But children learn and use the later, derived form first, at least partly because it is the most common version in their experience.

The complex syntactic constructions that children learn early in development are different from those same constructions as depicted in adult textbook accounts. Children's infinitival complement constructions are very similar to their existing simple constructions using modal verbs such as *must* and *should*. Their constructions with sentential complements involve matrix clauses that are highly formulaic and often express speaker attitudes (or else directives to listeners). Both of these complement constructions initially revolve around specific lexical items, in particular a relatively small (closed?) set of matrix verbs and complementizers. Children's early relative clauses come mostly in the form of presentational relatives, which employ very simple and well-mastered copular formulae (*Its the X, There's the X,* and so on) as main clauses and which have a very familiar topic-comment structure. Many early conjoined clauses seem to be learned as children initially produce just one of those clauses in response to an adult utterance expressing the other; the conjoining is thus across discourse turns in a dialogue and uses one of a few discourse connectives such as *and* and *but* and *because.*

In this chapter I have thus argued that children's complex constructions do not come out of nowhere. Although children learn these constructions as complex wholes with their own gestalt properties, they are aided in the acquisition process by the fact that many of the pieces out of which these constructions are built are in fact simpler constructions they have already mastered in other contexts. Children's acquisition of complex constructions may thus be explained with the same single-process, usage-based theory that was used earlier to explain their simpler syntactic constructions. Like those simpler constructions, children's complex constructions start out very concrete and item-based—revolving around a delimited number of matrix verbs and function words—and only gradually become more abstract. There is basically no evidence that the kind of highly abstract analysis of these constructions proposed by Pinker (1984) and others reflects psychological reality for young children.

Children's skills in using their simple and complex syntactic constructions to maintain topics during conversational interactions develop very slowly. Although children take turns appropriately from very early in their language development, their ability to participate in sustained conversational interactions continues to develop on into the school years. Converting these skills for use in producing personal narratives takes even longer, as children must use already known linguistic devices for new, mostly endophoric (within-text) functions. Much conversation and discourse thus places special demands on children's intention-reading and perspective-taking skills, as they must adapt what they want to say to the particular conversational context at hand. Determining the many functions of the plurifunctional grammatical items that are integral parts of mature conversation and discourse also places special demands on children's pattern-finding skills.

As children begin to master the use of a natural language, the process of acquisition takes in new directions the very same cognitive and social-cognitive skills that enabled its acquisition in the first place. This Vygotskian flip—interpersonal cultural processes, as in dialogue, are internalized into individual mental processes, as in conscious thinking—is a unique aspect of the human version of culture and cultural evolution and explains many of the most distinctive cognitive abilities of the species *Homo sapiens* (Tomasello, 1999). The influence of language on cognition is apparent first and most importantly in the new types of cognitive representations—

what I called in Chapter 2 perspectival cognitive representations—that processes of symbolic communication create. This influence is also apparent in the fact that children growing up learning different languages learn to conceptualize some aspects of the world in different ways—especially in the on-line cognitive processes they must employ in order to formulate an utterance in their language (thinking for speaking), but possibly in terms of more permanent cognitive representations as well. Finally, the acquisition of language—in particular the constant pressure to adjust utterance formulations for particular listeners in particular discourse circumstances—may also play a necessary, or at least a facilitative, role in children's emerging understanding that other persons are mental agents with thoughts and beliefs of their own (theory of mind).

Biological, Cultural, and Ontogenetic Processes

Putting together novel expressions is something that speakers do, not grammars. It is a problem-solving activity that demands a constructive effort and occurs when linguistic convention is put to use in specific circumstances.

—RONALD LANGACKER

TO DESCRIBE and explain an individual human being's linguistic competence, we must refer to processes that have occurred in three distinct time frames:

- *Phylogenetic:* the biological adaptations that have enabled members of this individual's species to communicate with one another linguistically.
- *Historical:* the cultural-historical forces that have changed and shaped the particular linguistic conventions of this individual's speech community.
- *Ontogenetic:* the developmental processes by means of which this individual has acquired competence with a language during her lifetime.

The difficult part comes in trying to figure out which aspects of linguistic competence to attribute to processes in which of these time frames.

Generative grammar holds that the essence of language is grammar, and that grammar is a product of human phylogeny. Individual languages change over historical time, but this is only superficial change in the linguistic "periphery," involving such things as the lexicon, the conceptual system, irregular constructions and idioms, and pragmatics. The underlying "core" of linguistic competence, in the form of an hypothesized universal grammar, is and has been at all times since some hypothesized evolutionary event the same for all members of the species. Likewise, children's linguistic performance changes over ontogenetic time, but this too is superficial. It is due only to the unfolding of a fixed maturational program for the universal grammar, the timing of the environmental "triggering" of the various parameters of the universal grammar, and children's growing competence with the linguistic periphery.

In contrast, usage-based linguistics holds that the essence of language is its symbolic dimension, that is, the ways in which human beings use conventional linguistic symbols for purposes of interpersonal communication. The ability to communicate with conspecifics symbolically (conventionally, intersubjectively) is almost certainly a species-specific biological adaptation, as the only species that communicates in this way in its natural environment is *Homo sapiens*, and human children all over the world begin using linguistic symbols at around the same age. In this view the grammatical dimension of language does not derive from a specific biological adaptation, but rather from historical and ontogenetic processes. When humans use symbols to communicate with one another, stringing them together into sequences, patterns of use emerge and are grammaticized into constructions. New generations of children inherit these linguistic constructions in the sense that they are exposed to utterances that instantiate them, from which they themselves must (re-)construct the abstract grammatical dimensions of the language they are learning. They do this using biologically inherited cognitive skills falling under the general headings of intention-reading and pattern-finding.

In this penultimate chapter, I take up again the issue of phylogenetic, historical, and ontogenetic processes, and their interrelations, in the genesis of linguistic structure—and different theories of how all of this might work.

8.1. Dual Inheritance

Many of the most thoughtful theorists in human behavioral ecology are exponents of what is known as Dual Inheritance Theory (e.g., Boyd and Richerson, 1985; Durham, 1991). Organisms inherit both their genes and their environments, including their social environments. Dual Inheritance Theory emphasizes, for example, that an ant is biologically adapted for following the pheromone trails that others have already laid down, for feeding the larvae that are already there, and for attending to the preexisting queen. In other words, an ant is biologically adapted for interacting with other ants and the things they have made or modified, which exist *a priori* in its species-typical environment. *Homo sapiens* of course follow the same general pattern of dual inheritance. But what is different about human beings is that they are not just adapted for specific preexisting structures in their environment such as pheromone trails and larvae, but rather they are adapted for acquiring totally new skills and knowledge from their social-cultural environments (Tomasello, Kruger, and Ratner, 1993).

And so there is no controversy. Everyone agrees that human beings can acquire a natural language only because they are biologically prepared to do so and only because they are exposed other people in the culture speaking a language. The difficult part is in specifying the exact nature of this biological preparation, including the exact nature of the cognitive and learning skills that children use during ontogeny to acquire competence with the language into which they are born.

8.1.1. The Role of Biology

The best-known theory about the role of biology in human linguistic competence is Chomsky's proposal that with respect to core grammar biology is everything. In this theory, the innate language module (universal grammar) does not contain things like special learning procedures and perceptual biases but rather real linguistic content; it is thus a theory of "representational innateness" (Elman et al., 1996). Specific lists of what might be in an innate language module are not common, but O'Grady (1997) offers the lists shown in Table 8.1. Pinker (1994) offers a very different list with very different kinds of entities: X-bar phrase structure; subject and object; noun and verb; movement rules; and grammatical morphology. No one who espouses principles and parameters has proposed anything resembling a complete list.

But representational innateness is a very unlikely theory. Most importantly, as argued earlier, the basic problem posed by linguistic diversity has yet to be adequately addressed. No one has described a mechanism that could link innate universal representations to the specific structures in specific languages, given that the language-particular structures are so various in their manifestations. Nor has anyone espousing a theory of representational innateness proposed a satisfactory way of dealing with developmental change. As documented in earlier chapters, children's language development is gradual and uneven in a way that is totally incompatible with a hypothesized mechanism in which universal parameters are instantaneously set. Nevertheless, taking a different tack, some theorists have recently compiled a number of more general lines of evidence for linguistic nativism having to do with such things as possible critical periods for language development, linguistic savants, language disorders, and brain localization (summarized by Pinker, 1994).

The problems with these lines of evidence are many and diverse, but perhaps the main one is a systematic confusion of representational innateness and other types of biological influence. Human beings are biologi-

Table 8.1   One list of the syntactic categories of universal grammar.

Lexical categories	Non-lexical (functional) categories
Noun (N)	Determiner (Det)
Verb (V)	Auxiliary (Aux)
Adjective (A)	Degree word (Deg)
Preposition/postposition (P)	Complementizer (Comp)
Adverb (Adv)	Pronoun (Pro)
	Conjunction

Source: From W. O'Grady, *Syntactic Development* (Chicago: University of Chicago Press, 1997), © 1997 by The University of Chicago Press.

cally prepared for language, but this may or may not involve the inheritance of specific linguistic structures. A sampling of some of the issues follows (see Tomasello, 1995c, for more detail).

GRAMMAR GENES

There is a British family many of whose members have difficulty with grammatical morphology, and indeed a relevant genetic marker has recently been identified (Fisher et al., 1998; Lai et al., 2001). Some linguists (e.g., Gopnik and Crago, 1991) have taken this to mean that the grammatical morphology component of the generative grammar module is genetically determined. The problem is that the afflicted members of the family have a serious expressive problem with their speech in general (Fletcher, 1990; Vargha-Khadem and Passingham, 1990), and moreover, virtually all of their documented deficits are in linguistic production, not comprehension (Marchman, 1993). The members of this family also have other motor problems, even in simple tasks. This all suggests that their problems derive not from deficits of specifically linguistic structures but rather from motoric problems in general, including most importantly an oral-facial apraxia that severely restricts their skills with human speech processing. The fact is that neither this case nor any other provides evidence that there are grammar genes that code for specific aspects of language structure (and Pinker, 1994, agrees with this negative assessment).

LINGUISTIC SAVANTS

There are persons who have low IQ scores but produce complex grammatical utterances nonetheless: so-called linguistic savants. This fact is taken by some (e.g., Yamada, 1981; Smith and Tsimpli, 1995) to indicate that there is an innate grammar module independent of general cognitive skills. But IQ is a ratio derived by dividing a number based on a person's raw score on an IQ test (so-called mental age) by the person's chronological age. And despite their low IQ scores, all the so-called savants who have been studied have been teenagers with mental ages equal to those of 4- to 6-year-old children—who, as virtually everyone agrees, have practically adult-level linguistic skills in many respects. Recent data also demonstrate that the language of Williams syndrome children—at one time thought by some to be linguistic savants—is actually much delayed and in general quite predictable from their mental age (Gosch, Stading, and Pankau, 1994).

BRAIN LOCALIZATION

There are parts of the brain that are for most people specialized for some aspects of language processing—and this fact is thought by some to imply an innate language module. But severely brain damaged children quite often develop language functions in atypical portions of the brain, and they go on to display almost normal language skills as older children and adults (Bates and Roe, 2001). And even if there were strict localization of specific language functions across all members of the human population, this would not imply anything about an innate language module. Many hypotheses could explain localization—for example, certain aspects of language processing may require a certain level of complexity of brain function, and certain parts of the brain are good with complex material of whatever type. Brain localization implies basically nothing about the origins of a cognitive function.

CRITICAL PERIOD

Newport and colleagues (Newport, 1999; Newport, Bavelier, and Neville, in press) examined the second-language acquisition skills of adults and children of different ages after they immigrated to a new country. After any given length of time in the new country, the children were more skillful with the new language than were adults. Newport et al. claimed to have found a sharp discontinuity in the data such that before adolescence language learning is faster and more natural. This led to the hypothesis that there is a biologically based critical period for language acquisition extending from around 1 year of age to early adolescence.

The problem is that reanalyses of these data, and some new data, do not support the claim that there is a well-defined critical period (e.g., Elman et al., 1996; Hakuta, Bialystock, and Wiley, in press). It is true that children typically make more progress in second-language acquisition in a given amount of time than do adults, but virtually all studies following Newport have found not a sharp but a continuous decline in skill as people get older. The reasons for this may be multiply determined. Most importantly, adults have a first language that has been learned and entrenched for a longer period of time, which creates more problems of interference. Second, in most immigrant situations children receive much more and much better experience with language in the social settings in which they participate (such as all-day school) than do adults (Snow and Hoefnagel-Höhle, 1978). And finally, children are more flexible learners than adults in many skilled activities. It is usually very easy to identify in a group of skiers or tennis players or piano players those who began learning their skill in early childhood and those who are adult learners—and language is no exception. This final consideration is especially important in explaining the relative lack of fluency of deaf persons who are not exposed to their first language (sign language) until later childhood or adulthood (Singleton and Newport, in press).

DEFICIENT INPUT

Bickerton (1984) claimed that the existence and structure of creole languages provides support for linguistic nativism. In some cultural situations people who speak different languages come together in specific activities and must create a common means of communication: a pidgin language, which lacks many of the syntactic features of natural languages. It is supposedly the case that some children have grown up exposed almost totally to pidgin languages, but they end up speaking a creole language, which is based on the pidgin but adds in many of the syntactic structures it is missing. But adult pidgin speakers by definition all have dominant languages that they use in some contexts, and it is unclear in published reports (all concerning cases from the relatively distant past, based on written records) to what extent the children heard these languages. Maratsos (1984) points out that a number of linguistic entities in the creole data Bickerton reports could *only* have come from one of the dominant natural language from which the pidgins derived, and Samarin (1984) and Seuren (1984) highlight a number of facts about the demographics of pidgins and creoles showing that the children in question had much more exposure to natural languages than Bickerton supposed. The case for children supplementing impoverished "input" cannot be made until we know what the "input" was.

Goldin-Meadow (1984) reported cases of deaf children whose parents do not believe in teaching them a conventional sign language, and whose families have developed idiosyncratic signing practices. Similar to the pidgin-creole example, as they are learning "home-sign" the children supposedly add some syntactic features that are not in their mothers' signing—presumably from an innate syntax module. However, Bates (1984) points out many of the interpretive problems involved in assigning formal syntactic descriptions to idiosyncratic forms of communication. For example,

Goldin-Meadow takes as evidence of a complex recursive sentence a gesture string such as "Susan/WAVE/Susan/CLOSE," but Bates notes that it might just be two simple sign duos concatenated and not recursively related. It is interesting and important that the remarkable Nicaraguan children who seem to have created their own creolized sign language (e.g., Senghas and Coppola, 2001) all came to the process with relatively well-developed systems of home sign developed with their parents. Even so, it seems that processes of grammaticalization can work very quickly in some cases.

POVERTY OF THE STIMULUS

Chomsky argues that, in general, even typically developing human beings have some kinds of very abstract knowledge about language for which there is no, or only ambiguous, evidence in the language they hear around them. The result is what is called the "poverty of the stimulus." A proposed case in point is English yes/no questions. Chomsky's (1980a: 4) account is that children begin with a statement such as *He is cold* and transform it, by various mechanical operations, into *Is he cold?* Leaving aside the question of whether this transformational, or "movement," account is psychologically realistic, when a child hears a question such as this she can infer either one of two rules: that the left-most auxiliary in the statement form begins the question or that the auxiliary of the main clause begins the question. Either rule is possible in this simple example since it contains only one auxiliary. But in more complex examples involving multiple clauses with auxiliaries it becomes clear that speakers of English use the second, structure-dependent rule—called structure-dependent because it requires the speaker to identify the head (main clause) of the sentence, whereas the first rule simply requires reference to the linear ordering. Chomsky's claim is that children never hear, or virtually never hear, the kinds of more complex examples that would allow them to see that the structure-dependent rule and not the linear-dependent rule is at work (e.g., 1980b: 40).

But in an analysis of some written corpora Pullum (1996, 2002) finds many of just the right kind of examples that children need. All that is needed is a sentence in which the subject NP contains a relative clause with an auxiliary (which is left-most) and in which the main clause contains an auxiliary as well. Some of his examples (the two auxiliaries are italicized and the position where the main auxiliary would be in the corresponding statement is underscored):

> *Can* those who *are* leaving early __ sit near the door?
> *Is* the boy who *was* crying __ still here?
> *Could* those who *are* coming __ raise their hands?

With mundane examples such as these so easy to come by, it would seem very likely that young children hear with some regularity the utterances they need to hear in order to induce the structure-dependent nature of English yes/no questions. (See van Valin, 1990, 1998, on the pragmatic bases of the subjacency constraint on "movement" in general.)*

SUMMARY

Overall, then, the case for linguistic nativism—in the form of representational innateness—is very poor. Combining all the data and arguments throughout this book, we can say that: (1) there are virtually no linguistic items or structures that are universal in the world's languages; (2) there is no poverty of the stimulus in language acquisition; (3) linking does not work; (4) parameters do not help; (5) the continuity assumption is demonstrably false; (6) performance factors and the maturation of universal grammar are simply unprincipled fudge factors used to explain recalcitrant data; (7) invoking extensive lexical learning as necessary for triggering parameters makes the theory basically indistinguishable from other learning theories—except that it has in addition the linking problem; and (8) although the empirical situations cited in support of biological bases for language acquisition mostly do demonstrate such bases, they do not demonstrate in any form representational innateness.

It would be possible to propose that human beings have evolved special learning mechanisms that enable them to acquire a natural language with special facility. But no one has proposed any such mechanisms (especially since the statistical learning of human infants has now been discovered in other primate species; see Chapter 2). The alternative to representational nativism, therefore, is to grant that indeed many human skills of cognition, social cognition, learning, and communication are grounded in our primate heritage and, in many cases, require very few particular experiences during ontogeny to operate normally. In addition, human beings' species-unique symbolic abilities may require only a basic social environment to emerge on time developmentally, and humans' species-unique

---

* The other example given by Chomsky (1980a: 4)—and the main other example used by generative grammarians to illustrate the "poverty of the stimulus" argument—concerns the way various types of pronouns connect to their antecedents, so-called binding theory (see also Crain and Pietroski, 2001). But it is difficult to see the problem here. There is no reason why children cannot simply learn the structure dependencies involved in the way the various pronouns work in their language when those are paired with the appropriate referential situations. It is also relevant that mastery of the binding principles is a fairly late accomplishment for most English-speaking children, typically not until school age (O'Grady, 1997)—which would imply extensive learning. (See van Hoek, 1997, 2002, for a critique of the generative account of binding in terms of C-command and for a very different proposal which provides a functional account of coreference based on the notion of conceptual reference points).

skills with speech may require nothing more than basic exercising of the vocal-auditory apparatus as well. But none of this involves innate linguistic structures or any other form of representational innateness. The biological foundations we are talking about involve a host of human capacities and human environments that conspire to make the learning and use of a natural language by developing human beings basically "inevitable" (Bates, 1979).

An especially interesting case in all of this is chimpanzees and other great apes raised in human-like cultural environments and exposed to human-like forms of symbolic communication (e.g., Savage-Rumbaugh et al., 1993). These apes are not biologically prepared to acquire linguistic symbols in the way that human beings are, of course, but they are given similar opportunities. The final word is not in on what apes can do in these situations, but they clearly learn to communicate with humans in some interesting ways. These studies demonstrate the power of a cultural environment—in which caretakers treat youngsters as intentional beings and attempt to share with them all that they know and can do—to potentiate certain cognitive and social-cognitive skills in beings closely related to humans. But these individuals do not then turn into humans, and their communicative skills differ from those of humans in many ways; for example, basically all of their productions are imperatives, to request things, to the neglect of the declarative sharing of information (Tomasello, 1994). The full story of the biological and cultural foundations of human linguistic communication is going to be a complicated one.

8.1.2. The Role of Culture and Cultural Learning

Human children are biologically prepared to learn any one of the world's 6,000+ natural languages—which differ from one another in profound ways—and this would seem to suggest a fairly broad and flexible biological adaptation. Indeed, Tomasello (1999) proposed that the acquisition of language is actually a part of an even wider adaptation for cultural learning in general. Human children differ from their nearest primate relatives not only in having language but also in being able to imitatively learn other types of social conventions, to communicate with others declaratively, to use material symbols such as pictures and maps, to make and use intentionally defined tools with a history, to collaborate using complementary roles, to teach one another, and to create social institutions such as governments and money. This suggests a fairly general human ability to interact with conspecifics culturally, that is, to create material, symbolic, and institutional artifacts historically and to acquire their use ontogenetically. No other species on the planet has this same propensity for things cultural.

Tomasello (1999) proposed that there is a single biological adaptation involved in all of these cultural skills, namely an understanding of the intentional and mental states of other persons (an ability which persons with severe cases of autism lack). When *Homo sapiens* began to understand that other people have intentional and mental states, they naturally wanted to manipulate these states for various cooperative and competitive purposes. This engendered the creation of symbolic conventions— uniquely human communicative devices not shared, even in part, by other animal species in their natural environments (who do not even point or show things to one another). This would seem to suggest that the adaptation enabling symbolic communication evolved only after humans diverged from other primates some 6 million years ago—perhaps even in the process of becoming modern humans some 200,000 years ago.

But when human beings started communicating with one another using symbols, they could not suppress their already existing primate skills of schematization, categorization, statistical learning, and analogy-making. It thus happened that as individuals started stringing together different symbols, they began constructing certain symbol sequences into larger units with their own communicative significance, that is, they began to grammaticize linguistic constructions. Specialized adaptations of the vocal-auditory system happening during the same time period—clearly geared for the rapid comprehension and production of the species-unique set of sounds known as human speech—served to facilitate the process. Regardless of details, some such account involving both a uniquely human cognitive adaptation for things cultural and symbolic (intention-reading) and a primate-wide set of skills of cognition and categorization (pattern-finding) would seem to be necessary to explain not only language universals, which are the sole concern of linguistic nativism, but also the many and intricate language particulars which characterize the variegated constructions of the many languages of the world.

Some people cannot believe that cultural-historical processes could possibly create abstract structures such as those embodied in the grammars of natural languages. But they can. The analogies are clearly not perfect, but again, as argued in Chapter 2, we may simply point to other cultural-historical phenomena such as algebra, money, and even such frivolous things as chess. Because not all cultures engage in these activities, they would not seem to be a part of the human genetic endowment. Of course, like language they all rest very firmly on a variety of biologically evolved cognitive and social-cognitive skills. It is just that the abstract structures that characterize them in the end are not given in the human genome at the beginning. The structures are created by human beings interacting with one another over historical time. The case of language may be very different in detail from these other much less fundamental human skills in the way this process takes place. The main point is simply that the creation of abstract symbolic structures via some version of a collective, cultural-historical process is something that can happen in a variety of domains of human activity. In the case of language, some of the relevant grammaticalization processes may have happened when the human species consisted of a single linguistic community, whereas others happened only after the geographical diversification of the species in the last 200,000 years—leading to the diversity we observe among modern-day languages.

8.1.3. Why Are Languages So Complicated?

In the context of thinking about the evolution and historical development of language for purposes of human communication, we may ask the straightforward yet revealing question: Why are languages so complicated? Why have natural languages evolved so many and such different and such complicated structures? Why can't we get by with *The cat is on the mat* and other such simple constructions? Why do we need all of the complexities of passive constructions, cleft constructions, auxiliary verbs, modal verbs, relative clauses, sentential complements, evidential markers, gender marking, incorporated nouns, and on and on? Oversimplifying considerably, we may answer these questions by specifying four basic reasons—functional pressures on the grammaticalization process, if you will. The point of this exercise is simply to demonstrate, contra many formal linguists, that there are good functional reasons for why human beings have conventionalized so many complex and seemingly arbitrary linguistic items and structures.

The first reason languages are so complicated is that people want to talk about events involving multiple participants, and these must be kept track of. In some cases the role being played by each participant in the event is not totally clear from context, and so the role must be specified, for example, by case marking or a conventional word order. Givón (1979) speculates that there are two basic approaches to this problem taken by the languages of the world—both present to some degree in all languages. The pragmatic way is to make a decision in each usage event whether syntactic marking is required, which saves trouble in cases where marking is not necessary, but requires continuous decision-making and pragmatic back-filling. In contrast, the syntactic way is just to mark participants every time obligatorily, which saves decision-making energy but means that the marking is sometimes done unnecessarily. Either way, the problem of specifying the role of participants makes for linguistic complications.

In addition, of course, in any kind of extended conversation or discourse these multiple participants must be kept track of across multiple events. Although it is not obvious at first glance, many linguists in fact believe that this is the main function of many of the most seemingly useless linguistic devices such as gender marking; that is to say, once a referent is introduced, if it may later be referred to with a gender-marked pronoun, determiner, or adjective, reference tracking is made significantly easier. And, naturally, when there are multiple events to be communicated about these need to be related to one another as well, especially in terms of their temporal and causal relations involving new uses of known linguistic items. And so the first point is simply that languages must be complicated because the situations and events people want to talk about are complicated.

Second, talking about particular events or states of affairs must be done in different ways in different circumstances if the speaker is to communicate effectively. In particular, speakers' acts of reference to "things" in nominal constructions and their acts of predication to "processes" in clausal constructions must be grounded in the immediate joint attentional frame in a manner sensitive to the current perspective, knowledge, and expectations of the listener—which involves all of the complexities of nominal choices (for example, the use of pronoun versus noun phrase versus noun with a relative clause) and tense-aspect-modality marking (for example, indicating time relative to now). In addition, the speaker's utterance as a whole must package information in a manner sensitive to the listener's perspective, knowledge, and expectations—which involves the appropriate use of certain constructions (such as passives) as well as many other conversational devices for expressing the given or presupposed or topical aspects of an utterance as opposed to the new or focused information, all from the perspective of the listener.

Importantly, this process takes on many new features in narrative discourse where these devices must be used with respect not to the perceptually shared context (since this is often irrelevant to a narrative about the past or future) but to the discourse context created by the narrative—often including many complex hypothetical worlds or "mental spaces" ("Once upon a time . . ."; Fauconnier, 1985). And so the second point is that languages are complicated because they must provide an array of linguistic items and constructions that may be flexibly deployed in the never-ending series of unique communicative partners and usage events—each requiring a different act of perspective-taking—that human beings face throughout their lives, including those involving the narration of events displaced in time and space, sometimes for unfamiliar listeners.

Third, in some cases speakers want, or need, to express their psychological attitude (or perhaps someone else's) to a given event or state of affairs. In a sense, it might be said that the speaker needs to ground an utterance in her own perspective, but the speaker's perspective is not just a cognitive affair but also includes her wants, desires, feelings, and attitudes. The expression of speaker attitude leads to many of the complexities of modal expressions (*might, should, must, ought, may, will,* and so on), as well as to a large percentage of the complex constructions such as infinitival and sentential complements (*I want to X, I think that X,* and so on). It might be interesting to ask exactly why people need to express so many different kinds of modal and psychological attitudes, involving such nuanced distinctions, but that would take us far afield into other areas of psychology. In general, the third point is simply that languages are complicated because they provide resources for speakers to express a wide variety of psychological attitudes toward the things they are talking about.

Fourth and finally, when people confront certain of these functions repeatedly many scores of times every day, they try to take advantage of the predictability of these recurrent communicative situations to find short-cuts of expression—mainly by reducing longer and more complex expressions to shorter and more compact ones. This process of grammaticalization creates some linguistic symbols that are perceptually relatively indistinct because they are shorter and often not stressed (grammatical morphemes). But more importantly, because the same morpheme may be grammaticalized within different expressions or constructions—and even within different genres of discourse such as conversation versus narrative—this process serves to create some of the many plurifunctionalities that so bedevil language learners, both adult and child. As opposed to the other three factors, in this case we are talking less about the complexities in the kinds of things people need to talk about, and more about issues of efficient information processing and the like. Highly grammaticized and plurifunctional morphology is indeed the weak link from an acquisition point of view in many situations. But it apparently serves its functions adequately and is not unlearnable—or else it would not be there.

And so the fourth point is that languages are complicated because language users in one generation exploit the predictability of certain communicative situations in order to abbreviate recurrent expressions, and this creates for the next generation of learners a set of perceptually indistinct and often plurifunctional linguistic symbols—and sometimes learners even confront expressions or constructions in the middle of the grammaticalization process.

Children thus encounter early in their lives a bewildering array of linguistic items and structures that have evolved historically to meet the many different communicative needs of their linguistic communities. In some cases, they experience a similar need and then go and find the appropriate linguistic devices to fill that need. In other cases, however, they learn a linguistic device first for a single function and only later discover some of its many other functions when they encounter it in some subtly different use, perhaps in a different mode of discourse. The late discovery of some of these other functions sometimes depends on children's further cognitive development and sometimes depends on their obtaining enough exposure to the relevant linguistic forms to enable them to sort out all the complexities—or both.

8.2. Pyscholinguistic Processes of Acquisition

In the current account of child language acquisition, we have done basically two things: (1) we have documented many of the most important kinds of linguistic items and structures that children initially acquire, and (2) we have argued and presented evidence for the existence of certain general cognitive processes—falling under the two overall headings of intention-reading and pattern-finding—that account for the acquisition process. In order to bring some coherence to the story, it is useful to now review, and to some degree synthesize, the different processes involved in children's language development. There are four basic sets of processes, each of which does its own job:

- *intention-reading* and *cultural learning,* which account for how children learn linguistic symbols in the first place;
- *schematization* and *analogy,* which account for how children create abstract syntactic constructions out of the concrete pieces of language they have heard;
- *entrenchment* and *competition,* which account for how children constrain their abstractions to those that are conventional in their linguistic community;
- *functionally based distributional analysis,* which accounts for how children form paradigmatic categories of various kinds of linguistic constituents.

These are the processes by means of which children construct a language, that is, a structured inventory of linguistic constructions. I should emphasize again that underlying all of these processes are children's skills of intention-reading. It is important to stress this because young children use communicative function (as determined by intention-reading) not only to acquire concrete words and expressions but also to make analogies among constructions and to form paradigmatic categories of various kinds of linguistic items. This is a crucial theoretical point that will help to distinguish the current approach both from generative grammar and from the otherwise very compatible approach of connectionism, which mainly operates with little attention to communicative function (a point to be revisited in Chapter 9).

8.2.1. Intention-Reading and Cultural Learning

Because natural languages are conventional, the most fundamental process of language acquisition is the ability to do things the way other people do them, that is, social learning broadly defined. Social learning in general is widespread in the animal kingdom (see Heyes and Galef, 1996), but social learning comes in many forms.

As argued in Chapter 2, the acquisition of most cultural skills, including skills of linguistic communication, depends on a special type of social learning involving intention-reading that is most often called cultural learning, one form of which is imitative learning (Tomasello, Kruger, and Ratner, 1993). This can be seen most clearly in experiments in which young children reproduce an adult's intended action even when she does not actually perform it (Meltzoff, 1995) and in which they selectively reproduce only an adult's intentional, but not her accidental, actions (Carpenter, Akhtar, and Tomasello, 1998a). To make matters more complicated, the acquisition of language involves the imitative learning of adult behaviors expressing not just simple intentions but communicative intentions (roughly, intentions toward my intentions—such as how you are trying to direct my attention). Children's ability to read and learn the expression of communicative intentions can be seen most clearly in word-learning studies in which young children have to identify the adult's intended referent in a wide variety of situations in which word and referent are not both present simultaneously (see Chapter 3). There is no evidence that any other animal species engages in social learning processes that take account of the intentions, much less the communicative intentions, of others (Tomasello, 1996).

In human linguistic communication the most fundamental unit of intentional action is the utterance as a relatively complete and coherent expression of a communicative intention, and so the most fundamental unit of language learning is stored exemplars of utterances. This is what children do in learning holophrases and other concrete and relatively fixed linguistic expressions (*Thank You, Don't mention it,* and so on). But as they are attempting to comprehend the communicative intention underlying an utterance, children are also attempting to comprehend the functional roles being played by its various components. This is a kind of "blame assignment" procedure in which the attempt is to determine the functional role of a constituent in the communicative intention as a whole—what we have called segmenting communicative intentions. Identifying the functional roles of the components of utterances is possible only if the child has some (perhaps imperfect) understanding of the adult's overall communicative intention—because understanding the functional role of X means understanding how X contributes to some larger communicative structure. This is the basic process by means of which children learn the communicative functions of particular words, phrases, and other utterance constituents—and, with help from pattern-finding skills, categories of these.

And so, the foundational process of language learning is hearing an adult utterance, reading the communicative intention embodied in that utterance, segmenting that communicative intention into component parts (in most cases), and storing the comprehended utterance and components. This is how all concrete pieces of language must be learned if they are later to be used conventionally and creatively in novel communicative circumstances. The basic reason that other animal species do not communicate with conspecifics using something like a human language is that they do not read the intentions or communicative intentions of others, much less segment these into component parts.

8.2.2. Schematization and Analogy

As documented in Section 4.1.4, young children hear and use—on a numbingly regular basis—the same utterances repeated over and over but with systematic variation, for example, as instantiated in item-based schemas such as *I wanna X, Let's X, Gimme X, I'm Xing it, Where's-the X? Can you X?* Forming schemas of this type means imitatively learning the recurrent concrete pieces of language for concrete functions, as well as forming a relatively abstract slot designating a relatively abstract function. This process is called schematization (see Chapter 4), and its roots may be observed in a variety of primate species who schematize everything from food-processing skills (Byrne, 1995; Whiten, 1998) to arbitrary sequences in the laboratory (Ramus et al., 2000; Hauser, Weiss, and Marcus, in press; see Conway and Christiansen, 2001, for a review).

The variable elements or slots in linguistic schemas correspond to the variable items of experience in the referential event for which that schema is used. Thus, in *Where's-the X* the speaker's seeking is constant across instances but the thing being sought changes across situations; in *I'm Xing it* the acting on an object is constant but the particular action varies. The communicative function of the item in a slot is thus constrained by the overall communicative function of the schema, but it is still somewhat open; it is a slot-filler category in the sense of Nelson (1985). This primacy of the schema leads to the kinds of functional coercion evidenced in creative uses of language in which an item is used in a schema that requires the listener to interpret that item in an unusual way; for example, under communicative pressure a child might say something like *Allgone sticky*, as she watches Mom wiping candy off her hands. The point is simply that the slots in item-based schemas are functionally defined (they have almost no phonological restrictions, as do many morphological schemas) but this functional definition can be stretched to fit individual cases—which is perhaps the major source of syntactic creativity in the language of 1- and 2-year-old children.

One special form of schematization is analogy—or, alternatively, we might say that one special form of analogy is schematization (see Chapter 5). Both exemplify the process by which children try to categorize, in the general sense of this term, whole utterances and/or significant other linguistic constructions (such as nominals). In general, we may say that an analogy can be made only if there is some understanding of the functional interrelations of the component parts of the two entities to be analogized across—at least in the case of syntax (in morphology there can be some analogies based on sound patterns). To understand the analogy "an atom is like a solar system" one has to understand something about the component parts of atoms and solar systems and how they work and relate to one another in each case; indeed the analogy effaces the particular objects involved altogether. Nonhuman primates can form relational categories of a sort (Tomasello and Call, 1997; Thompson and Oden, 2000), but the kinds of analogies that human children make are based on a much richer set of functional interrelations.

In the case of syntactic constructions, analogies are made not on the basis of surface form but on the basis of the functional interrelations among components in the two constructions being analogized. Thus, the *X is Y-ing the Z* and the *A is B-ing the C* are analogous because the same basic relational situation is being referred to in each case, and X and A play the role of actor, Y and B the activity, and Z and C the undergoer. In this way, different constructions develop their own syntactic roles, first locally in item-based constructions (such as "thrower" and "thing thrown"), and then more globally in abstract constructions (such as transitive-subject, ditransitive-recipient). There may even emerge late in development, in some languages, a super-abstract Subject-Predicate construction containing an abstract syntactic role such as "subject" more generally, based on abstractions across various abstract constructions. It is possible that perceptual similarity (or even identity) of the objects involved in analogies, while not strictly necessary, does in many cases facilitate human beings in their attempts to make analogies (see Childers and Tomasello, 2001). If so, this explains why children begin by schematizing across utterances with common linguistic material, thus creating item-based constructions, before they attempt to make totally abstract analogies based on a structure mapping involving little or no common linguistic material across utterances, thus creating abstract constructions.

An important part of item-based and abstract constructions is various kinds of syntactic marking, specifically indicating the syntactic roles that participants are playing in the scene or event as a whole. For example, English-speaking children learn at some point that *X's* VERB*ing me* means that X is doing something to me, *I'm* VERB*ing* X means that I am doing something to X, and *X's getting* VERB*ed* means that something is being done to X. The construction thus structures the interrelations among the basic events and participants in the referential scene, and children learn this. Indeed, one of the major functions of particular patterns of grammatical morphology in constructions (some instances of which seem to have only a very bleached-out meaning individually, as in the passive above) is to enable the recognition of the construction as an independent symbolic unit in which certain roles reside (Croft, 2001). Special symbols such as case markers and word order are the most common devices that languages use in general to mark the basic "who's doing what to whom" of an utterance. This kind of marking of roles may be thought of as the use of second-order symbols, since the function of the markers is to indicate how the linguistic items they mark should be construed in the meaning of the utterance as a whole. In their normal activities, including communicative activities, nonhuman animals would not seem to be using anything corresponding to syntactic marking in schemas (but see Zuberbühler, 2002, for an interesting observation involving a wild monkey species).

And so, the most fundamental process in the acquisition of abstract grammatical competence is schematizing or analogizing across utterances and significant utterance constituents and so forming syntactic constructions, some parts of which are concrete and some parts of which are abstract slots—the limiting case being totally abstract constructions with abstract syntactic roles. Since every language has different specific constructions, there is really no alternative to assuming that something like this is going on when children start to produce creative yet canonical utterances in their native language. Understanding the role of some syntactic symbols—applied either locally in item-based constructions or more generally in abstract constructions (or even more generally still)—is also an important part of the process.

8.2.3. Entrenchment and Competition

It is easy to just say that children learn concrete pieces of language and then generalize, without specifying how those generalizations are made. This is the kind of blind induction that Chomsky has argued so eloquently against, and indeed if that were the whole theory it would be little more than hand waving. But there are principles of categorization and analogy that determine the nature of the generalizations children make. These include both general principles (for example, Gentner's findings of the important role of causal structure in analogies) and some more language-specific principles (for example, findings about which kinds of verb meanings may be reasonably classified together; Pinker, 1989). Moreover, and importantly, additional constraints to the generalization process are provided by the information-processing principle of entrenchment and the pragmatic principle of competition (contrast, preemption; see Chapter 5).

Entrenchment simply refers to the fact that when an organism does something in the same way successfully enough times, that way of doing it becomes habitual and it is very difficult for another way of doing that same thing to enter into the picture. Preemption, or contrast, is a communicative principle of roughly the form: if someone communicates to me using Form X, rather than Form Y, there was a reason for that choice related to the speaker's specific communicative intention. This motivates the listener to search for that reason and so to distinguish the two forms and their appropriate communicative contexts. Together, entrenchment and preemption may be thought of as a single process of competition in which the different possible forms for effecting different classes of communicative functions compete with one another on the basis of a number of principles, including frequency/entrenchment.

It is nevertheless true that we know very little about the specifics of how all of this works. Thus, we know very little about the nature and frequency of the syntactic overgeneralization errors that children make at different developmental periods. Further, there is only one empirical study evaluating the effectiveness of entrenchment in preventing syntactic overgeneralizations (Brooks et al., 1999), and that study has no direct measures of the exact frequency of the verbs involved. Similarly, there is only one study of preemption and of semantic classes of verbs as constraining factors (Brooks and Tomasello, 1999a), and this study worked with only a narrow range of structures and verbs. And so, until we actually do some of the necessary empirical work, and see how these general principles actually work when applied to specific linguistic items and structures in specific languages, we will still be doing a fair amount of hand waving about how children make exactly the generalizations they do and not others. But of course it must be added that generative approaches engage in a fair amount of hand waving themselves in appealing to abstract principles of universal grammar to constrain children's generalizations.

In terms of evolutionary roots, entrenchment is very similar to a number of basic processes of animal learning investigated by learning theorists and going under such names as habit-formation; it is also similar to processes investigated by cognitive scientists under such names as routinization and automatization. Preemption or contrast might also be thought of as similar to some basic principles of animal learning, sometimes called blocking, in which one response tends to inhibit others to the same stimulus. However, contrast as we have conceptualized it here concerns a version of this as manifest in communicative intentions, which means that it has to do with understanding the choices other people intentionally make and why they make them. Construed in this way, contrast would be a uniquely human pragmatic principle.

It is probably true that constraining linguistic generalizations appropriately is the aspect of the current usage-based theory that, at the moment, is its weakest link. The two most important ways to help remedy this situation are: (1) a closer and more detailed analysis of the kinds of "errors" that children make and the kinds of linguistic experiences and communicative pressures that might lead to these (and constrain them); and (2) more experimental work on such things as the quantitative dimensions of how entrenchment and preemption work to constrain generalizations in the cases of many different particular constructions.

8.2.4. Functionally Based Distributional Analysis

Paradigmatic categories such and noun and verb provide language learners with many creative possibilities, as they enable learners to use newly learned items the way other "similar" items have been used in the past—with no direct experience. These categories are formed through a process of functionally based distributional analysis in which concrete linguistic items (such as words or phrases) that serve the same communicative function in utterances and constructions over time are grouped together into a category. Thus, noun is a paradigmatic category based on the functions that different words of this type serve within nominal constructions—with related categories being such things as pronouns and common nouns, based on the related but different functions these perform. Paradigmatic categories are thus defined in functional terms by their distributional-combinatorial properties: nouns are what nouns do in larger linguistic structures. This provides the functional basis by means of which these paradigmatic linguistic categories cohere.

It is important to emphasize that this same process of functionally based distributional analysis also operates on units of language larger than words. For example, what is typically called a noun phrase may be constituted by anything from a proper name to a pronoun to a common noun with a determiner and a relative clause hanging off it. But for many syntactic purposes these may all be treated as the same kind of unit. How can this be—given their very different surface forms? The only reasonable answer is that they are treated as units of the same type because they all do the same job in utterances: they identify a referent playing some role in the scene being depicted. Indeed, given the very different forms of the different nominals involved, it is difficult to even think of an alternative to this functionally based account.

And so again in this case, we find that children's basic pattern-finding processes work on linguistic items and structures understood as symbols with both a form and, importantly, a communicative function. Indeed, it may be said in general that the kinds of linguistic categorization that characterize human psycholinguistic processing depend most fundamentally on the functional dimension of linguistic symbols—since the members of many paradigmatic categories (for example, nouns or noun phrases) have no common elements of form at all. In the case of nonhuman primates, it is not even clear where to start to look for such categories—either with normal animals or with those raised by humans—since virtually all of the work on nonhuman primate categorization involves perceptual categories only (that is, detecting perceptual similarities among objects). Perhaps the closest thing would be studies of some human-raised apes categorizing objects on the basis of their function, for example, tools versus foods (see Tomasello and Call, 1997). But again, humans take this functionally based categorization to new levels in acquiring the conventional uses of the paradigmatic categories of a natural language.

Categorization is one of the most heavily researched areas in the cognitive sciences, including developmental psychology. But how children form categories in natural languages—a process of grouping together not items of perceptual or conceptual experience but rather items used in linguistic communication—has been very little investigated. The arguments made here suggest that future research on children's skills of linguistic categorization should focus on communicative function as an essential, indeed the essential, element—analogous to the focus on function in the work of Nelson and Mandler on event categories and slot-filler categories in non-linguistic domains. It is only by investigating how children identify and equate the functional roles linguistic items play in the different constructions of which they are a part that we will discover how children build the abstract categories responsible for so much of linguistic creativity.

8.2.5. But Is This Enough?

Chomsky and other generative grammarians have consistently maintained that psycholinguistic processes such as those just enumerated are not sufficient to enable a human being to acquire a natural language. But it is important to note that generative grammarians are not talking here about concrete pieces of language, schematic idioms, quirky constructions, or even the basic conventional syntactic constructions of a language. Indeed, in dual process approaches (words and rules; Pinker, 1999) it is specifically stated that basic psychological and learning processes are sufficient for acquisition of the items and structures of a language not participating in core grammar. Thus, children are said to use basic psycholinguistic processes not only to acquire words and idioms but also to acquire irregular rules such as forming the past tense of verbs like *sing* and *ring* with the irregular forms *sang* and *rang* (sometimes overgeneralized to things like *brang*). Everyone, of all theoretical persuasions, thus agrees that something like the account given here—with some arguing over details—is necessary for the acquisition of a major part of human linguistic competence.

So what is missing? Which aspects of linguistic competence cannot be acquired in this way? As presaged above, the predictable list from generative grammarians is things like question formation and other constructions where structure dependency is crucial, along with the binding principles and other so-called constraints on so-called movement. But what if structure dependence is a simple reflection of the fact that multiple items of a language can work together for a single communicative function and so can form a larger functional unit, such as a complex nominal containing a relative clause aimed at effecting a single act of reference? Then structure dependency would seem to arise quite naturally from functional, usage-based, psycholinguistic processes of language acquisition. And what if there is no such thing as movement—and therefore no need for constraints on movement? What if the formal linguists' practice of finding abstract patterns by formally transforming different constructions into one another is just a meta-linguistic game with no psychological significance? Then many of the linguistic structures that seem to demand an explanation over and above one based on basic psycholinguistic processes—that is, those that seem to require the invoking of formal principles, parameters, constraints, and features—simply do not exist. Then, it would be quite logical to propose that all aspects of language structure—from the more idiosyncratic to the more canonical—would all be acquired in the same basic way.

The other predictable charge from generative grammarians against approaches grounded in basic psycholinguistic processes is vagueness or lack of theoretical rigor. But if we think about other activities in which young children engage and how they are studied, we can ask: Vague relative to what? When developmental psychologists study children's development of mathematical skills, they do not take all of the mathematical complexities of the developmental endpoint, place them in the minds of 2-year-olds, and worry about vagueness when someone talks about such important processes as categorizing objects in the world, ordering objects with respect to some quantitative dimension, and psychologically chunking larger quantities so as to operate with big numbers more efficiently. So why should we worry about vagueness when we are providing a similar account of a domain that has no more formal properties than does the acquisition of mathematical competence? The answer is that we should not. We have much more important things to worry about, for example, all of the many unanswered empirical questions that have been enumerated in the preceding chapters.

And so we have before us the choice between a single process theory and a dual process theory. For reasons emanating mostly from the sociology of science and historical factors, the argument has been posed so that the burden of proof has been mainly placed on single process theorists to demonstrate that their approach can work. They have not succeeded in doing this completely, and the current theory is no exception. But the more normal conceptualization of this theoretical choice—based on Occam's Razor or some such—would be to place the burden of proof on the dual process theorists. Why do we need the phlogiston/ether of universal grammar—which is what necessitates the second process—at all? What is it doing anyway? Why not just chuck it?

It is possible that other usage-based theorists would argue that some of the acquisition processes just enumerated are not necessary, that some of them are redundant with one another or reducible to a more basic one, that others are needed, or that the understanding of communicative intentions is not a necessary component of some or any of them. These are all reasonable arguments. But the attempt in this book has been to show in each case why the hypothesized process is necessary. The basic justification is that each one deals with a different aspect of the process of language acquisition, such as acquiring concrete pieces of language, making abstractions of different kinds, constraining abstractions, and forming paradigmatic categories. It seems difficult to do without any of them—although perhaps they work in such different ways in the acquisition of specific structures or in specific languages that sub-types should be more clearly distinguished. These are all empirical questions.

8.3. Psycholinguistic Processes of Production

So far we have focused almost exclusively on how children build up their inventories of linguistic items and structures. But also important is the way they use this inventory to produce utterances on specific occasions of use. Thus, sometimes they produce relatively fixed concrete expressions. Perhaps this provides a production shortcut avoiding deep structural analyses, which may be especially helpful for young children whose skills in this regard are not great (see Wray and Perkins, 2000, on the role of formulaic language in human communication). Children also formulate many of their early utterances using some routinized expression as a kind of skeletal template, as in such pivot schemas as *Can-we X?*

In addition, of course, children construct some utterances in an even more creative manner from various bits and pieces whose functions they know from previous usage. This involves myriad cognitive processes falling under the general description of usage-based syntactic operations (or so-called cut and paste operations), including everything from filling a slot in an item-based construction to adding something onto a construction to integrating two constructions in a novel way. The cognitive dimension of these processes is sometimes called symbolic integration or conceptual blending (Langacker, 1987a; Fauconnier, 1997). The main difference here from traditional accounts is the recognition that children do not have to create each of their utterances from the ground up, using meaningful words and meaningless rules, but rather they integrate together in various ways many different kinds of already constructed constructions, each with an associated communicative function. Interestingly, aspects of this process may be indexed by various parameters of fluency in the way children produce utterances and pieces of utterances, and the process may be influenced in various ways by children's developing capacities with respect to working memory, presumably the processing locale for utterance construction.

8.3.1. Imitation, Formulaicity, and Fluency

As outlined in Chapter 2, children can hear an utterance used for a particular communicative purpose and when they have the same communicative purpose use that same utterance—perhaps with some small modifications appropriate to the discourse context. The question that remains about such productions is the degree to which the child understands the communicative functions of their constituents. This is obviously an empirical question in any particular case, but a number of researchers have noted that young children quite often produce what seem to be unanalyzed chunks that an adult would see as multi-morphemic. This is true in both morphologically rich languages, where children initially learn complex multi-morphemic words as wholes, and in more isolating languages where children learn some number of so-called frozen phrases such as *Lemme-see, I-wanna-do-it,* and *Gimme-that* (Peters, 1983; Lieven, Pine, and Dresner Barnes, 1992). In her classic and controversial paper, R. Clark (1974) called this "performance without competence" (see Perkins, 2000, for a review).

But in the usage-based view children can in addition learn chunks of language that are nevertheless analyzed. The basic idea is this. In spontaneous spoken speech, adults typically speak in what has been called intonation units (Chafe, 1994). These are relatively fluently produced stretches of language, typically containing six or seven words and no more than one new piece of information (DuBois, 1987). Intonation units correspond in the vast majority of cases (over 90 percent) to grammatical units such as clauses, noun phrases, and prepositional phrases (Croft, 1995). There is much evidence that stretches of language that a person uses repeatedly begin to approach unit status for purposes of language production, especially when they are used consistently for the same communicative function. For example, as noted above, Bybee and Scheibmann (1999) found that the highly frequent English expression *I-dunno* is pronounced in reduced form, with the constituent *don't* being pronounced in a totally different way from its pronunciation in other linguistic contexts. In a classic series of experiments, Goldman-Eisler (1968) had adults repeat novel expressions many times, and found that over time their productions became more fluent, suggesting a move toward unit status (similar to *I-dunno*).

The existence of multi-morphemic fluent units of speech that the child controls as single units is of tremendous theoretical importance for theories of linguistic competence and performance. It means that children do not have to put together every utterance from scratch and that their linguistic competence consists not just of individual morphemes and words but also of larger chunks of language with relatively complex internal structures. Obviously, children can be learning at the same time fluent units of speech that are mixed in the sense of having some analyzed and some unanalyzed parts (as in *Gimme-the X*). The hard part, as we will see below, is then in coordinating these prefabricated pieces of language in functionally coherent ways.

An interesting proposal by Elbers (1995), potentially relevant to these issues, is that much of children's syntactic development derives from their analysis of their own linguistic productions. Thus, if a child produces an utterance without a full adult-like understanding, upon hearing it (perhaps along with other related utterances), she performs analyses similar to those she would perform on adult utterances that she hears. Elbers argues that the analysis of one's own linguistic productions has many advantages over the analysis of the speech of others, the most important being that one always knows the underlying communicative intention. Perhaps of crucial importance are analyses that work both on the language the child hears and on that she produces.

8.3.2. Usage-Based Syntactic Operations

If children are not putting together creative utterances with meaningful words and meaningless rules, then what exactly are they doing? In the current usage-based view, what they are doing is constructing utterances out of various already mastered pieces of language of various shapes, sizes, and degrees of internal structure and abstraction—in ways appropriate to the exigencies of the current usage event. To engage in this process of symbolic integration, in which the child fits together into a coherent whole such things as an item-based construction and a novel item to go in the slot, the child must be focused on both form and function.

Lieven et al. (in press) addressed this issue in a naturalistic study of one 2-year-old child learning English. The novelty was that this child's language was recorded using extremely dense taping intervals: 5 hours per week for 6 weeks, roughly 5–10 times denser than most existing databases of child language and accounting for approximately 8–10 percent of all of the child's utterances during this period. In order to investigate this child's constructional creativity, all of her 537 utterances produced during the last one-hour taping session at the end of the 6-week period were designated as target utterances (295 multi-word utterances). Then, for each target utterance, there was a search for "similar" utterances produced by the child (not the mother) in the previous 6 weeks of taping. The main goal was thus to determine for each utterance recorded on the final day of the study what kinds of syntactic operations were necessary for its production, that is to say, in what ways the child had to modify things she had previously said (her "stored linguistic experience") to produce the thing she was now saying. We may call these operations "usage-based syntactic operations" since they explicitly indicate that the child does not put together each of her utterances from scratch, morpheme by morpheme, but rather, she puts together her utterances from a motley assortment of different kinds of preexisting psycholinguistic units.

What was found by this procedure was the following:

- 21 percent of all of this child's utterances on the target day (single word and multi-word) were novel utterances; 79 percent were things she had said before.
- 37 percent of the multi-word utterances on the target day were novel utterances; 63 percent were things she had said before (in exactly the same form).
- Of the novel multi-word utterances, 74 percent consisted of repetition of some part of a previously used utterance with only one small change, for example, some new word was "filled in" to a slot or "added on" to the beginning or end. For example, the child had said many hundreds of times previously *Where's the __?* and on the target tape she produced the novel utterance *Where's the butter?* The majority of the item-based, utterance-level constructions that the child used on the last day of the study she had used many times during the previous six weeks.
- 26 percent of the novel multi-word utterances on the last tape (5 percent of all utterances during the hour) differed from things this child had said before in more than one way. These mostly involved the combination of "filling in" and "adding on" to an established utterance-level construction, but there were several utterances that seemed to be novel in more complex ways.

It is important to note that there was also very high functional consistency across different uses of this child's utterance-level constructions, that is, the child filled a given slot with basically the same kind or kinds of linguistic items or phrases across the entire six-week period of the study. Figure 8.1 displays some examples of creative utterances of different types and their hypothesized precedents from the child's already mastered items and item-based constructions.

In view of these findings, we might say that children have three basic options for producing an utterance on a particular occasion of use:

- First, they might retrieve a functionally appropriate concrete expression and just say it as they have heard it said (and probably said it before themselves). For example, they say *Up!* or *There-ya-go*.
- Second, they might retrieve an utterance-level construction and simultaneously tweak it to fit the current communicative situation. The basic ways they can do this are: (1) filling a new constituent into a slot in the item-based construction (as when *I wanna ----* and *ball* combine to make *I wanna ball*); (2) adding a new constituent onto the beginning or end of an utterance-level construction or expression (as

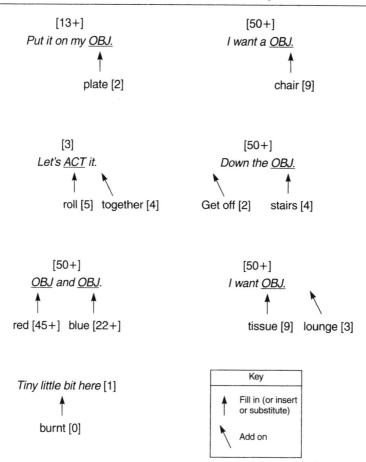

Figure 8.1. Some possible usage-based syntactic operations involving two operations, especially "filling in" and "adding on" (hypothetical frequencies in parentheses).

when *Throw it* and *here* combine to make *Throw it here*); and (3) inserting a new constituent into the middle of an utterance-level construction or expression (the way a German child might insert *auch* [too] into a schema position where nothing had ever before appeared).

· Third, a child might produce an utterance by combining constituent schemas without using an utterance-level construction. In the absence of an utterance-level construction, they presumably do this on the basis of various kinds of pragmatic principles governing the ordering of old and new information, and so forth—although there is very little relevant research here. The idea is very close to Braine's (1976) "groping patterns."

These processes of utterance production may be called usage-based syntactic operations because the child does not begin with words and morphemes and glue them together with contentless rules; rather, she starts with already constructed pieces of language of various shapes, sizes, and degrees of abstraction (and whose internal complexities she may control to varying degrees), and then "cuts and pastes" these together in a way appropriate to the current communicative situation. It is important to note in this metaphor that to cut and paste effectively a speaker is always making sure that the functions of the various pieces fit together functionally in the intended manner—one does not cut and paste indiscriminately in a word-processing document but in ways that "fit." These processes may also work at the level of utterance constituents and their internal structure.

There may be differences in the ways individual children use these three strategies, but it is likely that all children early in development learn at least some utterance-level constructions and expressions as production units that allow them to fluently and efficiently express entire communicative intentions (at the very least such things as *Thank-you* and *Bye-bye*, but also many frequent utterance schemas like *I wanna X* and *Where's-the X?*). Utterance-level constructions—both item-based and more abstract—are thus a major, if not the major, target of children's early language-learning efforts, a major way station on the road to more adult-like linguistic competence. Nominal and clausal constructions, as major constituents of utterance-level constructions, are also major targets of children's early language-learning efforts as they enable the fluent expression of recurrent utterance sub-functions flexibly in novel utterances (see Chapter 6). There are certainly important cross-linguistic differences in how all of this works, but in some languages it is simply a case of children working with bound morphemes rather than words, in many of the same ways outlined above. That is to say, there is no difference in principle between an English-speaking child learning an utterance-level construction with three adult words and an open slot, and an Inuktitut child learning an utterance-level construction with one free morpheme, two bound morphemes, and an open morpheme slot (see again Dabrowska, 2001, on syntactic constructions as "big words").

An intriguing source of evidence for identifying usage-based syntactic operations comes from a close study of the units one can see in their productions based on various parameters of intonation and fluency, involving such things as pauses, hesitations, false starts, and reformulations. In an enlightening review of stuttering and other speech disfluencies, Karniol (1999) provides strong evidence that young children's sentence-production strategies change in significant ways during the 2- to 3-year age period. The basic facts are these. Most children show an increase in disfluent utterances in the 2- to 3-year age period, with stutterers simply representing the end of a continuum. Significantly, the utterance-production problems experienced by normal children and stutterers are the same, and they have to do not with speech, as is commonly believed, but with utterance planning in general. Evidence for this proposal includes the following facts: (1) stuttering children show no problem imitating or reading utterances similar to those they have trouble producing; (2) stuttering children experience most difficulties at points requiring the most planning, that is, at utterance-initial and clause-initial locations (consistent with the behavior of normal children); (3) stuttering occurs most often with utterances that are more syntactically complex (also consistent with the behavior of normal children); and (4) more than three-quarters of all stuttering children recover spontaneously, and a therapy that focuses on utterance production in general (not speech) can be quite effective. In a recent study of normal children, Rispoli and Hadley (in press) showed that children produce the most disfluences in their most syntactically complex utterances.

Karniol (1999) argues that stuttering symptoms (word repetition, blocking, elongation) occur in both stuttering and non-stuttering children for the same reasons. They occur at a developmental point when children must change their utterance-production strategies because their competence with more and more complex constructions is increasing, as is their competence in more complex discourse interactions. Karniol argues that at this more advanced level, children cannot simply spit out an exemplar of an utterance-level construction, but rather they must coordinate such preplanned elements and active on-line revisions in discourse. Of special importance seem to be issues in coordinating the rhythmic (suprasegmental) properties associated with both the preplanned and the spontaneous linguistic structures often required in spontaneous discourse.

A study by Wijnen (1990) is generally supportive of this perspective. Wijnen presented evidence that there may be significant changes in normal children's utterance-production strategies at around this same 2- to 3-year age period. The language development of a single Dutch boy was followed from roughly age 2 to age 3. The fluency with which this child produced each of his utterances at different developmental periods was noted (especially in terms of repetitions, revisions, and incomplete phrases). Wijnen found that the number of disfluent utterances increased in the middle of the year and then decreased near the end of the year. The increase in disfluencies was explained in terms of a change of utterance-planning

312 Constructing a Language
312 Constructing a Language
312 Constructing a Language
312 Constructing a Language
312 Constructing a Language

strategies necessitated by the child's acquisition of ever more complex constructions. Interestingly, this child's disfluency rate began to decline in association with his acquisition of some new "syntactic frames" that enabled him to regain his fluency using larger chunks. There are virtually no other studies that investigate at this level of detail the relationship between children's emerging syntactic competence and their emerging skills of utterance production.

These findings on children's changing levels of fluency during the 2- to 3-year age period might suggest a reason why children seem to have an initial tendency to focus on utterance-level constructions as the major organizer for their spontaneous utterances. The reason is that these constructions contain—all in a single, at least partially prefabricated unit (either with or without some constant linguistic material)—the basic semantics and pragmatics that the child wishes to produce encapsulated in a well-known rhythmic structure. But when this strategy begins to be inadequate to meet the child's communicative needs in complex discourse contexts, typically as she nears her third birthday, she must begin to use more creative strategies in which utterances are produced out of a combination of prefabricated units and on-line adaptations, with no preexisting suprasegmental prosodic package for the whole.

8.3.3. Production Limitations and Working Memory

Many researchers believe that young children have much more competence with language than their child-like productions would lead one to believe. Despite the plausibility of positing that young children have fragile skills of working memory and language processing, the fact is that there are no cases in which children's limited productions have been explained by empirically identified processing limitations (and much evidence to the contrary; e.g., Braine, 1974; Bloom, 1973; Brown, 1973). Nevertheless, performance limitations continue to be used widely by some theorists as a way of explaining why young children's linguistic productions do not match with their hypothesized adult-like competence (see Section 5.4.1).

It is clearly not the case that children possess fully adult-like language processing and performance capabilities, and it is very likely that limitations of these kinds affect what they can and cannot learn. This is why measures of working memory correlate with children's early language skills (Adams and Gathercole, 1995, 1996, 2000). And this may well be why deficits in working memory appear to be at least partly responsible for language impairments (Bishop, North and Donlan, 1996; Botting and Conti-Ramsden, 2001). But, counterintuitively, there have been some proposals that a limited working memory may actually work to young children's advantage in the learning of complex linguistic structures (not production or performance). Thus, Newport (1990) argued that one of the reasons young children seem to be better language learners than adults is that "less is more": with a limited working memory, young children are not distracted by some of the syntactic complexities that adult learners cannot help attending to. Elman (1993) even found that simulating such a limitation in a connectionist model helped the computer program to learn.

In a recent review of many different lines of evidence—including first-language acquisition, second-language acquisition, and computational modeling—Brooks and Kempe (submitted) conclude, contrary to Newport and Elman, that a larger working memory can only be helpful in language learning. This is demonstrated by the facts that (1) adult learners learn more and learn more quickly than child learners when input is controlled (Snow and Hoefnagel-Höhle, 1978), (2) there are positive correlations between working memory and language learning (Adams and Gathercole, 2000), and (3) new computer simulations call into question the less-is-more hypothesis (Rohde and Plaut, 1999). Brooks and Kempe explain the well-known finding that child second-language learners attain higher levels of ultimate competence than adult second-language learners by pointing to the greater amount of input that children are normally exposed to, the simplifications in child-directed speech that children experience, and the lack of interference from a first language. They thus claim that less is indeed more, just not in the sense of a limited memory capacity; receiving simplified input and having less interference from a first language is what really helps. But there is a dearth of experimental studies with young children in which working memory is systematically manipulated (for example, by requiring them to perform some parallel task) and language learning is systematically assessed.

The overall conclusion would thus seem to be that more is more in terms of working memory. Having a larger working memory enables children to both comprehend and produce more complex syntactic structures. But less may be more when it comes to input and interference from another language, that is, it may be better to get simplified input initially no matter the size of working memory—and a less entrenched first language to interfere with the second seems to be a good thing as well.

8.3.4. Pragmatic Grounding

The other thing that children must manage in parallel as they produce an utterance in a particular usage event is the formulation of that utterance in terms appropriate to the particular communicative context. The child must pragmatically ground what she wants to say in the current joint attentional frame—which involves the choice of linguistic items and structures both to indicate speaker attitude and to accommodate to listener perspective. Accommodating to listener perspective means using appropriate morpho-syntax both at the level of the utterance (using the construction type that embodies the most felicitous perspective for the listener) and at the level of phrases (choosing the appropriate nominal form for felicitous reference and the appropriate tense-aspect-modality marking for felicitous predication). And all of these decisions take on even more complex dimensions at the level of larger stretches of discourse and narrative, where such things as topic maintenance and reference tracking across clauses are major concerns.

Communication within a dual level intentional structure—a joint attentional frame within which communicative intentions are expressed— seems to be uniquely human and based on uniquely human intention-reading skills. As noted in Chapter 6, children struggle for some time with pragmatic grounding (as do adults), and their skills seem to depend to some extent on perspective-taking skills that develop in significant ways during the preschool period. Our knowledge of how children learn these pragmatic strategies—involving an understanding of the choices other people make based on an assessment of the listener's knowledge and perspective—is very meager at this point. There are almost no experimental studies that manipulate the shared joint attentional scene between a child and an adult (perhaps created by discourse) and look at the constructions the child uses as a result.

8.4. The Development of Linguistic Representations

From a cognitive science point of view, the central issue in the study of language development is the nature of children's underlying linguistic representations and how these change during ontogeny. Obviously, to investigate this question we need a linguistic theory in which to couch our descriptions of children's linguistic representations.

From a cognitive-functional linguistics point of view the first stipulation is that all representations, from morphemes to words to syntactic constructions, are composed of a form and a function. The function is the communicative intention behind a linguistic item or structure, and it must be formulated in terms of the cognitive structures with which children conceptualize their worlds at different points in development. One example is the diagrams presented in Chapter 3 (taken from Tomasello, 1992a), which depict the meaning of children's early verb island constructions in terms of objects and their spatial and causal relations as they unfold over discrete moments of attention (for example, an object is first present and then absent, or is in one location and then another, or a person causes an object to change state, or a person engages in an activity). The constitutive elements of these diagrams—whose overall structure was taken from the theory of Langacker (1987a)—are based on hypotheses about what kind of cognitive structures young children have available to them at which developmental periods. The use of such iconic diagrams is justified by theoretical approaches in cognitive science which argue that human cognition is based, first and most importantly, in processes of human perception (Barsalou, 1999). In terms of form, we have depicted the structural form of children's linguistic constructions using Croft's (2001) radical construction grammar "formalism," which allows for a mixture of specific lexical items, construction-specific syntactic roles, and more construction-general paradigmatic categories. Future research should work to integrate these ways of representing linguistic form and function in a more intimate manner than has been effected in this book.

But regardless of formal representations, there are still things to be investigated in general about (1) how abstract children's linguistic representations are at different points in early development, and (2) how children organize their constructions cognitively at different points in development.

8.4.1. Exemplars into Abstractions

I have argued repeatedly throughout the preceding chapters that children's early linguistic representations are highly concrete, based in concrete and specific pieces of language, not in abstract categories (although they have some open slot-filler categories as well). The data supporting this conclusion are overwhelming. They include:

- analyses of children's spontaneous productions showing (1) very restricted ranges of application of many early linguistic items and structures, (2) asynchronous development of item-based constructions that from an adult point of view should have similar structures, and (3) gradual and continuous development within specific item-based structures;
- production experiments in which young children use nonce verbs in the way adults have used them, failing to generalize them to others of their existing constructions—suggesting that these existing constructions are item-based and not verb-general; and
- comprehension experiments in which young children, who know the activity they are supposed to act out in response to a nonce verb, fail to assign the correct agent-patient roles to the characters involved on the basis of canonical word-order cues (in English)—again suggesting

that their constructions at this point are item-based and not totally general.

One other recent finding supports this same conclusion. It is a priming study, and unlike most other experimental approaches it does not rely on introducing children to nonce words, but rather it exposes them to, and lets them use, their native language. Savage, Lieven, and Tomasello (in press) primed English-speaking children with either active or passive sentences, in some cases with high lexical overlap between the priming sentence and the sentence the child was likely to produce (that is, the prime used some pronouns and grammatical morphemes that the child could use in her target utterance even though different objects and actions were involved) and in some cases with very low lexical overlap (the prime used only nouns, which the child could not use in her target utterance since different objects were involved). In some ways, this method could be considered the most direct test yet of children's early syntactic representations, since successful priming in the "high lexical overlap" condition would suggest that their linguistic knowledge is represented more in terms of specific lexical items, whereas priming in the "low lexical overlap" condition would suggest that their linguistic knowledge is represented more abstractly. Following Bock and Griffin (2000), Pickering and Brannigan (1999), and other adult psycholinguists, the question is thus whether children are subject to so-called structural priming. The answer is that the older children, around 6 years of age, could indeed be structurally primed to produce a particular construction such as the passive. The younger children, who had just turned 3 years old, could not be primed structurally; but they were primed by the more lexically specific primes. Four-year-olds fell somewhere between these two extremes. So once more—in this case using a very different method, widely accepted in the adult psycholinguistic community—we find that children's early linguistic representations are very likely based in specific item-based constructions (with some abstract slots), and it is only in the late preschool period that their utterance-level constructions take on adult-like abstractness.

But rather than thinking of children's utterance-level constructions as either concrete or abstract, it is probably better to think of them as growing gradually in abstractness over time as more and more relevant exemplars are encountered and assimilated to the construction. Two sets of findings support this more developmental view. The first are the various preferential looking studies reviewed in Chapter 4, in which (some methodological problems aside) it seems that children display more abstract linguistic knowledge than in other experimental procedures (see especially Fisher, 2000, 2002). Overall this should not be surprising since in many domains

of cognitive development young children show skills in preferential looking experiments that they do not show under more demanding experimental conditions (Haith and Benson, 1997). It may thus be that preferential
looking studies of children's language are revealing very weak initial abstractions that are strong enough to govern their looking patterns but not
strong enough to guide their behavior in situations in which they must either act on the world or produce utterances. These stronger representations emerge gradually as children accumulate more linguistic experience.

The second set of studies are those of Akhtar (1999) and Abbot-Smith,
Lieven, and Tomasello (2001), as also reported in Chapter 4. In these
studies young children were exposed to nonce verbs in noncanonical English word orders (such as *Gaffing the girl the boy*). When later given the
opportunity to use the new verb with new characters, the 4-year-olds corrected the word order to canonical English SVO—ignoring the aberrant
input. The 2-year-olds, in contrast, did not correct the weird word order
but followed the input (even though they did correct to SVO order sentences in the same weird order but with a familiar verb, such as *push*). The
two groups of 3-year-olds were in between (see Figure 8.2), thus producing a very clear age trend. One interpretation of these results is that the
younger children could be driven by the weird input in their use of the
novel verb because their linguistic representations were not as abstract or
as "strong" as those of the older children who resisted the pull of the immediate input. Perhaps it is also useful in this context to mention the study
of Brooks et al. (1999), who found that young children could be induced
to make overgeneralization transitivity errors (such as *He disappeared it*)
much more readily with verbs they had heard very few times than with
those they had heard many times—with this tendency being more preva-
lent at younger ages (age 3 as opposed to age 6). Again this might imply
that the more experience children have with particular linguistic items and
structures—as a function of both frequency in the environment and time
(age)—the stronger is the underlying representation.

One reasonable interpretation of all the studies directly aimed at children's underlying linguistic representation is thus as follows. From about
2 or 2½ years of age children have only very weak verb-general representations of their utterance-level constructions, and so these show up only in
preferential looking tasks which require only weak representations. But
over the next months and years their linguistic representations grow in
strength and abstractness—on the basis of both the type and the token frequency with which they hear certain linguistic structures—and so these
now begin to show themselves in tasks requiring more active behavioral
decision-making or even language production, which require stronger representations. This hypothesis is in the general spirit of a number of pro-

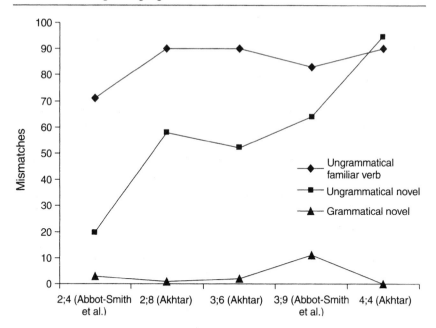

Figure 8.2. Mean percentage of utterances which were mismatches, as a function of condition and age group. Based on Akhtar (1999) and Abbot-Smith, Lieven, and Tomasello (2001).

posals suggesting that, if cognitive representations retain information about the variety of individual instances, they may be felicitously described as being either weaker or stronger mainly according to their type and token frequency (e.g. Munakata et al., 1997). It is also consonant with the view that "linguistic knowledge" and "linguistic processing" are really just different aspects of the same thing. Thus, things like frequency and the probabilistic distribution of lexical items in the input not only play a crucial role in how children build up their linguistic representations, but they also form an integral part of those representations themselves in the end state (see the papers in Barlow and Kemmer, 2000; Elman et al., 1996).

8.4.2. Building a Structured Inventory of Constructions

As their utterance-level constructions become gradually stronger and more abstract, children may begin to find links among them in various ways. We are not in a position to say much about this at the moment, as there is very little relevant research, and the issue is not even very well settled in adult

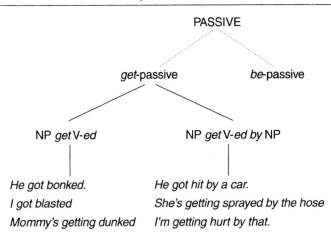

Figure 8.3. Hypothetical depiction of some sub-constructions of the English passive.

linguistics. But, as indicated in Chapter 4, there would seem to be two kinds of links of most importance: instance links and part-whole links.

Instance link simply refers to the kind of abstraction process just elaborated. As children make more abstractions, things lower in the hierarchy—more concrete pieces of language—are seen as instances of more general and abstract constructions and categories. And so, for example, we might observe something as in Figure 8.3 for the *get*-passive construction. In this diagram, at the bottom are individual utterances which a child could, if she heard any one of them often enough, produce as concrete expressions. At the second level are specified the versions of the construction with and without the *by* phrase. Finally, at the top of the hierarchy is a representation of the *get*-passive construction incorporating both of these variants. It is possible that there is still another level at which the *get*-passive is united with the *be*-passive.

Is there still another level at which the general passive construction is united with other constructions of the English language? Given the diversity of constructions involved—including everything from imperatives without subjects to *wh*-questions with the subject (as determined by agreement) following the verb to passives in which the subject is the recipient of the action semantically—one reasonable answer is that they are united in only a very loose way. Thus it is possible that there is something like a Subject-Predicate construction superseding the main abstract utterance-level constructions of English—for mature speakers, that is. But at the same time as this super-structure represents commonalities among abstract constructions, it also fails to represent any of the special properties of subjects and predicates in these diverse constructions. In any case, regardless of how many levels there might be and how abstract these might be, in particular instances it is very likely that human beings at all ages actually operate most of the time psycholinguistically with constructions near the lower end of the hierarchy (Langacker, 2000).

The other important types of links, as touched upon in Chapter 6, are the links that must be established between constructions in order to produce an utterance. Most importantly, mature individuals construct nominal constructions and clausal constructions in a partially modularized fashion which must then be coordinated with the utterance-level construction being used. Since a number of different utterance-level constructions use these in different ways—in particular tense-aspect-modality (TAM) marking in such things as questions in English—this can potentially be quite complicated.

The only substantive proposal made here is that children begin this process in an unmodularized fashion, at least for the things associated with verbs and clauses (nominals may be fairly modularized from the beginning since they are used as complete utterances so often and since their specific form has so little effect on the rest of the construction). The proposal is that children's TAM marking is initially done for each constructional island separately, and only gradually and in piecemeal fashion do children begin to abstract some notion of verb phrase or clause that is common across all different utterance-level constructions. But again in this case the abstraction only represents commonalities that exist at a very general level. People probably operate most often at a much lower level in which, for example, the TAM marking in *wh*-questions is done the way that particular construction does it—without much concern for other constructions (or the deep similarities that linguists can, with much time and effort, dig up).

8.5. Summary

It is clear from all that has been reported and discussed in the previous chapters that acquiring competence with a natural language requires children to do many different things. At the very least, they must be able to: comprehend communicative intentions as expressed in utterances; segment communicative intentions and ongoing speech and so extract individual words from these utterances; create linguistic schemas with slots; mark syntactic roles in item-based constructions; form abstract constructions across these schemas via analogy; perform distributional analyses to form paradigmatic categories; learn to take their current listener's perspective into account in both forming and choosing among conventional nominal and clausal constructions; learn to comprehend and express different modalities and negation (speaker attitude); acquire competence with complex constructions containing two or more predicates; learn to manage conversations and narratives, keeping track of referents over long stretches of discourse; cut and paste together stored linguistic units to produce particular utterances appropriate to the current communicative context; and on and on.

There are no fully adequate theoretical accounts of how young children do all of this, including the current theory. But the current approach holds out more promise than those based on formal linguistic models, mainly because it takes account of a wider range of biological, cultural, and psycholinguistic processes of language acquisition—including those involved in the symbolic dimensions of linguistic communication, which are programmatically ignored by formal linguists. In the current approach, the human capacity for language is best seen as a conspiracy of many different cognitive, social-cognitive, information-processing, and learning skills, some of which human beings share with other primates and some of which are unique products of human evolution. But these processes have something to work on during ontogeny only because linguistic symbols and constructions have evolved culturally and historically—and so exist as a part of the child's species-typical environment before she arrives on the scene. Over historical and ontogenetic time novel linguistic structures emerge (see papers in MacWhinney, 1999).

In this chapter I have summarized, and to some degree integrated, some of the ontogenetic processes involved children's language acquisition and use. These are: intention-reading and cultural learning, which account for how children learn linguistic symbols in the first place; schematization and analogy, which account for how children create abstract syntactic constructions out of the concrete pieces of language they have heard; entrenchment and competition, which account for how children constrain their abstractions to those that are conventional in their linguistic community; and functionally based distributional analysis, which accounts for how children form paradigmatic categories of various kinds of linguistic constituents. I have proposed that skills of intention-reading are foundational to all of these since they participate in most of the pattern-finding processes as well. Symbolically integrating (cutting and pasting) together in functionally appropriate ways pieces of language that children have learned or constructed through intention-reading and pattern-finding involves, in one way or another, all of these processes put to new uses, as well as other processes of working memory, motor planning, and like.

As a final theoretical point, it is important to stress once again that even if there were something like an innate universal grammar, children would still need to engage in processes such as those enumerated in this chapter—by everyone's admission—in order to acquire the many lexical symbols, fixed expressions, schematic idioms, and grammatical conventions of their particular language. The usage-based processes enumerated in this book thus play an important role in the language acquisition process, no matter one's theoretical orientation. Given the relative success of this approach and even of connectionist models—employing only a subset of the processes here enumerated—the question becomes why we need a second mechanism of acquisition or a universal grammar at all.

Toward a Psychology of Language Acquisition

For remember that in general we don't use language
according to strict rules—it hasn't been taught to us by
means of strict rules either.

—LUDWIG WITTGENSTEIN

IN THE INTRODUCTION to his 1984 book, *Language Learnability and Language Development,* Pinker expressed disappointment in the field of child language acquisition. Chomsky (1957, 1965) and others had argued that since language is the most important and distinctive cognitive skill of human beings, the study of its origins in human phylogeny and ontogeny should be a centerpiece of cognitive science and should lead to significant new insights into the workings of the human mind. But in the two decades between Chomsky's arguments and his own book, Pinker did not see the kind of progress anticipated. He attributed this lack of progress to a lack of linguistic sophistication in the field. The 1984 book was an attempt to rectify the situation by providing a rigorous treatment of major topics in language acquisition within the framework of a formal linguistic theory (lexical functional grammar). Pinker intended his approach to set us on a productive new course, and indeed there has been a fair amount of research activity in the general direction he envisaged. But one could reasonably argue that this approach has led to very little progress in discovering how human children become skilled users of a natural language.

One diagnosis of the reasons for this failure is as follows. In order to gain the theoretical rigor he wanted, Pinker (1984) invoked the theoretical tools of lexical functional grammar. But since these tools were developed to analyze adult language, and since children's language on the surface does not look like adult language, he had to make the continuity assumption: underneath, the language of children is structured by the same abstract categories and rules as that of adults. This was a mistake. There is not one shred of evidence for the continuity assumption. The reason children's language does not look like adult language is that it is not like it in terms of the underlying representations involved; children's language is structured by much weaker and more local linguistic abstractions. Perhaps, then, we should abandon the continuity assumption and instead adopt the developmental assumption that whereas the processes working at different developmental stages are constant, the actual structures and representations involved are different at these different stages.

In the modern study of child language acquisition the best-known theoretical alternative to generative grammar is of course connectionism (e.g., Elman, 2001). This approach has much to offer, as it is a single-mechanism theory, it does not depend on any *a priori* formal linguistic theory, and it is totally data-driven from the bottom up. But given what we have learned from the empirical studies reviewed in this book, connectionist models at the moment are psychologically unrealistic in two basic ways. First, they do not deal with communicative intentions or function. Admittedly, they do seem to be able to simulate many aspects of language acquisition simply by looking at patterns in the surface distribution of forms. But this is not the way children do it. Children are focused on the adult's communicative intentions as they attempt to comprehend her immediate utterance, and communicative function is the main basis for their linguistic generalizations over time (otherwise they would be totally baffled by a language's many homonyms and proforms, among other things). Connectionist modelers are aware of all this (e.g., MacWhinney, 1999); they are simply working for the moment with what is most tractable. But we can hope that in the not too distant future there will be ways of dealing with communicative intention and function in these computational models.

Second, at the moment connectionist models work only with very small units such as words and grammatical morphemes. But the data and theoretical arguments reviewed in this book suggest that children also work with larger units such as whole linguistic constructions. These also have functions, and it was argued above that making analogies across these linguistic gestalts requires reference to these functions (this is especially true in syntax, as opposed to morphology). It should also be noted that many connectionist modelers claim that a language can be learned and used without any linguistic abstractions at all. This is partly an issue of how one defines abstractions, as connectionist models contain weighted units whose weights are a direct function of the exemplars encountered—a kind of pseudo-abstraction, perhaps. The empirical point is simply that children's productivity with nonce forms after a certain age clearly suggests some form of emergent linguistic abstractions, however these might be conceived or implemented.

The usage-based approach advocated in this book is offered up as an alternative to both of these better-known theories. The novel features of the current theory—in contrast with both formal linguistic models and connectionist models—may be summarized in three emphases. First, the current model is thoroughly *functionalist*—based explicitly in the expression and comprehension of communicative intentions (intention-reading). This focus is shared by neither generative grammar nor connectionism (in its current instantiations), mainly because both are concerned much more with the acquisition of formal patterns than with the acquisition of concrete pieces of language for use in referring to and predicating things about phenomena in the real world. If human cognitive representations derive most directly from human perception (Barsalou, 1999), then our theoretical representations of linguistic representations should contain information about how language is used to direct people's attention to events and entities in the current joint attentional frame. Moreover, it is extremely difficult to see how either generative grammar or connectionism could ever deal adequately with the appropriate use of the many pragmatic grounding devices by means of which people take account of the knowledge, expectations, and perspective of their listeners. These are an integral part of everyday linguistic communication, and they are in fact the *raison d'être* for many important morphological and syntactic constructions of the language. Are these to simply be left out of account? Approaches that ignore function also ignore the apparent fact, as argued above, that children use function to make many of their most basic and important linguistic generalizations at all stages of development.

The current approach thus posits intention-reading—specifically, the understanding and segmenting of communicative intentions as they are expressed in all kinds of linguistic items and structures—as primary in the language acquisition process, including all of the most important processes of pattern-finding. The essential question, then, is whether we can explain how human beings create and find linguistic patterns without making reference to communicative function. This is an empirical question, and many people—from both the generativist and connectionist camps—are betting that we can. But my assessment is that we cannot, at least not if psychological reality is our ultimate goal.

Second, the current approach is *construction-based*. This has two important implications. First, it means that the focus is on whole utterances and constructions—not isolated words or morphemes—as the most fundamental units of language acquisition. Utterances are the primary reality of language from a communicative point of view because they are the most direct embodiment of a speaker's communicative intentions. And so it is utterances—not words or abstract categories—that children are initially focused on learning. Abstracting in various ways across these utterances and their constituents leads children to utterance-level, nominal, and clausal constructions, which are themselves meaningful linguistic symbols: linguistic gestalts. The process by which children do this involves as an essential component their cognitive skills at making analogies across complex relational structures. Unfortunately, this is a process of language acquisition that has received very little research attention from acquisition theorists of any persuasion, mainly because of the almost exclusive focus of most theorists on paradigmatic categories such as noun and verb or so-called grammatical relations (syntactic roles) such as subject and object (Tomasello, 1998d). These categories and syntactic roles are important as well, of course, but they can be induced only if children first have some comprehension of the larger utterances and constructions of which they form a part. Our conclusion in Chapter 5 was precisely that we cannot account for the facts of child language acquisition without positing some such larger structures across which children make analogies and within which they perform their functionally based distributional analyses.

The other main implication of a construction-based view is that we focus on children's learning and use of particular words, phrases, and expressions, as concrete linguistic entities—a focus shared with connectionism, but not with generative grammar. As children attempt to read the intentions of other persons as expressed in utterances, they extract words and functionally coherent phrases from these utterances, but they also create item-based constructions with open slots on the level of whole utterances. Few theorists of language acquisition deal with these humble creations, and those who have dealt with them (e.g., Braine, 1976) have not provided an account by means of which they evolve into more abstract and adult-like constructions. But item-based constructions are of crucial importance to syntactic development as an important way station, and indeed modern construction grammar accounts of adult linguistic competence emphasize that they constitute an important component of adult linguistic competence as well (e.g., Fillmore, Kaye, and O'Conner, 1988; Fillmore, 1989; Pawley and Syder, 1983). This means that we can posit our own kind of continuity in the process of child language acquisition. In this case, however, we are not talking about a continuity in linguistic representations across development, but rather a continuity of the processes by means of which human language users, at all stages of ontogeny, are storing linguistic units of various kinds and at the same time making many kinds of abstractions across them as well.

Third, the current approach is *usage-based*. This perspective entails a commitment to the proposition that language structure emerges from language use, both historically and ontogenetically. In ontogeny, the hypothesis is that a child hears and stores concrete utterances and then finds patterns in these stored utterances. This is a gradual and uneven process that depends crucially on the type and token frequency with which certain structures appear in the input—which itself depends on the rate at which they appear and on time (age). This means that over developmental time children's linguistic representations become stronger and more abstract, but they can—depending on input—do this very locally as children hear different numbers of exemplars, that vary from one another in different ways, for different construction types.

Focusing on production, a usage-based perspective means focusing on how children construct, from their stored linguistic experience, utterances that are adapted for their listener in the current usage event. Usage-based syntactic operations are the psycholinguistic mechanisms by means of which children symbolically integrate the various kinds of units in their linguistic inventories—from simple to complex, from concrete to abstract—in creative ways on particular occasions of use. We have only just begun to identify the specifics involved, but the focus on relatively complex linguistic expressions and constructions as available to children in prefabricated form—either with or without the knowledge of their internal constituency—leads us to posit a whole different set of operations from the meaningful words and meaningless rules posited by more formal approaches. We can thus talk about such things as filling slots in pivot schemas, adding things onto item-based constructions, concatenating clauses to create novel utterances without an utterance-level construction, inserting things into constructions, and on and on. The main theoretical point is simply that by taking this approach we may attempt to discover empirically the actual syntactic operations that children are using psycholinguistically rather than specifying all the possibilities ahead of time on the basis of an abstract formal theory.

Perhaps most radically, the current usage-based proposal, following those of Langacker (1987a) and Bybee (1995), claims that children and adults have access to their hierarchy of linguistic constructions at several levels of abstraction simultaneously. This means that in many cases children's comprehension and production of relatively complex utterances are based on a simple retrieval of stored expressions, whereas in other cases they are based on the cutting and pasting together of stored linguistic schemas and constructions of various kinds and degrees of abstraction. This would seem to be the way that people master a variety of cognitive skills, and there is no reason to think that language is any different in this regard. Importantly, when we focus in this way on language use and usage-based operations, we must perforce invoke in our acquisition theory a variety of cognitive and social-cognitive processes that originate from outside the domain of language per se (perception, memory, joint attention, intention-reading, categorization, analogy, and so on).

In all, these are exciting times in the language sciences, including the study of child language acquisition. New discoveries in a science often follow upon the development of novel methodologies and the new observations that these enable. And so, it is only in recent years that large corpora of both written and spoken language have become available—with even larger ones on the way—and many of these can be searched automatically, enabling larger quantities and thus the use of more powerful statistical techniques. In the study of language development, the CHILDES corpora make it "relatively" easy to answer specific questions about spontaneous spoken speech. In addition, new experimental approaches to child language acquisition are being devised at an ever-increasing rate, drawing on experience both from adult cognitive science (including adult psycholinguistics) and from other areas of developmental psychology. There are thus a variety of new measurement techniques to identify basic psycholinguistic representations and processes, ranging from priming techniques to the identification of the intonational contours encapsulating utterances to the tracking of eye movements during language comprehension and production to the computational modeling of various learning processes.

But these new methodological techniques will be of long-term benefit to the field only if we get our theoretical house in order. This involves, in my opinion, adopting a view of human linguistic competence based less on an analogy to formal languages and more on empirical research in the cognitive sciences. Of special importance is integrating our theories of child language acquisition with theory and research on children's cognitive, social-cognitive, and communicative development in general. How children become competent users of a natural language is not a logical problem but an empirical problem.

References

Abbot-Smith, K., Lieven, E., and Tomasello, M. 2001. What children do and do not do with ungrammatical word orders. *Cognitive Development 16*, 1–14.

——— Submitted. Training two-year-olds to produce the transitive.

Acredolo, L. P., and Goodwyn, S. W. 1988. Symbolic gesturing in normal infants. *Child Development 59*, 450–466.

Adams, A. M., and Gathercole, S. E. 1995. Phonological working memory and speech production in preschool children. *Journal of Speech and Hearing Research 38*, 403–414.

——— 1996. Phonological working memory and spoken language development in young children. *Quarterly Journal of Experimental Psychology 49A(1)*, 216–233.

——— 2000. Limitations in working memory: Implications for language development. *International Journal of Language and Communication Disorders 35*, 95–116

Akhtar, N. 1999. Acquiring basic word order: Evidence for data-driven learning of syntactic structure. *Journal of Child Language 26*, 339–356.

Akhtar, N., Carpenter, M., and Tomasello, M. 1996. The role of discourse novelty in early word learning. *Child Development 67*, 635–645.

Akhtar, N., Dunham, F., and Dunham, P. 1991. Directive interactions and early vocabulary development: The role of joint attentional focus. *Journal of Child Language 18*, 41–50.

Akhtar, N., Jipson, J., and Callanan, M. 2001. Learning words through overhearing. *Child Development 72*, 416–430.

Akhtar, N., and Montague, L. 1999. Early lexical acquisition: The role of cross-situational learning. *First Language 19*, 347–358.

Akhtar, N., and Tomasello, M. 1996. Two-year-olds learn words for absent objects and actions. *British Journal of Developmental Psychology 14*, 79–93.

——— 1997. Young children's productivity with word order and verb morphology. *Developmental Psychology 33*, 952–965.

Aksu-Koç, A. 1988. *The acquisition of aspects and modality.* Cambridge: Cambridge University Press.

——— 1998. The role of input vs. universal predispositions in the emergence of tense-aspect morphology: Evidence from Turkish. *First Language 18,* 255–280.

Aksu-Koç, A., and Slobin, D. 1986. A psychological account of the development and use of evidentials in Turkish. In W. Chafe and J. N. Chafe, eds., *Evidentiality: The linguistic coding of epistemology.* Norwood, NJ: Ablex.

Aksu-Koç, A., and von Stutterheim, C. 1994. Temporal relations in narrative: Simultaneity. In Berman and Slobin 1994.

Allen, S. 1996. *Aspects of argument structure acquisition in Inuktitut.* Amsterdam: Benjamins.

——— In press. A discourse-pragmatic explanation for the subject-object asymmetry in early null arguments: The principle of informativeness revisited. In R. Shillcock, A. Sorace, and C. Heycock, eds., *Proceedings of the Third GALA Conference.*

Allen, S. E. M., and Crago, M. B. 1996. Early passive acquisition in Inuktitut. *Journal of Child Language 23,* 129–156.

Allen, S. E. M., and Schröder, H. 2000. Preferred argument structure in early Inuktitut spontaneous speech data. In J. W. DuBois, L. E. Kumpf, and W. J. Ashby, eds., *Preferred argument structure: Grammar as architecture for function.* Amsterdam: Benjamins.

Ambalu, D., Chiat, S., and Pring, T. 1997. When is it best to hear a verb? The effects of timing and focus of verb models on children's learning of verbs. *Journal of Child Language 24,* 25–34.

Anglin, J. 1993. Vocabulary development: A morphological analysis. *Monographs of the Society for Research in Child Development 58(238),* 1–166.

Anisfeld, M., Rosenberg, E. S., Hoberman, M. J., and Gasparini, D. 1998. Lexical acceleration coincides with the onset of combinatorial speech. *First Language 18,* 165–184.

Anselmi, D., Tomasello, M., and Acunzo, M. 1986. Young children's responses to neutral and specific contingent queries. *Journal of Child Language 13,* 135–44.

Antinucci, F., and Miller, R. 1976. How children talk about what happened. *Journal of Child Language 3,* 167–189.

Appleton, M., and Reddy, V. 1996. Teaching three-year-olds to pass belief tests: A conversational approach. *Social Development 5,* 275–291.

Ariel, M. 1988. Referring and accessibility. *Journal of Linguistics 24,* 65–87.

Atkinson, M. 1996. Now, hang on a minute: Some reflections on emerging orthodoxies. In H. Clahsen, ed., *Generative perspectives on language acquisition.* Hillsdale, NJ: Erlbaum.

Bachrach, V. R., and Luszcz, M. A. 1979. Communicative competence in young children: The use of implicit linguistic information. *Child Development 50,* 260–263.

——— 1983. The emergence of communicative competence: Detection of conversational topics. *Journal of Child Language 10,* 623–637.

Baillargeon, R. 1995. Physical reasoning in infancy. In M. Gazzaniga, ed., *The cognitive neurosciences.* Cambridge, MA: MIT Press.

Bakeman, R., and Adamson, L. 1984. Coordinating attention to people and objects in mother-infant and peer-infant interactions. *Child Development 55,* 1278–89.

Baker, C. L., and McCarthy, J. J. 1981. *The logical problem of language acquisition.* Cambridge, MA: MIT Press.

Baldwin, D. 1991. Infants' contributions to the achievement of joint reference. *Child Development 62,* 875–90.

Baldwin, D. 1993a. Infants' ability to consult the speaker for clues to word reference. *Journal of Child Language 20,* 395–418.

—— 1993b. Early referential understanding: Young children's ability to recognize referential acts for what they are. *Developmental Psychology 29,* 1–12.

—— 2000. Interpersonal understanding fuels knowledge acquisition. *Current Directions in Psychological Science 9,* 40–45.

Baldwin, D. A., and Baird, J. A. 2001. Discerning intentions in dynamic human action. *Trends in Cognitive Sciences 5,* 171–178.

Barlow, M., and Kemmer, S., eds. 2000. *Usage based models of language acquisition.* Stanford: CSLI Publications

Barnes, S., Gutfreund, M., Satterly, D., and Wells, G. 1983. Characteristics of adult speech which predict children's language development. *Journal of Child Language 10,* 65–84.

Baron-Cohen, Simon 1995. *Mindblindness: An essay on autism and theory of mind.* Cambridge, MA: MIT Press.

Barrett, M. 1982. The holophrastic hypothesis: Conceptual and empirical issues. *Cognition 11,* 47–76.

—— 1986. *From education to segregation: An enquiry into the changing character of special provision for the retarded in England c. 1846–1918.* Ph.D. diss., University of Lancaster.

Barsalou, L. W. 1999. Perceptual symbol systems. *Behavioral and Brain Sciences 22,* 577–609.

Barton, M., and Tomasello, M. 1994. The rest of the family: The role of fathers and siblings in early language development. In C. Gallaway and B. Richards, eds., *Input and interaction in language acquisition.* Cambridge: Cambridge University Press.

—— 1991. Joint attention and conversation in mother-sibling infant triads. *Child Development 62,* 517–529.

Bartsch, K., and Wellman, H. 1995. *Children talk about the mind.* New York: Oxford University Press.

Bascelli, E., and Barbieri, M. S. 2002. Italian children's understanding of the epistemic and deontic modal verbs dovere (must) and potere (may). *Journal of Child Language 29,* 87–107.

Bassano, D. 1996. Functional and formal constraints on the emergence of epistemic modality: A longitudinal study on French. *First Language 16,* 77–113.

Bates, E. 1976. *Language and context: The acquisition of pragmatics.* New York: Academic Press.

—— 1979. *The emergence of symbols: Cognition and communication in infancy.* New York: Academic Press.

——— 1984. On the invention of language: An alternative view. *Monographs of the Society for Research in Child Development 49,* 130–142.

Bates, E., Bretherton, I., and Snyder, L. 1988. *From first words to grammar: Individual differences and dissociable mechanisms.* Cambridge: Cambridge University Press.

Bates, E., Camaioni, L., and Volterra, V. 1975. The acquisition of performatives prior to speech. *Merrill-Palmer Quarterly 21,* 205–224.

Bates, E., and Goodman, J. 1997. On the inseparability of grammar and lexicon: Evidence from acquisition, aphasia, and real time processing. *Language and Cognitive Processes 12,* 507–587.

——— 1999. On the emergence of grammar from the lexicon. In B. MacWhinney, ed., *The emergence of language.* Mahwah, NJ: Erlbaum.

Bates, E., and MacWhinney, B. 1979. The functionalist approach to the acquisition of grammar. In E. Ochs and B. Schieffelin, eds., *Developmental pragmatics.* New York: Academic Press.

——— 1982. A functionalist approach to grammatical development. In Wanner and Gleitman, 1982.

——— 1987. Competition, variation, and language learning. In B. MacWhinney, ed., *Mechanisms of language acquisition.* Hillsdale, NJ: Erlbaum.

——— 1989. Functionalism and the competition model. In B. MacWhinney and E. Bates, eds., *The cross-linguistic study of sentence processing.* Cambridge: Cambridge University Press.

Bates, E., MacWhinney, B., Caselli, C., Devoscovi, A., Natale, F., and Venza, V. 1984. A cross-linguistic study of the development of sentence comprehension strategies. *Child Development 55,* 341–354.

Bates, E., and Roe, K. 2001. Language development in children with unilateral brain injury. In C. A. Nelson and M. Luciana, eds., *Handbook of developmental cognitive neuroscience.* Cambridge, MA: MIT Press.

Bauer, P. 1996. What do infants recall of their lives? Memory for specific events by one- to two-year-olds. *American Psychologist 51,* 29–41.

Bavin, E. L., and Growcott, C. 2000. Infants of 24–30 months understand verb frames. In M. Perkins and S. Howard, eds., *New directions in language development and disorders.* New York: Kluwer and Plenum.

Bavin, E. L., and Kidd, E. 2000. Learning new verbs: Beyond the input. In C. Davis, T. J. van Gelder, and R. Wales, eds., *Cognitive science in Australia.* Adelaide: Causal.

Behrend, D. 1990. The development of verb concepts: Children's use of verbs to label novel and familiar events. *Child Development 61,* 681–696.

Behrend, D. A., Harris, L. L., and Cartwright, K. B. 1995. Morphological cues to verb meaning: Inflections and the initial mapping of verb meanings. *Journal of Child Language 22,* 89–106.

Behrens, H. 1998. Where does the information go? Paper presented at MPI workshop on argument structure, Nijmegen.

——— 2001a. Cognitive-conceptual development and the acquisition of grammatical morphemes. In M. Bowerman and S. Levinson, eds., *Language acquisition and conceptual development.* Cambridge: Cambridge University Press.

——— 2001b. Learning multiple regularities: Evidence from overgeneralization errors in the German plural. In A. H.-J. Do, L. Domínguez, and A. Johansen, eds., *Proceedings of the 26th Annual Boston University Conference on Language Development*. Somerville, MA: Cascadilla Press.

Behrens, H., and Gut, U. Submitted. The relationship between syntactic and prosodic organisation in early multiword speech.

Behrens, H., and Tomasello, M. 1999. And what about the Chinese? *Behavioral and Brain Sciences 22*, 1014.

Bennett-Kastor, T. 1983. Noun phrases and coherence in child narrative. *Journal of Child Language 10*, 135–149.

Berman, R. 1982. Verb-pattern alternation: The interface of morphology, syntax, and semantics in Hebrew child language. *Journal of Child Language 9*, 169–91.

———— 1993. Marking verb transitivity in Hebrew-speaking children. *Journal of Child Language 20*, 641–670.

Berman, R., and Armon-Lotem, S. 1995. How grammatical are early verbs? Paper presented at the Colloque International de Besançon sur l'Acquisition de la Syntaxe, Besançon, France, Nov.

Berman, R., and Slobin, D. 1994. *Relating events in narrative: A cross-linguistic developmental study*. Hillsdale, NJ: Erlbaum.

Bickerton, D. 1984. The language bioprogram hypothesis. *Behavioral and Brain Sciences 7*, 173–221.

Birch, S. A. J., and Bloom, P. 2002. Preschoolers are sensitive to the speaker's knowledge when learning proper names. *Child Development 73*, 434–444

Bishop, D. V. M. 1997. *Uncommon understanding: Development and disorders of language comprehension in children*. East Sussex, UK: Psychology Press.

Bishop, D. V. M., North, T., and Donlan, C. 1996. Nonword repetition as a behavioural marker for inherited language impairment: Evidence from a twin study. *Journal of Child Psychology and Psychiatry 37*, 391–403.

Bloom, L. 1970. *Language development: Form and function in emerging grammars*. Cambridge, MA: MIT Press.

———— 1971. Why not pivot grammar? *Journal of Speech and Hearing Disorders 36*, 40–50.

———— 1973. *One word at a time*. The Hague: Mouton.

———— 1992. *Language development from two to three*. Cambridge: Cambridge University Press.

———— 1993. *The transition from infancy to language: Acquiring the power of expression*. New York: Cambridge University Press.

———— 1994. Meaning and expression. In W. Overton and D. Palermo, eds., *The ontogenesis of meaning*. Hillsdale, NJ: Erlbaum.

Bloom, L., Lahey, M., Hood, L., Lifter, K., and Fiess, K. 1980. Complex sentences: Acquisition of syntactic connectives and the meaning relations they encode. *Journal of Child Language 7*, 235–261.

Bloom, L., Lifter, K., and Hafitz, J. 1980. The semantics of verbs and the development of verb inflections in child language. *Language 56*, 386–412.

Bloom, L., Lightbown, P., and Hood, L. 1975. Structure and variation in child language. *Monographs of the Society for Research in Child Development 40(2)*.

Bloom, L., Rispoli, M., Gartner, B., and Hafitz, J. 1989. Acquisition of complementation. *Journal of Child Language 16*, 101–120.

Bloom, L., Rocissano, L., and Hood, L. 1976. Adult-child discourse: Developmental interaction between information processing and linguistic knowledge. *Cognitive Psychology 8*, 521–551.

Bloom, L., Tackeff, J., and Lahey, M. 1984. Learning "to" in complement constructions. *Journal of Child Language 11*, 391–406.

Bloom, L., Tinker, E., and Margulis, C. 1993. The words children learn: Evidence for a verb bias in early vocabularies. *Cognitive Development 8*, 431–450.

Bloom, P. 1990. Subjectless sentences in child language. *Linguistic Inquiry 21*, 491–504.

——— 2000. *How children learn the meanings of words*. Cambridge, MA: MIT Press.

Bock, J. K., and Griffin, Z. M. 2000. The persistence of structural priming: Transient activation or implicit learning? *Journal of Experimental Psychology: General 129*, 177–192.

Bohannon, N., and Stanowicz, L. 1988. The issue of negative evidence: Adult responses to children's language errors. *Developmental Psychology 24*, 684–689.

Bonvillian, J. D., Garber, A. M., and Dell, S. B. 1997. Language origin accounts: Was the gesture in the beginning? *First-Language 17*, 219–239.

Botting, N., and Conti-Ramsden, G. 2001. Non-word repetition and language development in children with specific language impairment (SLI). *International Journal of Language and Communication Disorders 36*, 421–432.

Bowerman, M. 1973. *Early syntactic development*. Cambridge: Cambridge University Press.

——— 1978. Systematizing semantic knowledge: Changes over time in the child's organization of word meaning. *Child Development 49*, 977–987.

——— 1979. The acquisition of complex sentences. In P. Fletcher and M. Garman, eds., *Language acquisition*. Cambridge: Cambridge University Press.

——— 1982. Reorganizational processes in lexical and syntactic development. In Wanner and Gleitman, 1982.

——— 1985. What shapes children's grammars? In D. I. Slobin, ed., *The crosslinguistic study of language acquisition*. Hillsdale, NJ: Erlbaum.

——— 1988. The "no negative evidence" problem: How do children avoid constructing an overgeneral grammar? In J. A. Hawkins, ed., *Explaining language universals*. Oxford: Basil Blackwell.

——— 1990. Mapping thematic roles onto syntactic functions: Are children helped by innate linking rules? *Linguistics 28*, 1253–89.

——— 1996. Learning how to structure space for language: A cross-linguistic perspective. In P. Bloom, M. Peterson, L. Nadel, and M. Garret, eds., *Language and space*. Cambridge, MA: MIT Press.

——— 1997. Argument structure and learnability: Is a solution in sight? *Berkeley Linguistics Society 22*, 454–468.

Bowerman, M., and Choi, S. 2001. Shaping meanings for language: Universal and language-specific in the acquisition of spatial semantic categories. In M. Bowerman and S. C. Levinson, eds., *Language acquisition and conceptual development*. New York: Cambridge University Press.

Boyd, R., and Richerson, P. J. 1985. *Culture and the evolutionary process*. Chicago: University of Chicago Press.

Braine, M. 1963. The ontogeny of English phrase structure. *Language 39*, 1–14.

―――― 1971. On two types of models of the internalization of grammars. In D. I. Slobin, ed., *The ontogenesis of grammar.* New York: Academic Press.

―――― 1974. On what might constitute learnable phonology. *Language 50*, 270–299.

―――― 1976. Children's first word combinations. *Monographs of the Society for Research in Child Development 41(1).*

―――― 1992. What sort of innate structure is needed to bootstrap into syntax? *Cognition 45*, 77–100.

―――― 1994. Is nativism sufficient? *Journal of Child Language 21*, 9–31.

Braine, M., Brody, R. E., Fisch, S. M., Weisberger, M. J., and Blum, M. 1990. Can children use a verb without exposure to its argument structure? *Journal of Child Language 17*, 313–342.

Braine, M., and Brooks, P. 1995. Verb-argument structure and the problem of avoiding an overgeneral grammar. In Tomasello and Merriman 1995.

Braine, M. D. S., Brooks, P., Cowan, N., Samuels, M., and Tamis-LeMonda, C. 1993. The development of categories at the semantic/syntax interface. *Cognitive Development 8*, 465–494.

Brent, M., and Siskind, J. M. 2000. The role of exposure to isolated words in early vocabulary development. *Cognition 81*, B33–B44.

Bridges, A. 1984. Preschool children's comprehension of agency. *Journal of Child Language 11*, 593–610.

Brinkmann, U. 1995. *The locative alternation: Its structure and acquisition.* Nijmegen: Thesis Katholieke Universiteit Nijmegen.

Bronckardt, J., and Sinclair, H. 1973. Time, tense, and aspect. *Cognition 2* 107–130.

Brooks, P., and Kempe, V. Submitted. Less is more: Processing constraints or input adaptations?

Brooks, P., and Tomasello, M. 1999a. Young children learn to produce passives with nonce verbs. *Developmental Psychology 35*, 29–44.

―――― 1999b. How young children constrain their argument structure constructions. *Language 75*, 720–738.

Brooks, P., Tomasello, M., Lewis, L., and Dodson, K. 1999. Children's overgeneralization of fixed transitivity verbs: The entrenchment hypothesis. *Child Development 70*, 1325–37.

Brown, A., and Kane, M. 1988. Preschool children can learn to transfer: Learning to learn and learning from example. *Cognitive Psychology 20*, 493–523.

Brown, P. 2001. Learning to talk about motion *up* and *down* in Tzeltal: Is there a language-specific bias for verb learning? In M. Bowerman and S. Levinson, eds., *Language acquisition and conceptual development.* Cambridge: Cambridge University Press.

Brown, R. 1957. Linguistic determinism and the part of speech. *Journal of Abnormal and Social Psychology 55*, 1–5.

―――― 1973. *A first language: The early stages.* Cambridge, MA: Harvard University Press.

Brown, R., and Hanlon, C. 1970. Derivational complexity and order of acquisition in child speech. In J. R. Hayes, ed., *Cognition and the development of language.* New York: John Wiley and Sons.

Bruner, J. 1975. The ontogenesis of speech acts. *Journal of Child Language 2*, 1–20.

——— 1981. The pragmatics of acquisition. In W. Deutsch, ed., *The child's construction of language*. New York: Academic Press.

——— 1983. *Child's talk*. New York: Norton.

Buczowska, E. 1989. *The acquisition of temporal systems in English as a native language and English as a foreign language*. Doctoral diss., Adam Mickiewicz University, Poznan.

Budwig, N. 1990. The linguistic marking of nonprototypical agency: An exploration into children's use of passives. *Linguistics 28*, 1221–52.

Budwig, N., Stein, S., and O'Brien, C. 2001. Non-agent subjects in early child language: A crosslinguistic comparison. In K. Nelson, A. Aksu-Ko, and C. Johnson, eds., *Children's language*, vol. 11: *Interactional contributions to language development*. Mahwah, NJ: Lawrence Erlbaum.

Butterworth, G. 1991. The ontogeny and phylogeny of joint visual attention. In A. Whiten, ed., *Natural theories of mind*. Oxford: Basil Blackwell.

Bybee, J. 1985. *Morphology: A study of the relation between meaning and form*. Amsterdam: Benjamins.

——— 1995. Regular morphology and the lexicon. *Language and Cognitive Processes 10*, 425–455.

——— 2002. Sequentiality as the basis of constituent structure. In T. Givón and B. Malle, eds., *From Pre-language to language*. Amsterdam: Benjamins.

Bybee, J., Perkins, R., and Pagliuca, W. 1994. *The evolution of grammar*. Chicago: University of Chicago Press.

Bybee, J., and Scheibmann, J. 1999. The effect of usage on degrees of constituency: The reduction of *don't* in English. *Linguistics 37*, 575–596.

Bybee, J. L., and Slobin, D. I. 1982. Rules and schemas in the development and use of the English past tense. *Language 58*, 265–289.

Byrne, R. W. 1995. The thinking ape. Oxford: Oxford University Press.

Byrnes, J. P., and Duff, M. A. 1989. Young children's comprehension of modal expressions. *Cognitive Development 4*, 369–387.

Cameron-Faulkner, T., Lieven, E., and Tomasello, M. In press. A construction based analysis of child directed speech. *Cognitive Science*.

Campbell, A., Brooks, P., and Tomasello, M. 2000. Factors affecting young children's use of pronouns as referring expressions. *Journal of Speech, Language and Learning Research 43*, 1337–1349.

Campbell, A., and Tomasello, M. 2001. The acquisition of English dative constructions. *Applied Psycholinguistics 22*, 253–267.

Carey, S., and Bartlett, E. 1978. Acquiring a single new word. *Papers and Reports on Child Language Development 15*, 17–29.

Carpenter, M., Akhtar, N., and Tomasello, M. 1998. Sixteen-month-old infants differentially imitate intentional and accidental actions. *Infant Behavior and Development 21*, 315–330.

Carpenter, M., Nagell, K., and Tomasello, M. 1998. Social cognition, joint attention, and communicative competence from 9 to 15 months of age. *Monographs of the Society for Research in Child Development 255*.

Caselli, M. C., Bates, E., Casadio, P., Fenson, J., Fenson, L., Sanderl, L., and Weir,

J. 1995. A cross-linguistic study of early lexical development. *Cognitive Development 10*, 159–200.

Caselli, M. C., Casadio, P., and Bates, E. 1999. A comparison of the transition from first words to grammar in English and Italian. *Journal of Child Language 26*, 69–111.

Chafe, W. 1994. *Discourse, consciousness, and time: The flow and displacement of conscious experience in speaking and writing.* Chicago: University of Chicago Press.

Chang, F. In press. Symbolically speaking: A connectionist model of sentence production. *Cognitive Science.*

Chapman, R., and Miller, J. 1975. Word order in early two and three word utterances: Does production precede comprehension? *Journal of Speech and Hearing Research 18*, 355–371.

Cheney, D. L., and Seyfarth, R. M. 1990. *How monkeys see the world.* Chicago: University of Chicago Press.

Cheney, D. L., and Wrangham, R. W. 1987. Predation. In B. B. Smuts, D. L. Cheney, R. M. Seyfarth, R. W. Wrangham, and T. T. Struhsaker, eds., *Primate societies.* Chicago: University of Chicago Press.

Childers, J., and Tomasello, M. 2001. The role of pronouns in young children's acquisition of the English transitive construction. *Developmental Psychology 37*, 739–748.

——— In press. Two-year-olds learn novel nouns, verbs, and conventional actions from massed or distributed exposures. *Developmental Psychology.*

Choi, S. 1988. The semantic development of negation: A cross-linguistic study. *Journal of Child Language 15*, 517–532.

——— 1991. Children's answers to yes-no questions: A developmental study in English, French, and Korean. *Developmental Psychology 27(3)*, 407–420.

Choi, S., and Bowerman, M. 1991. Learning to express motion events in English and Korean: The influence of language-specific lexicalization patterns. *Cognition 41*, 83–121.

Choi, S., Bowerman, M., Mandler, J., and McDonough, L. 2001. Early sensitivity to language-specific spatial categories in English and Korean. *Cognitive Development 14*, 241–268.

Choi, S., and Gopnik, A. 1996. Early acquisition of verbs in Korean: A cross-linguistic study. *Journal of Child Language 22*, 497–530.

Chomsky, C. 1969. Linguistics and philosophy. In S. Hook, ed., *Language and philosophy.* New York: New York University Press.

Chomsky, N. 1957. *Syntactic structures.* The Hague: Mouton.

——— 1959. A review of B. F. Skinner's "Verbal behavior." *Language 35*, 26–58.

——— 1965. *Aspects of the theory of syntax.* Cambridge, MA: MIT Press.

——— 1968. *Language and mind.* New York: Harcourt Brace Jovanovich.

——— 1980a. Rules and representations. *Behavioral and Brain Sciences 3*, 1–61.

——— 1980b. Comments in Piatelli-Palmarini, ed., *Language and learning: The debate between Jean Piaget and Noam Chomsky.* Cambridge, MA: Harvard University Press.

——— 1981. *Lectures on government and binding.* Dortrecht: Foris.

——— 1986. *Knowledge of language.* Berlin: Praeger.

——— 1995. *Minimalism.* Cambridge, MA: MIT Press.

Clahsen, H. 1999. Lexical entries and rules of language: A multidisciplinary study of German inflection. *Behavioral and Brain Sciences 22,* 980–999.

Clahsen, H., Rothweiler, M., Woest, A., and Marcus, G. 1992. Regular and irregular inflection in the acquisition of German noun plurals. *Cognition 45,* 225–255.

Clancy, P. 1989. Form and function in the acquisition of Korean wh-questions. *Journal of Child Language 16,* 323–347.

——— 1993. Preferred argument structure in Korean acquisition. In E. Clark, ed., *Proceedings of the 25th annual child language research forum.* Stanford: Center for the Study of Language and Information.

——— 1995. Referential strategies and the co-construction of argument structure in Korean acquisition. *Typological Studies in Language 33,* 33–68.

——— 2000. The lexicon in interaction: Developmental origins of preferred argument structure in Korean. In J. DuBois, ed., *Preferred argument structure: Grammar as architecture for function.* Amsterdam: Benjamins.

Clancy, P., Lee, H., and Zoh, M. H. 1986. Parsing strategies in the acquisition of relative clauses: Universal principles and language-specific realizations. *Cognition 24,* 225–262.

Clark, E. 1971. On the acquisition of the meaning of before and after. *Journal of Verbal Learning and Verbal Behavior 10,* 266–275.

——— 1973. What's in a name? On the child's acquisition of semantics in his first language. In T. Moore, ed., *Cognitive development and the acquisition of language.* New York: Academic Press.

——— 1982. The young word maker: A case study of innovation in the child's lexicon. In Wanner and Gleitman, 1982.

——— 1983. Meanings and concepts. In J. Flavell and E. Markman, eds., *Handbook of child psychology,* vol. 3: *Cognitive development.* New York: John Wiley.

——— 1987. The principle of contrast: A constraint on language acquisition. In B. MacWhinney, ed., *Mechanisms of language acquisition.* Hillsdale, NJ: Erlbaum.

——— 1988. On the logic of contrast. *Journal of Child Language 15,* 317–336.

——— 1993. *The lexicon in acquisition.* Cambridge: Cambridge University Press.

——— 1997. Conceptual perspective and lexical choice in acquisition. *Cognition 64,* 1–37.

Clark, E., and Berman, R. 1984. Structure and use in the acquisition of word formation. *Language 60,* 542–590.

Clark, E. V., and Sengul, C. J. 1978. Strategies in the acquisition of deixis. *Journal of Child Language 5,* 457–475.

Clark, E. V., and Svaib, T. A. 1997. Speaker perspective and reference in young children. *First Language 17,* 54–73.

Clark, H. 1996. *Uses of language.* Cambridge: Cambridge University Press.

Clark, R. 1974. Performing without competence. *Journal of Child Language 1,* 1–10.

Coates, J. 1988. Introduction. In J. Coates and D. Cameron, eds., *Women in their speech communities.* London: Longman.

Cohen, L. B. 1998. An information-processing approach to infant perception and cognition. In F. Simion and G. Butterworth, eds., *The development of sensory, motor, and cognitive capacities in early infancy.* Hove, UK: Psychology Press.

Comrie, B. 1976. *Aspect: An introduction to the study of verbal aspect and related problems.* Cambridge: Cambridge University Press.

Conti-Ramsden, G., and Friel-Patti, S. 1987. Situational variability in mother-child conversations. In K. E. Nelson, ed., *Children's language,* vol. 6. Hillsdale, NJ: Erlbaum.

Conti-Ramsden, G., and Snow, C., eds., *Children's language,* vol. 7. Hillsdale, NJ: Erlbaum.

Conway, C. M., and Christiansen, M. H. 2001. Sequential learning in non-human primates. *Trends in Cognitive Sciences 5,* 529–546.

Corkum, V., and Moore, C. 1995. Development of joint visual attention in infants. In C. Moore and P. J. Dunham, eds., *Joint attention: Its origins and role in development.* Hillsdale, NJ: Erlbaum.

Correa, L. 1995a. The relative difficulty of children's comprehension of relative clauses: A procedural account. In K. Nelson and Z. Réger, eds., *Children's language,* vol. 3. Hillsdale, NJ: Erlbaum.

——— 1995b. An alternative assessment of children's comprehension of relative clauses. *Journal of Psycholinguistics Research 24,* 183–203.

Corrigan, R. 1988. Children's identification of actors and patients in prototypical and nonprototypical sentence types. *Cognitive Development 3,* 285–297.

Crain, S., and Pietroski, P. 2001. Nature, nurture and Universal Grammar. *Linguistics and Philosophy 24,* 139–185.

Croft, W. 1991. *Syntactic categories and grammatical relations: The cognitive organization of information.* Chicago: University of Chicago Press.

——— 1995. Intonation units and grammatical units. *Linguistics 33(5),* 839–882.

——— 2000. *Explaining language change: An evolutionary approach.* London: Longman.

——— 2001. *Radical construction grammar: Syntactic theory in typological perspective.* Oxford: Oxford University Press.

Cromer, R. F. 1971. The development of the ability to decentre in time. *British Journal of Psychology 62,* 353–365.

Cullicover, P. 1999. *Syntactic nuts.* Oxford: Oxford University Press.

Cziko, G. A. 1986. Testing the language bioprogram: A review of children's acquisition of articles. *Language 62,* 878–898.

Dabrowska, E. 2000. From formula to schema: The acquisition of English questions. *Cognitive Linguistics 11,* 1–20.

——— 2001. Learning a morphological system without a default: The Polish genitive. *Journal of Child Language 28,* 545–574.

Dale, P. S., and Crain-Thoreson, C. 1993. Pronoun reversals: Who, when, and why? *Journal of Child Language 20,* 573–589.

Dasinger, L., and Toupin, C. 1994. The development of relative clauses in narrative. In Berman and Slobin 1994.

Deacon, T. W. 1996. Prefrontal cortex and symbol learning: Why a brain capable of language evolved only once. In B. M. Velichkovsky and D. M. Rumbaugh, eds., *Communicating meaning: The evolution and development of language.* Mahwah, NJ: Erlbaum.

——— 1998. *The symbolic species: The co-evolution of language and the human brain.* London: Penguin.

Deak, G. O., and Maratsos, M. 1998. On having complex representations of things: Preschoolers use multiple words for objects and people. *Developmental Psychology 34(2),* 224–240.

DeLancey, S. 1981. An interpretation of split ergativity and related patterns. *Language 57,* 626–657.

de León, L. 2000. The emergent participant: Interactive patterns in the socialization of Tzotzil (Mayan) infants. *Journal of Linguistic Anthropology 8,* 131–161.

Dempster, F. 1996. Distributing and managing the conditions of encoding and practice. In E. Bjork and R. Bjork, eds., *Handbook of perception and cognition,* 2d ed. New York: Academic Press.

Demuth, K. 1989. Maturation and the acquisition of the Sesotho passive. *Language 65,* 56–80.

——— 1990. Subject, topic, and Sesotho passive. *Journal of Child Language 17,* 67–84.

DeVilliers, J. 1985. Learning how to use verbs: Lexical coding and the influence of input. *Journal of Child Language 12,* 587–596.

——— 2000. Language and theory of mind: What are the developmental relationships? In S. Baron-Cohen, H. Tager-Flusberg, and D. J. Cohen, eds., *Understanding other minds,* 2d ed. Oxford: Oxford University Press.

DeVilliers, J., and DeVilliers, P. 1973. Development of the use of word order in comprehension. *Journal of Psycholinguistic Research 2,* 331–341.

Dick, F., Bates, E., Wulfeck, B., Utman, J., Dronkers, N., and Gernsbacher, M. A. 2001. Language deficits, localization, and grammar: Evidence for a distributive model of language breakdown in aphasics and normals. *Psychological Review 108(4),* 759–788.

Didow, S. M., and Eckerman, C. O. 2001. Toddler peers: From nonverbal coordinated action to verbal discourse. *Social Development 10,* 170–188.

Diesendruck, G., and Markson, L. In press. Children's avoidance of lexical overlap: A pragmatic account. *Developmental Psychology 37(5),* 630–641.

Diesendruck, G., Markson, L., Akhtar, N., and Reudor, A. In press. Two-year-olds' sensitivity to speakers' intent. *Child Development.*

Diessel, H. 1999. *Demonstratives: Form, function, and grammaticalization.* Typological studies in languages, 42. Amsterdam: Benjamins.

——— In press. *The acquisition of complex sentences in English.* Cambridge: Cambridge University Press.

Diessel, H., and Tomasello, M. 2000. The development of relative constructions in early child speech. *Cognitive Linguistics 11,* 131–152.

——— 2001. The acquisition of finite complement clauses in English: A usage based approach to the development of grammatical constructions. *Cognitive Linguistics 12,* 97–141.

Dodson, K., and Tomasello, M. 1998. Acquiring the transitive construction in English: The role of animacy and pronouns. *Journal of Child Language 25,* 555–574.

Döpke, S. 1998. Competing language structures: The acquisition of verb placement by bilingual German-English children. *Journal of Child Language 25,* 555–584.

Drozd, K. F. 1995. Child English pre-sentential negation as metalinguistic exclamatory sentence negation. *Journal of Child Language 22,* 583–610.

Dryer, M. 1997. Are grammatical relations universal? In J. Bybee, J. Haiman, and S. Thompson, eds., *Essays on language function and language type.* Amsterdam: Benjamins.

DuBois, J. 1987. The discourse basis of ergativity. *Language 63,* 805–855.

—— In press. Discourse and grammar. In M. Tomasello, ed., *The new psychology of language,* vol. 2: *Cognitive and functional approaches to language structure.* Mahwah, NJ: Erlbaum.

Dunbar, R. 1996. *Grooming, gossip and the evolution of language.* London: Faber and Faber.

Dunham, P., Dunham, F., and Curwin, A. 1993. Joint attentional states and lexical acquisition at 18 months. *Developmental Psychology 29,* 827–831.

Dunn, J. 1988. *The beginnings of social understanding.* Oxford: Blackwell.

Dunn, J., Brown, J., and Beardsall, L. 1991. Family talk about feeling states and children's later understanding of others' emotions. *Developmental Psychology 27,* 448–455.

Dunn, J., and Shatz, M. 1989. Becoming a conversationalist despite (or because of) having an older sibling. *Child Development 60,* 339–410.

Durham, W. 1991. *Coevolution, genes, culture and human diversity.* Palo Alto: Stanford University Press.

Eckerman, C. O., and Didow, S. M. 1996. Nonverbal imitation and toddlers' mastery of verbal means of achieving coordinated action. *Developmental Psychology 32,* 141–152.

Edwards, D., and Goodwin, R. 1986. Action words and pragmatic functions. In S. Kuczaj and M. Barrett, eds., *The development of word meaning.* New York: Springer-Verlag.

Elbers, L. 1995. Production as a source of input for analysis: Evidence from the developmental course of a word-blend. *Journal of Child Language 22,* 47–71.

Elman, J. L. 1990. Finding structure in time. *Cognitive Science 14,* 179–211.

—— 1991. Distributed representations, simple recurrent networks, and grammatical structure. *Machine Learning 7,* 195–224.

—— 1993. Learning and development in neural networks: The importance of starting small. *Cognition 48,* 71–99.

—— 2001. Connectionism and language acquisition. In M. Tomasello and E. Bates, eds., *Language development.* Oxford: Blackwell.

Elman, J. L., Bates, E., Johnson, M., Karmiloff-Smith, A., Parisi, D., and Plunkett, K. 1996. *Rethinking innateness: A connectionist perspective on development.* Cambridge, MA: MIT Press.

Emslie, H., and Stevenson, R. 1981. Pre-school children's use of the articles in definite and indefinite referring expressions. *Journal of Child Language 8,* 313–328.

Erreich, A. 1984. Learning how to ask: Patterns of inversion in yes-no and wh-questions. *Journal of Child Language 11,* 579–592.

Erteschik-Shir, N. 1979. Discourse constraints on dative movements. In T. Givón, ed., *Syntax and semantics*, vol. 12: *Discourse and syntax*. New York: Academic Press.

Ervin-Tripp, S. M. 1996. Context in language. In D. I. Slobin, J. Gerhardt, A. Kyratzis, and J. Guo, eds., *Social interactions, social context, and language*. Hillsdale, NJ: Erlbaum.

Ewers, H. 1999. Schemata im mentalen Lexikon: Empirische Untersuchungen zum Erwerb der deutschen Pluralbildung. In J. Meibauer and M. Rothweiler, eds., *Das Lexikon im Spracherwerb*. Tübingen: Francke.

Fabian-Kraus, V., and Ammon, P. 1980. Assessing linguistic competence: When are children hard to understand? *Journal of Child Language 7*, 401–412.

Fantz, R. L. 1963. Pattern vision in newborn infants. *Science 140*, 296–297.

Farrar, J. 1990. Discourse and the acquisition of grammatical morphemes. *Journal of Child Language 17*, 607–624.

—— 1992. Negative evidence and grammatical morpheme acquisition. *Developmental Psychology 28*, 90–98.

Farrar, M. J., Freund, M., and Forbes, J. 1993. Event knowledge and early language acquisition. *Journal of Child Language 20*, 591–606.

Fauconnier, G. 1985. *Mental spaces*. Cambridge, MA: MIT Press.

—— 1997. *Mappings in thought and language*. Cambridge: Cambridge University Press.

Fenson, L., Dale, P., Reznick, J. S., Bates, E., Thal, D., and Pethick, S. 1994. Variability in early communicative development. *Monographs of the Society for Research in Child Development 59(5)*, v–173.

Fernald, A., Pinto, J. P., Swingley, D., Weinberg, A., and McRoberts, G. 1998. Rapid gains in speed of verbal processing by infants in the second year. *Psychological Science 9*, 228–231.

Figueira, R. A. 1984. On the development of the expression of causativity: A syntactic hypothesis. *Journal of Child Language 11*, 109–127.

Fillmore, C. 1977a. Topics in lexical semantics. In R. Cole, ed., *Current issues in linguistic theory*. Bloomington: Indiana University Press.

—— 1977b. The case for case reopened. In P. Cole, ed., *Syntax and semantics 8: Grammatical relations*. New York: Academic Press.

—— 1988. The mechanisms of construction grammar. *Berkeley Linguistics Society 14*, 35–55.

—— 1989. Grammatical construction theory and the familiar dichotomies. In R. Dietrich and C. F. Graumann, eds., *Language processing in social context*. Amsterdam: North Holland/Elsevier.

Fillmore, C., Kaye, P., and O'Conner, M. 1988. Regularity and idiomaticity in grammatical constructions: The case of let alone. *Language 64*, 501–538.

Fisher, C. 1996. Structural limits on verb mapping: The role of analogy in children's interpretations of sentences. *Cognitive Psychology 31*, 41–81.

—— 2000. *Who's blicking whom? Word order in early verb learning*. Poster presented at the 11th International Conference on Infant Studies, Brighton, England.

—— 2002. Structural limits on verb mapping: The role of abstract structure in 2.5-year-olds' interpretations of novel verbs. *Developmental Science 5(1)*, 55–64.

Fisher, C., Gleitman, H., and Gleitman, L. R. 1991. On the semantic content of subcategorization frames. *Cognitive Psychology 23*, 331–392.

Fisher, S. E., Vargha-Khadem, F., Watkins, K. E., Monaco, A. P., and Pembrey, M. E. 1998. Localisation of a gene implicated in a severe speech and language disorder. *Nature Genetics 18(2)*, 168–170.

Flavell, J. 1997. *Cognitive development*. Englewood Cliffs, NJ: Prentice Hall.

Fleischman, S. 1982. *The future in thought and language: Diachronic evidence from romance*. Cambridge: Cambridge University Press.

Fletcher, P. 1981. Description and explanation in the acquisition of verb-forms. *Journal of Child Language 8*, 93–108.

——— 1985. *A child's learning of English*. Oxford: Basil Blackwell.

——— 1990. Speech and language defects. *Nature 346*, 226.

Fodor, J. 2001. Setting syntactic parameters. In M. Baltin and C. Collins, eds., *The handbook of contemporary syntactic theory*. Oxford: Blackwell.

Foley, W., and Van Valin, R. 1984. *Functional syntax and universal grammar*. Cambridge: Cambridge University Press.

Forbes, J. N., and Farrar, M. J. 1993. Children's initial assumptions about the meaning of novel motion verbs: Biased and conservative? *Cognitive Development 8*, 273–290.

Foster, S. H. 1986. Learning discourse topic management in the preschool years. *Journal of Child Language 13*, 231–250.

Foulkes, D. 1978. *A grammar of dreams*. New York: Basic Books.

Fox, B., and Thompson, S. 1990. A discourse explanation of "the grammar" of relative clauses in English conversation. *Language 66*, 297–316.

Franco, F., and Butterworth, G. 1996. Pointing and social awareness: Declaring and requesting in the second year. *Journal of Child Language 23*, 307–336.

French, L., and Nelson, K. 1985. *Young children's understanding of relational terms: Some ifs, ors and buts*. New York: Springer-Verlag.

Furrow, D., Nelson, K., and Benedict, H. 1979. Mothers' speech to children and syntactic development: Some simple relationships. *Journal of Child Language 6*, 423–442.

Gallagher, T. 1977. Revision behaviors in the speech of normal children developing language. *Journal of Speech and Hearing Research 20*, 303–318.

——— 1981. Contingent query sequences within adult-child discourse. *Journal of Child Language 8*, 51–62.

Galligan, R. 1987. Intonation with single words: Purposive and grammatical use. *Journal of Child Language 14*, 1–22.

Galloway, C., and Richards, B. J. 1994. *Input and interaction in language acquisition*. Cambridge: Cambridge University Press.

Garton, A. 1983. An approach to the study of determiners in early language development. *Journal of Psycholinguistic Research 12*, 513–525.

Garvey, C. 1977. The contingent query: A dependent act in conversation. In M. Lewis and L. A. Rosenblum, eds., *Interaction, conversation, and the development of language*. New York: Wiley.

Gathercole, V. 1986. The acquisition of the present perfect: Explaining difference in the speech of Scottish and American children. *Journal of Child Language 13*, 537–560.

Gathercole, V., Sebastián, E., and Soto, P. 1999. The early acquisition of Spanish verbal morphology: Across-the-board or piecemeal knowledge? *International Journal of Bilingualism 3*, 133–182.

Gee, J., and Savasir, I. 1985. On the use of "will" and "gonna": Towards a description of activity-types for child language. *Discourse Processes 8*, 143–175.

Gelman, S. A., and Taylor, M. 1984. How two-year-old children interpret proper and common names for unfamiliar objects. *Child Development 55*, 1535–40.

Gentner, D. 1982. Why nouns are learned before verbs: Linguistic relativity versus natural partitioning. In S. Kuczaj, ed., *Language development*, vol. 2. Hillsdale, NJ: Erlbaum.

Gentner, D., and Boroditsky, L. 2001. Individuation, relativity, and early word learning. In M. Bowerman and S. C. Levinson, eds., *Language acquisition and conceptual development*. New York: Cambridge University Press.

Gentner, D., and Markman, A. 1995. Similarity is like analogy: Structural alignment in comparison. In C. Cacciari, ed., *Similarity in language, thought and perception*. Brussels: BREPOLS.

——— 1997. Structure mapping in analogy and similarity. *American Psychologist 52*, 45–56.

Gentner, D., and Medina, J. 1998. Similarity and the development of rules. *Cognition 65*, 263–297.

Gergely, G., Nádasdy, Z., Csibra, G., and Biró, S. 1995. Taking the intentional stance at 12 months of age. *Cognition 56*, 165–193.

Gerhardt, J. 1985. An interpretive approach to the study of modality: What child language can tell the linguist. *Studies in Language 9*, 127–229.

——— 1988. From discourse to semantics: The development of verb morphology and forms of self-reference in the speech of a two-year-old. *Journal of Child Language 15(2)*, 337–393.

——— 1991. The meaning and use of the modals hafta, needta and wanna in children's speech. *Journal of Pragmatics 16(6)*, 531–590.

Gerhardt, J., and Savasir, I. 1986. The use of simple present in the speech of two three-year-olds: Normativity not subjectivity. *Language in Society 15*, 501–536.

Gerken, L. A. 1990. A metrical account of children's subjectless sentences. *Proceedings of the North East Linguistics Society 20*, 121–134.

——— 1991. The metrical basis for children's subjectless sentences. *Journal of Memory and Language 30*, 431–451.

——— 1994. Child phonology: Past research, present questions, future directions. In M. A. Gernsbacher, ed., *Handbook of psycholinguistics*. New York: Academic Press.

Gillette, J., Gleitman, H, Gleitman, L., and Lederer, A. 1999. Human simulations of vocabulary learning. *Cognition 73(2)*, 135–176.

Givón, T. 1979. *On understanding grammar*. New York: Academic Press.

——— 1984. *Syntax: A functional-typological introduction*, vol. 1. Amsterdam: Benjamins.

——— 1993. *English grammar: A function-based introduction*. Amsterdam: Benjamins.

——— 1995. *Functionalism and grammar*. Amsterdam: Benjamins.

Gleitman, L. 1990. The structural sources of verb meaning. *Language Acquisition 1*, 3–55.

Gleitman, L. R., Newport, E. L., and Gleitman, H. 1984. The current status of the motherese hypothesis. *Journal of Child Language 11*, 43–79.

Gleitman, L. R., and Wanner, E. 1982. Language acquisition: The state of the art. In Wanner and Gleitman, 1982.

Goldberg, A. 1995. *Constructions: A construction grammar approach to argument structure*. Chicago: University of Chicago Press.

Goldberg, A., and Sethuraman, N. Manuscript. Learning argument structure generalizations.

Goldin-Meadow, S. 1984. Gestural communication in deaf children. *Monographs of the Society for Research in Child Development 49(3–4)*, 143–151.

——— 1997. When gestures and words speak differently. *Current Directions in Psychological Science 5*, 138–143.

Goldin-Meadow, S., Seligman, M. E. P., and Gelman, R. 1976. Language in the two-year-old: Receptive and productive stages. *Cognition 4(2)*, 189–202.

Goldman-Eisler, F. 1968. *Psycholinguistics: Experiments in spontaneous speech*. New York: Academic Press.

Golinkoff, R. M. 1983. The preverbal negotiation of failed messages. In R. M. Golinkoff, ed., *The transition from prelinguistic to linguistic communication*. Hillsdale, NJ: Erlbaum.

——— 1993. When is communication a meeting of the minds? *Journal of Child Language 20*, 199–208.

Golinkoff, R., Hirsh-Pasek, K., and Hollich, G. 1999. Emergent cues for early word learning. In B. MacWhinney, ed., *Emergence of language*. Hillsdale, NJ: Erlbaum.

Golinkoff, R., Hirsh-Pasek, K., Mervis, C., Frawley, W., and Parillo, M. 1995. Lexical principles can be extended to the acquisition of verbs. In Tomasello and Merriman 1995.

Golinkoff, R., Mervis, C., and Hirsh-Pasek, K. 1994. Early object labels: The case for a developmental lexical principles framework. *Journal of Child Language 21*, 125–156.

Gomez, R., and Gerken, L. 1999. Artificial grammar learning by 1-year-olds leads to specific and abstract knowledge. *Cognition 70*, 109–135.

Goodwyn, S., and Acredolo, L. 1993. Symbolic gesture versus word: Is there a modality advantage for onset of symbol use? *Child Development 64*, 688–701.

Gopnik, A. 1988. Three types of early word. *First Language 8*, 49–70.

Gopnik, A., and Choi, S. 1995. Names, relational words, and cognitive development in English and Korean speakers: Nouns are not always learned before verbs. In Tomasello and Merriman 1995.

Gopnik, A., and Meltzoff, A. 1986. Relations between semantic and cognitive development in the one word stage: The specificity hypothesis. *Child Development 57*, 1040–53.

Gordon, P., and Chafetz, J. 1990. Verb-based versus class-based accounts of actionality effects in children's comprehension of passives. *Cognition 36*, 227–254.

Gosch, A., Städing, G., and Pankau, R. 1994. Linguistic abilities in children with Williams-Beuren Syndrome. *American Journal of Medical Genetics 52*, 291–296.

Greenfield, P. M., Reilly, J., Leaper, C., and Baker, N. 1985. The structural and functional status of single-word utterances and their relationship to early one-word speech. In M. Barrett, ed., *Children's single-word speech*. London: Wiley.

Greenfield, P. M., and Smith, J. H. 1976. *The structure of communication in early language development*. New York: Academic Press.

Grice, H. 1975. Logic and conversation. In P. Cole and J. Morgan, eds., *Syntax and semantics*, vol. 3. New York: Academic Press.

Gropen, J., Pinker, S., Hollander, M., and Goldberg, R. 1991a. Affectedness and direct objects: The role of lexical semantics in the acquisition of verb argument structure. *Cognition 41*, 153–195.

—— 1991b. Syntax and semantics in the acquisition of locative verbs. *Journal of Child Language 18*, 115–151.

Gropen, J., Pinker, S., Hollander, M., Goldberg, R., and Wilson, R. 1989. The learnability and acquisition of the dative alternation in English. *Language 65*, 203–257.

Gumperz, J. J., and Levinson, S. C. 1996. *Rethinking linguistic relativity*. Cambridge: Cambridge University Press.

Gundel, J., Hedberg, N., and Zacharski, R. 1993. Cognitive status and the form of referring expressions. *Language 69(2)*, 274–307.

Haith, M., and Benson, J. 1997. Infant cognition. In D. Kuhn and R. Siegler, eds., *Handbook of child psychology*, vol. 2. New York: Wiley.

Hakuta, K. 1982. Interaction between particles and word order in the comprehension and production of simple sentences in Japanese children. *Developmental Psychology 18*, 62–76.

Hakuta, K., Bialystock, E., and Wiley, E. In press. Critical evidence: A test of the critical period hypothesis for second language acquisition. *Psychological Science*.

Hall, G. 1991. *Perceptual and associative learning*. Oxford: Clarendon Press.

—— 1999. Semantics and the acquisition of proper names. In R. Jackendoff, P. Bloom, and K. Wynn, eds., *Language logic, and concepts: Essays in honor of John MacNamara*. Cambridge, MA: MIT Press.

Harner, L. 1976. Children's understanding of linguistic reference to past and future. *Journal of Psycholinguistic Research 5*, 65–84.

—— 1981. Children's talk about the time and aspect of actions. *Child Development 52*, 498–506.

Harris, F., and Flora, J. 1982. Children's use of *get* passives. *Journal of Psycholinguistic Research 11*, 297–311.

Harris, M., Barlow-Brown, F., and Chasin, J. 1995. The emergence of referential understanding: Pointing and the comprehension of object names. *First Language 15*, 19–34.

Harris, M., Barrett, M. D., Jones, D., and Brookes, S. 1988. Linguistic input and early word meaning. *Journal of Child Language 15*, 77–94.

Harris, P. 1996. Desires, beliefs, and language. In P. Carruthers and P. Smith, eds., *Theories of theories of mind*. Cambridge: Cambridge University Press.

Hart, B., and Risley, T. R. 1995. *Meaningful differences in the everyday experience of young American children.* Baltimore: Paul Brookes.

Haspelmath, M. 1989. From purposive to infinitive—A universal path of grammaticization. *Folia Linguistica Historica 10(1–2),* 287–310.

Hauser, M. D., Weiss, D., and Marcus, G. In press. Rule learning by cotton-top tamarins. *Cognition.*

Heibeck, T. H., and Markman, E. M. 1987. Word learning in children: An examination of fast mapping. *Child Development 58,* 1021–34.

Herriot, P. 1969. The comprehension of active and passive sentences as a function of pragmatic expectations. *Journal of Verbal Learning and Verbal Behavior 8(2),* 166–169.

Heyes, C. M., and Galef, B. G., Jr., eds. 1996. *Social learning in animals: The roots of culture.* New York: Academic Press.

Hickmann, M. 1995. Discourse organization and the development of reference to person, space, and time. In P. Fletcher and B. MacWhinney, eds., *Handbook of child language.* Oxford: Basil Blackwell.

Hickmann, M., and Hendriks, H. 1999. Cohesion and anaphora in children's narratives: A comparison of English, French, German, and Mandarin Chinese. *Journal of Child Language 26,* 419–452.

Hirsh-Pasek, K., and Golinkoff, R. M. 1991. Language comprehension: A new look at some old themes. In N. Krasnegor, D. Rumbaugh, M. Studdert-Kennedy, and R. Schiefelbusch, eds., *Biological and behavioral aspects of language acquisition.* Hillsdale, NJ: Erlbaum.

——— 1996. *The origins of grammar: Evidence from early language comprehension.* Cambridge, MA: MIT Press.

Hirst, W., and Weil, J. 1982. Acquisition of the epistemic and deontic meaning of modals. *Journal of Child Language 9,* 659–666.

Hoff-Ginsberg, E. 1985. Some contributions of mothers' speech to their children's syntactic growth. *Journal of Child Language 12,* 367–385.

Hoff-Ginsberg, E., and Shatz, M. 1982. Linguistic input and the child's acquisition of language. *Psychological Bulletin 92,* 3–26.

Hopper, P. 1997. Discourse and category 'verb' in English. *Language and Communication 17,* 93–102.

Hopper, P., and Thompson, S. 1980. Transitivity in grammar and discourse. *Language 56(2),* 215–299.

——— 1984. The discourse basis for lexical categories in universal grammar. *Language 60,* 703–752.

——— 1985. The iconicity of the universal categories noun and verb. In J. Haiman, ed., *Iconicity in syntax.* Amsterdam: Benjamins.

Hopper, P. J., and Traugott, E. C. 1993. *Grammaticalization.* Cambridge: Cambridge University Press.

Hornstein, D., and Lightfoot, N. 1981. *Explanation in linguistics.* London: Longman.

Houston, D., Jusczyk, P. W., and Tager, J. 1997. *Talker-specificity and the persistence of infants' word representations.* Paper presented at the 22nd Annual Boston University Conference on Language Development.

Howe, C. 1976. The meaning of two-word utterances in the speech of young children. *Journal of Child Language 3,* 29–48.

Hudson, R. 1995. Competence without comp? In B. Aarts and C. F. Meyer, eds., *The verb in contemporary English*. Cambridge: Cambridge University Press.

Hummer, P., Wimmer, H., and Antes, G. 1993. On the origins of denial negation. *Journal of Child Language 20*, 607–618.

Huttenlocher, J., Hedges, L., and Duncan, S. 1991. Categories and particulars: Prototype effects in estimating spatial location. *Psychological Review 98*, 352–376.

Huttenlocher, J., Smiley, P., and Charney, R. 1983. Emergence of action categories in the child: Evidence from verb meanings. *Psychological Review 90*, 72–93.

Huttenlocher, J., Smiley, P., and Ratner, H. 1983. What do word meanings reveal about conceptual development? In T. Seiler and W. Wannenmacher, eds., *Conceptual development and the development of word meaning*. Berlin: Springer Verlag.

Huttenlocher, J., Vasilyeva, M., Cymernan, E., and Levine, S. In press. Language input and child syntax. *Cognitive Psychology*.

Hyams, N. 1984. The acquisition of infinitival complements: A reply to Bloom, Tackeff, and Lahey. *Journal of Child Language 11*, 679–684.

——— 1994. Non-discreteness and variation in child language: Implications for principle and parameter models of language development. In Y. Levy, ed., *Other children, other languages*. Hillsdale, NJ: Erlbaum.

Imai, M., and Gentner, D. 1993. What we think, what we mean, and how we say it. *Chicago Linguistic Society 29*, 171–186.

Imai, M., and Haryu, E. 2001. Learning proper nouns and common nouns without clues from syntax. *Child Development 72(3)*, 787–803.

Ingham, R. 1993. Critical influences on the acquisition of verb transitivity. In D. Messer and G. Turner, eds., *Critical influences on child language acquisition and development*. London: Macmillan.

——— 1993/94. Input and learnability: Direct-object omissibility in English. *Language Acquisition 3(2)*, 95–120.

Ingram, D., and Tyack, D. 1979. The inversion of subject NP and Aux in children's questions. *Journal of Psycholinguistic Research 4*, 333–341.

Israel, M., Johnson, C., and Brooks, P. J. 2000. From states to events: The acquisition of English passive participles. *Cognitive Linguistics 11(1–2)*, 103–129.

Iverson, J. M., Capirci, O., and Caselli, M. C. 1994. From communication to language in two modalities. *Cognitive Development 9*, 23–43.

Iverson, J. M., and Goldin-Meadow, S. 1998. Why people gesture when they speak. *Nature 396*, 228.

Jackendoff, R. 1990. *Semantic structures*. Cambridge, MA: MIT Press.

——— 1996. Twistin' the night away. *Language 73*, 534–559.

Jaswal, V. K., and Markman, E. M. 2001. Learning proper and common names in inferential versus ostensive contexts. *Child Development 72*, 768–786.

Jenkins, J., and Astington, J. 1996. Cognitive factors and family structure associated with theory of mind development in children. *Developmental Psychology 32*, 70–78.

Jisa, H., and Kern, S. 1998. Relative clauses in French children's narrative texts. *Journal of Child Language 25*, 623–652.

Johnson, M. 1987. *The body in the mind*. Chicago: University of Chicago Press.

Johnston, J. R., and Slobin, D. I. 1979. The development of locative expressions in English, Italian, Serbo-Croatian and Turkish. *Journal of Child Language 16*, 529–545.

Jones, S. S., and Smith, L. B. 2002. How children know the relevant properties for generalizing object names. *Developmental Science 5(2)*, 219–232.

Jusczyk, P. W. 1997. *The discovery of spoken language*. Cambridge, MA: MIT Press.

Jusczyk, P. W., and Aslin, R. N. 1995. Infants' detection of the sound patterns of words in fluent speech. *Cognitive Psychology 29*, 1–23.

Jusczyk, P. W., and Hohne, E. A. 1997. Infants' memory for spoken words. *Science 277*, 1984–86.

Jusczyk, P. W., Hohne, E. A., and Bauman, A. L. 1999. Infants' sensitivity to allophonic cues for word segmentation. *Perception and Psychophysics 61*, 1465–76.

Kail, M., and Hickmann, M. 1992. On French children's ability to introduce referents in discourse as a function of mutual knowledge. *First Language 12*, 73–94.

Kaper, W. 1976. Pronominal case-errors. *Journal of Child Language 3*, 439–442.

Karmiloff-Smith, A. 1979. *A functional approach to language acquisition*. Cambridge: Cambridge University Press.

—— 1986. From meta-process to conscious access: Evidence from children's metalinguistic and repair data. *Cognition 23*, 95–147.

Karniol, R. 1999. Stuttering, language, and cognition: A review and a model of stuttering as suprasegmental sentence plan alignment (SPA). *Psychological Bulletin 117*, 104–124.

Katz, N., Baker, E., and McNamara, J. 1974. What's in a name? A study of how children learn common and proper names. *Child Development 45*, 469–473.

Kawashima, M., and Prideaux, G. 1992. The function of local cues in the acquisition of Japanese temporal sentences. *Language Sciences 14*, 29–53.

Kay, P., and Fillmore, C. 1999. Grammatical constructions and linguistic generalizations. *Language 75*, 1–33.

Keenan, E. L., 1976. Towards a universal definition of subject. In C. Li, ed., *Subject and topic*. New York: Academic Press.

Kemler Nelson, D., Russell, R., Duke, N., and Jones, K. 2000. Two-year-olds will name artifacts by their functions. *Child Development 71*, 1271–88.

Kemmer, S. 1993. *The middle voice*. Amsterdam: Benjamins.

Kessel, F. S. 1970. The role of syntax in children's comprehension from ages six to twelve. *Monographs of the Society for Research in Child Development 35*, 457.

Kim, Y. 1989. Theoretical implications of complement structure acquisition in Korean. *Journal of Child Language 16*, 573–598.

Kirkham, N. Z., Slemmer, J. A., and Johnson, S. P. 2002. Visual statistical learning in infancy: Evidence for a domain general learning mechanism. *Cognition 83(2)*, 335–342.

Klein, W., and Perdue, C. 1997. The basic variety; or, Couldn't natural languages be much simpler? *Second Language Research 13(4)*, 301–347.

Klima, E., and Bellugi, U. 1966. Syntactic regularities in the speech of children. In

J. Lyons and R. J. Wales, eds., *Psycholinguistic papers: The proceedings of the 1966 Edinburgh Conference*. Edinburgh: Edinburgh University Press.

Köpcke, K. 1998. The acquisition of plural marking in English and German revisited: Schemata versus rules. *Journal of Child Language 25*, 293–319.

Krug, M. 1998. String frequency: A cognitive motivating factor in coalescence, language processing, and language change. *Journal of English Linguistics 26*, 286–320.

———— 2000. Emerging English modals: A corpus-based study of grammaticalization. *Topics in English linguistics 32*. Berlin/New York: Mouton de Gruyter.

Kuczaj, S. 1977. The acquisition of regular and irregular past tense forms. *Journal of Verbal Learning and Verbal Behavior 16*, 589–600.

———— 1987. Deferred imitation and the acquisition of novel lexical items. *First Language 7*, 177–182.

Kuczaj, S., and Daly, M. 1979. The development of hypothetical reference in the speech of young children. *Journal of Child Language 6*, 563–580.

Kuczaj, S., and Maratsos, M. P. 1975. What children can say before they will. *Merrill-Palmer Quarterly 21*, 89–111.

Kuhl, P. K., and Miller, J. D. 1975. Speech perception by the chinchilla: Voiced-voiceless distinction in alveolar plosive consonants. *Science 190*, 69–72.

Kyratzis, A., and Ervin-Tripp, S. M. 1999. The development of discourse markers in peer interaction. *Journal of Pragmatics 31*, 1321–1338.

Lai, C. S. L., Fisher, S. E., Hurst, J. A., Vargha-Khadem, F., and Monaco, A. P. 2001. A forkhead-domain gene is mutated in a severe speech and language disorder. *Nature 413*, 519–523.

Lakoff, G. 1978. Some remarks on AI and linguistics. *Cognitive Science 2*, 267–275.

———— 1987. *Women, fire, and dangerous things: What categories reveal about the mind*. Chicago: University of Chicago Press.

Lambrecht, K. 1988. Presentational cleft construction in spoken French. In J. Haiman and S. A. Thompson, eds., *Clause combining in grammar and discourse*. Amsterdam: Benjamins.

———— 1994. *Information structure and sentence form*. Cambridge: Cambridge University Press.

Langacker, R. 1987a. *Foundations of cognitive grammar*, vol. 1. Stanford: Stanford University Press.

———— 1987b. Nouns and verbs. *Language 63*, 53–94.

———— 1988. A usage-based model. In B. Rudzka-Ostyn, ed., *Topics in cognitive linguistics*. Amsterdam: Benjamins.

———— 1991. *Foundations of cognitive grammar*, vol. 2. Stanford: Stanford University Press.

———— 2000. A dynamic usage-based model. In M. Barlow and S. Kemmerer, eds., *Usage-based models of language*. Stanford: SLI Publications.

Lederer, A., Gleitman, L., and Gleitman, H. 1995. Verbs of a feather flock together: Structural properties of maternal speech. In M. Tomasello and E. Merriman, eds., *Acquisition of the verb lexicon*. New York: Academic Press.

Legerstee, M. 1991. The role of person and object in eliciting early imitation. *Journal of Experimental Child Psychology 51*, 423–433.

Leonard, L. B. 1998. *Children with specific language impairment.* Cambridge, MA: MIT Press.

Levin, B., and Rappaport Hovav, M. 1991. Wiping the slate clean: A lexical semantic exploration. *Cognition 41*, 123–151.

Levinsky, S., and Gerken, L. A. 1995. Children's knowledge of pronoun usage in discourse. In E. Clark, ed., *Proceedings of the 26th annual child language research forum.* Palo Alto: Stanford University Press.

Levy, E., and Nelson, K. 1994. Words in discourse: A dialectical approach to the acquisition of meaning and use. *Journal of Child Language 21*, 367–389.

Lewis, L. B., Antone, C., and Johnson, J. S. 1999. Effects of prosodic stress and serial position on syllable omission in first words. *Developmental Psychology 35*, 45–59.

Li, P., and Shirai, Y. 2000. *The acquisition of lexical and grammatical aspect.* Berlin/New York: Mouton de Gruyter.

Lieberman, P. 1985. *The biology and evolution of language.* Cambridge, MA: Harvard University Press.

Lieven, E. 1994. Crosslinguistic and crosscultural aspects of language addressed to children. In C. Gallaway and B. J. Richards, eds., *Input and interaction in language acquisition.* Cambridge: Cambridge University Press.

———— 1997. Variation in a crosslinguistic context. In D. I. Slobin, ed., *The crosslinguistic study of language acquisition,* vol. 5. Hillsdale, NJ: Erlbaum.

———— Submitted. The development of English auxiliaries.

Lieven, E., Behrens, H., Speares, J., and Tomasello, M. In press. Early syntactic creativity: A usage-based approach. *Journal of Child Language.*

Lieven, E., Pine, J., and Baldwin, G. 1997. Lexically-based learning and early grammatical development. *Journal of Child Language 24*, 187–220.

Lieven, E., Pine, J., and Dresner Barnes, H. 1992. Individual differences in early vocabulary development. *Journal of Child Language 19*, 287–310.

Lieven, E., Pine, J., and Rowland, C. 1998. Comparing different models of the development of the English verb category. *Linguistics 36*, 807–830.

Limber, J. 1973. The genesis of complex sentences. In T. Moore, ed., *Cognitive development and the acquisition of language.* New York: Academic Press.

———— 1976. Syntax and sentence interpretation. In R. Wales and E. C. T. Walker, eds., *New approaches to language mechanisms.* Amsterdam: North Holland.

Linder, K. In press. The development of sentence interpretation strategies in monolingual German-learning children with and without specific language impairment. *Linguistics 41*.

Littschwager, J. C., and Markman, E. M. 1993. *Young children's understanding of proper versus common nouns.* Paper presented at the Biennial Meeting of the Society for Research in Child Development, New Orleans.

Lloyd, P. 1991. Strategies used to communicate route directions by telephone: A comparison of the performance of 7-year-olds, 10-year-olds and adults. *Journal of Child Language 18*, 171–190.

Locke, A. 1978. The emergence of language. In A. Locke, ed., *Action, gesture, and symbol: The emergence of language.* New York: Academic Press.

Lord, C. 1979. Don't you fall me down: Children's generalizations regarding cause and transitivity. *Papers and Reports on Child Language Development 17*, 81–89.

Loveland, K., and Landry, S. 1986. Joint attention in autism and developmental language delay. *Journal of Autism and Developmental Disorders 16*, 335–349.

Loveland, K. A. 1984. Learning about points of view: Spatial perspective and the acquisition of 'I/you.' *Journal of Child Language 11*, 535–556.

——— 1993. Autism, affordances, and the self. In U. Neisser, ed., *The perceived self*. Cambridge: Cambridge University Press.

Lucariello, J., and Nelson, K. 1986. Context effects on lexical specificity in maternal and child discourse. *Journal of Child Language 13*, 507–522.

Lyons, J. 1968. *Introduction to theoretical linguistics*. London: Cambridge University Press.

MacWhinney, B. 1978. The acquisition of morphophonology. *Monographs of the Society for Research in Child Development 43*.

——— 1999. The emergence of language from embodiment. In B. MacWhinney, ed., *Emergentist perspectives on language acquisition*. Mahwah, NJ: Erlbaum.

MacWhinney, B., and Bates, E. 1978. Sentential devices for conveying givenness and newness. *Journal of Verbal Learning and Verbal Behavior 17*, 539–558.

Mandler, J. 1992. How to build a baby II: Conceptual primitives. *Psychological Review 99*, 587–604.

——— 2000. Perceptual and conceptual processes in infancy. *Journal of Cognition and Development 1*, 3–36.

Mannle, S., Barton, M., and Tomasello, M. 1992. Two-year-olds' conversations with their mothers and preschool-aged siblings. *First Language 12*, 57–71.

Maratsos, M. 1974. Preschool children's use of definite and indefinite articles. *Child Development 45*, 446–455.

——— 1976. *The use of definite and indefinite reference in young children*. Cambridge: Cambridge University Press.

——— 1982. The child's construction of grammatical categories. In Wanner and Gleitman, 1982.

——— 1984. How degenerate is the input to Creoles and where do its biases come from? *Behavioral and Brain Sciences 7*, 200–201.

——— 2000. More overregularizations after all. *Journal of Child Language 28*, 32–54.

Maratsos, M., Gudeman, R., Gerard-Ngo, P., and DeHart, G. 1987. A study in novel word learning: The productivity of the causative. In B. MacWhinney, ed., *Mechanisms of language acquisition*. Hillsdale, NJ: Erlbaum.

Marchman, V. 1993. Constraints on plasticity in a connectionist model of the English past tense. *Journal of Cognitive Neuroscience 5*, 215–234.

Marchman, V., and Bates, E. 1994. Continuity in lexical and morphological development: A test of the critical mass hypothesis. *Journal of Child Language 21*, 339–366.

Marcos, H. 1991. Reformulating a request at 18 months: Gestures, vocalizations and words. *First Language 11*, 361–375.

Marcos, H., and Bernicot, J. 1994. Addressee co-operation and request reformulation in young children. *Journal of Child Language 21*, 677–692.

Marcus, G. 1995. The acquisition of inflection in children and multilayered connectionist networks. *Cognition 56*, 271–279.

Marcus, G. F., Brinkman, U., Clahsen, H., Wiese, R., and Pinker, S. 1995. German inflection: The exception that proves the rule. *Cognitive Psychology 29*, 189–256.

Marcus, G. F., Pinker, S., Ullman, M., Hollander, M., Rosen, T. J., and Xu, F. 1992. Overregularization in language acquisition. *Monographs of the Society for Research in Child Development 57*, 34–69.

Marcus, G. F., Vijayan, S., Bandi Rao, S., and Vishton, P. M. 1999. Rule learning by seven-month-old-infants. *Science 283*, 77–80.

Markman, E. 1989. *Categorization and naming in children.* Cambridge, MA: MIT Press.

———— 1992. Constraints on word learning: Speculations about their nature, origins, and word specificity. In M. Gunnar and M. Maratsos, eds., *Modularity and constraints in language and cognition.* Hillsdale, NJ: Erlbaum.

Markman, E. M., and Wachtel, G. A. 1988. Children's use of mutual exclusivity to constrain the meanings of words. *Cognitive Psychology 20*, 121–157.

Markson, L. 1999. *Mechanisms of word learning in children: Insights from fast mapping.* Doctoral diss., University of Arizona.

Markson, L., and Bloom, P. 1997. Evidence against a dedicated system for word learning in children. *Nature 385(6619)*, 813–815.

Mazuka, R. 1996. How can a grammatical parameter be set before the first word? In J. Morgan and K. Demuth, eds., *Signal to syntax: Bootstrapping from speech to grammar in early acquisition.* Mahwah, NJ: Erlbaum.

McCune, L. 1992. First words: A dynamic systems view. In C. Ferguson, L. Menn, and C. Stoel-Gammon, eds., *Phonological development: Models, research, and implications.* Parkton, MD: York Press.

McCune-Nicolich, L. 1981. The cognitive basis of relational words in the single word period. *Journal of Child Language 8*, 15–34.

McNeil, D. 1992. *Hand and mind: What gestures reveal about thought.* Chicago: University of Chicago Press.

McNeill, D. 1966. The creation of language by children. In J. Lyons and R. J. Wales, eds., *Psycholinguistic papers: The proceedings of the 1966 Edinburgh Conference.* Edinburgh: Edinburgh University Press.

McNeill, D., and McNeill, N. B. 1968. What does a child mean when he says no? In E. M. Zale, ed., *Proceedings of the conference on language and language behavior.* New York: Appleton-Century-Crofts.

McPherson, L. 1991. "A little" goes a long way: Evidence for a perceptual basis of learning for the noun categories COUNT and MASS. *Journal of Child Language 18*, 315–338.

McRae, K., Ferretti, T. R., and Amyote, L. 1997. Thematic roles as verb-specific concepts. *Language and Cognitive Processes 12*, 137–176.

McShane, J., and Whittaker, S. 1988. The encoding of tense and aspect by 3- to 5-year-old children. *Journal of Experimental Child Psychology 45*, 52–70.

McWhorter, J. H. 1998. Identifying the Creole prototype: Vindicating a typological class. *Language 74*, 788–818.

Meisel, J. 1987. Reference to past events and actions in the development of natural second language acquisition. In C. Pfaff, ed., *First and second language acquisition processes*. Cambridge, MA: Newbury House.

―――― 1995. Parameters in acquisition. In P. Fletcher and B. MacWhinney, eds., *The handbook of child language*. Cambridge, MA: Basil Blackwell.

Meltzoff, A. 1995. Understanding the intentions of others: Re-enactment of intended acts by 18-month-old children. *Developmental Psychology 31*, 838–850.

Meltzoff, A., and Moore, K. 1977. Imitation of facial and manual gestures by newborn infants. *Science 198*, 75–78.

―――― 1989. Imitation in newborn infants: Exploring the range of gestures imitated and the underlying mechanisms. *Developmental Psychology 25*, 954–962.

―――― 1994. Imitation, memory, and the representation of persons. *Infant Behavior and Development 17*, 83–99.

Menyuk, P. 1969. *Sentences children use*. Cambridge, MA: MIT Press.

Merriman, W. E., Marazita, J., and Jarvis, L. 1995. Children's disposition to map new words onto new referents. In Tomasello and Merriman 1995.

Mervis, C. B., and Bertrand, J. 1995. Early lexical acquisition and the vocabulary spurt: A response to Goldfield and Reznick. *Journal of Child Language 22*, 461–468.

Mervis, C. B., Golinkoff, R. M., and Bertrand, J. 1994. Two-year-olds readily learn multiple labels for the same basic level category. *Child Development 65*, 1163–77.

Michaelis, L., and Lambrecht, K. 1996. Toward a construction-based theory of language function: The case of nominal extraposition. *Language 72*, 215–247.

Moore, C., Angelopoulos, M., and Bennett, P. 1999. Word learning in the context of referential and salience cues. *Developmental Psychology 35*, 60–68.

Moore, C., and D'Entremont, B. 2001. Developmental changes in pointing as a function of parent's attentional focus. *Journal of Cognition and Development 2(2)*, 109–129.

Morford, M., and Goldin-Meadow, S. 1992. Comprehension and production of gesture in combination with speech in one-word speakers. *Journal of Child Language 19(3)*, 559–580.

Munakata, Y., McClelland, J. L., Johnson, M. H., and Siegler, R. S. 1997. Rethinking infant knowledge: Toward an adaptive process account of successes and failures in object permanence tasks. *Psychological Review 104*, 686–713.

Mundy, P., Sigman, M., and Kasari, C. 1990. A longitudinal study of joint attention and language development in autistic children. *Journal of Autism and Developmental Disorders 20*, 115–128.

Naigles, L. 1990. Children use syntax to learn verb meanings. *Journal of Child Language 17*, 357–374.

―――― 1996. The use of multiple frames in verb learning via syntactic bootstrapping. *Cognition 58*, 221–251.

Naigles, L., Gleitman, L., and Gleitman, H. 1993. Children acquire word meaning components from syntactic evidence. In E. Dromi, ed., *Language and cognition: A developmental perspective*. Norwood, NJ: Ablex.

Naigles, L., and Hoff-Ginsberg, E. 1995. Input to verb learning: Evidence for the plausibility of syntactic bootstrapping. *Developmental Psychology 5*, 827–837.

—— 1998. Why are some verbs learned before others? *Journal of Child Language 25*, 95–120.

Naigles, L., and Kako, E. 1993. First contact in verb acquisition: Defining a role for syntax. *Child Development 64*, 1665–87.

Namy, L. L., and Waxman, S. R. 1998. Words and gestures: Infants' interpretations of different forms of symbolic reference. *Child Development 69(2)*, 295–308.

Nelson, K. 1973. Structure and strategy in learning to talk. *Monographs of the Society for Research in Child Development 38(149)*.

—— 1974. Concept, word, and sentence: Interrelations in acquisition and development. *Psychological Review 81*, 267–285.

—— 1976. Some attributes of adjectives used by young children. *Cognition 4*, 13–30.

—— 1977. Facilitating children's syntax acquisition. *Developmental Psychology 13*, 101–107.

—— 1985. *Making sense: The acquisition of shared meaning.* New York: Academic Press.

—— 1986. *Event knowledge: Structure and function in development.* Hillsdale, NJ: Erlbaum.

—— 1995. The dual category problem in the acquisition of action words. In Tomasello and Merriman 1995.

—— 1996. *Language in cognitive development.* New York: Cambridge University Press.

Nelson, K., Hampson, J., and Shaw, L. K. 1993. Nouns in early lexicons: Evidence, explanations and implications. *Journal of Child Language 20*, 61–84.

Nelson, K. E. 1986. Some observations from the perspective of the rare event cognitive comparison theory of language acquisition. In K. E. Nelson and A. van Kleek, eds., *Children's language.* Hillsdale, NJ: Erlbaum.

Nelson, K. E., and Bonvillian, J. D. 1978. Early semantic development: Conceptual growth and related processes between 2 and 4½years of age. In K. E. Nelson, ed., *Children's language,* vol. 1. New York: Gardner.

Newman, J. 1996. *Give: A cognitive linguistic study.* Berlin/New York: Mouton de Gruyter.

Newport, E. 1990. Maturational constraints on language learning. *Cognitive Science 14*, 11–28.

Newport, E. L. 1999. Reduced input in the acquisition of signed languages: Contributions to the study of creolization. In M. DeGraff, ed., *Language creation and language change: Creolization, diachrony, and development.* Cambridge, MA: MIT Press.

Newport, E. L., Aslin, R. N., and Hauser, M. D. 2001. Learning at a distance: Statistical learning of non-adjacent regularities in humans and tamarin monkeys. Boston University Conference on Language Development, Nov.

Newport, E. L., Bavelier, D., and Neville, H. J. In press. Critical thinking about critical periods: Perspectives on a critical period for language acquisition. In

E. Dupoux, ed., *Language brain and cognitive development: Essays in honor of Jacques Mehler.* Cambridge, MA: MIT Press.

Newport, E. L., Gleitman, H., and Gleitman, L. R. 1977. Mother I'd rather do it myself: Some effects and non-effects of maternal speech style. In C. E. Snow and C. A. Ferguson, eds., *Talking to children: Language input and acquisition.* Cambridge: Cambridge University Press.

Ninio, A. 1992. The relation of children's single word utterances to single word utterances in the input. *Journal of Child Language 19*, 87–110.

——— 1993. On the fringes of the system: Children's acquisition of syntactically isolated forms at the onset of speech. *First Language 13*, 291–314.

——— 1999. Pathbreaking verbs in syntactic development and the question of prototypical transitivity. *Journal of Child Language 26*, 619–653.

Ninio, A., and Bruner, J. 1978. The achievement and antecedents of labelling. *Journal of Child Language 5*, 1–15.

Nomura, M., and Shirai, Y. 1997. Overextension of intransitive verbs in the acquisition of Japanese. In E. Clark, ed., *Proceedings of the 28th annual child language research forum.* Stanford: Center for the Study of Language and Information.

Noveck, I. A, Ho, S., and Sera, M. 1996. Children's understanding of epistemic modals. *Journal of Child Language 23*, 621–643.

Nunberg, G., Sag, I., and Wasow, T. 1994. Idioms. *Language 70*, 491–538.

Ochs, E., and Schieffelin, B. 1986. *Language socialization across cultures.* Cambridge: Cambridge University Press.

O'Grady, W. 1997. *Syntactic Development.* Chicago: Chicago University Press.

O'Neill, D. K. 1996. Two-year-old children's sensitivity to a parent's knowledge state when making requests. *Child Development 67*, 659–677.

O'Neill, D., and Atance, C. 2000. "Maybe my daddy give me a big piano": The development of children's use of modals to express uncertainty. *First Language 20*, 29–52.

Oshima-Takane, Y. 1988. Children learn from speech not addressed to them: The case of personal pronouns. *Journal of Child Language 15*, 94–108.

——— 1992. Analysis of pronominal errors: A case study. *Journal of Child Language 19*, 111–131.

——— 1999. The learning of first and second person pronouns in English. In R. Jackendoff, P. Bloom, and K. Wynn, eds., *Language, logic, and concept: Essays in memory of John MacNamara.* Cambridge, MA: MIT press.

Oshima-Takane, Y., and Benaroya, T. 1989. An alternative view of pronominal errors in autistic children. *Journal of Autism and Developmental Disorders 19*, 73–85.

Owings, D., and Morton, E. 1998. *Animal vocal communication.* Cambridge: Cambridge University Press.

Owren, M. J., and Rendell, D. 2001. Sound on the rebound: Bringing form and function back to the forefront in understanding nonhuman primate vocal signaling. *Evolutionary Anthropology 10*, 58–71.

Pan, B. A., Imbens-Bailey, A., Winner, K., and Snow, C. 1996. Communicative intents expressed by parents in interaction with young children. *Merrill-Palmer Quarterly 42(2)*, 248–266.

Pan, B. A., and Snow, C. E. 1999. The development of conversation and discourse. In M. Barrett, ed., *The development of language*. London: UCL Press.

Pappas, A., and Gelman, S. A. 1998. Generic noun phrases in mother-child conversations. *Journal of Child Language 25,* 19–33.

Park, T. 1979. Some facts on negation: Wode's four-stage developmental theory of negation revisited. *Journal of Child Language 6,* 147–151.

Pawley, A., and Syder, F. 1983. Two puzzles for linguistic theory. In J. Richards and R. Smith, eds., *Language and communication*. New York: Longman.

Pea, R. D. 1982. Origins of verbal logic: Spontaneous denials by two- and three-year-olds. *Journal of Child Language 9,* 597–626.

Pearson, B. Z., Fernandez, S. C., Lewedeg, V., and Oller, D. K. 1997. The relation of input factors to lexical learning by bilingual infants. *Applied Psycholinguistics 18,* 41–58.

Perkins, M. R. 2000. Productivity and formulaicity in language development. In C. Schelletter, C. Letts, and M. Garman, eds., *Issues in normal and disordered child language: From phonology to narrative*. Special issue of The New Bulmershe Papers, University of Reading.

Perner, J., Ruffman, T., and Leekam, S. R. 1994. Theory of mind is contagious: You catch it from your sibs. *Child Development 65(4),* 1228–38.

Peters, A. 1983. *The units of language acquisition*. Cambridge: Cambridge University Press.

Peters, A., and Boggs, S. 1986. Interactional routines as cultural influences on language acquisition. In E. Ochs and B. Schieffelin, eds., *Language socialization across cultures*. Cambridge: Cambridge University Press.

Peterson, C. 1990. The who, when and where of early narratives. *Journal of Child Language 17,* 433–455.

Peterson, C., and Dodsworth, P. 1991. A longitudinal analysis of young children's cohesion and noun specification in narratives. *Journal of Child Language 18,* 397–415.

Peterson, C., and McCabe, A. 1987. The connective *and*: Do older children use it less as they learn other connectives? *Journal of Child Language 14,* 375–381.

—— 1991a. Linking children's connective use and narrative macrostructure. In A. McCabe and C. Peterson, eds., *Developing narrative structure*. Hillsdale, NJ: Erlbaum.

—— 1991b. On the threshold of the story realm: Semantic versus pragmatic use of connectives in narratives. *Merrill-Palmer Quarterly 37,* 445–464.

Peterson, C. C., and Siegal, M. 1999. Representing inner worlds: Theory of mind in autistic, deaf, and normal hearing children. *Psychological Science 10,* 126–129.

Petitto, L. A. 1988. "Language" in the prelinguistic child. In F. Kessel, ed., *The development of language and of language researchers*. Hillsdale, NJ: Erlbaum.

Piaget, J. 1935/1952. *The origins of intelligence in children*. New York: Norton.

—— 1937/1954. *The construction of reality in the child*. New York: Basic Books.

—— 1970. Piaget's theory. In P. H. Mussen, ed., *Carmichael's manual of child psychology*, 3d ed., vol. 1. New York: Wiley.

Pickering, M. J., and Branigan, H. P. 1999. Syntactic priming in language production. *Trends in Cognitive Sciences 3,* 136–141.

Piéraut-Le Bonniec, G. 1980. *The development of modal reasoning: Genesis of necessity and possibility notions.* New York: Academic Press.

Pine, J. 1994. The language of primary caregivers. In C. Gallaway and B. J. Richards, eds., *Input and interaction in language acquisition.* Cambridge: Cambridge University Press.

Pine, J., and Lieven, E. 1993. Reanalysing rote-learned phrases: Individual differences in the transition to multi word speech. *Journal of Child Language 20,* 551–571.

———— 1997. Slot and frame patterns in the development of the determiner category. *Applied Psycholinguistics 18,* 123–138.

Pine, J., Lieven, E., and Rowland, G. 1998. Comparing different models of the development of the English verb category. *Linguistics 36,* 4–40.

Pine, J., and Martindale, H. 1996. Syntactic categories in the speech of young children: The case of the determiner. *Journal of Child Language 23,* 369–395.

Pine, J., Rowland, C., Lieven, E., and Theakston, A. Submitted. Testing the agreement/tense omission model. Manuscript.

Pinker, S. 1981. A theory of graph comprehension. In R. Freedle, ed., *Artificial intelligence and the future of testing.* Hillsdale, NJ: Erlbaum.

———— 1984. *Language learnability and language development.* Cambridge, MA: Harvard University Press.

———— 1987. The bootstrapping problem in language acquisition. In B. MacWhinney, ed., *Mechanisms of language acquisition.* Hillsdale, NJ: Erlbaum.

———— 1989. *Learnability and cognition: The acquisition of verb-argument structure.* Cambridge, MA: Harvard University Press.

———— 1991. Rules of language. *Science 253,* 530–535.

———— 1994. *The language instinct: How the mind creates language.* New York: Morrow.

———— 1999. *Words and rules.* New York: Morrow.

Pinker, S., and Bloom, P. 1992. Natural language and natural selection. In J. H. Barkow, L. Cosmides, and J. Tooby, eds., *The adapted mind.* Oxford: Oxford University Press.

Pinker, S., Lebeaux, D. S., and Frost, L. A. 1987. Productivity and constraints in the acquisition of the passive. *Cognition 26,* 195–267.

Pinker, S., and Prince, A. 1988. On language and connectionism: Analysis of a parallel distributed processing model of language acquisition. *Cognition 28,* 73–193.

Pizzuto E., and Caselli, M. C. 1992. The acquisition of Italian morphology: Implications for models of language development. *Journal of Child Language 19,* 491–557.

———— 1994. The acquisition of Italian verb morphology in a cross-linguistic perspective. In Y. Levy, ed., *Other children, other languages: Issues in the theory of language acquisition.* Hillsdale, NJ: Erlbaum.

Pizzuto, E., and Volterra, V. 2000. Iconicity and transparency in sign languages: A cross-linguistic cross-cultural view. In K. Emmorey and H. Lane, eds., *The signs of language revisited.* Mahwah, NJ: Erlbaum.

Plunkett, K., and Marchman, V. 1991. U-shaped learning and frequency effects in a multi-layered perceptron: Implications for child language acquisition. *Cognition 38*, 43–102.

—— 1993. From rote learning to system building: Acquiring verb morphology in children and connectionist nets. *Cognition 48*, 21–69.

Poplack, S. 2001. Variability, frequency and productivity in the irrealis domain of French. In J. Bybee and P. Hopper, eds., *Frequency effects and emergent grammar.* Amsterdam: Benjamins.

Power, R., and Dal Martello, M. F. 1986. The use of the definite and indefinite articles by Italian pre-school children. *Journal of Child Language 13*, 145–154.

Premack, D. 1983. The codes of man and beasts. *Behavioral and Brain Sciences 6*, 125–167.

Pullum, G. 1996. Learnability, hyperlearning, and the poverty of the stimulus. *Proceedings of the Berkeley Linguistics Society 22*, 498–513.

—— 2002. Empirical assessment of stimulus poverty arguments. *Linguistic Review 19*, 9–50.

Pye, C., Loeb, D., Redmond, S, and Richardson, L. 1994. When do children learn verbs? In E. Clark, ed., *Proceedings of the 25th annual child language research forum.* Stanford: CSLI Publications.

Pye, C., and Quixtan Poz, P. 1988. Precocious passives and antipassives in Quiche Mayan. *Papers and Reports on Child Language Development 27*, 71–80.

Quine, W. 1960. *Word and object.* Cambridge, MA: Harvard University Press.

Quinn, P. C., Cummins, M., Kase, J., Martin, E., and Weissman, S. 1996. Development of categorical representations for above and below spatial relations in 3- to 7-month-old infants. *Developmental Psychology 32*, 942–950.

Quirk, R., Greenbaum, S., Leech, G., and Svartvik, J. 1985. *A grammar of contemporary English.* London: Longman.

Radford, A. 1990. *Syntactic theory and the acquisition of English syntax.* Cambridge, MA: Blackwell.

Rakison, D. H., and Oakes, L. M. In press. *Early category and concept development: Making sense of the blooming, buzzing confusion.* Oxford: Oxford University Press.

Ramus, F., Hauser, M. D., Miller, C., Morris, D., and Mehler, J. 2000. Language discrimination by human newborns and by cotton-top tamarin monkeys. *Science 288*, 349–351.

Rappaport, M., and Levin, B. 1988. What to do with theta-roles. In W. Wilkins, ed., *Syntax and semantics,* vol. 21: *Thematic relations.* New York: Academic Press.

Ratner, N., and Bruner, J. 1978. Games, social exchange, and the acquisition of language. *Journal of Child Language 5*, 391–402.

Redington, M., Chater, N., and Finch, S. 1998. Distributional information: A powerful cue for acquiring syntactic categories. *Cognitive Science 22*, 425–469.

Reznick, J. S., and Goldfield, B. 1992. Rapid change in lexical development in comprehension and production. *Developmental Psychology 28*, 406–413.

Rice, M. L. 1990. Preschoolers' QUIL: Quick incidental learning of words. In

G. Conti-Ramsden and C. Snow, eds., *Children's language,* vol. 7. Hillsdale, NJ: Erlbaum.

Rice, M. L., Wexler, K., and Hershberger, S. 1998. Tense over time: The longitudinal course of tense acquisition in children with specific language impairment. *Journal of Speech, Language and Hearing Research 41,* 1412–31.

Richards, B. J. 1990. *Language development and individual differences: A study of auxiliary verb learning.* Cambridge: Cambridge University Press.

Rispoli, M. 1987. The acquisition of verbs in Japanese. *First Language 7,* 183–200.

——— 1991. The mosaic acquisition of grammatical relations. *Journal of Child Language 18,* 517–551.

——— 1992. Discourse and the acquisition of eat. *Journal of Child Language 19,* 581–595.

——— 1994. Structural dependency and the acquisition of grammatical relations. In Y. Levy, ed., *Other children, other languages: Issues in the theory of language acquisition.* Hillsdale, NJ: Erlbaum.

——— 1998. Patterns of pronoun case error. *Journal of Child Language 25,* 533–544.

Rispoli, M., and Hadley, P. In press. The leading-edge: The significance of sentence disruptions in the development of grammar. *Journal of Speech, Hearing and Language Research.*

Roberts, K. 1983. Comprehension and production of word order in stage 1. *Child Development 54,* 443–449.

Roeper, T. 1996. The role of merger theory and formal features in acquisition. In H. Clahsen, ed., *Generative perspectives on language acquisition: Empirical findings, theoretical considerations and crosslinguistic comparison.* Amsterdam: Benjamins.

Rohde, D. L. T., and Plaut, D. C. 1999. Language acquisition in the absence of explicit negative evidence: How important is starting small? *Cognition 72,* 67–109.

Rollins, P. R., and Snow, C. E. 1998. Shared attention and grammatical development in typical children and children with autism. *Journal of Child Language 25,* 653–654.

Rowland, C., and Pine, J. M. 2000. Subject-auxiliary inversion errors and wh-question acquisition: "What children do know?" *Journal of Child Language 27,* 157–181.

Rubino, R., and Pine, J. 1998. Subject-verb agreement in Brazilian Portuguese: What low error rates hide. *Journal of Child Language 25,* 35–60.

Rumelhart, D., and McClelland, J. 1986. On learning the past tenses of English verbs. In J. McClelland, D. Rumelhart, and the PDP Research Group, eds., *Parallel distributed processing: Explorations in the microstructure of cognition,* vol. 2. Cambridge, MA: MIT Press.

Sachs, J. 1983. Talking about the there and then: The emergence of displaced reference in parent-child discourse. In K. E. Nelson, ed., *Children's language,* vol. 4. Hillsdale, NJ: Erlbaum.

Saffran, J., Aslin, R., and Newport E. 1996. Statistical learning by 8-month old infants. *Science 274,* 1926.

Saffran, J. R., Johnson, E. K., Aslin, R. N., and Newport, E. L. 1999. Statistical learning of tone sequences by human infants and adults. *Cognition 70(1)*, 27–52.

Saffran, J. R., Newport, E. L., Aslin, R. N., Tunick, R. A., and Barrueco, S. 1997. Incidental language learning: Listening (and learning) out of the corner of your ear. *Psychological Science 8*, 101–105.

Samarin, W. 1984. Socioprogrammed linguistics. *Behavioral and Brain Sciences 7*, 206–207.

Sampson, G. 1997. *Educating Eve: The language instinct debate*. London: Casell Academic.

Samuelson, L. K., and Smith, L. B. 1998. Memory and attention make smart word learning: An alternative account of Akhtar, Carpenter and Tomasello. *Child Development 1*, 94–104.

Saussure, F. 1916/1959. *Course in general linguistics*. New York: Philosophical Library.

Savage, C., Lieven, E., and Tomasello, M. In press. Priming active and passive constructions in young English-speaking children. *Developmental Science*.

Savage-Rumbaugh, S. 1990. Language as a cause-effect communication system. *Philosophical Psychology 3*, 55–76.

Savage-Rumbaugh, S., Murphy, J., Sevcik, R., Brakke, K., Williams, S., and Rumbaugh, D. 1993. Language comprehension in ape and child. *Monographs of the Society for Research in Child Development 58(3–4)*.

Saxton, M. 2000. Negative evidence and negative feedback. *First Language 20*, 221–252.

Saxton, M., Kulscar, B., Marshall, G., and Rupra, M. 1998. Longer-term effects of corrective input: An experimental approach. *Journal of Child Language 25*, 701–722.

Saylor, M. M. 2000. Time-stability and adjective use by child and adult English speakers. *First Language 20*, 91–120.

Schlesinger, I. 1971. Learning of grammar from pivot to realization rules. In R. Huxley and E. Ingram, eds., *Language acquisition: Models and methods*. New York: Academic Press.

———— 1988. The origin of relational categories. In Y. Levy, I. Schlesinger, and M. Braine, eds., *Categories and processes in language acquisition*. Hillsdale, NJ: Erlbaum.

Schneider, W. 1999. Automaticity. In *MIT encyclopedia of the cognitive sciences*. Cambridge, MA: MIT Press.

Schuetze, C., and Wexler, K. 1996. Subject case licensing and English root infinitives. In D. MacLaughlin and S. McEwen, eds., *Proceedings of the 20th annual Boston University conference on language development*. Boston: Cascadilla.

Schwartz, R., and Leonard, L. 1983. Some further comments on reduplication in child phonology. *Journal of Child Language 10*, 441–448.

Schwartz, R., and Terrell, B. 1983. The role of input frequency in lexical acquisition. *Journal of Child Language 10*, 57–66.

Schwe, H., and Markman, E. 1997. Young children's appreciation of the mental impact of their communicative signals. *Developmental Psychology 33*, 630–635.

Scollon, R. 1973. *Conversations with a one year old.* Honolulu: University of Hawaii Press.

Scott, C. M. 1984. Adverbial connectivity in conversations of children 6 to 12. *Journal of Child Language 11,* 423–452.

Senghas, A., and Coppola, M. 2001. Children creating language: How Nicaraguan sign language acquired a spatial grammar. *Psychological Science 12(4),* 323–328.

Serrat, E. 1997. Acquisition of verb category in Catalan. Ph.D. diss., University of Barcelona.

Seuren, P. 1984. The bioprogram hypothesis: Fact and fancy. *Behavioral and Brain Sciences 7,* 208–209.

Shanker, S. G., Savage-Rumbaugh, S., and Taylor, T. J. 1999. Kanzi: A new beginning. *Animal Learning and Behavior 27(1),* 24–25.

Shatz, M., Wellman, H., and Silber, S. 1983. The acquisition of mental verbs: A systematic investigation of the first reference to mental state. *Cognition 14,* 301–321.

Sheldon, A. 1974. The role of parallel function in the acquisition of relative clauses in English. *Journal of Verbal Learning and Verbal Behavior, 13,* 272–281.

Shirai, Y. 1994. On the overgeneralization of progressive marking on stative verbs: Bioprogram or input? *First Language 14,* 67–82.

——— 1998. The emergence of tense-aspect morphology in Japanese: Universal predisposition? *First Language 18,* 281–309.

Shirai, Y., and Andersen, R. W. 1995. The acquisition of tense/aspect morphology: A prototype account. *Language 71,* 743–762.

Sigman, M., and Capps, L. 1997. *Children with autism: A developmental perspective.* Cambridge, MA: Harvard University Press.

Siller, M., and Sigman, M. 2002. The behaviors of parents of children with autism predict the subsequent development of their children's communication skills. *Journal of Autism and Developmental Disorders 32(2),* 77–89.

Silva, M. 1991. Simultaneity in children's narratives: The case of when, while and as. *Journal of Child Language 18,* 641–662.

Singleton, J. L., and Newport, E. L. In press. When learners surpass their models: The acquisition of American Sign Language from inconsistent input. *Cognitive Psychology.*

Skinner, B. F. 1957. *Verbal learning.* New York: Appleton-Century-Croft.

Slobin, D. 1970. Universals of grammatical development in children. In G. Flores D'Arcais and W. Levelt, eds., *Advances in psycholinguistics.* Amsterdam: North Holland.

——— 1973. Cognitive prerequisites for the development of grammar. In C. Ferguson and D. Slobin, eds., *Studies of child language development.* New York: Holt, Rinehart, Winston.

——— 1982. Universal and particular in the acquisition of language. In Wanner and Gleitman, 1982.

——— 1985a. Crosslinguistic evidence for the language-making capacity. In Slobin, ed., *The crosslinguistic study of language acquisition,* vol. 2. Hillsdale, NJ: Erlbaum.

——— 1985b. *The crosslinguistic study of language acquisition,* vols. 1 and 2. Hillsdale, NJ: Erlbaum.

———— 1992. *The crosslinguistic study of language acquisition:* vol. 3. Hillsdale, NJ: Erlbaum.

———— 1996. Talking perfectly: Discourse origins of the present perfect. In W. Pagliuca and G. Davis, eds., *Essays in semantics.* Oxford: Oxford University Press.

———— 1997. *The crosslinguistic study of language acquisition,* vols. 4 and 5: *Expanding the contexts.* Mahwah, NJ: Erlbaum.

Slobin, D., and Bever, T. 1982. Children use canonical sentence schemas: A crosslinguistic study of word order and inflections. *Cognition 12,* 229–265.

Smiley, P., and Huttenlocher, J. 1995. Conceptual development and the child's early words for events, objects and persons. In Tomasello and Merriman 1995.

Smith, C. B., Adamson, L. B., and Bakeman, R. 1988. Interactional predictors of early language. *First Language 8,* 143–156.

Smith, C. S. 1980. The acquisition of time talk: Relations between child and adult grammars. *Journal of Child Language 7,* 263–278.

Smith, L. B. 2000. Learning how to learn words: An associative crane. In R. M. Golinkoff and K. Hirsh-Pasek, eds., *Becoming a word learner.* Oxford: Oxford University Press.

Smith, N., and Tsimpli, I. 1995. *The mind of a savant.* Oxford: Blackwell.

Snow, C. E., and Ferguson, C. A. 1977. *Talking to children.* Cambridge: Cambridge University Press.

Snow, C. E., and Goldfield, B. 1983. Turn the page please: Situation specific language acquisition. *Journal of Child Language 10,* 551–570.

Snow, C. E., and Hoefnagel-Höhle, M. 1978. The critical period hypothesis: Evidence from second language learning. *Child Development 49,* 1114–28.

Snow, C. E., Pan, B., Imbens-Bailey, A., and Herman, J. 1996. Learning how to say what one means: A longitudinal study of children's speech act use. *Social Development 5,* 56–84.

Snyder, W., and Stromswold, K. 1997. The structure and acquisition of English dative constructions. *Linguistic Inquiry 28,* 281–317.

Soja, N. 1992. Inferences about the meanings of nouns: The relationship between perception and syntax. *Cognitive Development 7,* 29–45.

Soja, N., Carey, S., and Spelke, E. 1991. Ontological categories guide young children's inductions of word meaning: Object terms and substance terms. *Cognition 38,* 179–211.

Spelke, E. S., Katz, G., Purcell, S. E., Ehrlich, S. M., and Breinlinger, K. 1994. Early knowledge of object motion: Continuity and inertia. *Cognition 51,* 131–176.

Sperber, D., and Wilson, D. 1986. *Relevance: Communication and cognition.* Cambridge, MA: Harvard University Press.

Spooren, W., and Sanders, T. Submitted. Relations between coherence relations: evidence from acquisition data.

Stephany, U. 1981. Verbal grammar in modern Greek early child language. In P. Dale and D. Ingram, eds., *Child language: An international perspective.* Baltimore: University Park Press.

———— 1993. Modality in first language acquisition: The state of the art. In

N. Dittmar and A. Reich, eds., *Modality in language acquisition*. Berlin: de Gruyter.

Stoll, S. 1998. The acquisition of Russian aspect. *First Language 18*, 351–378.

Sudhalter, V., and Braine, M. 1985. How does comprehension of passives develop? A comparison of actional and experiential verbs. *Journal of Child Language 12*, 455–470.

Suzman, S. M. 1985. Learning the passive in Zulu. *Papers and Reports on Child Language Development 24*, 131–137.

Sweetser, E. E. 1990. *From etymology to pragmatics*. Cambridge: Cambridge University Press.

Swingley, D., Pinto, J. P., and Fernald, A. 1999. Continuous processing in word recognition at 24 months. *Cognition 71*, 73–108.

Talmy, L. 1985. Lexicalization patterns: Semantic structure in lexical forms. In T. Shopen, ed., *Language typology and syntactic description*, vol. 3. Cambridge: Cambridge University Press.

——— 1988. The relation of grammar to cognition. In B. Rudzka-Ostyn, ed., *Topics in cognitive linguistics*. Amsterdam: Benjamins.

——— 1996. The windowing of attention in language. In M. Shibatani and S. Thompson, eds., *Grammatical constructions*. Oxford: Oxford University Press.

Tam, C., and Stokes, S. F. 2001. Form and function of negation in early developmental Cantonese. *Journal of Child Language 28(2)*, 373–391.

Tanz, C. 1974. Cognitive principles underlying children's errors in pronominal case-marking. *Journal of Child Language 1*, 271–276.

——— 1980. *Studies in the acquisition of deictic terms*. London: Cambridge University Press.

Tardif, T. 1996. Nouns are not always learned before verbs: Evidence from Mandarin speakers' early vocabularies. *Developmental Psychology 32(3)*, 492–504.

Tardif, T., Gelman, S., and Xu, F. 1999. Putting the noun bias in context: A comparison of English and Mandarin. *Child Development 70*, 620–635.

Tavakolian, S. 1981. *Language acquisition and linguistic theory*. Cambridge, MA: MIT Press.

Tfouni, L. V., and Klatzky, R. L. 1983. A discourse analysis of deixis: Pragmatic, cognitive and semantic factors in the comprehension of 'this,' 'that,' 'here' and 'there.' *Journal of Child Language 10*, 123–133.

Theakston, A., Lieven, E., Pine, J., and Rowland, C. 2001. The role of performance limitations in the acquisition of verb argument structure. *Journal of Child Language 28*, 127–152.

Thomas, M. 1989. The acquisition of English articles by first- and second-language learners. *Applied Psycholinguistics 10*, 335–355.

Thompson, R. K. R., and Oden, D. 2000. Categorical perception and conceptual judgements by nonhuman primates: The paleological monkey and the analogical ape. *Cognitive Science 24*, 363–396.

Thompson, S. A., and Mulac, A. 1991. A quantitative perspective on the grammaticization of epistemic parentheticals in English. In E. Heine and E. Traugott, eds., *Approaches to grammaticalization*, vol. 2. Amsterdam: Benjamins.

Tinbergen, N. 1951. *The study of instinct*. New York: Oxford University Press.

Tomasello, M. 1987. Learning to use prepositions: A case study. *Journal of Child Language 14*, 79–98.

—— 1988. The role of joint attentional process in early language development. *Language Sciences 10*, 69–88.

—— 1992a. *First verbs: A case study of early grammatical development*. New York: Cambridge University Press.

—— 1992b. The social bases of language acquisition. *Social Development 1*, 67–87.

—— 1994. Can an ape understand a sentence? A review of *Language Comprehension in Ape and Child* by E. S. Savage-Rumbaugh et al. *Language and Communication 14*, 377–390.

—— 1995a. Joint attention as social cognition. In C. Moore and P. J. Dunham, eds., *Joint attention: Its origins and role in development*. Hillsdale, NJ: Erlbaum.

—— 1995b. Pragmatic contexts for early verb learning. In Tomasello and Merriman 1995.

—— 1995c. Language is not an instinct. *Cognitive Development 10*, 131–156.

—— 1996. Do apes ape? In J. Galef and C. Heyes, eds., *Social learning in animals: The roots of culture*. New York: Academic Press.

—— 1998a. *The new psychology of language*, vol. 1: *Cognitive and functional approaches to language structure*. Mahwah, NJ: Erlbaum.

—— 1998b. Reference: Intending that others jointly attend. *Pragmatics and Cognition 6*, 219–243.

—— 1998c. One child's early talk about possession. In J. Newman, ed., *The linguistics of giving*. Amsterdam: Benjamins.

—— 1998d. The return of constructions. *Journal of Child Language 75*, 431–447.

—— 1999. *The cultural origins of human cognition*. Cambridge, MA: Harvard University Press.

—— 2000a. First steps in a usage based theory of language acquisition. *Cognitive Linguistics 11*, 61–82.

—— 2000b. Do young children have adult syntactic competence? *Cognition 74*, 209–253.

—— 2002. *The new psychology of language*, vol. 2: *Cognitive and functional approaches to language structure*. Mahwah, NJ: Erlbaum.

—— In press. Could we please lose the mapping metaphor, please? *Behavioral and Brain Sciences*.

Tomasello, M., and Abbot-Smith, K. 2002. A tale of two theories: Response to Fisher. *Cognition 83*, 207–214.

Tomasello, M., and Akhtar, N. 1995. Two-year-olds use pragmatic cues to differentiate reference to objects and actions. *Cognitive Development 10*, 201–224.

Tomasello, M., Akhtar, N., Dodson, K., and Rekau, L. 1997. Differential productivity in young children's use of nouns and verbs. *Journal of Child Language 24*, 373–87.

Tomasello, M., Anselmi, D., and Farrar, J. 1984/85. Young children's coordination of gestural and linguistic reference. *First Language 5*, 199–210.

Tomasello, M., and Barton, M. 1994. Learning words in non-ostensive contexts. *Developmental Psychology 30*, 639–650.

Tomasello, M., and Brooks, P. 1998. Young children's earliest transitive and intransitive constructions. *Cognitive Linguistics 9*, 379–395.

———— 1999. Early syntactic development: A construction grammar approach. In M. Barrett, ed., *The development of language*. London: Psychology Press.

Tomasello, M., Brooks, P., and Stern, E. 1998. Learning to produce passive sentences through discourse. *First Language 18*, 223–237.

Tomasello, M., and Call, J. 1997. *Primate cognition*. Oxford: Oxford University Press.

Tomasello, M., Call, J., and Gluckman, A. 1997. The comprehension of novel communicative signs by apes and human children. *Child Development 68*, 1067–81.

Tomasello, M., and Camaioni, L. 1997. A comparison of the gestural communication of apes and human infants. *Human Development 40*, 7–24.

Tomasello, M., and Farrar, J. 1984. Cognitive bases of lexical development: Object permanence and relational words. *Journal of Child Language 11*, 477–493.

———— 1986a. Joint attention and early language. *Child Development 57*, 1454–63.

———— 1986b. Object permanence and relational words: A lexical training study. *Journal of Child Language 13*, 495–506.

Tomasello, M., Farrar, J., and Dines, J. 1984. Children's speech revisions for a familiar and an unfamiliar adult. *Journal of Speech and Hearing Research 27*, 359–363.

Tomasello, M., and Kruger, A. 1992. Joint attention on actions: Acquiring verbs in ostensive and non-ostensive contexts. *Journal of Child Language 19*, 311–333.

Tomasello, M., Kruger, A., and Ratner, H. 1993. Cultural learning. *Behavioral and Brain Sciences 16*, 495–552.

Tomasello, M., and Mannle, S. 1985. Pragmatics of sibling speech to one year olds. *Child Development 56*, 911–917.

Tomasello, M., Mannle, S., and Barton, M. 1989. The development of communicative competence in twins. *Revue Internationale de Psychologie Sociale 2*, 49–59.

Tomasello, M., Mannle, S., and Kruger, A. 1986. Linguistic environment of one to two year old twins. *Developmental Psychology 22*, 169–176.

Tomasello, M., Mannle, S., and Werdenschlag, L. 1988. The effect of previously learned words on the child's acquisition of words for similar referents. *Journal of Child Language 15*, 505–515.

Tomasello, M., and Merriman, W., eds. 1995. *Beyond names for things: Young children's acquisition of verbs*. Hillsdale, NJ: Erlbaum.

Tomasello, M., and Mervis, C. 1994. The instrument is great, but measuring comprehension is still a problem. *Monographs of the Society for Research in Child Development 59*, 174–179.

Tomasello, M., and Rakoczy, H. In press. What makes human cognition unique? *Mind and Language*.

Tomasello, M., Striano, T., and Rochat, P. 1999. Do young children use objects as symbols? *British Journal of Developmental Psychology 17*, 563–584.

Tomasello, M., Strosberg, R., and Akhtar, N. 1996. Eighteen-month-old children learn words in non-ostensive contexts. *Journal of Child Language 23*, 157–176.

Tomasello, M., and Todd, J. 1983. Joint attention and lexical acquisition style. *First Language 4*, 197–212.

Tomasello, M., and Zuberbühler, K. 2002. Primate vocal and gestural communication. In M. Bekoff, C. Allen, and G. Burghardt, eds., *The cognitive animal: Empirical and theoretical perspectives on animal cognition*. Cambridge, MA: MIT Press.

Trask, L. 1996. *Historical linguistics: An introduction*. New York: St Martin's.

Traugott, E. 1989. On the rise of epistemic meanings in English: An example of subjectification in semantic change. *Language 65*, 31–55.

Traugott, E., and Heine, B. 1991. *Approaches to grammaticalization*, vols. 1 and 2. Amsterdam: Benjamins.

Trevarthen, C. 1979. Communication and cooperation in early infancy: A description of primary intersubjectivity. In M. M. Bullowa, ed., *Before speech: The beginning of interpersonal communication*. New York: Cambridge University Press.

Vaidyanathan, R. 1988. Development of forms and functions of interrogatives in children: A longitudinal study in Tamil. *Journal of Child Language 15*, 533–549.

———— 1991. Development of forms and functions of negation in the early stages of language acquisition: A study in Tamil. *Journal of Child Language 18*, 51–66.

Valian, V. 1991. Syntactic subjects in the early speech of American and Italian children. *Cognition 40*, 21–81.

van Hoek, K. 1997. *Anaphora and conceptual structure*. Chicago: University of Chicago Press.

———— 2002. Pronouns and point of view: Cognitive principles of coreference. In M. Tomasello, ed., *The new psychology of language,* vol. 2: *Cognitive and functional approaches to language structure*. Mahwah, NJ: Erlbaum.

Van Valin, R. 1990. Semantic parameters of split intransitivity. *Language 66*, 221–260.

———— 1992. An overview of ergative phenomena and their implications for language acquisition. In D. I. Slobin, ed., *The crosslinguistic study of language acquisition,* vol. 3. Hillsdale, NJ: Erlbaum.

———— 1993. A synopsis of role and reference grammar. In R. Van Valin, ed., *Advances in role and reference grammar*. Amsterdam: Benjamins.

———— 1998. The acquisition of wh-questions and the mechanisms of language acquisition. In M. Tomasello, ed., *The new psychology of language,* vol. 1: *Cognitive and functional approaches to language structure*. Mahwah, NJ: Erlbaum.

Vargha-Khadem, F., and Passingham, R. 1990. Speech and language defects. *Nature 346*, 226.

Vear, D., and Ramos, E. 2001. Pragmatic and semantic variation in children's earliest uses of verbs. Paper presented at Society for Research in Child Development.

Vihman, M. M. 1996. *Phonological development: The origins of language in the child.* Oxford: Blackwell.

Wagner, L. 2001. Aspectual influences on early tense comprehension. *Journal of Child Language 28,* 661–682.

Wanner, E., and L. Gleitman, eds. 1982. *Language acquisition: The state of the art.* Cambridge: Cambridge University Press.

Warden, C., and Warner, L. 1928. The sensory capacities and intelligence of dogs with a report on the ability of the noted dog "Fellow" to respond to verbal stimuli. *Quarterly Review of Biology 3(1),* 1–29.

Warden, D. 1976. The influence of context on children's use of identifying expressions and references. *British Journal of Psychology 67(1),* 101–112.

Watson-Gegeo, K. A., and Gegeo, D. W. 1986. The social world of Kwara'ae children: Acquisition of language and values. In J. Cook-Gumperz, W. Corsaro, and J. Streeck, eds., *Children's worlds and children's language.* New York: Mouton de Gruyter.

Weist, R. 1983. Prefix versus suffix information processing in the comprehension of tense and aspect. *Journal of Child Language 10,* 85–96.

——— 1986. Tense and aspect. In P. Fletcher and M. Garman, eds., *Language acquisition,* 2d ed. Cambridge: Cambridge University Press.

Weist, R., and Konieczna, E. 1985. Affix processing strategies and linguistic systems. *Journal of Child Language 12,* 27–35.

Weist, R., Lyytinen, P., Wysocka, J., and Atanassova, M. 1997. The interaction of language and thought in children's language acquisition: A crosslinguistic study. *Journal of Child Language 24,* 81–121.

Weist, R., Wysocka, H., and Lyytinen, P. 1991. A cross-linguistic perspective on the development of temporal systems. *Journal of Child Language 18,* 67–92.

Weist, R., Wysocka, H., Witkowska-Stadnik, K., Buczowska, E., and Konieczna, E. 1984. The defective tense hypothesis: On the emergence of tense and aspect in child Polish. *Journal of Child Language 11,* 347–374.

Wells, G. 1983. *Learning through interaction: The study of language development.* Cambridge: Cambridge University Press.

Werker, J. F., and Desjardins, R. N. 1995. Listening to speech in the first year of life: Experiential influences on phoneme perception. *Current Directions in Psychological Sciences 4(3),* 76–81.

Whiten, A. 1998. Imitation of the sequential structure of actions by chimpanzees (Pan troglodytes). *Journal of Comparative Psychology 112,* 270–281.

Wierzbicka, A. 1985. "Oats and wheat": The fallacy of arbitrariness. In J. Haiman, ed., *Iconicity in syntax.* Amsterdam: Benjamins.

Wijnen, F. 1990. On the development of language production mechanisms. Doctoral diss., University of Nijmegen.

Wilcox, J., and Webster, E. 1980. Early discourse behaviors: Children's response to listener feedback. *Child Development 51,* 1120–25.

Wilcox, S., and Palermo, D. 1975. "In," "on," and "under" revisited. *Cognition 3,* 245–254.

Wilson, S. In press. Lexically specific constructions in the acquisition of inflections in English. *Journal of Child Language.*

Wittek, A., and Tomasello, M. Submitted (a). German-speaking children's productivity with case-marking: A test of the local cues hypothesis.

———— Submitted (b). Referential choice by two-year-olds.

Wittgenstein, L. 1955. *Philosophical investigations.* Oxford: Basil Blackwell.

Wode, H. 1977. Four early stages in the development of L1 negation. *Journal of Child Language 4,* 87–102.

Woodward, A. L., and Markman, E. M. 1997. Early word learning. In W. Damon, D. Kuhn, and R. Siegler, eds., *Handbook of child psychology,* vol. 2: *Cognition, perception and language.* New York: Wiley.

Woodward, A. L., Markman, E. M., and Fitzsimmons, C. M. 1994. Rapid word learning in 13- and 18-month-olds. *Developmental Psychology 30,* 553–566.

Wray, Alison, and Perkins, M. 2000. The functions of formulaic language: An integrated model. *Language and Communication 20,* 1–28.

Xu, F., Carey, S., and Welch, J. 1999. Infants' ability to use object kind information for object individuation. *Cognition 70,* 137–166.

Yamada, J. 1981. Evidence for the independence of language and cognition: Case study of a "hyperlinguistic" adolescent. *UCLA Working Papers in Cognitive Linguistics 3,* 93–115.

Zuberbühler, K. 2002. A syntactic rule in forest monkey communication. *Animal Behaviour 63,* 293–299.

Acknowledgments

The first version of this book was intended to be a textbook. But it turns out that I am incapable of writing about things I think are either boring or wrong. So I undertook a major revision and turned the project into an extended theoretical proposal—much of which was implicit in the first version anyway. What this means is that I wrote my theoretical account around a fairly systematic review of the research in child language acquisition—at least the part of it that does not view children's language through the lens of adult formal grammars—and so I think the book can still be used as an advanced textbook by a significant portion of researchers in the field.

To the extent that this final version is a better book, the credit goes in large part to discussions I have had over the past year with a number of my colleagues, some of whom read portions or even all of the manuscript. Of special importance is my colleague and social conscience, Elena Lieven, whose thoughts on language acquisition are at this point inextricably intertwined with my own. Thank you, Elena. For discussions and feedback I would also like to single out Gina Conti-Ramsden, Kirsten Smith, Ewa Dabrowska, Nancy Budwig, Holger Diessel, Heike Behrens, and Angelika Wittek. Also, the two reviewers from Harvard University Press— Adele Goldberg and Stephen Wilson—provided very useful feedback, as did Elizabeth Knoll at HUP, especially on the first chapter. I thank you all. In addition, Jenny Speares was a big help with the references, and Camille Smith at HUP edited the manuscript and corrected many an awkward phrasing. I also express my deepest gratitude to Henriette Zeidler. She did innumerable things to facilitate the birthing of this book, including providing expert help with the figures and references, securing permissions, and the like. But most important, she basically ran the department administratively—with great skill and good cheer, natürlich—while I was at home writing in relative peace and quiet.

Index